THE LOST DECADE

By Merlyn Vandervort

2007 thru 2017

A failed Experiment in Progressive Government

Also by Merlyn Vandervort

Make It Happen!—ISBN 1493713531

RS Means—Repair & Remodeling Estimating Methods, third edition-
Contributing Author, Disaster Reconstruction - ISBN 0-87629-454-9

1997 International Edition of the Blue Book- Contributing Author, "The
10 & 10 Myth" – ISBN 0-918767-00-8

Columnist, "The Vandervort Report," *Lake Ozark Business Journal*

Contact Merlyn Vandervort:
Merlyn@Atlasbizcoach.com

Websites:
www.MetroRenovators.com
www.Atlasbizcoach.com

Introduction

By the time Barack Obama leaves office on January 20th, 2017, he will have increased our national debt by more than every single US President before him, combined! When Barack Obama took office, his party, the 110th, "Democrat controlled" Congress had increased the National Debt to $9 trillion dollars. That amount included the national debt that all 43 other presidents from George Washington to George W. Bush, inherited from their predecessors, combined! In six short years, Barack Obama and the Democrats will have doubled that debt to $18 trillion dollars! By the time Obama leaves office, the debt will have increased to nearly $20 trillion dollars. In other words, it took all 43 presidents, and 110 Congresses before Barack Obama; 219 years, to increase our debt to $9 trillion dollars, and it has taken Barack Obama and the Democrats, only six years to double that amount.

Most voters quickly forgot that the Democrats actually took control of two thirds of the US government on January 3rd, 2007; two years before Barack Obama was elected, and two years before the Great Recession devastated our economy. Not since the 103rd congress in 1995, had the Democrat Party controlled a majority in both chambers of Congress. This left President Bush, a lame duck president, with little if any power. Understand, whichever party controls two thirds of our government has complete control. It doesn't matter if it's the White house and the Senate, or the White house and the House of Representatives, or the House and the Senate. The Congress has the power of the purse, and the power to introduce legislation. The President can only sign or veto bills that the Congress passes, and if Congress has enough votes, they can even override a Presidential veto. Congress can impeach a President, but the President can't impeach Congress.

I realize that Barack Obama, and his fellow liberal Democrats, along with the liberally biased, so called "main stream" media, have done a pretty good job in blaming Bush for the Great Recession, but the facts simply don't support that conclusion. When the Democrats took control of two thirds of our government on January 3rd, 2007 the DOW Jones closed at a very strong 12,621.77. The GDP for the previous quarter was a very strong 3.5%, and the unemployment rate was 4.6%. George Bush's economic policies had set a record of 52 straight months of job growth! All of that positive economic growth and momentum, changed on January 3rd, 2007 when the 110th Congress took the majority control of our government. On that day, Nancy Pelosi took control as the Speaker of the House, Harry Reid took control as the Majority Leader of the Senate. Barney Frank took over the House Financial Services Committee, and Chris Dodd took over the Senate Banking Committee.

From that day forward, America's economic demise was imminent. A year later, our economy began to contract, and two years later we were in a full blown recession, the likes America hadn't experienced since the Great Depression. When Barack Obama took office on January 22, 2009 Democrats had a "trifecta" super control of the entire government, and complete power to enact their "big government" progressive polices that would soon prove to cripple America, and send us on a death spiral.

Why did our economy have a complete melt down? Because of the banking and financial services! Who had complete control of the US banking and financial services, for over a year prior to the crisis? No it certainly wasn't George Bush, and it certainly wasn't the Republicans. The Speaker of the House of Representatives was none other than Democrat Nancy Pelosi, and the Majority Leader of the Senate was none other than Democrat Harry Reid. Democrat Barney Frank was in charge of the House Financial Services Committee, and Democrat Chris Dodd was in control of the Senate Banking Committee. These are the committees that have complete control and direct oversight of Fannie Mae, (Federal National Mortgage Association – FNMA) and Freddie Mac (Federal Home Loan Mortgage Corporation – FHLMC) both of which are government sponsored enterprises (GSE). It was precisely the poor lending policies, and practices, and the lack of oversight that led to the toxic loans held by Fannie Mae and Freddie Mac that were directly responsible for the housing bubble that caused the Great Recession.

President Bush asked Congress seventeen times to implement much tighter restrictions and oversight on Fannie and Freddie, starting all the way back in 2001, because of the financial risk for the US economy. So who in congress fought against making reforms to Fannie and Freddie? None other than Senator Barack Obama, and his allies. Freddie and Fannie used huge lobbying budgets and political contributions to keep regulators off of their backs. The Center for Responsive Politics, keeps track of which politicians get political contributions from Fannie and Freddie, and in the ten years prior to 2008, Barack Obama was number two at the top of their list. Keep in mind, that Obama had only been a one term Senator, so he was only in the Senate for four of the ten years, and still received the second most. Less than a year later, Barack Obama gave them a big pay back, by bailing them out, with our tax dollars.

Here is an interesting statistic, in the six years that George Bush was President, before the Democrats took control of the House and Senate on

January 3rd, 2007 there had been 22 failed banks that the FDIC had to close. Keep in mind, that George Bush also inherited a recession from Bill Clinton, and the 2000 technology bubble. In contrast, since the time that the democrats took control of the House and Senate, and the Banking and Financial Services, there have been 508 bank failures! That's an astonishing 23 times more bank failures after the democrats took control, than prior to them taking control. It's worth pointing out that there were zero bank failures in 2005 & 2006, so what the democrats inherited was a stable financial market. So the next time, you hear Barack Obama and his allies blame Bush, and proclaim that they "inherited" a bad economy, please remind them of the facts, and what Barack Obama actually inherited, was of his and his parties own making.

I realize that most people don't see eye to eye on many things, and certainly not on politics. I have several friends and family members whom I care deeply about, and I recognize and respect their right to see the world through a different pair of glasses than I do. If you do agree with my politics, I suspect you will greatly appreciate this book. That said, I really wrote this book for the rest of the population who don't agree with my politics, are uninformed about the country they live in, or, very likely, both. America is the greatest country on earth, and I love this country very much; but it doesn't take a rocket scientist to see that as a country, we are on the brink of a fiscal death spiral that will lead to our own demise if we don't get our house in order!

In the words of John F. Kennedy:

"Our most basic common link is that we all inhabit this planet. We all breathe the same air, we all cherish our children's future. And we are all mortal."

President Kennedy's insightful speech identified at least four of the very few things that most people would agree on. I have little doubt that all Americans, certainly all parents, "cherish our children's future." Can we all at least agree on that? The question is: Are we, as parents or grandparents or even future parents, willing to make hard choices and sacrifices today to protect our children's futures? No doubt, most parents would lay their lives on the line to protect their children. No doubt every parent wants better for his or her children than he or she has had for himself or herself. I truly believe that about most every parent; that he or she wants his or her children and grandchildren to inherit a better, more prosperous world than the one we inherited from our parents. If you truly believe that, you owe it to your children and our future generations to at least read this book with an open mind, regardless of whether you agree with my politics or not.

Have you ever been wrong about anything? Have you ever been shocked or surprised? Have you ever had an epiphany? Have you ever found religion or lost it? Unfortunately most people gain (notice I didn't say *learn*) their political leanings from their parents, peers, entertainment TV, biased teachers, biased news organizations, or just because someone likes the way one politician or another looks or talks. All of which might be factors, but if you truly do "cherish your children's future," you need to open your eyes, have an open mind to the facts, and ask some hard questions.

Do you vote for a politician because he or she tells you what you want to hear? That your troubles in life are someone else's fault, and a vote for him or her will right any wrongs you have? Or a politician who promises to give you something back if only you would help him or her get elected? The sad truth is, that works. My question is, how could "we the people" be so gullible? Do you realize that we have an $18 trillion debt? Do you realize that we have $120 trillion in unfunded liabilities? That is the world we are leaving to our children! By the time our next president takes office, our national debt will be approaching $20 trillion, and we are now spending a $1.5 trillion more than what we bring in each year! That is completely irresponsible, and completely unsustainable!

As I began writing this book, I really tried to put a great deal of effort into not losing half of my potential readers, as is easy to do when talking politics. I initially tried to write this book in as much of a non-offensive, nonpartisan, "politically correct" way as possible; but you just can't sugarcoat the reality. America needs a good shaking and a wake-up call, and my intent with this book is to contribute to that wake-up call. If you do disagree with my politics, I respect that; but I would strongly encourage you to give this book a good, open-minded read. You don't have anything to lose and can only gain by hearing another perspective. If you vote, our children's future depends on it.

The Democrats acted as if they were merely innocent bystanders of the economic meltdown, and American voters were all too happy to buy into "Hope and Change" from a cool, handsome, young, "historic" candidate with an undeniable talent to speak as if he were Bill Clinton, John F. Kennedy, and Dr. Martin Luther King all wrapped up in one inspirational candidate. America would soon come to realize that a cool, handsome politician with a keen ability to give a good speech does not a president make. Unfortunately for America, the majority of people didn't come to that conclusion nearly soon enough.

In full disclosure, I've never been a supporter of Barack Obama, but I did understand the historic moment of Americans electing our first black president. After catching my breath from the 2008 elections, I prayed and hoped that our new president would be able to deliver on his promises to bring the country together, and truly lead our country. That hope of promise soon became despair. Obama's reelection in 2012 would result in America enduring four more years of a failed "big government," progressive ideology. Failure of leadership soon diminished our standing on the world stage. The Obama administrations continuous lies, incompetence, scandals, corruption, and cover-ups have left our president, and our country, impotent.

As you read this book, you will likely sense a lot of emotion in my words. I wrote this book because of my children, and your children, and our future generations. As such it's hard not to write with a lot of emotion. I am extremely aggravated about what "we the people" have allowed to happen to this great country, and I'm very concerned about the country our children are inheriting. The intent of this book is to provide an in-depth analysis of why we got here, how we got here, where "here" really is, and some thoughts on how we can take our country back, and repair the damages that have been done!

I must say that when I started writing this book, I didn't think it was possible for things to get any worse, but even through the course of writing this book, things under this administration have gone from really bad to a complete and utter disaster! Lack of American leadership, has left America, and the world, a very dangerous place.

In the words of Adolph Hitler:

"How fortunate for governments that the people they administer, don't think!"

If you are wondering how on earth our country got into this terrible state, those chilling words from Adolph Hitler do a pretty good job of explaining it. Unfortunately, all too often many Americans, don't think!

About the Author

Merlyn Vandervort has been a successful business entrepreneur for over twenty-five years. In addition to being a successful builder and developer, Merlyn is an accomplished author, motivational speaker, a professional business coach & consultant, and a rancher. By the age of thirty-two, Merlyn was a self-made millionaire; ten years later his net worth had grown to nearly $40 million. When the economy crashed in late 2008 and 2009, the majority of his wealth evaporated overnight. Down but not out, Merlyn spent the next five years navigating his way out of the eye of the hurricane and survived the Great Recession.

"The Great Recession was terrible, but what followed was unimaginable incompetence, and corruption; I know first-hand just how devastating progressive policies have been to the businesses that are the economic engine of America." – Merlyn Vandervort

At the age of twenty-four, with nothing more than a few thousand dollars, a pickup truck, and a box of tools, Merlyn founded Metro Renovators Inc., working out of a small office in the back of his garage. Metro Renovators specialized in disaster cleanup and reconstruction, and rebuilt properties and communities all over the country that had been destroyed by natural disasters. His company quickly outgrew the back of Merlyn's garage, and within a few years Metro Renovators had grown to be one of the largest disaster reconstruction companies in the country, having multiple offices and employing hundreds of people. In 1998, his Kansas City and Springfield Missouri based construction companies were acquired by Inrecon/Belfor USA.

After fulfilling a four-year contract as the regional vice president for Belfor USA, Merlyn reluctantly turned down a lucrative offer to continue his career path with Belfor and instead relocated to Missouri's Lake of the Ozarks region and continued his construction and development endeavors, rebranding his construction company as Metro Renovators & Construction Services, Inc., and focusing on designing and building luxury waterfront homes and high-quality commercial projects. He also focused his business attention on owning several restaurants in the Lake of the Ozarks region and Kansas City. His hospitality successes led him to develop a $60 million five-star resort hotel and yacht club, Camden on the Lake, adjacent to the world famous Horny Toad entertainment complex, which he had developed several years earlier. Merlyn also excelled as an event promoter for such events as the National Championship Powerboat Races, the Lake of the Ozarks Bike-Fest, and over a hundred benefit concerts featuring legendary recording artists such as Willie Nelson and the Beach Boys, to name a few. The luxury resort development he founded was completed in the third quarter of 2008, amid the worst economic collapse since the Great Depression, which created a tremendous challenge; fortunately Merlyn's extensive business experience and tenacity enabled him to meet the challenge head on and overcome it.

Merlyn is still actively involved in construction and development, as well as various real estate ventures, but he now spends much of his time paying it forward through his books and motivational speaking, and by consulting and coaching other successful business owners and entrepreneurs to assist them in growing and maximizing the success of their business.

This book is dedicated to my three children and my future grandchildren and great-grandchildren.

Dear Malari, Merlyn III, and Gunner,

I can't tell you all enough just how very proud I am of each of you. You are all so very talented and intelligent, and I have greatly enjoyed watching you all grow into the productive and self-sufficient young adults you've become, and are still becoming. I know a lot of what's in this book you've grown up hearing me say over and over, and as you've become older and self-reliant, I know you can now appreciate the life lessons that I've tried to instill in each of you.

I deeply regret that you and your generation are inheriting the financial irresponsibility of my generation. As you all know, I have always been a staunch opponent of the progressive "big government" policies that have gotten our country into such a mess, and you can be assured that I will continue that fight until the day I pass from this earth. Unfortunately the heavy lifting will now be up to all of you and your generation. It will be up to all of you to scream from the rooftops if need be to try to get America to open its eyes, see the peril we are in, and change the trajectory we are on. I know you all have the strength and courage to carry the fight. I hope this book is a positive contribution to the cause.

I love you all very much,

Dad

Contents

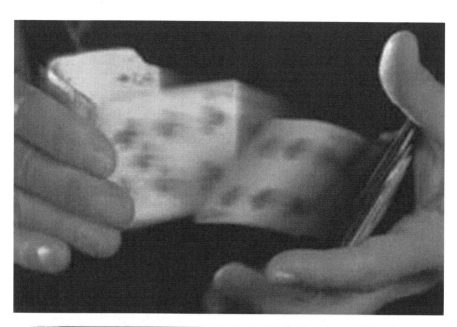

CHAPTER ONE

Sleight of Hand: Politics 101

"As parents, we can have no joy, knowing that this government is not sufficiently lasting to ensure anything which may bequeath posterity: and by a plain method of argument, as we are running the next generation into debt, we ought to do the work of it, otherwise we use them meanly and pitifully. In order to discover the line of our duty rightly, we should take our children in our hand, and fix our station a few years farther into life; that eminence will present a prospect, which a few present fears and prejudices conceal from our sight."—Thomas Paine, *Common Sense*, 1776

Our Founding Fathers had the foresight to understand that "we the people" of America could easily "bequeath" our debts, our fears, and our prejudices to our children and future generations. Paine wisely recommended that we "take our children in our hand, and fix our station a few years farther into life." In other words, think ahead. Americans have become complacent, and all too often we fail to think ahead and instead live only for today. And why shouldn't we? Today's politicians certainly lack the character and fortitude of our Founding

Fathers. I would suggest that we all take a lesson from history and read the words of our Founding Fathers. As such, I will begin each chapter with some words of wisdom from our Founding Fathers and will end this book with some of the greatest words of our Founding Fathers: words that have held our republic together for more than two centuries. I might suggest that we all remind our elected politicians today of the lessons of our history and the words of our forefathers.

Every magician knows that the secret to any good magic trick is sleight of hand—keeping the audience focused on something insignificant or irrelevant just long enough to pull off the trick and pull the wool over everyone's eyes. This is the same principle that politicians use every day. Keep the majority of voters focused on something relatively insignificant or even nonexistent just long enough to fool them and gain power.

Slick politicians (and I use that term derogatorily) pick one or two small-ball issues that specifically target their base or a specific group of voters—issues such as "the war on women" or "spread the wealth" or "income inequality"—and exploit those issues to get those voters worked up in a frenzy, overlooking all other rational thoughts on the really important issues of the day.

Does anyone really believe that either party has a war on women? It's a ridiculous argument. As if the only thing that women care about is getting free contraceptives, and having completely unrestricted access to abortion. I'm not a woman, but I would certainly think that the "war on women" argument is an insult to any informed, self-reliant woman. But yet a slick, liberal politician would falsely argue that conservatives want to limit access to birth control, and completely eliminate a woman's right to choose. The Supreme Court recently ruled in favor of religious freedoms in the Hobby Lobby case, and liberals immediately twisted the ruling as a war on women, because the high court ruled that a privately held business with a moral objection to abortion, can choose not to have their group health insurance plan cover abortion inducing drugs such as the morning after pill, as a means of contraception. Hobby Lobby is a family owned business who has strong religious convictions, and has always offered their employees a very good health insurance plan that does provide over a dozen different types of contraception; the only contraception's Hobby Lobby objected to, were those that they believed caused an abortion. However if you listen to Harry Reid or Nancy Pelosi or most any other liberal for that matter, they completely fail to point out all the facts, and they do so in an effort to distort the facts and scare uninformed women into believing that the Supreme Court and conservatives are trying to eliminate their access to birth control, when nothing could be further from the truth. It's also worth pointing out that the high court's ruling didn't do anything to limit access to all forms of contraception including abortion inducing drugs; the Supreme Court simply said that a privately held business, can't be forced by the government to include it in their group health insurance coverage.

Income inequality is another argument liberals try to use to get uninformed voters riled up. The fact is, that income inequality has gotten much worse over recent years under the party that pretends to champion it. No president has ever touted the issue as emphatically as President Obama. In his 2012 State of the Union address, Obama said; "The defining issue of our time is how to keep that promise alive. No challenge is more urgent. No debate is more important. We can either settle for a country where a shrinking number of people do really well, while a growing number of Americans barely get by, or we can restore an economy where everyone gets a fair shot, and everyone does their fair share, and everyone plays by the same set of rules." One thing for sure, Barack Obama sure can give a good speech. The problem is, that he doesn't have a clue on how to make his rhetoric a reality, and has done exactly the opposite of what it would take to restore our economy. The fact is, under President Obama's progressive policies the income gap has only gotten worse, much worse.

Back in 1928, the top one percent of earners received about a quarter of all pre-tax income. The bottom 90 percent received just over half of it. The Great Depression and Franklin D. Roosevelt's "New Deal" progressive policies, stripped wealth from most everyone across the board. By 1955, as the economy continued to recover as a result of America's rearmament for World War II, the top 1 percent saw their share of the wealth shrink to 11 percent, while the bottom 90 percent grew to 67 percent. Through the '50s, '60s, and early '70s, decades of economic growth brought prosperity for all, and each economic group's income share remained fairly constant. Then came the late '70s under President Carter; the top 1 percent saw their share begin to rise and the bottom 90 percent saw theirs begin to fall. Between the mid-1980s through the end of 2008 income distribution returned to the pre-carter era of prosperity for all. Since Barack Obama's inauguration in 2009 income inequality has gotten drastically worse; in-fact not since the pre-Great Depression era has income inequality ever been so far apart. Under Barack Obama, the top 1 percent was back to where they were over eighty five years ago taking in about a quarter of all pre-tax income. And for the very first time in history, the bottom 90 percent saw their share drop below 50 percent. According to Emmanuel Saez, a professor at the University of California, Berkley; during the post-recession years of 2009-2012, the top earners took in a greater share of total income growth than during the boom years of 2002-2007. The conclusion is clear, big government progressive policies, inevitably harm the middle class.

Gay rights is an issue that has been exploited by both sides of the aisle. In 2000 the Republicans used it to get out the conservative vote, and twelve years later, as the issue has evolved, the Democrats equally exploited it to get out the liberal vote. Not that all of these issues aren't important, but it is pretty scary when one party or another is in charge of our national security or controls our entire economy based on what they have to say about one or two social issues.

Unfortunately economics and foreign policy are somewhat complicated issues, and most voters choose not to pay too much attention to them until they blow up in our faces and the economy collapses or we find ourselves in the middle of a war, at which point voters immediately, and understandably, hold whomever is in power accountable. Unfortunately war and economic collapse are often several elections in the making and are often the inevitable consequences of bad policies and weak leadership that usually go back more than one administration or election cycle. Case in point, while it may appear that Barack Obama has gotten the US out of two wars, and refused to engage or show American leadership in areas of conflict around the world; his ineptitude and failure of leadership, will almost certainly force our next Commander in Chief to face military conflicts or God forbid, attacks on our homeland; that may have been avoided. Our national debt has doubled under President Obama, and our economy is still in total havoc; it will likely take several years for our next President to clean up the mess he will undoubtedly inherit.

Bad economic policies, such as the policies that led up to the Great Recession, often take many years before they actually come to a head and blow up in our faces. Weak leadership on foreign policy in one administration only emboldens our enemies, puts American interests in jeopardy, and can easily lead to the next administration having to clean up the mess and pick up the pieces, often at great risk of military force.

The simple truth about politics is that everything is all about buying votes and politicians doing and saying whatever they can to hang on to power and their jobs! Far too many politicians from both sides of the aisle will do and say just about anything to get a majority vote and gain power. Not only do politicians buy votes from their constituents, they buy votes called earmarks from other politicians: "you vote for this bill, regardless of whether you agree with it or not, and in return for your vote, I will add to the bill the funding for your pet project back home." It happens every day in Washington. This type of "pork barrel spending" only balloons our national debt.

Politics, plain and simple, is all about buying votes. The problem is that we, the American taxpayers, aren't paying close enough attention to our national treasure or the crooks we put in charge of spending it. That is a terrible flaw in our democracy and is precisely the reason we have nearly an $18 trillion debt and an economy that is only limping along. According to the US debt clock, we are spending $1.5 trillion every year more than we are bringing in, and that should scare the hell out of everyone! Politicians are masters at making promises on the backs of hardworking taxpayers and at the expense of future generations.

Things in Washington have never been worse off since the time of the Civil War. Not only is our national debt threatening our security as a nation and the very future of our democracy; we are on an unsustainable spending path that can only end in disaster unless we make some hard choices, and some serious changes, very quickly! Our entire government is out of control: the Internal Revenue Service, the National Security Agency, the Veterans Administration, the Justice Department, the State Department, Health and Human Services, the list goes on and on, all the way to Capitol Hill and the White House. Our scandal-riddled government is plagued with corruption and incompetence! I for one say enough is enough, it's high time that "we the people" take our country back!

Politicians are very reluctant to address the difficult issues of our time, because as soon as they do, they get hammered by another politician who either wants their job or wants their political party to gain power. Unfortunately, far too many voters are naïve and vote only for politicians who will tell them whatever it is that they want to hear. So the can keeps getting kicked down the road; but what happens when the road runs out? Armageddon.

Look at what happens to any responsible politician who ever even brings up the topic of making any adjustments to help preserve Social Security or Medicare; he or she gets crucified by the opposition, so the time bomb keeps on ticking away. All too often, American voters choose to ignore the serious problems and turn a blind eye because they don't want to face the reality. The attitude of far too many people is that if it isn't broke, don't fix it. Unfortunately that's kind of like driving a car and never paying any attention to your gauges; the car seems to be running along just fine, and so long as it keeps going I'm going to ignore the red oil light that keeps coming on. That works just fine, until it doesn't; sooner or later your engine locks up. Folks, this is a wake-up call; our red light has been blinking for the past eight years, and our engine is on the brink of locking up!

Most people think of Social Security as their retirement fund. It isn't; it's a social safety net. By the way the official name for the Social Security program is; "Old-age, Survivors, and Disability Insurance" (OASDI). Most think they pay into Social Security all of their working lives and they are able to draw the money back out once they retire. While that might have been the basic principle when the program was implemented, there are three big holes in the program. First of all, many people never really put in enough throughout his or her working lifetime that it would be enough for them to live off of when he or she retires, so others paying into the system are forced to subsidize those individuals. Social Security was always intended to have enough young workers to subsidize older Americans when they retired. According to the Social Security Board of Trustee's; in 1945 there were 42 workers paying into the program for every one person collecting benefits, and today there is less than 3 workers paying in for every one person collecting benefits. That is totally unsustainable. The math works poorly at best, and for it to work at all requires that the working population grow at a rate faster than the number of people who are retiring, and that the retired persons live for only a short period of time after they retire. People are living much longer than they were fifty years ago. The baby boom generation is now reaching retirement age, and they far outnumber the workers coming into the workforce. To add insult to injury, politicians have been looting the Social Security fund for the past thirty years to buy votes!

In 1983, Congress passed legislation on a bi-partisan vote, which amended the Social Security Act, and increased the amount of Social Security tax that workers and their employers contribute to the Social Security fund. They did this, recognizing that in the year 2010, the first of the baby boom generation would start to retire, and the Congressional Budget Office had determined that if they didn't raise the amount going into the fund, that it wouldn't be able to sustain the huge influx of baby boomers who would start to draw benefits in large numbers. Sounds like a pretty good idea; politicians actually thinking ahead? Well, if they were thinking ahead when they passed the bill, they quickly lost all sense of reason a few years later, when they decided it would be a good idea to stop putting the revenue into a separate Social Security trust fund, and decided that putting those funds into the general fund, might be a good idea. This lumped all of the American people's retirement safety net in with everything else the government brought in, and spent.

Every single politician and every president since Ronald Reagan have been complicit in looting the Social Security fund for everything under the sun. So how does that equate to using our retirement safety net for buying votes? Any time a politician is spending money out of the general fund, for whatever reason, they have been ultimately diminishing our Social Security fund. What do politicians spend money on? Buying votes. Regardless if it's funding a "pork barrel" pet project, or hiring more unionized government employees, or giving one company or another a government contract, or increasing government entitlements; it's all done to buy the votes of their constituents, or pay back their supporters for getting them elected.

So how much has been looted from the Social Security Fund? As of 2012, the number was at a whopping $2.7 trillion dollars! In year 2010, the government had to borrow $49 billion dollars, just to meet the Social Security commitment, another $45 billion was borrowed in 2011. The Congressional Budget Office projects that, during the years 2012-2021, Social Security will run cumulative deficits totaling $547 billion. The CBO further projects that between 2022 and 2033, redemption of the Trust Fund balance to pay retirees will have to draw approximately $3 trillion in government funds from sources other than payroll taxes! The point is, if politicians had left their grubby little hands off of our Social Security fund, it would be solvent, but unfortunately it isn't. It's gone!

So you are probably asking yourself, if politicians took the money, surely they were simply borrowing the money and intend to put it back? Yea right... Yes they did simply borrow it, but what they replaced it with was nothing more than an IOU. Our cash was replaced with non-marketable Treasury securities, backed by "the full faith and credit of the US government." In other words, "we the people" owe the money back to our own Social Security fund. I don't know if you caught the "non-marketable" Treasury securities? What the heck good is anything that is "non-marketable"? It's all smoke and mirrors; but politicians who were getting elected for the past thirty years; all knew that they would likely be long out of office when this all blows up in everyone's face, and it would be someone else's problem. You know what, they were right; and that someone else is us; "we the people". We are the ones that owe it, not the politicians who pilfered it.

President George W. Bush called for a transition to a combination of a government-funded program and personal accounts (individual accounts or private accounts) through partial privatization of the system. Progressives hated the idea, because it took some control out of the hands of the government, and put it in the hands of the people. I don't know about you, but I would much prefer to be in control of my own life, and my own retirement than to depend on the government. I mean, the government has already showed us just how good of a job they will do. No thanks.

Let's look at the idea of private or individual accounts as opposed to our forced dependence on a Social Security system that is no longer a viable solution. To begin with, this type of a program wouldn't work for the majority of folks in the work force today, but it could have real potential for the younger generation who is just now coming into the workforce and has forty years to build a retirement fund. According to the Social Security Administration's August 2010 published statistics, the average monthly paid benefit paid to a worker whom had paid into the Social Security system and is now retired and collecting benefits was $1,171.60. Let's bump that number up to $1,250 a month for cost of living increases. According to the Social Security Administration Office, a 65 year old man today, can expect to live to age 84, and a 65 year old woman can expect to live to age 85. So let's assume that if a person starts collecting benefits at age 65, that they will collect benefits for an average of twenty years. At $1,250 per month the benefit would be $15,000 a year, and if the retiree collects benefits for an average of twenty years, they will have collected $300,000 in Social Security benefits throughout their retirement years.

Let's face it, it would be damn difficult for anyone to live off of $1,250 a month in their retirement years, and one would hope that most Americans only plan on using Social Security as a supplement to other retirement savings. Smart Americans shouldn't be depending on Social Security to be there for them at all.

The average American worker today earns just shy of $50,000 a year. That number varies greatly in different areas of the country, but for sake of this exercise let's use that number. American workers pay into the Social Security fund via a Social Security payroll tax of 7.65 percent; additionally, the American workers employer has to contribute an equal amount of 7.65 percent. For those who might not have realized that their employer is paying into each of their employees Social Security retirement fund, in an equal contribution as the employee; it's worth making note of. In any event, the total paid into Social Security is 15.3 percent. So if the American worker is earning $50 thousand dollars a year; the worker and their employer are collectively contributing $7,650.00 annually, into the Social Security fund for the benefit of the employee. Let's assume that employee only earns an average of $50 thousand a year throughout his or her career of let's use forty years. If you were to invest that $7,650.00 each year into a fairly conservative financial portfolio that earns, let's say only 4 percent; that fund would be worth slightly over $750,000.00 in forty years! If you never even touch that principal amount, and only continue collecting the 4 percent your retirement fund is earning; it would provide $30,000.00 a year of investment income, or $2,500.00 per month. That is over double the average Social Security payment; not to mention the fact that you would also have three quarters of a million dollars in the bank!

Social Security is a ticking time bomb that isn't going to fix itself. The American public needs a major reality check and needs to quit voting for politicians who refuse to tackle this problem. Ask yourself, if you had been working for a company all your life and thought you had a nice retirement fund to look forward to, wouldn't you much prefer knowing the truth—that the fund is running out of money—and dealing with it while you were still young enough to do something about it? Or would you prefer not knowing so you could keep your head buried in the sand until one day a few years into your retirement when you get a letter saying, "Sorry, there are no funds available to continue paying you your retirement check; best of luck." Wouldn't you much prefer, for example, receiving 95 percent of what you were promised and knowing that change is what it will take to keep your retirement fund solvent? Wouldn't you much prefer that over the very real possibility of someday receiving nothing?

If you were supposed to get a 1 percent cost of living increase every two years, wouldn't you prefer getting that only once every three years if that is what it takes to keep the program solvent? Those are the kinds of reasonable decisions everyone needs to start thinking about very soon. Unfortunately most people would just prefer that politicians keep lying to them, because people don't want to hear what they don't want to hear. It's time we all start accepting the fact that those of us who haven't started collecting Social Security are going to have to make some concessions in order to preserve this much-needed social safety net. And the next time some "slick politician" wants to dip into the Social Security fund for any reason, he should be tarred and feathered and immediately thrown out of office!

Oh, but then there is the "it's not fair" issue: "I've paid into this fund for years, and I'm due what I'm due! Social Security isn't an entitlement, I've paid my dues, and now I want what I'm due!"

Guess what, folks? Life isn't fair. And regardless of what's fair or what's not fair, "we the people" are responsible for the mess we are in! We've elected politicians time and time again because they told us what we wanted to hear! American voters have no one to blame but themselves. No point in sugarcoating it; that's the hard truth.

Social Security, isn't an entitlement, at least not for most recipients. American workers pay into Social Security all of their lives, as do their employers, and those who have paid in all of their lives should certainly have the expectation of being able to depend on it when they need it later in life. Unfortunately that ship has sailed. Social Security is doomed to fail, because it operates the exact same way a Ponzi scheme operates, and it is a mathematical certainty that it will fail for the very same reason; unless "we the people" demand that our elected leaders do something about it. The Social Security debate, is definitely a debate we all need to buck up and have. No doubt Social Security, or at least some form of a retirement social safety net, is imperative. There are a few very smart leaders who want to fix it, and know how to fix it, and "we the people" need to have the courage to help them fix it. So the next time you hear some progressive politician trying to demagogue the conversation, tell him or her to shut up and sit down!

Unfortunately most Americans have little concept of economics or even where money comes from. We'll get more in depth into this issue in chapter 2, but we need to at least scratch the surface of it here, because it is relative to how slick politicians play the sleight-of-hand game to keep voters in the dark. Many Americans think that the US Treasury can simply print an unlimited supply of currency, so many voters don't give much thought to the debt and the unsustainable deficits we continue to run up.

So where does the US government get money from? After all, the United States is by far the largest economy in the world, so who on earth would have the ability to loan the United States money? A lot of it we borrow from China. That's right, America's banker is China. Or maybe more accurately stated, America's drug dealer is China, because America is addicted to spending money like it's a drug that we can't get enough of. What happens to a junkie who can no longer get a fix? He or she goes into very painful withdraws. That's what America has to look forward to if we don't soon start weaning ourselves off of our spending addiction.

Think about the fact that China is America's banker, or loan shark, if you will. We may have friendly relations with China today, but make no mistake; China is our geopolitical foe. Anyone who's ever borrowed any money understands the leverage a lender has over a borrower, and it's not a good thing. Our national debt has doubled since Barack Obama took office, and our level of spending increases every day. The United States spends far more than it brings in, and it doesn't take a mathematician to understand that is a recipe for disaster. What happens if China and everyone else stops loaning us money? Surely no one thinks that the world has an unlimited supply of money to keep supporting America's spending.

America's national debt is by far the single biggest threat to our national security. Our national debt puts every single American's life and future in jeopardy. Worse yet, it puts our children, grandchildren, and great-grandchildren's futures in jeopardy. There is no question that the next generation is going to inherit the wrath of our sins. That's right, I said *sins*, because what else would you call it when a parent burdens his or her heirs with overwhelming debt and a world much worse than the one the parent inherited? Isn't it the dream of every parent that our children live a better life than we have? I know that is what I want for my kids, and that is one of the main reasons I'm writing this book: to scream from the top of my lungs and try to wake up my fellow Americans and encourage everyone to help me do something about this terrible mess we are now in!

So why not just raise taxes to lower our national debt? That may be the campaign slogan of many slick-talking politicians, because it buys votes. But it wouldn't do anything to solve the problem, and in fact it would only make the problem much worse. Politicians love to pretend that they are going to be Robin Hood and often proclaim "raise the taxes on the rich," or that the rich aren't paying their fair share. Nothing could be further from the truth, but politicians seldom care about the truth. Making that argument, however, accomplishes two things for a slick-talking politician: a) it convinces some voters to believe that it will somehow solve the problem, and b) it enables some voters to place the blame for all the problems in their life on people who have more money than they do. There are dozens of good arguments why raising taxes are never a good idea, and history has taught us that raising taxes never solves the problem, and inevitably has an adverse impact on the US economy.

Here's the best argument for not raising taxes on anyone, including the wealthy. It is no secret how completely inefficient the federal government is at nearly everything it does. For crying out loud, they spent four years and over $100 million trying to build a website, and it crashed the first week it went online. Then they had to turn around and hire private contractors just to get it working. The government has now spent a whopping eight hundred and forty million dollars on Healthcare.gov. Can you imagine the ramifications of any company making that big of a blunder? Imagine Google or Facebook making that big of a mistake; their stock would plummet and the chief executive officer would be terminated in short order. The private sector simply would not accept that kind of incompetence, and heads would roll. But sadly we've come to expect that kind of a result when our government tries to take on something that it knows nothing about.

The US government is an enormous bureaucracy, with dysfunctional oversight, limited transparency, ramped fraud and abuse, and no accountability. When it's next to impossible to fire a federal employee, there is no accountability. So why on earth would it be a good idea to raise taxes just to give it all to an inefficient machine to squander away and fund our elected politicians' ability to keep buying votes?

People or businesses with money don't keep it in a shoe box under their bed, and they don't hide it in their mattresses. To the contrary, they put that money to work and keep it working twenty-four hours a day, seven days a week, and 365 days a year! No one with money simply keeps it in a bank, either, unless he or she is afraid of an uncertain economic climate, such as the one we've been in since 2008.

When the climate in Washington is pro-business, businesses and people with money invest that money in the stock market, technology, innovation, real estate, infrastructure, and businesses. That, my friends, is what creates jobs and opportunity for everyone. That is what increases everyone's retirement accounts, grows the economy, creates wealth, and helps improve the life of every man, woman, and child in America! Success doesn't happen by accident; success is achieved because smart people make smart decisions and take smart risks. However, that doesn't happen when the movers and shakers of this world are stifled by the same bureaucracy that makes our government so inefficient. Successful businesses have to create their own wealth, which promotes ingenuity and efficiency. Successful businesses have to be transparent and accountable to their customers and their stockholders, or they will quickly find themselves out of business.

So once you understand and accept the fact of just how inefficient and wasteful the government is with the people's treasure, why on earth would anyone think that it's a good idea to take money out of the hands of successful people and businesses who are efficiently and effectively putting that money to work in the economy and creating jobs and opportunity?

The question is, who does a better and more responsible job with flowing money through the economy? Hands down, no question, it is the private sector. When you take more money from people and business who have money, it drastically stifles our economic growth, because the private sector does a much better job in growing our economy and creating opportunity than the government does.

Keeping taxes low unties the hands of capitalism and the American economy and enables growth and prosperity, which in the long run is without question the very best way to increase tax revenue.

Here is another way to look at this. You can call this the Sam Walton theory. Sam Walton believed that as a retailer, if he could keep his prices down by having a much lower margin of profit, his sales would soar and his overall profit dollars would be much greater. In other words, if he had a 20 percent profit margin and his sales were $1 million, he would generate $200,000 in gross profit. However, if he cut his profit margin by twenty five percent and it resulted in doubling his sales to $2 million, then it would increase his gross profit by 50 percent to $300,000. This logic works precisely the same when it comes to taxes. If you can keep taxes very low, it allows entrepreneurs and capitalists the ability to invest more of their money into the economy, which quickly grows the economy and greatly increases the total tax revenue generated, even though the percent of tax is lowered. You grow the tax base and grow prosperity for everyone all at the same time.

If you still aren't convinced that lower taxes for everyone, including the wealthy, is the best policy, consider this: Everyone in America is a consumer. We all engage in commerce in some form or another. We all purchase products from a wide range of businesses in nearly every single industry. Wealthy Americans purchase goods and services from businesses you and your family and friends either work for or possibly own. You cannot tax a business without it being passed along to the consumer; that is virtually impossible. The more money the government tries to take from businesses or wealthy Americans, the less they are going to spend on goods and services from the very companies you, your family, and your friends work for or own. If you think you can take more from businesses and wealthy people without it quickly trickling down to everyone else in the economy, you're being very naive.

America has one of the highest corporate tax rates in the world, and it is stifling our economic growth. High corporate tax rates make it very difficult for American companies to compete on the world stage, and that isn't good for America or our economy.

According to an April 2014 Reuters report, foreign profits held by American companies overseas more than doubled from 2008 to 2013 to top over $2.1 trillion due to the United States' uncompetitive tax rates. Lowering the corporate tax rates would likely result in that $2 trillion quickly coming back to the United States to be invested here, which would surely jumpstart our economy and create millions of jobs immediately! Again, politics keeps that from happening because it makes a good political "sound bite" to say, "Would you rather give a tax cut to businesses and wealthy Americans, or would you rather invest in infrastructure, education, and research?" It sounds good, but it's a ridiculous argument, because lower taxes spur economic growth, which not only ultimately increases tax revenue, but also enables the private sector to invest in infrastructure, education, and research, greatly increasing the total revenue invested across the board.

To really point out just how much of a political ploy or "talking point" it is to drum up their liberal base when Democrats start beating the "raise taxes on the rich" drum, look at the facts: according to IRS tax return and Treasury Department data in 2009 and 2010, if you taxed all millionaires 100 percent of their adjusted gross income, it wouldn't fund our government for even three short months! And it wouldn't cut a penny off of our national debt. I would add that if you taxed the wealthy that much, I'm pretty sure that they would all leave the country, retire, or sit back until wiser minds got into office.

In the early 1960s the top marginal tax rate was at 90 percent. Then-actor Ronald Reagan decided that he would only work half the year, because that was the point at which he hit that high tax threshold.

Reagan expressed that he much preferred riding his horse half of the year than to be paying the government 90 percent of what he worked for. He later expressed that was a real wake-up call for him on the damages that high taxes imposed on America.

The current tax code needs to be completely eviscerated and rewritten from scratch. Or, better yet, do away with the IRS altogether and come up with a good flat tax, or a national sales tax. Oh, wait a minute; that would have everyone putting a little skin in the game, which would be way too fair for politicians to ever support. But surely there has got to be a better solution than what our current tax code is.

On a personal note, I'm a developer, and at the time the Great Recession hit, I had a lot of balls in the air and owned a lot of flourishing businesses. No question the economic collapse put a major hurt on me, as it did any developer or entrepreneur that had anything at risk. By the end of 2009 I had lost over $25 million. As much as that hurt, it didn't completely wipe me out, and I was able to survive it. That said, just prior to the economic collapse, I had upward of 250 people working for my various businesses, and I was pumping tens of millions of dollars back into my local economy every year. No doubt the success of my businesses had a positive trickle-down success effect for my community, as well as the hundreds of other businesses I purchased goods and services from. It certainly had a positive impact on the 250 or so employees that worked for my companies as well as the families that they were supporting. In 2010, I started liquidating most of my business assets to ensure that I survived the fall out of the recession. Fortunately I got through it, and was able to start rebuilding my life.

My point in telling my personal story is, as much as I got hurt by the recession, it didn't completely change my life or how I live. Sure, I had to cut back on a lot of things; I sold off whatever I could to eliminate my debt, and did whatever else I could to get back on my feet.

That said, all in all, I still live pretty comfortably. What has changed, however, and what I'm not doing today, is employing 250 people; nor am I pumping tens of millions of dollars back into the economy every year, the way I was five or six years ago. That definitely does trickle down and adversely affects a lot of people's lives in my community. It's not that I'm not ready to jump back into the game. As hard as the economic collapse hit me, I went to great lengths to protect my good credit, to enable me to take advantage of some potentially great opportunities that were created due to the Great Recession; the price of real estate dropped in half, and it created an incredible buying opportunity, for those able to take advantage of it. I certainly haven't lost the knowledge or ability to jump back in and re-build my war chest, and that is certainly what I intend to do.

Unfortunately, progressive policies aren't helping our economy recover, as we are still in the "lost decade." I have grave concerns that our country is on a collision course of our own making. The enormous national debt, Obamacare, corruption and incompetence in government—the list goes on and on. The Obama administration and their policies and regulations are the most antibusiness administration I've ever witnessed in my twenty-five-plus years of being in business. The world is in total chaos, the threat of a terrorist attack on our homeland is a very real and present danger, and our president is nothing short of being derelict in his duties. I don't scare easily, but the Obama administration's failure of leadership at home and across the globe, scares the living hell out of me!

In full disclosure, in case it's not obvious thus far, I'm a conservative, and I always have been ever since I knew anything about politics. When I was nineteen I voted for Ronald Reagan in my first presidential election. Ironically, when I was twelve years old, I took my first after-school job washing dishes at a restaurant called "Reagan's Restaurant," owned by a man named Ronald Reagan. I'll never forget when I first met him; he introduced himself, "Hi, my name's Ronald Reagan, you know, like the actor." I was twelve, I had no idea who Ronald Reagan the actor was, but when Ronald Reagan ran for president a few years later, I paid close attention.

Here's an overly simplified explanation of politics you have probably heard: "If you're not a liberal before you're thirty, you have no heart. If you're not a conservative by the time you're forty, you have no brain." That doesn't mean that if you're a liberal you're stupid, or if you're a conservative you're heartless; good people can love this country and their fellow Americans and still disagree on what's best for America. What it does mean, however, is that most liberal or progressive ideas and ideology often sound good and compassionate in theory or in academic circles but, as practical, "real world" solutions, they inevitably fall way short of delivering their intended objective and almost always create unintended consequences that adversely impact the majority of the population.

Let me try to explain this another way: Responsible parents inevitably think much differently than their children. They have to. Someone has to be the adult in the room; someone has to be responsible; someone has to make the family work, pay the bills, keep a roof over the family's head, keep food on the table, live within their budget, and create a safety net for the future security of the family. Very seldom do any of the real-life responsibilities of building a strong and secure family ever resonate with our children until they are self-reliant, productive members of society with their own families that they themselves are responsible for.

Most kids, given the choice, would "live for themselves and live for today" without giving tomorrow much thought or concern and completely take for granted the responsibility Mom and Dad have in providing for the family. As responsible parents, we understand and accept the naiveté and free spirit of our children and their sometimes grand ideas about life. As parents, we not only understand it, at times we embrace it, encourage it, and even envy it, knowing that all too soon they will be exposed to the realities of life, and as parents we can only hope that we have given them the tools to make the transition to becoming strong, self-sufficient members of society as they become adults and are someday prepared to take care of themselves and able to be responsible for families of their own.

My point is that some of us grow up, and some of us don't. Some of us take responsibility for our own lives, and understand that no one owes us anything, and that it is totally up to us to be self-sufficient. Others however, never reach that level of maturity, and like children still living under their parents roof, fail to take responsibility for themselves, and are all too happy to be co-dependent on the government, or whomever is willing.

Let's use the same "family analysis" and compare it to how our democracy works. Let's start with a typical family of five (two parents and three children). Let's suppose that the typical American family operated the same way as our democracy and that each member of the family gets an equal vote, regardless of the fact that only Mom and Dad are contributing to the family piggy bank. Suppose the kids voted that they wanted more of an allowance every week and didn't want to go to school every day, or voted to go to Disneyland twice a year, regardless, keep in mind, of whether or not Mom and Dad could afford it. If the family worked the same as our democracy, the parents would be forced to pay whatever until the piggy bank was completely empty. Our democracy works exactly that way; only about half of Americans contribute to the national piggy bank, but yet everyone has a say on how the national treasure is spent. America is on the tipping point of having the people who pay into the piggy bank be outnumbered by the voters who are dependent on the piggy bank but don't contribute to it.

What happens as that non-taxpaying majority votes and demands that the taxpaying minority keep increasing their allowance through social entitlements? Things would eventually come to a head, and the very same thing that would happen to that family or any business that operated in the same irresponsible fashion will inevitably happen to our country.

Let's take the family analogy one step further. Say these parents are able to charge up everything their children are demanding on the family credit card. Pretty soon the credit cards get maxed out, but suppose the parents are able to work things out with their banker to keep increasing their line of credit on that credit card. Pretty soon the parents are borrowing money off of the credit card just to pay the interest payment on the credit card. What happens when all of a sudden one day the bank doesn't allow the parents to charge anything more and cuts their credit cards up? The family is forced into bankruptcy, the bank forecloses on their family home, repossesses all of their assets, the parents can no longer support their family, and everything is lost. That is exactly what our country is doing right this second, every single day: borrowing money from China or wherever else we can get it just to pay the interest on our debt and to allow politicians to keep buying votes from naïve voters who don't know any better.

Have you ever known anyone who takes money off of one credit card, just to pay the minimum interest payment on another? Or writes one bad check to cover another bad check he or she wrote two days earlier? You could do that only for a short period of time before everything came crushing down on your head. That's what America is doing right now, just to keep the lights on.

If you can't quite relate to the family analogy, take any business you have any association with at all; a company you own, manage, or work for. How long do you think that company would stay in business if they were spending more money than they were bringing in? How long do you think that same company would be able to keep the doors open if all of the employees had an equal say on how the business was run or how every penny was spent, regardless of the fact that the employees didn't have a vested interest? No skin in the game? They would all vote themselves a big raise and a lucrative benefit package, and the company would be out of business in no time.

That's the way our democracy works; everyone gets an equal vote regardless if he or she has made any investment in our country or our economy, and yet voters who pay absolutely nothing into the national treasury cheer the loudest when politicians want to raise taxes on the upper income earners in this country. Like children lobbying their parents for a bigger allowance.

According to the Tax Federation's chief economist, the top 10 percent of earners in America already pay over 70 percent of all taxes in America, meaning the vast majority of earners, 90 percent, pay less than 30 percent of all taxes. Forty-seven percent of working-age Americans pay virtually nothing in income taxes every year. Yet politicians have the audacity to claim that the wealthy aren't paying their fair share.

Don't get me wrong; I'm all for giving people a hand up in life. What I'm not for is giving a handout. I also believe that we must always take care of those who can't take care of themselves due to age or disability, and I firmly believe that every child in America be given every opportunity America can afford him or her. But I squarely believe that America and our elected officials should make every effort to promote self-reliance and prevent government dependency for those able to work and provide for themselves.

Hey, I will be the first to admit that, in theory, some liberal ideas may sound pretty good! Until reality sets in and you have to take a realistic look at the costs, the unintended consequences, or both. Wouldn't it be just great if everyone in America made the same amount as everyone else—let's say $100,000 a year—and could never lose his or her job? As much as that might sound great in theory, it would be an economic disaster! It's no secret that some people put forth a lot more effort in getting training and education, work harder, and apply themselves more than others. Where's the incentive for people to be more educated or work harder than their coworkers or apply themselves more if they can only earn the same as those who don't educate themselves or don't apply themselves?

The minimum wage argument always draws voters out of the woodwork because it sounds like a great idea in theory. However, the unintended consequences cause more harm than good to those who need and may deserve a pay increase the most. In fact a recent study by the Free-Market American Action Forum found that the states with minimum wages higher than the federal minimum suffer from higher unemployment.

Researchers looked at labor data from both the nineteen states that as of 2013 had enforced minimum wages above $7.25 per hour and the thirty-one states that had minimum wages equal to $7.25. Overall, they found that just a $1 increase in the minimum wage was "associated with a 1.48 percentage point increase in the unemployment rate, and a "0.18 percentage point decrease in the net job growth rate."

A higher minimum wage thus led to the unemployment of 747,700 workers and a job growth reduction of 83,300 jobs, the study claims. The study went on to note that the minimum wage hikes especially took a toll on the employment opportunities for young and low-skill workers. Focusing in on sixteen- to nineteen-year-olds, researchers found that the "mean annual average teenage unemployment rate in states with minimum wages above $7.25 per hour in 2013 was 22.5 percent, which was 2 percentage points above the mean annual average unemployment rate in states with minimum wages at $7.25 per hour." Furthermore, "in high minimum wage states, the net job growth rate for teenagers was actually a negative in 2013, with a mean annual average rate of -0.5 percent." In states that held to the $7.25 per hour minimum wage, the same age group actually increased by 1.8 percent from 2012 to 2013.

The conclusion is unmistakable: when you raise the minimum wage, the unintended consequences are that you stifle job creation and adversely impact economic growth. A low minimum wage offers young and low-skill workers the opportunity to have a stepping-stone and get that first job and gain some marketable skills so that they can earn a higher wage. Employers are far less likely to hire young and lower-skilled workers if the minimum wage is too high.

I would add that when you raise the minimum wage, you inadvertently raise the cost of products that minimum wage earners purchase.

The very best way to increase wages is to lower the unemployment rate. Lower minimum wages provide employers the incentive to give young and low-skilled workers opportunities to enter the workforce and gain the experience and skills needed to work their way up the workforce ladder.

Anyone who has ever been in the workforce or has even observed people in the workforce recognizes that some workers should be paid more than others and that there has to be a low starting point for workers without any job experiences or skills. The higher the minimum wage, the less likely it is that some people will ever have any real opportunity to enter the workforce. A lower-paying starting wage with an opportunity to improve oneself is far better than no opportunity at all.

The progressive logic that all workers should be paid the same as anyone else working the same job has created a real problem with most unions today. For many, there is limited incentive to work harder or smarter than your coworker who is going to make the same pay as you are just by putting in the minimum performance.

Take the teachers union for example; anyone who's been to school or has had their kids in school knows that there are some really great teachers who do a fantastic job because they love teaching and helping their students develop into better, smarter students. However, we also know that there are also other teachers who shouldn't be teaching at all! The problem is that you have two teachers who've been working at the same school for the same amount of time and they are making the same income regardless of who is doing the better job. Worse yet, most union employees (teachers, government, or other) are difficult if not impossible to fire. Regardless of whatever industry you are in, most unions look out only for the union members and not necessarily the companies who employ the union workers, or the taxpayers who employ the federal employees, or the consumer who is purchasing union-made products, or our children who are being taught.

The federal government is almost completely made up of union employees, and the fact is that a federal employee is more likely to be killed on the job than he or she is to be fired! To add insult to injury, government employees earn nearly 50 percent more salary and benefits than their private-sector counterparts. Think about that fact for a minute. We, the taxpayers, are paying government employees; they work for us, not the other way around. Imagine owning your own business and paying your employees more than you earn yourself. That is exactly what the American taxpayer is doing every day.

Don't get me wrong, unions have been an important part of our country's history and union workers can still provide a valuable service to our country and our economy. But if unions intend to survive in this global economy, it would certainly be in their best interest of their own self-preservation if they evolved into a twenty-first-century force that allows American companies to be competitive on the world stage. Unions have been on the decline for the past couple of decades. American companies are moving to "right to work" friendly states in droves in order to stay competitive. That should be a very loud alarm bell that most unions need to make some serious changes. When an employer, or the US government can't hold an employee accountable, because of a union; that is a travesty.

I can speak on unions with some firsthand knowledge. When I began my construction career some thirty years ago, I joined the carpenters union, and went through their carpenter's apprenticeship program, and I did get a lot out of the education I received. When I founded my own construction company, I also started a sister company that was a unionized shop, to enable me to do government construction projects. So I have a pretty good perspective of unions both from the unionized workers point of view, and the point of view of a company who employs unionized workers. The advantage of joining a union is supposed to be job security, and collective bargaining. There is an old saying, "he who would give up freedom for security deserves neither." That so called job security and collective bargaining comes at a cost. Personally, I would much prefer to be in complete control of making my own job security, and I certainly don't want anyone else negotiating what my job performance is worth, and having my earnings tied to that of my co-workers. From an employer's point of view, unions are a disadvantage, because it limits an employer's ability to demand accountability from their employees, and what employer wants to be dictated to about what they pay their employees, that's what the free market should dictate. From a consumer's point of view, unions typically increase the cost of products, for example most would agree that Walmart offers some of the most competitive prices on the products they sell; Walmart is a non-union retailer. From a parent's point of view, unionized teachers are a big part of the problem with many failing public schools, because it forces schools to keep teachers based on tenure, instead of who the best teachers actually are. From a tax payer's point of view, unionized government workers greatly increase the tax burden on the American tax payers, increase our national debt, and keep the majority of our government completely unaccountable. So I guess you might say, that my experiences as an employee, an employer, a consumer, a parent, and a tax payer; I am not pro-union.

Politics plays a big role in unions. Unions notoriously support progressive politicians, using union dues regardless of how the union workers feel about issues or how they vote. And in turn, the unions expect the politicians that they have purchased to support pro-union ideology and spend America's treasure supporting union projects, schools, government employees, and so on. The next time you hear a politician proclaiming that we need to raise taxes so we can spend money on infrastructure, etc., that's what they are talking about: funding union jobs, to thank the unions for getting them elected!

Not that our country doesn't need ongoing infrastructure improvements; but as a taxpayer, knowing how indebted we are as a country, I want any contracting that my taxpayer dollars are going toward to go to the most qualified and competitive bid without dictating to a private company just what its employee compensation package must be.

If the federal government would cut just one single penny from every dollar spent every year, just 1 percent, the federal budget would be balanced in less than ten years! We will explore that a little more in depth later in this book, but my point is that politicians scream bloody murder anytime someone tries to have an adult conversation about reducing spending or trying to balance the budget. Think about that as you consider that the average federal employee makes one and a half times that of someone doing a similar job in the private sector.

In 2011 Congress ended up with sequestration after their inability to agree on responsible spending cuts. Sequestration was basically an agreement between the Democrats and the Republicans, that if they couldn't come up with a responsible way to cut spending in a given period of time; that a trillion dollars of spending cuts would automatically take place; half of which effected domestic spending cuts, and the other half effected cuts to the military. Politicians from both sides of the aisle screamed that the world was going to come to an end; in fact Senate Majority Leader Harry Reid proclaimed that it was going to cost more than a million and a half jobs. According to the Congressional Budget Office, sequestration cost only one government job! That's right, just one. Kind of funny how they were able to figure out where they were able to cut back a trillion dollars without losing more than one single government employee. Kind of makes you wonder how much more waste could have been cut if the government payroll was a serious consideration.

On the point of spending cuts; the Obama administration in July 2014 had the military send out pink slips to soldiers who were actually in battle. Notices telling our brave Americans defending our way of life, that their service would no longer be needed, and when they returned to America, they would be out of a job! That is absolutely pathetic if you ask me. While every segment of our government, in nearly every government agency other than our military; is growing and expanding their work force; their unionized government workforce; we are sending pink slips to the brave (non-unionized) American soldiers who have made our very democracy possible.

America doesn't have a revenue problem; we have an out-of-control government spending problem.

I will end this chapter with another quote from our Founding Fathers that I think is particularly relevant:

"I must study politics and war that my sons may have liberty to study mathematics and philosophy. My sons ought to study mathematics and philosophy, geography, natural history and naval architecture, navigation, commerce, and agriculture, in order to give their children a right to study painting, poetry, music, architecture, statuary, tapestry, and porcelain." —John Adams in a letter to his wife, Abigail Adams, 1780

CHAPTER TWO

It's the Spending, Stupid!
The Dollar and the Debt

"But with respect to future debt; would it not be wise and just, for that nation to declare in the constitution they are forming that neither the legislature, nor the nation itself, can validly contract more debt; than they may pay within their own age, or within the term of 19 years."—Thomas Jefferson, September 6, 1789

Just imagine how much better off we would be today as a country if our government couldn't borrow any more than it could afford to pay off in less than twenty years.

Please read this entire chapter very carefully. I realize that the topic of the debt and our economy can be boring, and most would prefer not to think about economics, but that's the problem: most Americans don't give this much thought, and that's why as a country we find ourselves on the brink of a disaster with consequences beyond comprehension. We allow ourselves to falsely believe that brighter minds than our own are in charge of our nation's treasure, and that simply isn't always the case.

Regardless of your politics, and regardless of whether you agree at all with conservative ideology, we are all Americans, and just as we should all be keenly aware of our own personal income and expenses, we should be equally keenly aware of our country's income and expenses. If you don't get anything else out of this book, I strongly encourage you to carefully read and make sure you understand the critically important information in this chapter.

Can you guess who said the following statement?

> The fact that we are here today to debate raising America's debt limit is a sign of leadership failure. It is a sign that the US government can't pay its own bills. It is a sign that we now depend on ongoing financial assistance from foreign countries to finance our government's reckless fiscal policies. Increasing America's debt weakens us domestically and internationally. Leadership means that "the buck stops here." Instead, Washington is shifting the burden of bad choices today onto the backs of our children and grandchildren. America has a debt problem and a failure of leadership. Americans deserve better.

That statement sounds like a fiscally conservative politician that I would agree with. It's completely unfathomable that those words came out of the mouth of then Senator Barack Obama on March 20, 2006, in a speech from the Senate floor. While I completely agreed with Barack Obama when he expressed that sentiment, I soon found out that he was neither sincere nor honest about his thoughts about the national debt and spending.

Then Senator Obama was arguing against raising the national debt ceiling to $9 trillion. That was the total amount that our national debt would be allowed to increase to through the end of George Bush's presidency, and it included the amount of the national debt that George Bush had inherited from every single president before him.

Six years into Barack Obama's presidency, he and his administration have spent that much alone—the amount he said would be reckless fiscal policy and a failure of leadership if the national debt ever reached that height. The amount it took forty-three presidents and over two centuries to accumulate, Barack Obama spent in just six years.

At some point while you are reading this book, and now might be a good time, so you are aware of the validity of what you're reading, I strongly encourage you to take a few minutes and go online and look at our national debt clock: www.usdebtclock.org. Take a really good look at all of the information that's available to you. This is America's national debt clock, and it shows you exactly how much debt our country owes, what revenue our country is bringing in, and what expenses we are incurring every single second of every single day. It also shows you what our unfunded liabilities are. You can also see just how much that debt calculates into what each taxpayer would have to pay to eliminate our debt. This site has a lot of good information and, more importantly, it allows "we the people" to see firsthand just how much trouble we are in as a country.

Before we get any further in talking about the national debt and the most important part of this chapter, which is the very real possibility of America losing the US dollar as the world reserve currency, which would result in Armageddon almost overnight, I want to do a quick Economics 101 to refresh your understanding of economics.

I'm not an economist, so I'll try to keep this lesson short, to the point, and very elementary. I know that this is a boring topic for the most part, but it's important that we make sure that we all understand how our currency works. I mean, where does our money actually come from? Where does it originate? And how do we know if our economy is growing or contracting?

Up until 1971, gold was the basis for our entire monetary system. Today, however, the Federal Reserve requires its member banks to keep specific amounts of money on reserve as a means of keeping a lid on the uncontrolled expansion of fiat (printed) money; in other words, these cash reserve requirements are the major safeguard to keep the money supply from exploding the system.

Central banks can create money by buying bonds in the treasury market. When central banks buy bonds, they usually buy their own country's treasury bonds, and their purchases are made from various banks that own bonds. The money from the central banks is held in vaults and is used for loan-making capital.

When the economy starts to slow down, the Fed can try to jump-start the economy by lowering interest rates and injecting money into the system. This money is injected into the economy by the Fed buying bonds from the banks.

When the Fed wants to increase the money supply in the United States, it buys bonds from banks on the open market and uses a pretty simple formula to calculate how much money it is actually creating.

All of this policy, however, can be very dangerous to our economy if not managed effectively by the Fed and can very easily lead to inflation (swift rise in prices because of a weaker dollar). To try to avoid inflation, the Fed keeps a tight rein on how much banks can actually lend out by using a bank reserve management system. This is far from an exact science, but it is what our monetary system is.

The reserve requirements work as follows:

If the current formula calls for a 10 percent reserve ratio, it means that for every dollar that a bank keeps in reserve, it can lend $10 to its clients.

At the same time, if the Fed buys $500 million in bonds on the open market, it creates $5 billion in new money that makes its way to the public via bank loans. In other words, if the Fed buys $500 million in bonds, that gives banks $500 million in cash reserves, which allows the banks to loan out ten times that amount, which puts $5 billion into the economy.

The reverse, or opposite, is true when the Fed wants to tighten credit and slow down the economy. It sells bonds to banks, thus draining money from the system, again based on the reserve formula.

All of this monetary system works OK until it doesn't. There are a multitude of considerations that take effect in our economy every day that can derail this system, resulting in huge shifts in our economy. Printing too much money is not at all a good thing, as it drastically weakens the American dollar, which results in inflation. The weaker the dollar, the less it buys.

So what is the primary indicator used to gauge the health and strength of our economy? Gross domestic product, or GDP. GDP represents the total dollar value of all goods and services produced over a specific time period, such as a year or a quarter. You can think of it as the size of our economy. The GDP is usually expressed as a comparison to the previous year or quarter. If from one year to another our GDP is up 2 percent, that means that our economy has grown by 2 percent in a year's time.

Measuring GDP is pretty complicated, which is why we have economists. The most basic calculation can be derived in two ways: either by adding up what everyone in the country spent in a given year (the expenditure method) or by adding up what everyone in the country earned in a given year (the income method). Either measure should arrive at about the same outcome.

The most common approach is the expenditure method, and it is calculated by adding the total consumption, investment, government spending, and net exports.

The income approach, which is often referred to as GDP (I), is calculated by adding up the total compensation to employees, gross profits for incorporated and non-incorporated firms, and taxes less any subsidies.

So you can start to see how important a growing GDP is to any economy and how it affects everyone's life within that economy. Any significant change in the GDP will have an almost immediate effect on the economy, everything from the value of stocks to unemployment. If the GDP is growing each year, it results in a lower unemployment rate, higher wages, and profitable companies. A healthy growth in GDP would be about 4 percent per year. A negative or flat GDP, however, is detrimental to our economy, which is why a recession is identified as any two quarters in a row of zero or negative GDP.

Now that you've looked at the debt clock, if seeing firsthand just how serious our troubles are doesn't scare the hell out of you, please read the rest of this chapter and then give that a bit more consideration. I suggest you look at that site every Monday morning, and hopefully it will be a blaring wake-up call to you to take a stand with me to try to take our country back from the vultures at the gate! Or, you can bury your head in the sand and wait for the tide to come in. Either way, if you don't pull your head out of the sand, sooner or later you are going to suffocate or drown.

As I'm writing this book, it is currently mid-2014, and I anticipate finishing this book and having it published by year's end, so the numbers I'm using have been rounded off based on the minimum numbers the US debt clock anticipates that our country will be at on its current trajectory at the end of 2014.

Imagine spending over 17 percent more than you earn every year. And instead of tightening up your belt and cutting back on spending, you convince yourself that it's better to rob Peter to pay Paul. First maxing out your credit cards, then a second mortgage on your home. Pretty soon your creditworthiness is stretched to the limit, your interest payments steadily increase, and soon you are at the point you can't pay your bills or borrow any more money. It doesn't take long until the house of cards comes crashing down on your head! Can you think of anything more irresponsible than living that far beyond one's means? Me neither, but that is exactly what our government is doing with our economy and the fate of our future generations. It is completely irresponsible and completely unsustainable!

I know most people couldn't care less about the national debt, and most people have their hands full just trying to figure out how to keep their own households above water. Besides, what does $18 trillion in debt really mean anyway? Let's start by actually writing out the number: $18,000,000,000,000.00. Let's put this another way: if you had spent $1 million each and every day since the birth of Jesus Christ, you would have spent about $735 billion by the end of 2014. But wait a minute; we have an $18 trillion debt at the end of 2014;

that's about 24.5 times more than $735 billion. So what that tells us is that if we had spent a million dollars every single hour, twenty-four hours a day, seven days a week, and 365 days a year, since the very first Christmas; it would still be less than what our national debt is today! Christ's birth in year one, times 365, times 2014, equals $735,010,000,000.00. Multiply that number times twenty-four hours a day and it gets you $17.640 trillion. That's a heck of a lot of money, but it is still less than what our national debt is today. Try to wrap your head around that for a minute.

OK, let's say we can forget about our national debt, even though it's going up by about $1.5 trillion every year. Let's set that number aside for a minute and take a look at our country's unfunded liabilities. What is an unfunded liability? That's the amount we ("We the people") are going to have to pay at some point in the future, one way or the other. Actually, let me restate that: there is virtually no way "we" are ever going to be able to pay that, but our children, our grandchildren, and their grandchildren are going to have to pay it at some point in the future.

That is what "We the people" have left to our next generation. The vast majority of unfunded liabilities are in entitlements: Social Security, Medicare, prescription drugs, etc. That number is now approaching $120 trillion! That's right, look for yourself: $120,000,000,000,000.00! That number is nearly seven times greater than what our national debt is. That number basically represents America's unfunded retirement fund (social security, Medicare, and Prescription drug liabilities).

Let's break down just how much it would take every single taxpayer to pay off America's unfunded liabilities. Make sure you are sitting down. In order for us to be able to pay our unfunded liabilities, it would take every single taxpayer in America contributing over $1,000,000! As many people don't make $1 million in their working lifetimes, it is virtually impossible that there is anyone alive on this planet today that will ever see the day that our unfunded liabilities are ever paid off. Plus keep in mind that that number is exploding every second of every day.

So, not only do we have $18 trillion in debt that we currently owe out, a lot of which we owe to foreign countries; we're spending about $8.5 trillion a year while only bringing in about $7 trillion a year. And we have nearly $120 trillion in unfunded liabilities! Yes, that is correct, but please don't take my word for it; look at the debt clock for yourself, and do your own math. Or you can chose not to believe your lying eyes, because how on earth can this be right? It doesn't take a mathematician or an economist to see the tragedy that is looming.

If you've allowed yourself to become complacent, as many Americans unfortunately have, you might be asking yourself right now, how can this possibly be true? Why aren't our elected officials sounding the alarm bells from the rooftops of Capitol Hill and the White House? Why isn't this in the news every day? The unfortunate truth is that most Americans don't want to hear about it because it is unfathomable to most people to believe. There are, however, some courageous politicians who have been sounding the alarms loud and clear; but when they do, they are attacked from all directions by progressives, and accused of wanting to "throw Granny over the cliff."

Here is a wake-up call to everyone: if we don't take some serious and immediate action to get our spending under control, Granny is going to jump off the cliff, because before long, America won't be able to provide for her the way we have promised.

Talking about politicians who have taken a responsible position and have been sounding the alarm bells, Paul Ryan, House budget chairman and a former vice presidential candidate, has been pummeled by the left when he's introduced a responsible budget every year since he's been budget chairman. His budget addresses the issue and balances the budget in ten years. House Republicans have passed his budget every year; however, Senate Majority Leader Harry Reid has axed it the second it reached the Senate. Why, you ask? Because Harry Reid would rather use the issue as a political tool to scare older Americans into thinking that Ryan's budget will take from their retirement. The truth is that Ryan's budget is the first real, responsible move to try to save entitlements from their own pending demise. If you have any doubt about that fact whatsoever, you should take another look at the $130 trillion we currently have in unfunded liabilities. Harry Reid would have you believe that it's not a big deal, and that if we'd just raise taxes on the rich, the problem would go away. That's nonsense! As I've previously outlined, you could tax every millionaire in the country at 100 percent and not only would it not shave a penny off of our national debt, it wouldn't even fund the government for three months. So, the only responsible way to address the issue is to figure out some smart solutions that don't affect our seniors who are currently receiving benefits, but do make responsible adjustments to future recipients.

So, does everyone in America just keep his or her blinders on? Until what? Imagine driving a car with no brakes that is on cruise control with a blindfold on. Sooner or later you are going to crash. You know you are going to crash, but it's too hard to think about, so you just hang on to the wheel as long as you can. Or, you could consider the consequences, take the blindfold off, and try to avoid the crash. Our economy is on cruise control, we're headed for the abyss, and our elected officials have removed the brakes. The question is, are we going to take control, make the hard decisions, and take our blinders off, or just hang on until our demise?

I seriously doubt that no one saw the Great Depression coming; no doubt, there had to have been signs of it, and I'm confident that good people tried to sound the alarm bells. But, hey, the Roaring Twenties that led up to the Great Depression had everyone thinking that such a demise could never happen in America. They too chose to keep their blinders on. Well, disaster did come, and thanks to the failed New Deal progressive policies of then President Franklin D. Roosevelt and his big-government ideas, the Depression lingered on for an entire decade.

The lead-up to the Great Recession wasn't much different than that of the Great Depression. For many Americans, 2002 through 2007 were a lot like the roaring twenties age of prosperity. There were signs that things could be about to boil over, and some politicians and some economists were sounding the alarms, but darn few. When times are good, no one wants to believe that disaster is looming, and they attack anyone and criticize anyone trying to rain on their parade. Our current failed policies of big government are very similar to those failed big-government policies that followed the Great Depression, and they have resulted in the same lingering detriment to America that has stifled any chance of real recovery, resulting in another "lost decade" in our country's history.

We'll talk in much greater detail about the Great Recession and the Great Depression in another chapter, but I bring them up now because all too often, as Americans we tend to have selective memory and fail to learn the lessons history should have taught us. We've allowed our government to get so out of control that the very future and security of our country and our democracy are in serious jeopardy.

Now let's talk about the possible looming nail in our coffin. I intentionally italicized that sentence for you speed readers because you need to pay special attention to this topic, because if this happens it could lead to the end of America as the world's largest economy and only superpower, at least for the rest of any of our lives. I'm talking about the fact that the US dollar is the world's reserve currency and that it is in jeopardy of being replaced by a single world "super-currency."

Wikipedia defines a reserve currency as a currency that is held in significant quantities by governments and institutions as part of their foreign exchange reserves and that is commonly used in international transactions. Persons who live in a country that issues a reserve currency can purchase imports and borrow across borders more cheaply than persons in other nations because they need not exchange their currency to do so. According to economists such as Valery Giscard d'Estaing, a former French minister and president, a reserve currency gets certain benefits called "the exorbitant privilege."

At present, the US dollar is the world's reserve currency, and the world's need for dollars has allowed the US government as well as Americans to borrow at lower costs, granting them an advantage in excess of $100 billion per year.

So, in elementary terms, what is the "world currency"? It is the dominant currency around the world that commerce is traded in, including oil. What that means is that to purchase oil, for example, anywhere around the world, most foreign currency must first be traded for, or converted into, the US dollar. That gives the US dollar and America a significant advantage, because it gives us an almost unlimited ability to print money, buy up bonds, and use those funds to subsidize our economy and apply to our debt. That is the only reason that our country didn't go into another Great Depression as a result of the housing bubble, and why we are able to keep the lights on, so to speak. But that certainly won't last forever for America any more than it ever has for any other dominant economies throughout history.

Reserve currencies come and go. International currencies in the past have included the Chinese liang and Greek drachma, coined in the fifth century BC, the silver punch-marked coins of fourth-century India, the Roman dinar, the Byzantine solidus and Islamic dinar of the Middle Ages, the Venetian ducato of the Renaissance, the seventeenth-century Dutch guilder, and the Spanish dollar, which dominated world currency for about a two-hundred-year period prior to the nineteenth century. Throughout the nineteenth century the world currency was the gold standard, which basically meant that all of the nation's currency represented a measurement of gold.

The United States has only been the largest economy in the world for less than a hundred years. Great Britain was considered to hold that spot for a brief time between World War I and World War II; China, however, was the largest economy in the world prior to 1900 and had maintained the position as the dominant economy for nearly two hundred years after they took the spot as the dominant world economy from India in the early 1700's.

My point in reciting the history of how many other countries have been the dominant world economy and how many times that the world currency has changed is that I would just about bet that any of the before-mentioned countries never thought that their economy would decline to the point that they were surpassed by another. America's the dominant world economy today, and that may be so for now, but if so, why is it that we owe China $1.5 trillion? If your finances are healthier than your neighbor's, you probably aren't needing to borrow money from them just to pay your bills. Just a thought.

From World War I until 1944, the world currency had been the British pound sterling. As the British economy had been in decline, and after America's victory in World War II, the US dollar became the recognized world currency at the Bretton Woods Conference of 1944. Between 1944 and 1971 the US dollar was backed by gold and silver, but following the Smithsonian Agreement in 1971, the US dollar became backed by nothing more than "the full faith and credit of the US government." Then President Richard Nixon basically told the world to take our paper or don't. At the time, there wasn't much any other country could do about the United States' decision to abandon the dollar being backed by metal. At the time, no other country had any economic standing to step in and replace the dollar. Times have changed.

This is worth your serious consideration. It is from the Board of Governors of the Federal Reserve System (this is posted on the Federal Reserve's website):

> Federal Reserve notes are not redeemable in gold, silver, or any other commodity. Federal Reserve notes have not been redeemable in gold since January 30, 1934, when the Congress amended Section 16 of the Federal Reserve Act to read: "The said (Federal Reserve) notes shall be obligations of the United States…They shall be redeemed in lawful money on demand at the Treasury Department of the United States, in the city of Washington, District of Columbia, or at any Federal Reserve bank." Federal Reserve notes have not been redeemable in silver since the 1960s.

> The Congress has specified that Federal Reserve Banks must hold collateral equal in value to the Federal Reserve notes that the Federal Reserve Bank puts into circulation. This collateral is chiefly held in the form of US Treasury, federal agency, and government-sponsored enterprise securities.

Pay attention to what the Federal Reserve is saying; it states that Congress has specified that the Federal Reserve banks (the US government) must hold collateral equal in value to the notes it puts into circulation. In simple terms, I read that to say that US financial obligations cannot exceed the value of their assets. Pretty simple; you can look at a balance sheet and see what any company's total assets are and what its liabilities are. I would direct you back to the US debt clock; it clearly shows that all US assets are valued at about $113 trillion. However, it also shows our unfunded liabilities at $120 trillion. I'm pretty darn good at looking at a balance sheet, and what that tells me is that we have $7 trillion more in liabilities than we have in assets, making America's net worth negative $7 trillion! Which seriously questions the value of the US dollar.

Let's put this into a simpler thought: If your neighbor was living far beyond his means, spending far more than he earned, and was up to his nose in debt, would you accept an IOU from him? Probably not, but that's what the US dollar is; it's an IOU from "the full faith and credit of the United States of America," which is living far beyond its means and has a debt that couldn't possibly be satisfied.

While you are looking at the US debt clock, also pay attention to what we are paying out in interest each year just to cover our payments. Six hundred billion dollars a year! That's right, 40 percent of our deficit (the amount we owe out over the amount we take in) is simply paying interest on our debt! In 2011 America's creditworthiness was downgraded for the first time in American history. Any consumer knows the weaker your credit, the more interest you pay. If the interest on our debt increases by just a tenth of a percent, it would be catastrophic! If the dollar loses its spot as the world reserve currency, our interest on our debt would skyrocket overnight!

China is on a comeback as the dominant economy in the world. The Asian giant has experienced an average 10 percent growth rate since it initiated market reforms in 1978, while lifting nearly half of its 1.3 billion people out of poverty to become the undisputed second largest economy behind the United States. A 2012 published authoritative study on global long-term growth prospects by the Organization for Economic Cooperation and Development (OECD) stated specifically that China's GDP (based on purchasing power parity, or PPP) was forecast to hit $15.26 trillion in 2015 and, for the very first time in over a century, exceeding the United States' forecast GDP, which at the time of the study was projected to be $15.24 trillion in 2015. It is important to point out, however, that this is not necessarily comparing GDP to GDP, as the PPP measure takes into consideration the implied exchange rate at which one country would have to convert currency into that of the other country. However, regardless of how you measure it, China is nipping at our heels as the dominant world economy, and if we don't take some very quick action, America could be at risk of losing the dollars position as the world reserve currency.

On the twenty-fourth of March, 2009, Zhou Xiaochuan, president of the People's Bank of China, called for "creative reform of the existing international monetary system toward an international reserve currency," arguing that it would "significantly reduce the risks of a future crisis and enhance crisis management capability." He further suggested that the International Monetary Fund's special drawing rights (a currency basket comprising dollars, euros, yen, and sterling) could serve as a "super-sovereign reserve currency" not easily influenced by the policies of individual countries, specifically the United States. Two days later, on March 26, 2009, a United Nations panel of expert economists called for a new global currency reserve scheme to replace the current US dollar-based system. Similar discussions have been had in Europe by the Board for Global Fiscal Stability.

A few weeks earlier, on March 16, 2009, in connection with the April 2009 G20 summit, the Kremlin called for a supranational reserve currency as part of a reform of the global financial system. In a document containing proposals for the G20 meeting, the Kremlin suggested that the IMF (or an ad hoc working group of the G20) should be instructed to carry out specific studies to review and consider the introduction of a supranational reserve currency to be issued by international financial institutions, indicating that it seems appropriate to consider the role of the IMF in this process and to review the feasibility of, and the need for, a "super-reserve" currency by the whole world community.

In its 2012–2013 Global Competitiveness Report, the World Economic Forum ranked the US economy as seventh most competitive out of 144 countries. While the United States still remains in the top ten, why is it that, as the world's largest economy, the United States has slipped to being only the seventh most competitive country to do business in? High taxes and anti-business policies and regulations.

I realize that this may all sound a little out there to some, but there is no denying that the drums are beating louder and louder about the very real possibility of replacing the US dollar as the world currency. The 2009 G20 summit was just the beginning, and the calls for a new world currency have only gotten louder and louder ever sense. Russian President Putin has made no bones about the fact that he sees President Obama as a weak leader, and he clearly has absolutely no respect for the United States.

Putin continues to one up President Obama on the world stage at every turn. No doubt; Putin is playing chess while Obama is playing marbles. Russia's economy right now might be relatively insignificant, but you get Russia and China cooperating with one another, as they are now, and that's a whole different story.

As recently as thirty years ago, Russia and China were both referred to as superpowers right alongside the United States, and they had been throughout most of the century. Then along came Ronald

Reagan, and his policies and leadership around the world catapulted America beyond the reach of any foreign power and ended the Cold War.

Barack Obama is definitely no Ronald Reagan and has reversed America's course of strength and prosperity to a position of leading from behind—or, more accurately, being left behind, or "following". I have little doubt that both China and Russia see the real "reset button" as the opportunity to take advantage of America's fledgling economy and weak leadership, reverse the gains America has made over the past thirty years, and regain their position on the world stage as dominant forces. Replacing the US dollar as the world reserve currency would be the proverbial nail in America's coffin if they are successful in their objective.

If the US dollar is replaced as the world reserve currency, life as we have come to know in America will be over. We are the only country in the world that can print money that is accepted all over the world. The very minute that ability stops, the jig is up; the smoke and mirrors will shatter and the game is over!

Our annual deficit is at $1.5 trillion a year. We have nearly $120 trillion in unfunded liabilities, which is $7 trillion more than our total assets. Any banker or anyone who's ever gotten a business loan will tell you that's not a good debt-to-worth ratio. If the US dollar loses its standing as the world reserve currency, America would not be able to satisfy our obligations, the value of our assets would be gravely diminished, and even if the government seized every single asset and every single dollar of every man, woman, and child in the country, it wouldn't be enough. We would be a bankrupt country.

There is no question that America's standing in the world has been drastically diminished ever since Barack Obama took office—from

Hillary Clinton's reset with Russia to our unsustainable national debt to our feckless foreign policy of leading from behind and drawing red lines in the sand that are meaningless. While some might think it's OK for America to be knocked down a few notches; that is an extremely dangerous place for America to be.

So how do we prevent this from happening? The simple answer is to get our fiscal house in order! That may be the simple answer, but actually implementing it is a real challenge. America has gotten complacent. We've gotten used to all the entitlements that politicians give to buy our votes, and once someone gets used to getting something for nothing, it's damn hard to get him or her to give it up. The dollar is in jeopardy of losing its standing as the world reserve currency because the rest of the world has serious questions and concerns about America's ability to honor its commitments due to our out-of-control spending and lack of leadership. There is very good cause for this concern. Why should the rest of the world be beholden to America's inability to live within our means? My guess is that they won't be. Now is the time for change—"hope for change." Real change.

CHAPTER THREE

Mission Not Accomplished: It All Begins

"If men through fear, fraud or mistake, should in terms renounce and give up any essential natural right, the eternal law of reason and the great end of society, would absolutely vacate such renunciation; the right to freedom being the gift of God Almighty, it is not in the power of Man to alienate this gift, and voluntarily become a slave."— John Adams, *Rights of Colonists*, 1772

Regardless of how you feel about George W. Bush, no one can deny that he agreed with those words of John Adams that freedom is the gift of God and it should not be within the power of man to alienate this gift. I have little doubt that George W. Bush was "just" in his cause of spreading democracy around the globe. Unfortunately people who have been oppressed for centuries and know no other life find it hard to embrace or even really understand freedom; they have, in a sense, "voluntarily enslaved themselves to a life without freedom."

So how did we as Americans allow ourselves to get into this terrible predicament we find ourselves in today? What in our recent history has led up to many of our country's people being so naïve that they would tolerate, even embrace the same progressive government policies that our grandparents and great-grandparents endured for the first lost decade of the Great Depression?

What was it that put all the pieces in place for the perfect storm? How on earth did we allow this to happen to our country? As I've said before, unfortunately people get complacent, and we can be a bit fickle. Most of us don't pay a lot of close attention to what's going on in the world, and the liberally biased media have long set the narrative of whatever propaganda they choose to peddle to the American people. All too often, people don't pay attention, until they do pay attention, usually because of something so significant that it immediately and adversely impacts their life and they are forced to pay attention. All too often, however, we only pay attention to the immediate facts at hand without getting what Paul Harvey used to refer to as "the rest of the story." For the younger generation whom might not remember Paul Harvey, he had a syndicated weekly radio address that talked in a very plain spoken manner about the issues of the time, but always added the behind the scenes side of the story or the other side of the story, and always ended his program with; "so now you know the rest of the story."

Unfortunately the event or the outcome of a tragedy that was long in the making is irrelevant without understanding what really brought the event or tragedy about. We fail to really evaluate the what, when, where, and why. We all too often are happy to accept the quick, clean, expedient explanation so we can put the matter behind us and get back to our own obtuse existence. If the liberal media yell loud enough, we hold whomever is in office at the time of the event account-able, regardless of whether he or she is actually to blame or not, and vote him or her out of office. We then pat ourselves on the back as we convince ourselves that we exercised our responsibility as voters, and then wash our hands of it.

In our most recent history, we have had two such events that were significant enough that everyone in America stopped what he or she was doing, at least long enough to realize that the event had taken place. First was September 11, 2001, which led to the war in Afghanistan and the invasion of Iraq. Nearly every adult in America remembers exactly the day that two airliners crashed into the World Trade Center, a third into the Pentagon, and a fourth into a field in Shanksville, Pennsylvania, after the passengers attempted to take back the aircraft from terrorists, effectively launching the first retaliatory strike against our enemy.

Secondly, no one can deny that the Great Recession adversely impacted every Americans life, and although we might not specifically recall the precise day it hit us the same way we do 9/11, we all remember the impact it had on our life and our country, and most of us are still feeling the impacts of it to this day. Unfortunately, however, very few of us ever bothered to understand "the rest of the story."

September 11, 2001, occurred just less than eight months after George W. Bush was inaugurated. The country was in shock, and for a period of time America was united. Americans not only wanted action, they were increasingly demanding it. George Bush responded decisively and, with bipartisan support in both houses of Congress and overwhelming international support, launched a war against Al-Qaeda in Afghanistan—a war that would last over a decade.

When I say that there was bipartisan support in both houses of Congress, that is understated. The fact is there has seldom if ever been a time in our democracy when the country, the president, and both houses of Congress were so completely united. Only three days after the attacks of 9/11, on September 14, both houses of Congress passed resolutions authorizing President Bush to use the US armed forces. The resolution stated:

> IN GENERAL—That the President is authorized to use all necessary and appropriate force against those nations, organizations, or persons he determines planned, authorized, committed, or aided the terrorist attacks that occurred on September 11, 2001, or harbored such organizations or persons, in order to prevent any future acts of international terrorism against the United States by such nations, organizations, or persons.

It's worth noting that out of all of the 435 members of the House of Representatives and all one hundred members of the Senate, there was only one single nay vote (Barbara Lee, D-CA). Surprisingly even ultra-liberal Barack Obama called Afghanistan "the good war." Of course Barack Obama was not yet a US senator, so he didn't have a vote.

Even the biased liberal media had to bite their tongues for a while. America was in mourning; we wanted decisive action and we wanted those who would attack us brought to justice. The media would have to hold their britches and choke on embracing American exceptionalism, faith, values, and the flag. That was the mood of the country. Unfortunately all good things come to an end, and the liberal media would not have to wait long for that mood to chill. America started to grow war weary, which opened the door for the media to jump back on the assault, just in time for President Bush's reelection campaign. Fortunately Americans weren't yet completely sold on the idea of changing their commander in chief while we were still at war.

Four days after Congress passed authorization for the use of military force, President Bush issued the following statement:

Today I am signing Senate Joint Resolution 23, the "Authorization for Use of Military Force."

On September 11, 2001, terrorists committed treacherous and horrific acts of violence against innocent Americans and individuals from other countries. Civilized nations and people around the world have expressed outrage at, and have unequivocally condemned, these attacks. Those who plan, authorize, commit, or aid terrorist attacks against the United States and its interests— including those who harbor terrorists—threaten the national security of the United States. It is, therefore, necessary and appropriate that the United States exercise its rights to defend itself and protect United States citizens both at home and abroad.

In adopting this resolution in response to the latest terrorist acts committed against the United States and the continuing threat to the United States and its citizens from terrorist activities, both Houses of Congress have acted wisely, decisively, and in the finest tradition of our country. I thank the leadership of both houses for their role in expeditiously passing this historic joint resolution. I have had the benefit of meaningful consultations with members of the Congress since the attacks of September 11, 2001, and I will continue to consult closely with them as our Nation responds to this threat to our peace and security.

Senate Joint Resolution 23 recognizes the seriousness of the terrorist threat to our Nation and the authority of the President under the Constitution to take action to deter and prevent acts of terrorism against the United States. In signing this resolution, I maintain the longstanding position of the executive branch regarding the President's constitutional authority to use force, including the Armed Forces of the United States regarding the constitutionality of the War Powers Resolution.

Our whole Nation is unalterably committed to a direct, forceful, and comprehensive response to these terrorist attacks and the scourge of terrorism directed against the United States and its interests.

GEORGE W. BUSH

The WHITE HOUSE

September 18, 2001

I point this out because I find that all too often, too many Americans have extremely selective memory and often see things through rose-colored glasses. The Left and their constituents often pick and choose what parts of history they elect to recall and spin the rest of it to fit their narrative.

To President Bush's credit, you seldom heard him criticize his predecessor, Bill Clinton, about his administration's responsibility, which led up to 9/11. Most Americans forget that President Bush also inherited a recession from Bill Clinton; they don't remember that because you hardly ever heard President Bush blame Clinton, certainly not the way Obama goes out of his way with every failed policy he makes to blame Bush. And America quickly had bigger problems than the recession Bush inherited when we were attacked eight months into the Bush presidency on September 11, 2001. It's worth noting that not only did President Bush seldom ever criticize his predecessor or blame him for whatever crisis Bush inherited; to his credit, he has declined to criticize President Obama. And as history has uncovered, there was a heck of a lot of blame and criticism due to both President Clinton and President Obama.

Congressional Democrats were wisely cautious to not immediately point the finger at George Bush as being responsible for the attacks on 9/11; and they were all too glad that President Bush didn't dwell on the reality of the Clinton administration's failed foreign policy and impotence in dealing with the threat Al-Qaeda posed to the security of America. The Al-Qaeda threat began a few months after President Clinton was elected and grew stronger every year throughout his presidency.

You've heard me criticize many Americans for becoming complacent and failing to learn the lessons of history. Here we are, only a little over a decade from the tragic events of 9/11, and how quickly we have forgotten. As President Obama touted during his 2012 reelection campaign, "Osama bin Laden is dead, and Al-Qaeda is on the ropes and on the run." Well, the 2012 anniversary of 9/11 put an end to that claim when our embassy in Benghazi, Libya, was attacked by terrorists, killing the first US ambassador to be killed in over thirty years, along with three other brave Americans. ISIS, a terrorist organization whom Al-Qaeda deemed too brutal for them; has now taken over half of Iraq and half of Syria. In short the world is in shambles because of a real lack of American Presidential leadership, and America is at greater risk than we ever have been.

Spin Master President Obama, along with co-conspirator Hillary Clinton, was unbelievably able to spin the Benghazi tragedy with a false narrative that it wasn't a terrorist attack, but rather some protest gone awry due to some Internet video. The left-wing media again failed to do their job, so that narrative floated just long enough to get past the election a few weeks later. The fact that President Obama was president when US Navy SEALs killed Osama bin Laden in May 2011 was squeezed for all it was worth.

After winning reelection, Obama then had the audacity to suggest that America is safe enough that we no longer need the same military presence around the world that we once did, so he suggested military cuts that would put us to pre–World War II levels. That sounds like the same pre–9/11 mentality that brought the devastating attacks on our homeland. That kind of talk scares the hell out of me and is proof that far too many Americans have forgotten the lessons we should have learned from 9/11. Let me take this opportunity to remind everyone:

On the morning of September 11, 2001, nineteen Muslim extremists hijacked four commercial passenger airliners and brutally attacked America. Two of the planes, American Airlines Flight 11 and United Airlines Flight 175, were crashed into the north and south towers of the World Trade Center in New York City. Within two hours, both towers collapsed. A third plane, American Airlines Flight 77, was crashed into the Pentagon. A fourth plane, United Flight 93, was targeted at Washington, DC, but crashed in a field near Shanksville, Pennsylvania, after the passengers—who, via cell phones, had already heard about the attacks on the World Trade Center and Pentagon—tried to overcome the terrorists and take back control of the plane. The brave passengers of United Flight 93 risked and gave everything to effectively launch the first retaliatory strike against the terrorists on that horrific day. In all, 2,977 people lost their lives, as did the nineteen hijackers. US intelligence quickly concluded that the attacks were launched by the terrorist group Al-Qaeda, led by Osama bin Laden.

Most Americans had never heard of Osama bin Laden or Al-Qaeda prior to America being attacked on September 11; however, we were all quickly forced to open our eyes, take note of who they were, and deal with the fact that they were intent on killing us and destroying our way of life. Those attacks on that fateful morning were far more successful at destroying the American way of life than most anyone realizes, or certainly than any of us wants to admit.

Shortly after Bill Clinton was elected in late 1992, Al-Qaeda launched its first attack on American interests when, on December 29,

1992, just three weeks prior to Clintons inauguration; Al-Qaeda successfully carried out an attack in Aden, Yemen, at the Gold Mohur hotel, where US troops had been staying while en route to Somalia (the troops had already left when the bomb exploded). The bombers targeted a second hotel, the Aden Movenpick, where they believed American troops might also be staying. The bomb detonated prematurely in the hotel parking lot around the same time as the other bomb explosion, killing two Australian tourists. Bin Laden later claimed that he and Mohamed Khan were responsible for the 1992 Yemen hotel bombings.

It's worth pointing out, that Bill Clinton's continued responses to the then growing Al-Qaeda threat, was very similar to Barack Obama's current policies of doing nothing. How did that work out for us on September 11, 2001? Not very good. Are we all so naïve that we don't pay any attention to history? I pray God I'm wrong, but mark my words; if America doesn't suffer another attack on our homeland before the end of Barack Obama's presidency, our next Commander in Chief will inherit that pending catastrophe.

Many Americans forgot that Al-Qaeda first attacked the World Trade Center in New York eight years prior to September 11, 2001. Al-Qaeda first attacked the World Trade Center on February 26, 1993, when Ramzi Yousef parked a rented van full of explosives in the parking garage beneath the World Trade Center. The explosion claimed six victims, and over one thousand people were wounded. Ramzi Yousef, the nephew of 9/11 planner Khalid Sheikh Mohammed, had trained in Afghanistan, although Khalid Sheikh Mohammed did not join Al-Qaeda until 1998. Yousef worked in cooperation with the blind sheikh Omar Abdul-Rahman, who was living across the Hudson in Jersey City at the time of the attack.

In November 1995, five Americans and two Indians were killed in the truck bombing of a US-operated Saudi National Guard training center in Riyadh, Saudi Arabia. A year later, in 1996, the al-Khobar Towers in Saudi Arabia were bombed, killing nineteen and injuring two hundred US military personnel. Two years later, in 1998, Al-Qaeda operatives carried out the bombings of US embassies in Nairobi, Kenya, and Dar es Salaam, Tanzania, killing more than 250 people and injuring more than five thousand others. Jordanian authorities thwarted a planned terrorist attack to kill US and Israeli tourists visiting Jordan for the millennial celebration and put twenty-eight suspects on trial. In October 2000, Al-Qaeda succeeded in bombing a US warship, the USS *Cole*. A day later a grenade was thrown at the British embassy in Yemen.

My point in reciting these terrible tragedies is that the Clinton administration chose to handle these terrorist attacks as nuisances, rather than the very real and present dangers to American sovereignty that they obviously were. And other than a lot of bluster and lobbing a couple of missiles into some empty tents and an aspirin factory, no action was taken by President Clinton, and no one was ever brought to justice. And, the American people paid little attention.

After the 1993 World Trade Center bombing, then President Bill Clinton promised that those responsible would be hunted down and punished. After the 1995 Saudi Arabia bombing, President Clinton made the American people the very same promise. Again, after the 1996 al-Kohbar Towers bombing, President Clinton again made the very same commitment to hunt down those responsible and bring them to justice. And when the USS *Cole* was bombed, killing seventeen sailors and injuring three more—you guessed it, the pattern of all talk and no action is pretty obvious by now. In Bill Clinton's radio address following the attack on the USS *Cole*, Clinton told Americans that we shouldn't overreact.

Eleven months after Clinton telling the American public not to overreact, nineteen Al-Qaeda terrorists hijacked four planes and launched the horrific terrorist attacks on our homeland, killing nearly three thousand citizens and leading to two wars that lasted more than a decade.

Maybe if President Clinton had kept his promises to hunt down the terrorists and bring them to justice, we could have avoided the tragedy of September 11, 2001, and very likely the wars in Afghanistan and Iraq, collectively saving over ten thousand lives.

If President Clinton had kept his commitment to hunt down and bring Al-Qaeda to justice, it might have also saved trillions of dollars in American treasure. According to a Congressional Budget Office (CBO) report published in October 2007, the US wars in Iraq and Afghanistan could cost taxpayers a total of $2.4 trillion by 2017 when counting the huge interest costs because of the combat being financed with borrowed money.

The Clinton machine quickly started circling the wagons, knowing that there was no way the American public wouldn't connect the dots to his responsibility in allowing for the Al-Qaeda threat to fester for the entire eight years of his presidency, and that he would have a lot of accountability. But then again, the Clintons are very experienced spin masters. Clinton first started his spin by having *Time* magazine publish a story claiming that the Clinton administration had handed off to the Bush administration an elaborate plan to go after bin Laden and Al-Qaeda; the claim was quickly refuted.

Clinton's responsibility in 9/11 started to come under close scrutiny as some honest journalists and politicians began to analyze why the United States was so vulnerable. Articles by the Associated Press charged that the Clinton administration had opportunities to eliminate bin Laden but failed to do so. In the final days of the Clinton presidency, senior officials received specific intelligence about the whereabouts of

Usama bin Laden and weighed a military plan to strike the terrorist's location, but the administration ultimately opted against such an attack.

The information spurred a high-level debate inside the White House in December 2000 about whether the classified information provided the last, best chance for President Clinton to take out bin Laden before Clinton left office, officials said. Sandy Berger, former national security advisor to Clinton, told the Associated Press that "there were a couple of points, including in December, where there was intelligence indicative of bin Laden's whereabouts. But I can tell you that at no point was it ripe enough to act."

A story by the *Philadelphia Inquirer* reported that the United States had for years both the knowledge and capability to kill bin Laden. It said that the US Special Forces and CIA operatives had been in Afghanistan but were prohibited by the White House from going after bin Laden. The Associated Press later reported that the Pentagon told President Clinton that they knew the location of bin Laden and could take him out, but Clinton decided it was too risky and refused to authorize such action. Clinton was later asked about that claim by Fox News and he denied it, indicating that his best shot at killing bin Laden was when he bombed training camps in 1998. Central Intelligence Agency Director James Woolsey revealed that he never had a private personal meeting with Clinton during the first two years of his tenure as head of the CIA—exactly the key time frame in investigating the 1993 WTC attacks. Do you think that might have been a good idea?

Under Clinton there were at least three opportunities to have bin Laden handed over to the United States, but all three were inexplicably rejected. According to the *Sunday Times* of London, Clinton himself said his refusal to accept the offer to hand over bin Laden was the "biggest mistake" of his presidency. According to anonymous sources in the CIA, Clinton didn't want bin Laden arrested. Two CIA officials who were involved in secret negotiations between Washington and Khartoum to take bin Laden into custody offered the damning accounts to New York's *Village Voice*. Other intelligence officials corroborated the charge that there was a deliberate effort to let bin Laden escape from the Sudan to Afghanistan, saying that "someone let this slip up." And a second official lamented that the United States had lost a treasure trove of intelligence on the elusive Al-Qaeda chief when it let him slip away. "It was not a matter of arresting bin Laden, but of access to information," he told the *Voice*.

The first instance the CIA official cited was Sudan's offer to extradite bin Laden in 1996, but the Clinton administration turned Sudan down, saying that there wasn't enough evidence to convict him in an American court. This was originally denied by administration officials, but, according to the *Times*, senior sources from within the administration now confirm it was true. In a January 2012 issue of *Vanity Fair* magazine, former Ambassador to Sudan Timothy Carney confirmed it, saying it had serious implications regarding the US Embassy bombings in 1998 and that the United States had lost access to a gold mine of material on bin Laden and his organization.

The second offer the *Times* article details involved Mansoor Ijaz, a Pakistani American who contributed to Clinton's presidential campaign and served as a go-between for the administration and various powers in the Middle East. Ijaz presented an exchange of e-mails as evidence to prove that he had in fact met with Clinton officials and intelligence officers from the United Arab Emirates who were offering to help deliver bin Laden to the United States. Ijaz says the deal was blown when Clinton sent his top counterterrorism advisor to meet the Arab leader directly rather than continuing to go through back channels.

The third offer, described as mysterious, was said to come from Saudi Arabian intelligence agencies. It was said to involve putting a tracking device in the luggage of bin Laden's mother while she was in Afghanistan visiting her son, but it was turned down. Richard Shelby, at the time the highest ranking Republican on the Senate Intelligence Committee, said he was aware of a Saudi offer to help, but was not able to talk about the specifics.

In a chilling irony, the very day before the attacks of September 11, 2001, former President Bill Clinton, openly acknowledged that he turned down a chance to kill Usama bin Laden, according to a recording that was released in July 2014. Clinton's words can be herd admitting that he could have killed bin Laden in a speech to Australian business leaders on September 10th, 2001. Clinton's eerie words had not been made public for thirteen years, but a businessman who had access to the recording handed it over to Sky News Australia.

Clinton's words; "I'm just saying, you know, if I were Usama bin Laden, he's a very smart guy, I've spent a lot of time thinking about him, and I nearly got him once. I nearly got him. And I could have killed him, but I would have to destroy a little town called Kandahar in Afghanistan and kill 300 innocent women and children, and then I would have been no better than him. And so, I didn't do it." Clinton added. I can't help but wonder what was going thru Bill Clinton's thoughts the morning after giving that speech, when the terrorist he chose not to kill, had nineteen terrorist hijack four airliners and attack the United States.

Former CIA head of the Bin Laden Unit, Michael Scheuer, who headed up the bin Laden unit from 1995 to 1999, said President Clinton is a "liar"! "If you looked up the definition of the word lie, Clinton's face would be right next to it" he continued. Scheuer's outrage was over his personal knowledge that Clinton did have opportunities to kill bin Laden, including the time Clinton refers to in the recorded speech. Scheuer, also persists that targeting bin Laden, at the time Clinton refers to in Kandahar, would not have killed three hundred innocent women and children, and would have only killed a few dozen fellow terrorists. Clinton didn't act on the bin Laden intelligence according to Scheuer, "because he's a coward, and because he's more concerned, like Obama, with what the world thinks about him."

The final report of the National Commission on Terrorist Attacks Upon the United States, otherwise known as the 9/11 Report, confirms that there were conflicting testimonies, and information about whether the administration had taken Al Qaeda threats seriously and had turned down a chance to have bin Laden extradited to the US on terrorism charges. In the end, the 9/11 panel found that there were several missed opportunities to go after bin Laden and Al Qaeda, including a point in which the Central Intelligence Agency had tracked bin Laden to a hunting camp in Afghanistan in 1999. The Clinton administration declined to launch an attack for fear of hitting officials from the United Arab Emirates, who were at the camp on a hunting trip.

OK, now we are slightly more up to speed on "the rest of the story" regarding 9/11 and the fact that there was plenty of blame to go around, including laying some if not much of the responsibility at the feet of Bill Clinton. OK, everyone who's been a big fan of Bill Clinton, please take a deep breath. I'm not blaming September 11 on Bill Clinton. I would imagine that had President Clinton had a crystal ball and if he could have foreseen the tragic events with any degree of certainty, he would have very likely acted far more aggressively than he did and may have been able to have averted the attacks. The point is that the dots weren't connected. The next attack on our homeland, will fall squarely at the feet of Barack Obama, and there will be absolutely no excuse for his ineptness during the entire term of his presidency.

I think we'd all agree that our vision is much clearer in hindsight than in foresight. This is likely part of the reason that President Bush reacted to the attacks of 9/11 so decisively and deliberately. It may also be part of the rationale considered when President Bush led us to war in Iraq. America had already been to war in Iraq a decade earlier, and it's no secret that the entire world saw Saddam Hussein as a serious threat to the world.

It is an undisputed fact that Saddam Hussein gassed some four hundred thousand of his own people in previous years, and every intelligence agency in the world believed that Hussein continued to have weapons of mass destruction (WMDs) and was willing to use them. The kind of threat Saddam Hussein posed, especially in light of the 9/11 attacks, was too much to overlook. Ironically Saddam Hussein underestimated America's resolve after 9/11 and actually thought that we wouldn't invade because of the fear of chemical and biological weapons, which is why he never made any credible argument that his WMD stockpiles had been diminished.

Actually weapons of mass destruction were found in Iraq; just far fewer than the world intelligence communities purported there were. In an American Forces Press Service article on June 29, 2006, the five hundred munitions discovered throughout Iraq since 2003 and discussed in a National Ground Intelligence Center report meet the criteria of weapons of mass destruction, the center's commander said. "These are chemical weapons as defined under the Chemical Weapons Convention, and yes...they do constitute weapons of mass destruction," army Col. John Chu told the House Armed Services Committee.

The Chemical Weapons Convention is an arms control agreement that outlaws the production, stockpiling, and use of chemical weapons. It was signed in 1993 and entered into force in 1997.

The munitions found contained sarin and mustard gases, army Lt. Gen. Michael D. Maples, director of the Defense Intelligence Agency, said. Sarin attacks the neurological system and is potentially lethal.

"Mustard is a blister agent (that) actually produces burning of any area (where) an individual may come in contact with the agent," he said. It also is potentially fatal if it gets into a person's lungs.

The munitions addressed in the report were produced in the 1980s, Maples said. Badly corroded, they could not currently be used as originally intended, Chu added.

While that's reassuring, the agent remaining in the weapons would be very valuable to terrorists and insurgents, Maples said. "We're talking chemical agents here that could be packaged in a different format and have a great effect," he said, referencing the sarin-gas attack on a Japanese subway in the mid-1990s.

This is true even considering any degradation of the chemical agents that may have occurred, Chu said. It's not known exactly how sarin breaks down, but no matter how degraded the agent is, it's still toxic.

Regardless of how much material in the weapon is actually a chemical agent, any remaining agent is toxic, he said. "Anything above zero (percent agent) would prove to be toxic and, if you were exposed to it long enough, lethal."

Maples went on to say that he doesn't believe Iraq is a "WMD-free zone." "I believe the former regime did a very poor job of accountability of munitions, and certainly did not document the destruction of munitions," he said. "The recovery program goes on, and I don't believe we have found all the weapons."

It is now widely accepted that Saddam Hussain ended his nuclear program in 1991 following the Gulf War and that, pursuant to the destruction of the Al-Hakam facility, Iraq abandoned its ambition to obtain advanced biological warfare weapons.

On May 1, 2003, just two short months after the invasion into Iraq, President Bush landed a navy fighter jet on the flight deck of the USS *Abraham Lincoln*. Having changed out of his combat flight uniform into a suit and tie, President Bush represented a commanding presence as the commander in chief of the US armed forces. Surrounded by admiring men and women in uniform, President Bush declared the end to major combat operation in Iraq. Under the backdrop of the infamous "Mission Accomplished" banner. Bush called Operation Iraqi Freedom "a job well done" and further went on to say, "In the battle of Iraq, the United States and our allies have prevailed." The thought of toppling Saddam Hussein in only two months was an astonishing accomplishment by anyone's standards. That said, if there was a day President Bush would like to have a do over, it might be that day. As well as the day appeared to have gone for President Bush politically, it may have well been the day that derailed his presidency, and allowed the Democrats to take control of both houses of Congress in the 2006 midterm elections.

The "Mission Accomplished" banner gave Americans the impression that all was great and our young men and women sailors serving in harm's way would be coming home from battle soon. Bush was reelected in 2004, but the American public was angry that "Mission Accomplished" hadn't been accomplished, and they would inevitably hold the president and his party accountable two years later.

That day, May 1, 2003 was a pivotal day in America and led to the Democrats taking control of both the House and the Senate in the 2006 midterm elections, resulting in the beginning of the lost decade.

President Bush should have taken the podium and thanked the sailors for the enthusiasm represented in the "Mission Accomplished" banner, but then immediately made it very clear to the sailors he was addressing, as well as the American public, that while we may have prevailed in taking down Saddam Hussein and diminishing his army, we were far from "mission accomplished" and still had a tough challenge ahead.

The American public would have understood that and continued their support much longer than they did; but when the public realized that "Mission Accomplished" was far from reality, Bush lost credibility, and once a president loses credibility with the public, it's nearly impossible to regain. President Bush fell into a terrible political trap of setting expectations so high that the American public believed we would be out of Iraq by year's end. That "Mission Accomplished" day would dog President Bush through the end of his presidency.

The fallout from "Mission Accomplished" went from bad to worse in the coming years. When the stockpiles of weapons of mass destruction that Iraq was believed to have had didn't materialize, the public felt that they had been misled. The Democrats were quick to smell the blood in the air and took full advantage of it.

Selective memory quickly set in; Democrats were successful in promoting the narrative that they somehow had no responsibility in the wars, and the voters bought it. Democrats and Republicans overwhelmingly supported the invasion of Iraq on a bipartisan vote. Then Senator Hillary Clinton, having been an actively involved first lady in the White House during the previous eight years of the Clinton administration, surely had as much intelligence as the Bush administration about Iraq's weapons of mass destruction, and she enthusiastically voted for the invasion of Iraq. Progressive voters should keep that in mind when considering Hillary Clinton for President in 2016; had she been President in 2003, she too would have invaded Iraq.

CHAPTER FOUR

The Perfect Storm: The Economic Death Spiral

"A rigid economy of the public contributions and absolute inter-diction of all useless expenses will go far towards keeping the govern-ment honest and unoppressive." —Thomas Jefferson, 1823

Thomas Jefferson understood that a good economy and doing away with all useless spending would be the key to keeping the gov-ernment honest and unoppressive. Unfortunately today's politicians haven't inherited the same wisdom of our Founding Fathers, because they do spend very uselessly and our government is anything but hon-est or unoppressive.

The Great Recession was unquestionably the worst economic crisis since the Great Depression. It affected virtually every business and taxpayer in the United States, and its global reach caused havoc all over the world. Unfortunately most Americans, and certainly most voters, have little understanding of what caused the global economic collapse. Most understand that it had something to do with a housing bubble and Wall Street, but they generally have little if any real or practical appreciation of the facts.

Admittedly it is more complicated than most want to take the time to understand, and most are just glad that the worst of it is behind us. But what if the worst isn't behind us? History has a funny way of repeating itself when the population a) doesn't take the time to understand why something happened, b) doesn't understand how to prevent it from happening in the future, c) doesn't take necessary action to prevent it from happening in the future, or d) over time, simply forgets that it ever happened or how bad it really was.

As Americans, we had better understand the what, when, where, and why of our economic collapse and make damn sure we don't allow it to happen again by making sure we elect politicians that truly understand it and are accountable to us to ensure that it never happens again.

I'm the first to admit that I'm not an economist, but I have gone to great lengths to get a real understanding of what happened and why it happened and how we can prevent it from happening again in the future. Contrary to what many may think when they play the blame game, the economic collapse was a bipartisan problem, and both parties are equally to blame.

There are a great number of components to why our economy collapsed, including the corruption between Wall Street, the regulators in charge of overseeing Wall Street, and the credit agencies. All of them were coconspirators in the economic collapse. However, that is only what the instruments of the collapse were. The bigger question is what legislation has passed or been amended over the past ten-plus years that all but assured "too big to fail," resulting in an economic collapse and a government bailout.

I realize that economics is most likely not very many people's favorite topic or area of study, but I think that as voters and Americans we all have a responsibility to know a little something about it. We owe it to ourselves, and more importantly our children. This chapter should provide you a fairly comprehensive explanation of what happened and why it happened. I encourage you to make every effort to get a clear understanding of what exactly happened.

The Levin–Coburn bipartisan report provides us a really good study of all the factors that came together with regard to the financial sector of our economy and those in charge of regulating it, all of which greatly contributed to the Great Recession.

The financial crisis was not an act of nature; it was a man-made economic assault that cost millions of jobs, evaporated billions of dollars in retirement savings, and put our nation in the worst economic tailspin since the Great Depression.

In April 2010, the Permanent Subcommittee on Investigations held a series of hearings in order to examine some of the causes and consequences of the crisis. The goals of the hearings were threefold: to construct a public record of the facts to deepen public understanding of what happened and to try to hold some of the perpetrators accountable; to inform the legislative debate about the need for financial reform; and to provide a foundation for building better defenses to protect Main Street from the excesses of Wall Street.

The hearings were based on an in-depth bipartisan investigation that began in November 2008. The subcommittee conducted over one hundred detailed interviews and depositions, consulted with dozens of experts, and collected and initiated review of millions of pages of documents. Given the extent of the economic damage and the complexity of its root causes, the subcommittee's approach has been to develop detailed case studies to examine each stage of the crisis.

The first hearing examined the role of high-risk home loans and the mortgage-backed securities that those loans produced, using as a case history the policies and practices of Washington Mutual Bank.

The second hearing examined the role of the banking regulators charged with ensuring the safety and soundness of the US banking system, again using Washington Mutual as a case history.

The third hearing focused on the role of the credit rating agencies (CRAs), specifically the two largest CRAs: Moody's and Standard & Poor's.

The final hearing focused on the role of investment banks, using Goldman Sachs as a case study.

Hearing One: The Role of High-Risk Home Loans

The first hearing, April 13, 2010, focused on the role of high-risk loans, using Washington Mutual Bank as a case history. It showed how the bank originated and sold hundreds of billions of dollars in high-risk loans to Wall Street in return for big fees, polluting the financial systems with toxic mortgages.

The subcommittee investigation reached the following findings of fact:

1. High-risk lending strategy. Washington Mutual ("WaMu") executives embarked upon a high-risk lending strategy and increased sales of high-risk home loans to Wall Street because they projected that high-risk home loans, which generally charged higher rates of interest, would be more profitable for the bank than low-risk home loans.

2. Shoddy lending practices. WaMu and its affiliate, Long Beach Mortgage Company ("Long Beach"), used shoddy lending practices riddled with credit, compliance, and operational deficiencies to make tens of thousands of high-risk home loans that too often contained excessive risk, fraudulent information, or errors.

3. Steering borrowers to high-risk loans. WaMu and Long Beach too often steered borrowers into home loans they could not afford, allowing and encouraging them to make low initial payments that would be followed by much higher payments, and presumed that rising home prices would enable those borrowers to refinance their loans or sell their homes before the payments shot up.

4. Polluting the financial system. WaMu and Long Beach securitized over $77 billion in subprime home loans and billions more in other high-risk home loans, used Wall Street firms to sell the securities to investors worldwide, and polluted the financial system with mortgage-backed securities that later incurred high rates of delinquency and loss.

5. Securitizing delinquency-prone and fraudulent loans. At times, WaMu selected and securitized loans that it had identified as likely to go delinquent without disclosing its analysis to investors who bought the securities, and also securitized loans tainted by fraudulent information without notifying purchasers of the fraud that was discovered.

6. Destructive compensation. WaMu's compensation system rewarded loan officers and loan processors for originating large volumes of high-risk loans, paid extra to loan officers who overcharged borrowers or added stiff prepayment penalties, and gave executives millions of dollars even when its high-risk lending strategy placed the bank in financial jeopardy.

Hearing Two: The Role of Bank Regulators

The second hearing, on April 16, 2010, focused on regulators, using as a case study the role of the Office of Thrift Supervision (OTS) and the Federal Deposit Insurance Corporation (FDIC) in exercising oversight of Washington Mutual Bank.

Feeble oversight by regulators, combined with regulatory standards and agency infighting, allowed Washington Mutual Bank, a $300 billion thrift and the sixth largest US depository institution, to engage in high-risk and shoddy lending practices and the sale of toxic and sometimes fraudulent mortgages that contributed to both the bank's demise and the 2008 financial crisis.

The subcommittee investigation reached the following findings of fact:

1. Largest US bank failure. From 2003 to 2008, OTS repeatedly identified significant problems with Washington Mutual's lending practices, risk management, and asset quality, but failed to force adequate corrective action, resulting in the largest bank failure in US history.

2. Shoddy lending and securitization practices. OTS allowed Washington Mutual and its affiliate Long Beach Mortgage Company to engage year after year in shoddy lending and securitization practices, failing to take enforcement action to stop its origination and sale of loans with fraudulent borrower information, appraisal problems, errors, and notoriously high rates of delinquency and loss.

3. Unsafe option ARM loans. OTS allowed Washington Mutual to originate hundreds of billions of dollars in high-risk option adjustable rate mortgages (ARMs), knowing that the bank used unsafe and unsound teaser rates, qualified borrowers using unrealistically low loan payments, permitted borrowers to make minimum payments resulting in negatively amortizing loans (i.e., loans with increasing principal), relied on rising house prices and refinancing to avoid payment shock and loan defaults, and had no realistic data to calculate loan losses in markets with flat or declining house prices.

4. Short-term profits over long-term fundamentals. OTS abdicated its responsibility to ensure the long-term safety and soundness of Washington Mutual by concluding that short-term profits obtained by the bank precluded enforcement action to stop the bank's use of shoddy lending and securitization practices and unsafe and unsound loans.

5. Impeding FDIC oversight. OTS impeded FDIC oversight of Washington Mutual by blocking its access to bank data, refusing to allow it to participate in bank examinations, rejecting requests to review bank loan files, and resisting FDIC recommendations for stronger enforcement action.

6. FDIC shortfalls. FDIC, the backup regulator of Washington Mutual, was unable to conduct the analysis it wanted to evaluate the risk posed by the bank to the Deposit Insurance Fund, did not prevail against unreasonable actions taken by OTS to limit its examination authority, and did not initiate its own enforcement action against the bank in light of ongoing opposition by the primary federal bank regulators to FDIC enforcement authority.

7. Recommendations over enforceable requirements. Federal bank regulators undermined efforts to end unsafe and unsound mortgage practices at US banks by issuing guidance instead of enforceable regulations limiting those practices, failing to prohibit many high-risk mortgage practices, and failing to set clear deadlines for bank compliance.

8. Failure to recognize systemic risk. OTS and FDIC allowed Washington Mutual and Long Beach to reduce their own risk by selling hundreds of billions of dollars of high-risk mortgage-backed securities that polluted the financial system with poorly performing loans, undermined investor confidence in the secondary mortgage market, and contributed to massive credit rating downgrades, investor losses, disrupted markets, and the US financial crisis.

9. Ineffective and demoralized regulatory culture. The Washington Mutual case history exposed the regulatory culture at OTS, in which bank examiners were frustrated and demoralized by their inability to stop unsafe years of serious bank deficiencies and in which regulators treated the banks they oversaw as constituents rather than arm's-length, regulated entities.

Hearing Three: The Role of Credit Rating Agencies

The third hearing, on April 23, 2010, focused on the role of the credit ratings agencies (CRAs). Moody's and Standard & Poor's, the two largest credit ratings agencies, rated tens of thousands of residential mortgage-backed securities (RMBSs) and collateralized debt obligations (CDOs) that were based on high-risk home loans.

While making record profits from 2004 to 2007, CRAs, which are paid by the issuers of the securities they rate, gave the highest possible ratings to securities underpinned by high-risk home loans. In 2007, after delinquencies rose and the subprime market began to collapse, the CRAs had to massively downgrade many of these securities, resulting in major shocks to the financial system.

The subcommittee reached the following findings of fact:

1. Inaccurate rating models. From 2004 to 2007, Moody's and Standard & Poor's used credit rating models with data that were inadequate to predict how high-risk residential mortgages, such as subprime, interest only, and option adjustable rate mortgages, would perform.

2. Competitive pressures. Competitive pressures, including the drive for market share and need to accommodate investment bankers bringing in business, affected the credit ratings issued by Moody's and Standard & Poor's.

3. Failure to reevaluate. By 2006, Moody's and Standard & Poor's knew of increased credit risks due to mortgage fraud, lax underwriting standards, and unsustainable housing price appreciation, but failed adequately to incorporate those factors into their credit rating models.

4. Failure to factor in fraud, laxity, or the housing bubble. From 2004 to 2008, Moody's and Standard & Poor's knew of increased credit risks due to mortgage fraud, lax underwriting standards, and unsustainable housing price appreciation but failed to incorporate those factors into their credit rating models.

5. Inadequate resources. Despite record profits from 2004 to 2008, Moody's and Standard & Poor's failed to assign sufficient resources to adequately rate new products and test the accuracy of existing ratings.

6. Mass downgrades shocked market. Mass downgrades by Moody's and Standard & Poor's including downgrades of hundreds of subprime RMBSs over a few days in July 2007, downgrades by Moody's of CDOs in October 2007, and downgrades by Standard & Poor's of over sixty-three hundred RMBSs and nineteen hundred CDOs on one day in January 2008, shocked the financial markets, helped cause the collapse of the subprime secondary market, triggered sales of assets that had lost investment grade status, and damaged holdings of financial firms worldwide, contributing to the financial crisis.

7. Failed ratings. Of twelve thousand RMBSs that, from 2006 to 2007, received AAA ratings from Moody's or Standard & Poor's, about one third have since received a rating downgrade, some within six months of their initial rating.

8. Statutory bar. The US Securities and Exchange Commission is barred by statute from conducting needed oversight into the substance, procedures, and methodologies of the credit rating models.

Hearing Four: The Role of Investment Banks

The final hearing, held on April 27, 2010, focused on the role of investment banks, using Goldman Sachs as a case study. Goldman Sachs and other investment banks played a crucial role in building and running the conveyor belt that fed toxic mortgages and mortgage-backed securities into the financial system.

For Goldman Sachs, this role included underwriting securities backed by or related to mortgages from some of the most notorious sub-prime mortgage lenders, including Long Beach. Goldman Sachs also designed and sold billions of dollars of collateralized debt obligations (CDOs) that further spread the risks associated with toxic mortgages, and issued derivative financial products, such as synthetic collateralized debt obligations (CDOs), which had no underlying assets and were merely bets that referenced mortgage-backed securities. In several cases, Goldman was marketing deals to its clients as good investment opportunities while simultaneously betting that these vary same deals would fail.

The subcommittee reached the following findings of fact:

1. Securitizing high-risk mortgages. From 2004 to 2007, in exchange for lucrative fees, Goldman Sachs helped lenders such as Long Beach, Fremont, and New Century securitize high-risk, poor-quality loans, obtain favorable credit ratings for the resulting residential mortgage-backed securities (RMBSs), and sell the RMBS securities to investors, pushing billions of dollars of risky mortgages into the financial system.

2. Magnifying risk. Goldman Sachs magnified the impact of toxic mortgages on financial markets by resecuritizing RMBS securities in collateralized debt obligations (CDOs), referencing them in synthetic CDOs, selling the CDO securities to investors, and using credit default swaps and index trading to profit from the failure of the same RMBS and CDO securities it sold.

3. Shorting the mortgage market. As high-risk mortgage delinquencies increased and RMBS and CDO securities began to lose value, Goldman Sachs took a net short position on the mortgage market, remaining net short throughout 2007, and cashed in very large short positions, generating billions of dollars in gain.

4. Conflict between client and proprietary trading. In 2007, Goldman Sachs went beyond its role as market maker for clients seeking to buy or sell mortgage-related securities, traded billions of dollars in mortgage-related assets for the benefit of the firm without disclosing its proprietary positions to clients, and instructed its sales force to sell mortgage-related assets, including high-risk RMBS and CDO securities that Goldman Sachs wanted to get off its books, creating a conflict between the firm's proprietary interests and the interests of its clients.

5. Abacus transaction. Goldman Sachs structured, underwrote, and sold a synthetic CDO called Abacus 2007–AC1, did not disclose to the Moody's analyst overseeing the rating of the CDO that a hedge fund client taking a short position in the CDO had helped to select the referenced assets, and also did not disclose that fact to other investors.

6. Using naked credit default swaps. Goldman Sachs used credit default swaps (CDS) on assets it did not own to bet against the mortgage market through single-name and index CDS transactions, generating substantial revenues in the process.

The Levin–Coburn report does a great job of providing us a clear study of fact as to what transpired in the years leading up to the Great Recession; however, the fact that it is a bipartisan report fails to contribute the direct correlation to what it was that allowed banks, investment companies, insurers, regulators, and credit agencies the ability to conspire with one another, or what it was that created this culture of corruption throughout the financial sector of our economy.

Before we can figure out how to prevent another economic disaster in the future, we definitely need to evaluate what brought

America—and the world, for that matter—to the brink of a worldwide depression, and it unfortunately goes much deeper than Wall Street corruption. It's a systemic problem that goes back more than a decade.

The Great Recession was a result of a combination of housing policies, legislation, overregulation, failed regulation, deregulation, fraud and corruption, and government incompetence that started decades ago and continued up until the 2008 economic collapse. This has been a bipartisan debacle supported by both sides of the aisle and both Republican and Democratic presidents. It was very unfortunate, however, for President George W. Bush's legacy, because it all came to a head on his watch and at the end of his presidency, making it easy for his critics to blame it all on Bush. It would be convenient if it were that easy, but it certainly wouldn't be the reality of it.

It's generally understood by the public, and it's accepted by virtually every respected economist, that the Great Recession was brought on by the bursting of the US housing bubble, which began in late 1999 and peaked in July 2006, after which the median price for real estate home sales in the United States started to decline. This caused the values of securities tied to US real estate pricing to plummet, which damaged financial institutions globally and ultimately resulted in the subsequent interbank credit crisis. The first sign of the lurking interbank credit crisis came in March 2007, when the US subprime mortgage industry collapsed due to higher than expected home foreclosure rates, resulting in more than twenty-five subprime lenders declaring bankruptcy, announcing significant losses, or putting themselves up for sale.

The Great Recession adversely affected the entire world economy, with greater detriment to some countries than others, but overall to a degree that made it the worst global recession since the Great Depression.

Increasing home ownership has been the goal of every president for at least the last four decades. While that is certainly a noble cause and makes for a good campaign promise, it has brought about some not-so-smart legislation, and certainly some terrible unintended consequences.

This can be tracked as far back as the Community Reinvestment Act of 1977, signed by then President Jimmy Carter. The Community Reinvestment Act was then revised and amended in the 1990s and signed by President Clinton. These revisions included language that pressured private banks to make risky loans and HUD affordable housing goals for the government-sponsored enterprises (GSEs) Fannie Mae and Freddie Mac, which resulted in the GSEs purchasing risky loans and led to a general breakdown in underwriting standards for all lenders. The Financial Crisis Inquiry Commission (FCIC), tasked with investigating the causes of the crisis, reported in January 2011: "We had a 21st-century financial system, with 19th-century safeguards."

The Housing and Community Development Act of 1992 established an affordable housing loan purchase mandate for Fannie Mae and Freddie Mac, and that mandate was to be regulated by HUD. Initially, the 1992 legislation required that 30 percent or more of Fannie's and Freddie's loan purchases be related to affordable housing. However, HUD was given the power to set future requirements. In 1995 HUD mandated that 40 percent of Fannie's and Freddie's loan purchases would have to support affordable housing. In 1996, HUD directed Freddie and Fannie to provide at least 42 percent of their mortgage financing to borrowers with income below the median in their area. This target was increased to 50 percent in 2000 and 52 percent in 2005.

To satisfy theses mandates, Fannie and Freddie eventually announced low-income and minority loan commitments totaling $5 trillion. Critics argue that to meet these commitments, Fannie and Freddie promoted a loosening of lending standards industrywide.

In the mid-1990's Fannie and Freddie also promoted automated valuation systems (AVMs), which meant that in many cases no onsite physical inspections for appraisals were needed. Rather, the AVM, which relied mostly on comparable sales data, would suffice. Some analysts believe that the use of AVMs, especially for properties in distressed neighborhoods, led to overvaluation of the collateral-backing mortgage loans.

In 1995 Fannie and Freddie introduced automated underwriting systems, designed to speed up the underwriting process. These systems, which soon set underwriting standards for most of the industry, greatly relaxed the underwriting approval process. An independent study of about one thousand loans found that the same loans were 65 percent more likely to be approved by the automated processes versus the traditional processes. Single-family lenders doing business with Freddie and Fannie were soon required to use these same liberalized systems.

The Democratic-controlled Financial Crisis Inquiry Commission placed significant blame for the crisis on deregulation, reporting: "We conclude widespread failures in financial regulation and supervision proved devastating to the stability of the nation's financial markets." The sentries were not at their posts, in no small part due to the widely accepted faith in the self-correcting nature of the markets and the ability of financial institutions to effectively police themselves. More than thirty years of deregulation and reliance on self-regulation by financial institutions, championed by former Federal Reserve Chairman Alan Greenspan and others, supported by successive administrations and Congresses, and actively pushed by the powerful financial industry at every turn, had stripped away key safeguards, which could have helped avoid the catastrophe. This approach had opened up gaps in oversight of critical areas with trillions of dollars at risk. In addition, the government permitted financial firms to pick their preferred regulators in what became a race to the weakest supervisor.

In a working paper released in late 2012, the National Bureau of Economic Research (NBER), the arbiters of the business cycle, presented "Did the Community Reinvestment Act Lead to Risky Lending?" The economists compared "the lending behavior of banks undergoing CRA exams within a given census tract in a given month to the behavior of banks operating in the same census tract month that did not face these exams. This comparison clearly indicated that the adherence to the CRA led to riskier lending by banks." The NBER concluded: "The evidence shows that around the CRA examinations, when incentives to conform to CRA standards are particularly high, banks not only increase lending rates but also appear to originate loans that are markedly riskier."

Let me sum all of this up: The US government, through legislation, regulation, and deregulation, decided that they wanted low-income voters to be able to purchase a home regardless of whether they could afford the loan or qualify for it. Lenders got used to the easy money that these loans made them, and most of the risk was covered by the American taxpaying public (thru Fannie and Freddie), so they went along for the ride. And when it all came crashing down, you guessed it, the American taxpayers footed the bill.

In the words of Rahm Emanuel, "Never let a good crisis go to waste." The Democrats definitely didn't let the Great Recession go to waste and cleverly convinced the American voters that the economic collapse was all the fault of President Bush and the Republicans, conveniently glossing over the fact that they controlled two thirds of the government a full year prior to when the recession officially began, so they had every opportunity to put the brakes on and didn't. This crisis set the stage for Democrats to take complete control of all branches of the government, with full and unfettered reign to enact their liberal, progressive, big government policies. The same kind of irresponsible policies, I might add, that got us into the crisis to begin with.

The lost decade might have officially begun a full year prior to the economic collapse—on January 3, 2007, when Nancy Pelosi became the speaker of the US House of Representatives and Harry Reid became the majority leader of the US Senate. The Great Recession became the crisis that kept on giving to the Democrats. The economic collapse in 2008 set America on course for the real era of big government, and on a collision course for disaster that America would have to endure for at least another eight years.

Not that Democrats were entirely responsible for the worst recession since the Great Depression; no, the Republicans were equally responsible, and there was plenty of blame to go around on both sides of the aisle. The two pieces of legislation that caused the economic collapse were both bipartisan bills that were supported by both Democratic and Republican lawmakers (the Housing and Community Development Act of 1992 and the Gramm–Leach–Bliley Act of 1999, which repealed the 1933 Glass–Steagall Act). However, the Democrats again seem to have selective memory, as they've forgotten that they do have a lot of responsibility for the economic collapse and the fact that they did control the majority of the government for a full year before the Great Recession hit. But with the never-ending support of the liberally biased, mainstream media, they were able to set all the blame squarely at the feet of George W. Bush, as if they had no part in it whatsoever and were somehow innocent bystanders. To add insult to injury, their progressive policies stagnated any possibility for a real recovery or any robust growth for the entire time in which they've held power.

I know…it's a whole heck of a lot easier if we can just keep using the "blame Bush" slogan that the Dems have so articulately pinned on him; but even if you feel better blaming Bush, we really need to at least understand what happened. I certainly don't want to lay the blame at the feet of Bill Clinton, either, because, as I've said, there was plenty of blame to go around for everyone. That said, if you had to pinpoint the start of the change in policies that led to the global economic collapse that hit on the watch of George Bush, Nancy Pelosi, and Harry Reid, it actually started on Bill Clinton's watch. In addition to revisions made to the Community Reinvestment Act, President Clinton also signed into law the Commodity Futures Modernization Act of 2000, which limited the regulation and over-sight of financial derivatives.

At about the same time the Community Reinvestment Act was revised, further easing lending restrictions to home buyers and pres-suring banks to make loans to lower-income buyers, Bill Clinton also signed the Gramm–Leach–Bliley Act of 1999, which repealed the Glass–Steagall Act, which effectively removed the separation between investment banks and depository banks in the United States. This opened the flood gates and made "too big to fail" inevitable.

The banking industry had been seeking the repeal of the 1933 Glass–Steagall Act since the 1980s, if not earlier. The Glass–Steagall Act limited commercial bank securities activities and affiliations within commercial banks and security firms. In 1987 the Congressional Research Service prepared a report that explored the cases for and against preserving the Glass–Steagall Act. The critics of the bill on both sides of the aisle argued that the bill would result in banks becoming "too big to fail" and further argued that this would result in a bailout by the federal government. Pretty sound foresight, as history soon taught us. The bipartisan bill was signed into law by President Clinton on

November 12, 1999. Eight years later, this bill would prove to bring America to the brink of collapse.

In 1998, a year before President Bill Clinton signed the Gramm–Leach–Bliley Act into law, Citicorp, a commercial bank holding company, merged with the insurance company Travelers Group to form the conglomerate Citigroup, a corporation combining banking, securities, and insurance services under a house of brands that included Citibank, Smith Barney, Primerica, and Travelers. Because this merger was a violation of the Glass–Steagall Act and the Bank Holding Company Act of 1956, the Federal Reserve gave Citigroup a temporary waiver in September 1998. Less than a year later, the Gramm–Leach–Bliley Act was passed to legalize these types of mergers on a permanent basis. The law also repealed Glass–Steagall's conflict of interest prohibitions "against simultaneous service by any officer, director, or employee of a securities firm as an officer, director, or employee of any member bank."

Yes, the Democrats found it easy to lay the blame of the economic collapse at the feet of George W. Bush and the wars in Iraq and Afghanistan, and the American public bought it hook, line, and sinker! Why wouldn't they buy into that narrative? After all, the mainstream media was all too happy to peddle that line of blaming Bush nonstop, and the war-weary American public had grown disenchanted with President Bush and his policies on Iraq and Afghanistan. Don't get me wrong; George Bush was president of the United States at the time the economy collapsed, so he does have a lot of responsibility—after all, if you're the president of the United States, the buck stops with you. That said, the 2006 midterm elections left George Bush a lame-duck president for the last two years of his presidency with greatly diminished power, and the Democrats virtually controlled the government for the last two years of President Bush's presidency, and a full year before the Great Recession hit, I might add.

For as much as President Bush has gotten most of the blame for the economic collapse, he ironically has little ownership in it. In fact, the Bush administration repeatedly warned Congress from the time he took office of the systematic consequences of financial turmoil at the housing government-sponsored enterprise (GSE). President Bush even put forth comprehensive plans to reduce the risk that either Fannie Mae or Freddie Mac would encounter such difficulties. Unfortunately his warnings and plans to rectify the problems fell on deaf ears.

In April 2001, the Bush administration's 2002 budget declared that the size of Fannie Mae and Freddie Mac is "a potential problem" because "financial trouble of large GSE[s] could cause strong repercussions in financial markets, affecting federally insured entities and economic activity."

In May 2002, President Bush called for the disclosure and corporate governance principles contained in his ten-point plan for corporate responsibility to apply to Fannie Mae and Freddie Mac (OMB/ Office of Management and Budget Prompt Letter to OFHEO/Office of Housing Enterprise Oversight, May 29, 2002).

January 2003: Freddie Mac announced it had to restate financial results for the previous three years.

February 2003: The Office of Housing Enterprise Oversight (OFHEO) released a report warning that unexpected problems at GSEs could immediately spread into financial sectors beyond the housing market, creating a "Systematic Risk" from Freddie Mac and Fannie Mae.

September 2003: Fannie Mae disclosed an SEC investigation and acknowledged that OFHEO's review found earnings manipulation.

September 2003: Bush administration Treasury Secretary John Snow testified before the House Financial Services Committee to recommend that Congress enact "legislation to create a new federal agency to regulate and supervise the financial activities of our housing-related government sponsored enterprises" and set prudent and appropriate minimum capital adequacy requirements.

October 2003: Fannie Mae disclosed a $1.2 billion accounting error.

November 2003: The Bush administration upgraded its warning to a "systematic risk" that could very well extend beyond the confines of the housing market.

Also in November of 2003, Council of Economic Advisors (CEA) Chairman Greg Mankiw explained that "legislation to reform GSE regulation needs to empower the new regulator with sufficient strength and credibility to reduce systematic risk" (Bank Supervisors State Banking Summit and Leadership Conference, November 6, 2003).

February 2004: President Bush's 2005 budget again highlighted the risk posed by the explosive growth of the GSEs and their low levels of required capital, and called for creation of a new, world-class regulator. "The Administration has determined that the safety and soundness regulators of the housing GSEs lack sufficient power and stature to meet their responsibilities, and therefore...should be replaced with a new strengthened regulator." Additionally in February, CEA Chairman Mankiw cautions Congress to "not take the financial market's strength for granted." Again, the call from the Bush administration was loud and clear: to reduce the risk by ensuring that the housing GSEs are overseen by an effective regulator (op-ed in the *Financial Times*, February 24, 2004).

June 2004: Bush administration Deputy Secretary of the Treasury Samuel Bodman spotlighted the risk posed by the GSEs and called for reform, saying:

> We do not have a world class system of supervision of the housing government sponsored enterprises (GSEs), even though the importance of the housing financial system the GSEs serve demands the best in supervision to ensure the long term vitality of that system. Therefore, the Administration has called for a new, first class, regulatory supervisor for three housing GSEs: Fannie Mae, Freddie Mac, and the Federal Home Loan Banking system. (House Financial Services Subcommittee on Oversight and Investigations Testimony, June 16, 2004)

April 2005: Treasury Secretary John Snow repeated his call for GSE reform, saying:

> Events that have transpired since I testified before this Committee in 2003 reinforce concerns over the systemic risks posed by the GSEs and further highlight the need for real GSE reform to ensure that our housing finance system remains a strong and vibrant source of funding for expanding homeownership opportunities in America...Half measures will only exacerbate the risks to our financial system. (Testimony before the House Financial Services Committee, April 13, 2005)

January 2007: The Democrats take control of two thirds of the government.

July 2007: Two Bear Stearns hedge funds invested in mortgage securities collapse.

August 2007: President Bush emphatically calls on Congress to pass a reform package for Fannie Mae and Freddie Mac, saying, "First things first when it comes to those two institutions. Congress needs to get them reformed, get them streamlined, get them focused, and then I will consider other options" (George W. Bush, press conference at the White House, August 9, 2007).

September 2007: Realty Trac announced foreclosure filings were up 243,000 in August, up 115 percent from the previous year.

September 2007: Single-family existing home sales decreased 7.5 percent from the previous month, the lowest level in nine years. Median sales prices of existing homes fell 6 percent from the year before.

December 2007: President Bush again warned the Democratic-controlled Congress of the need to pass legislation reforming GSEs, saying:

> These institutions provide liquidity in the mortgage market that benefits millions of homeowners, and it is vital they operate safely, and operate soundly. So I've called on Congress to pass legislation that strengthens independent regulation of the GSEs and ensures they focus on their important housing mission. The GSE reform bill passed by the House earlier this year is a good start but the Senate has not acted. And the United States Senate needs to pass this legislation soon. (President Bush meets with lawmakers to discuss housing at the White House, December 6, 2007)

January 2008: Bank of America announced it would buy Countrywide.

January 2008: Citigroup announced its mortgage portfolio lost $18.1 billion in value.

February 2008: Assistant Secretary David Nason reiterated the urgency of reforms, saying, "A new regulatory structure for the housing GSEs is essential if these entities are to continue to perform their public mission successfully" (testimony on reforming GSE regulation, Senate Committee on Banking, Housing, and Urban Affairs, February 7, 2008).

March 2008: Bear Stearns announced it would sell itself to JPMorgan Chase.

April 2008: President Bush again called on Congress to take action and "move forward with reforms on Fannie Mae and Freddie Mac. They need to continue to modernize the FHA, as well as allow State housing agencies to issue tax-free bonds to homeowners to refinance their mortgages" (President Bush meets with lawmakers at White House, April 14, 2008).

May 2008: President Bush again issued several pleas to Congress to pass legislation reforming Fannie Mae and Freddie Mac before the situation deteriorated any further:

> Americans are concerned about making their mortgage payments and keeping their homes. Yet Congress has failed to pass legislation I have repeatedly requested to modernize the Federal Housing Administration that will help more families stay in their homes, reform Fannie Mae and Freddie Mac to ensure they focus on their housing mission, and allow State Housing agencies to issue tax-free bonds to refinance subprime loans. (President Bush's radio address, May 3, 2008)

"Congress needs to pass legislation to modernize the Federal Housing Administration, reform Fannie Mae and Freddie Mac to ensure they focus on their housing mission, and allow State housing agencies to issue tax-free bonds to refinance subprime loans" (President Bush's radio address, May 31, 2008).

June 2008: As foreclosure rates continued to rise in the first quarter, the president once again asked Congress to take the necessary measures to address this challenge, saying, "We need to pass legislation to reform Fannie Mae and Freddie Mac."

July 2008: Congress finally heeded the president's call for action and passed reform of Fannie Mae and Freddie Mac as it became clear that the institutions were failing. Up until the economy started to become unhinged, the Democratic-controlled Congress thwarted President Bush's every attempt to address the lingering crisis and emphatically continued to deny that there was any crisis.

It is also worth pointing out that President Bush's decisive action to stabilize the banking industry at the time of the collapse did help divert a lot of pain that could have been much worse if he hadn't acted when he did.

I wouldn't be at all surprised if this is the first time you've heard about President Bush's many attempts to get Congress to pass legislation that very likely could have averted the Great Recession. Why haven't you heard all of this before, you ask? It's pretty simple, really; when President Bush was pointing out these problems and requesting that Congress act, most people didn't really even have a clue what he was talking about, and since it wasn't adversely impacting anyone at the time he was saying it, no one paid attention. It's kind of like your doctor warning you for years that you need to take better care of your health with a better diet and more exercise. Most people don't really pay close attention until it's too late. And once it is too late, it doesn't really do much good for the doctor to say, "I told you so."

This all came crashing down on the eve of the 2008 presidential elections and President Bush's final months in office, which meant President Bush was old news. America was all caught up in electing the first African American president, and it was just much easier to blame Bush.

So now, every time you hear Barack Obama blame Bush for the recession Obama "inherited," someone needs to remind him that if he inherited it from anyone, it was the very democratically controlled Congress of which he was a big part of.

By the time President Obama took office, the Band-Aid was already on; financial markets were starting to stabilize, and a recovery was already in motion. However, what little recovery we may have had was quickly stifled by the Democrats' progressive policies. That said, any recovery we've seen has been minimal at best and at this point would be nonexistent without the Fed pumping trillions of dollars into the economy, which greatly weakens the value of the dollar, which leads to inflation, and that is not good for the consumer or the taxpayer.

Interestingly enough, most people have forgot that President Bush himself inherited a recession from former President Bill Clinton as a result of the tech and dot-com bubble. I would suggest that it's because President Bush took ownership of the job the American people elected him to do and didn't spend his entire presidency blaming Clinton for whatever he inherited, including a recession and the failed policies that contributed to 9/11 and the economic collapse. Unfortunately, six years into President Obama's presidency, he has failed to show any character or leadership in this arena and never misses an opportunity to blame his predecessor. Can you imagine an NFL football team hiring a new coach after a disastrous losing season and six years later the team is still struggling along and the new coach is still blaming the guy he replaced six years ago? I would submit that if an NFL coach tried laying the blame of his poor performance on his predecessor to the owner of the team, the press, or the fans, he would be held accountable and fired!

I'm not sure that anyone could have avoided the Great Recession, no more than I think we might have avoided the events of 9/11. That destiny was already cooked into the books, ten years in the making when Washington politicians decided that it was a good idea for every American to own his or her own home and started easing lending restrictions and pressuring lenders to make loans to people with low credit scores and with little or no down payment. These loans were insured by the government through Fannie Mae and Freddie Mac, so lenders were all too happy to accommodate and, in essence, became coconspirators with Washington in their own pending demise.

This ease in lending restrictions created a huge short-term economic boom throughout most of the 2000s, because money was easy for pretty much anyone to get, so people borrowed more on their homes than they could afford until it blew up in everyone's face. It all worked out great, until it didn't. One thing led to another and the housing bubble burst, and it all came crumbling down in December of 2007 in what would become the worst recession since the Great Depression.

We all should have seen the writing on the wall. I mean, on what planet did it ever make good sense for a lender to loan 100 percent of the purchase price of a house, especially to a borrower who has only a six hundred credit score? Unbelievably there were even lenders out there loaning 125 percent of the value of a home, banking on an unsustainable appreciation. No economy could ever sustain that kind of stupidity. But, hey, we were all living high on the hog during that time period; the housing market was exploding, unemployment was practically nonexistent, and nobody wanted to upset that apple cart.

You would think that surely we learned the painful lessons that caused the worst recession since the Great Depression. Unfortunately I don't think so. This is evidenced by a lot of factors, least of all the fact that President Obama is calling for the same relaxed homeowner lending policies that got us into this mess in the first place. Everyone wants to believe that the recession era is behind us, but it's not! This has been the weakest recovery of any other recession in history except for the Great Depression. Ironically, both eras suffered from the same progressive policies.

It would certainly be much easier for everyone if it were just as simple as blaming Bush. Hell, I voted for President Bush twice, and I wish it was all his fault! That would be the easiest solution; because he's no longer president, somehow everything is all better. That wraps everything up in a nice, neat package with a pretty red bow around it. Unfortunately that just isn't the reality of the situation. The hard truth is that we are all accountable for what happened, and if we don't all open our eyes and start taking on the hard challenges of our time, it will no doubt happen again, and much sooner than any of us want to admit, and when it does it will make the Great Recession look like a minor bump in the road.

What am I talking about? People get complacent, and that keeps them from opening their eyes and asking the hard questions and accepting the hard answers and finding the will to effect real change. It's human nature for us to "just want everything to be OK," and we want that so badly that we convince ourselves that it is, because the alternative reality is often too hard to accept or too great a task to wrap our heads around, so we pretend that it isn't there. The Great Recession occurred from a housing bubble that was brought on by about $2 trillion of bad loans. According to the US debt clock outlook, shortly after our next president takes office, our national debt will be over *$20 trillion*! That is nearly ten times the amount of the problem that nearly pushed this country into another Depression, and yet we keep spending like a bunch of drunken sailors! We blame the people we elect for not fixing the problem but fail to take any responsibility ourselves! Many people won't vote for a politician who levels with them and tells them what they don't want to hear. It's much easier to vote for smooth-talking politicians who promise the world, all on the backs of hardworking taxpayers and at the expense of our next generations. And when any politician does try to make a stand and act responsibly, such as not raising the debt ceiling unless it's tied to spending cuts, the opposition crucifies him or her for it, and the public sits back and lets it happen.

Let's dig a little deeper. Everyone thinks it's a good idea to cut government spending, so long as the government doesn't make any cut to anything that will affect him or her personally one little bit whatsoever. The vast majority of government spending is entitlements. Mark my words, if we don't immediately demand as a country that we get a good handle on entitlement spending and curb its growth, we are destined for a disaster that we will be unable to borrow our way out of. The problem, however, is that no one wants to hear about this problem, because it might make him or her have to make adjustments or concessions in his or her personal life, so we all put blinders on and pretend that the eight-hundred-pound gorilla in the room is invisible, like children with absolutely no care or consideration of what tomorrow will bring. If it's not affecting me today, I'm not going to worry about it until I have to. That is not only a childish and naïve position, it is an extremely dangerous position.

Make no mistake about it, we are all responsible for the Great Recession; we all let it happen. Times were good, the economy was roaring, and if any politician had even suggested diverting the path we were on, he or she would have been pummeled by his or her opposition and quickly voted out of office! We let it happen then, and, as was evidenced by the 2012 presidential elections, we have continued to drink the Kool-Aid.

CHAPTER FIVE

Hope and Change?
The Coming of the Messiah

"I Pray Heaven to Bestow The Best of Blessings on THIS HOUSE, and on All that shall hereafter Inhabit it. May none but Honest and Wise Men ever rule under This Roof!"—John Adams, 1800

Those words of John Adams were certainly wishful thinking that all who would inhabit the White House would be honest and wise. That unfortunately has not always been the case, and it certainly isn't the case with Barack Obama.

Who is Barack Hussein Obama? Before the 2004 Democratic National Convention for then presidential candidate John Kerry, few people in America had ever heard of Barack Obama. When Barack Obama took the stage to deliver his speech to the convention, not only Democrats, but anyone who watched the speech was nothing short of mesmerized. Four years later, this one-term senator from Illinois left the supposedly inevitable Democratic nominee, Hillary Clinton, dumbfounded when he snatched victory away from her. Barack Obama had a very unique ability to communicate that could only be compared to the likes of Bill Clinton, John F. Kennedy, Dr. Martin Luther King, and even the "Old Gipper," Ronald Reagan. America would soon find out, however, that the ability to give a good speech does not a leader make. Unfortunately, it took just over four years before the majority of Americans would wake up and come to that reality.

Adolf Hitler was also a charismatic public speaker—a great communicator who turned out to be the devil in disguise. OK, slow down, I'm not comparing President Obama to Adolf Hitler. My point, however, is that being a great orator doesn't mean anything other than that someone can communicate well. Being able to give a good speech certainly doesn't qualify someone to be commander in chief.

"Here comes the Orator! With his flood of words, and his drop of reason."—Benjamin Franklin, *Poor Richard's Almanac*, 1735

Barack Obama captured the hearts and attention of Americans and people all over the world. His campaign of "Hope and Change" set just the right tone and offered America a historic opportunity to elect our first African American president, break a glass ceiling, and further mend the sins of America's history. Unfortunately Barack Obama chose to squander that opportunity to unite and bring America together, and America has never been more divided than we are today.

Admittedly, I became extremely skeptical of Barack Obama just as soon as I found out about the radical left people within his inner circle. I've invested a lot of time learning about just who Barack Obama is, and I've tried to summarize who he is, what his positions on the issues are, and who he's been affiliated with. I've tried to summarize this information as briefly as possible in this chapter, and I apologize for the lengthiness of this chapter, but there is an awful lot of pertinent information that you should know. Unfortunately the American people didn't take much time to get to know who they were electing as commander in chief not just once, but twice. Unfortunately for "we the people," Barack Obama and his political machine were able to effectively play the "politically correct" race card any time the hard questions came up, and the biased media ended up in a love fest with Barack Obama and failed to do their job.

So who is Barack Obama? According to his certificate of live birth, Barack Hussein Obama II was born August 4, 1961, in Honolulu, Hawaii, on the island of Oahu, United States of America. His birth certificate lists his mother as Stanley Ann Dunham and her race as Caucasian. His father is listed as Barack Hussein Obama, and his race is listed as African.

Barack Obama's birth certificate has been the subject of considerable question, speculation, and possible conspiracy theory. For whatever reason, the Obama campaign refused to release a copy of his birth certificate during the 2008 campaign, and only after intense criticism from the likes of Donald Trump and others during his 2012 reelection campaign did they finally but reluctantly agree to release it. The obvious question from looking at the birth certificate the Obama campaign finally provided is, if that's all there was to it, why the cloak and dagger and reluctance to provide it in the first place? Barack Obama's father was from Kenya Indonesia, and as a child Barack Obama lived in Kenya for a period of time. The speculation has always been about whether Barack Obama was actually born in the United States or if he was born in Kenya. Obviously, if he was born in Kenya and not the United States, the US Constitution wouldn't allow for him to run for or be elected to the office of the president of the United States.

To add to the speculation and give even more ammunition to the conspiracy theorists, Barack Obama has refused to ever provide his college grade transcripts. So why is that such a big deal? There could only be three reasons not to provide them:

a) He (Obama) had poor grades. If that's the case, what's the big deal, especially now that he's already been reelected? Many presidents have had mediocre grades; heck, Truman never even went to college. And it would actually add to his legacy or his story to have come from being a mediocre student to the high-est office in the nation. He admitted to doing drugs when he was younger, so why not admit to struggling in college? Good question.

b) He was able to get into college or advance in college despite whatever grades he may have had because of affirmative action. If so, who cares? What's the big deal about that? So he got a hand up in life and took advantage of that; who could blame him?

c) He applied for or was accepted into college as a foreign student from Kenya. Did he take advantage of any foreign exchange student programs? That would certainly be a big deal! That would certainly be something that he wouldn't want to get out. If that was the case, it would mean that he either lied on his application and committed fraud or that he was actually born in Kenya and would be precluded from holding high office.

I'm not going to buy into any conspiracy theories, and I'm going to accept the president at his word that he was born in the state of Hawaii as he attests he was. But I must say that his lack of transparency on these issues, his refusal to provide something as simple as a birth certificate for as long as he did, and his refusal to provide his college transcripts do raise legitimate questions as to why. And why if as his birth certificate indicates, he was in-fact born in Hawaii; why didn't he provide his birth certificate when he ran for president in 2008, but did finally provide it when he ran for re-election in 2012? Some have speculated that it was because when he first ran in 2008, that he didn't have the ability to obtain a US birth certificate, because he was actually born in Kenya, and four years later after being president of the United States for four years, he was able to finally produce a US birth certificate confirming that he was born in Hawaii. Some have speculated, that if anyone could get a good phony birth certificate, you would expect it to be the man in charge of the government. But again, that's all just speculation, and it's obviously a moot point.

Regardless of what his college transcripts might or might not confirm, Barack Obama did graduate from Columbia University in 1983 with a bachelor of arts in political science and later graduated from Harvard Law School in 1991. It's worth noting that he was president of the *Harvard Law Review* and was the first African American ever elected to that position.

After graduating from Harvard Law, Barack Obama's experience includes being a community organizer and being a lecturer at the University of Chicago Law School from 1992 to 2004. While a law professor at the University of Chicago Law School, Barack Obama was also an associate attorney for Davis, Miner & Barnhill in Chicago, where he litigated employment discrimination, housing discrimination, and voting rights cases.

Barack Obama served as an Illinois state senator from 1997 through 2004 and was then elected as a US senator in 2005. Then, three short years later, Barack Obama was elected to the highest office in the land—becoming the most powerful person in the world. As president of the United States, Barack Obama was entrusted with the largest economy in the world and was elevated to the commander in chief of the strongest military in the world.

No doubt, Barack Obama has a pretty impressive resume for a law professor or a community organizer. The problem, however, is that nowhere in his resume does he have any management experience whatsoever! Never has he had to make a payroll. He's never even held an administrative or managerial position in his life. Even as a lawyer, he was an associate lawyer and not even a partner. He has had zero experience in capitalism, and yet we hired him to be in control of the largest economy in the world! What on earth qualified Barack Obama to be the president of the United States? The commander in chief of the largest, most powerful military in the world? Nothing! But he is a really good public speaker, you've got to give him that!

What are Barack Obama's position on the issues? During his eight years as an Illinois state senator, Barack Obama avoided making controversial votes approximately 130 times, which, according to other Illinois state senators, is much higher than average. Rather than having to take a position and vote yea or nay on legislation, Obama often chose to simply vote "present," which was the equivalent of a nay vote when tallying up support or opposition for a bill. A "present" vote avoids giving critics the ammunition to say you are for or against a specific bill. I would call it lack of leadership that started in Obama's earliest days of politics.

Gun control: While teaching at the University of Chicago, Obama told then colleague John Lott directly, "I don't believe people should be able to own guns." As a candidate for Illinois state senate in 1996, Obama promised to support a ban on "the manufacture, sale, and possession of handguns." Senator Obama supported Washington, DC's comprehensive gun ban, which prevented district residents from possessing handguns even in their own homes; required that long guns be kept locked and disassembled; and lacked a provision allowing the guns to be reassembled in the event of an emergency.

Affirmative action: Obama favors racial preferences for minorities in university admissions, public employment, and state contracting. "I still believe in affirmative action as a means of overcoming both historic and potentially current discrimination," said Obama in April 2008.

Same-sex marriage: In the wake of a May 2008 California Supreme Court decision legalizing same-sex marriage in that state (similar to a 2003 decision by the high court of Massachusetts), Obama issued a call to "fully repeal" the Defense of Marriage Act (signed by President Clinton in 1996), a move that would have the effect of legalizing same-sex marriage nationwide. The Defense of Marriage Act currently protects states from having to recognize same-sex marriage contracted in other states.

Abortion: As a state senator Obama voted "present" twice on a ban of partial-birth abortions, and in 2000 voted against a bill that would have ended state funding of partial-birth abortions. On April 4, 2002, Obama challenged the sponsor of the Born Alive Infant Protection Act, a bill designed to protect infants who had been intended for abortion but had not died (prior to exiting the mother's body) as expected. Obama knew quite well that children were being born alive and were not looked after by the abortion doctors; that in 10 percent to 20 percent of the cases where induced-labor abortion was practiced, the infants survived and were then left, uncared for, to die; and that these facts were precisely what had prompted the legislation that he challenged. On July 17, 2007, Obama declared, "The first thing I'd do as president is sign the Freedom of Choice Act." This bill would effectively terminate all state restrictions on government funding for abortion. It would also invalidate state laws that currently protect medical personnel from losing their jobs if they refuse to participate in abortion procedures.

Criminal justice: Obama as a lawmaker opposed the death penalty and authored legislation requiring police to keep records of the race of everyone questioned, detained, or arrested. In 1999 Obama was the only state senator in Illinois to oppose a bill prohibiting early prison releases for offenders convicted of sex crimes.

Education: Obama toes the anti-voucher party line and thus the special interest of the Democratic Party's biggest funding and activist base, the National Education Association (the teachers union). Obama's view is that virtually all schooling-related problems can be ameliorated or solved with an infusion of additional cash.

Welfare reform: In 1997 Obama opposed an Illinois welfare-reform bill, proposed by Republican Senator Dave Syverson, which sought to move as many people as possible off the state welfare rolls and into paying jobs. He tried to weaken the legislation by calling for exceptions not only to the requirements that welfare recipients make an effort to find employment, but also to the bill's proposed five-year limit on benefits. Obama eventually had to add his name to the bill, because the senate had to pass it in order to conform to the federal welfare-reform laws.

Health care: At an AFL-CIO conference in 2003, Obama said, "I happen to be a proponent of a single-payer health care plan" (which basically means that the government completely controls health care, including the hospitals and the doctors, similar to the Veterans Administration). On April 3, 2007, Obama said:

> Let's say I proposed a plan that moved to a single-payer system.
> Let's say Medicare Plus. It'd be essentially everybody can buy

into Medicare, for example...Transitioning a system is a very difficult and costly and lengthy enterprise. It's not like you can turn on a switch and you go from one system to another. So it's possible that upfront you would need not just, I mean, you might need an additional $90 [billion] or $100 billion a year.

In the summer of 2008, when asked by a campaign audience about single-payer health care, Obama said, "If I were designing a system from scratch, I would probably go ahead with a single-payer (government-run) system." Obama would reiterate this sentiment again in June 2009 when he told an unreceptive American Medical Association, "I'll be honest, there are countries where a single-payer system works pretty well."

Gender discrimination: The Obama campaign asserted that gender-based "discrimination on the job" was a big problem in America. "For every $1.00 earned by a man, the average woman receives only $0.77," said the campaign website. "A recent study estimates it will take another forty-seven years for women to close the wage gap with men." To rectify this, Obama "believes the government needs to take steps to better enforce the Equal Pay Act, fight job discrimination, and improve child care options and family medical leave to give women equal footing in the workplace." But Obama's claim that women are underpaid (in comparison to men) by American employers was untrue.

As longtime employment lawyer William Farrell, who served as a board member of the National Organization for Women from 1970 to 1973, explains in his 2005 book, *Why Men Earn More*, the gender pay gap is actually twenty cents per dollar, not twenty-three cents. And that gap can be explained entirely by the fact that women as a group tend, to a much greater degree than men, to make employment choices that involve certain tradeoffs (i.e., choices that suppress incomes but, by the same token, afford tangible lifestyle advantages that are highly valued). In other words, if you compare apples to apples, job for job and skill level for skill level, women make on average the same as men make for the exact same job. A male history teacher who teaches at a particular school for five years will be making the exact same income as his female counterpart working the same job for the same amount of time in the same school district. You can go to just about every industry and that rule plays out. Where the discrepancy comes in is in the fact that men and women tend to choose different career paths that pay much differently, which skews the numbers to make it appear that there is a discrepancy. Men often chose more dangerous careers that might pay more. Men are more likely to travel for different job opportunities than women in general are. There are far more male professional athletes, for example, who make a great deal of money, and that skews the income discrepancy. Women, especially mothers, tend to take more jobs with more flexibility and may chose not to put in as much overtime in order to spend more time with their family, compared to what their male counterparts might choose. Construction work pays much more than most clerical or housekeeping jobs, but more men tend to work construction jobs, and more females tend to work clerical or housekeeping jobs. My point is that it's easy but completely disingenuous for Mr. Obama to take raw data and make claims and assertions without telling the whole story.

Energy: Obama voted against permitting the United States to drill for oil and natural gas in the Arctic National Wildlife Refuge (ANWR). At a July 30, 2008, campaign stop in Missouri, Obama said, "There are things that you can do individually...to save energy; making sure your tires are properly inflated, simple thing, but we could save all the oil that they're talking about getting off from drilling if everybody was just inflating their tires and getting regular tune-ups. You could actually save just as much." In 2008 Obama said the following about the future of the coal industry, which currently accounts for half of all the electricity in America: "If somebody wants to build a coal-powered plant, they can, it's just that it will bankrupt them because they will be charged a huge sum for all that greenhouse gas that's being emitted." It's no secret that Obama has yet to approve the Keystone Pipe Line.

Environment: Obama's position on the issue of global warming is unambiguous. His campaign website declared;

> Global warming is real, is happening now and is the result of human activities. The number of Category 4 and 5 hurricanes has almost doubled in the last 30 years. Glaciers are melting faster; the polar ice caps are shrinking; trees are blooming earlier; oceans are becoming more acidic, threatening marine life; people are dying in heat waves; species are migrating, and eventually many will become extinct. Scientists predict that absent major emission reductions, climate change will worsen famine and drought in some of the poorest places in the world and wreak havoc across the globe. In the US, sea-level rise threatens to cause massive economic and ecological damage to our populated coastal areas.

Homeland security/war on terror: In 2004 Obama spoke against the Republican-led Congress's budgets generally, and against the 2001 anti-terrorism bill known as the Patriot Act specifically, suggesting that the act infringed upon American's civil liberties. Obama voted no on a bill to remove the need for a FISA (Foreign Intelligence Surveillance Act) warrant before the government may proceed with wiretapping in defiance of FISA, describing it as "unlawful and unconstitutional." Obama campaigned on closing Guantanamo Bay prison, which holds terrorists captured in battle; however, since becoming president, he has come to the realization that Guantanamo Bay is the only realistic solution.

The war in Afghanistan and the Iraq war: In August 2007, Obama suggested that as a result of President Bush's poor military leadership, US troops in Afghanistan had done a disservice to their mission by "just air raiding villages and killing civilians, which caused enormous problems there." As for the war in Iraq, Obama was an outspoken opponent of the invasion at the outset. Over time, however, he made a number of statements that seemed to contradict his position. In a 2007 airing of *Meet the Press*, newsman Tim Russert reminded him of some of those statements: "In July of '04 you said when asked what would you have done in terms of how you would have voted for the war in Iraq" and Obama responded; "I'm not privy to Senate intelligence reports." Russert continued: "And then this, 'There's not much of a difference between my (Obama's) position on Iraq and George Bush's position at this stage." That was July of 2004. Russert concluded, "It doesn't seem that you are firmly wedded against the war, and that you left some wiggle room that, if you had been in the Senate, you may have voted for it." In 2008 the Obama campaign website declared that Obama as president would immediately begin to pull out troops engaged in combat operations at a pace of one or two brigades every month, to be completed by the end of 2009. Obama further claimed that the US presence in Iraq was "illegal." When President Bush announced the surge of twenty thousand additional troops, Obama said, "I'm not persuaded that twenty thousand additional troops in Iraq is going to solve the sectarian violence there. In fact, I think it will do the reverse." Throughout 2007, Obama argued that the surge was ill advised. In July 2007, Obama said, "Here's what we know. The surge has not worked." In July 2008, by which time the surge had proven to be extremely effective in reducing the violence in Iraq, newscaster Katie Couric asked Obama, "But yet you're saying...given what you know now, you still wouldn't support the surge...so I'm just trying to understand this." The only argument Obama could then make was in regard to the cost it would have saved to have not done the surge. In mid-July 2008, the portions of Obama's campaign website that emphasized his opposition to the troop surge and his statement that more troops would not change the course of the war were suddenly removed.

Israel: While running for Congress in 2000, Obama prepared a position paper on Israel in which he stated, "Jerusalem should remain united and should be recognized as Israel's capital." Obama continued to express that sentiment in January and June of 2008 while on the presidential campaign trail. The day after his June '08 comment, a number of Arab sources criticized Obama's comments, and an unnamed Obama advisor tried to "clarify" the candidate's statement by suggesting that it left room for Palestinian sovereignty. Soon thereafter, Obama said, "The truth is that this was an example where we had some poor phrasing in the speech." He then went on to say that his point had been "simply" that "we don't want barbed wire running through Jerusalem, similar to the way it was prior to the 1967 war."

Military and missile defense: Obama has consistently opposed America's development of a missile defense system. In a February 2008 campaign ad, he stated:

> I will cut tens of billions of dollars in wasteful spending. I will cut investments in unproven missile defense systems. I will not weaponize space. I will slow our development of future combat systems. I will institute an independent Defense Priorities Board to ensure that the Quadrennial Defense Review is not used to justify unnecessary defense spending...I will set a goal of a world without nuclear weapons. To seek that goal, I will not develop new nuclear weapons. I will seek a global ban on the production of fissile material.

Redistribution of wealth: Obama's comment to Joe the Plumber about wanting to "spread the wealth" on the campaign trail in 2008 was pretty telling and pretty much sums up Obama's position on wealth redistribution. He wants to tax everyone as much as he possibly can, so he can escalate the growth of government and entitlements.

Taxes: Obama generally favors significant increases in the tax rates paid by Americans. In 2001 he said, "I consider the Bush tax cuts for the wealthy to be both fiscally irresponsible and morally troubling." Obama has been known to characterize high earners' reluctance to pay more money in taxes as evidence of their racial insensitivity or bigotry. In a 1995 interview, for instance, he made a disparaging reference to a hypothetical "white executive living out in the suburbs, who doesn't want to pay taxes to inner-city children for them to go to school." In the same interview, he condemned the widespread "tendency," both in the United States and elsewhere, "for one group to try to suppress another group in the interest of power or greed or resources or what have you." While in the US Senate, Obama voted several dozen times for tax increases. You can't fund a progressive "big government" ideology without an increase in taxes.

Earmarks: Earmarking refers to the commonplace congressional practice of directing federal tax dollars to local projects that are often frivolous and of extremely limited utility. In fiscal year 2008, Obama was the sole Senate sponsor of twenty-nine earmarks whose aggregate sum was $10.7 million. Earmarks are often informal quid pro quo arrangements, where recipients show gratitude by giving money to the political official who steered the earmarks their way. For example, after Obama inserted earmarks into a 2008 defense appropriations bill, the recipients sent $16,000 in contributions to Obama's presidential campaign. On another occasion, in 2007 Obama earmarked $1 million for the University of Chicago Medical Center, where his wife, Michelle Obama, served as vice president of the center. It's also worth pointing out, that shortly after Barack Obama took office as a US Senator in 2005, Michelle Obama received a $200,000 pay raise. I'm not suggesting that Michelle Obama wasn't worth such a substantial pay raise, but I'm sure it didn't hurt that she was married to an influential US Senator; it certainly paid off for the University of Chicago Medical Center two years later when Senator Obama delivered a $1 million ear mark to them.

Voting rights: In September 2005, Obama sponsored Senate Concurrent Resolution 53, which expressed "the sense of Congress that any effort to impose photo identification requirements for voting should be rejected."

Immigration: Obama's voting record clearly reflects his desire to expand entitlements for illegal aliens.

The English language: Obama voted against a bill to declare English the official language of the US government. Under this bill, no person would be entitled to have the government communicate with him (or provide materials for him) in any language other than English. Nothing in the bill, however, prohibited the use of a language other than English.

The US Constitution: In his 2006 book, *The Audacity of Hope*, Obama expressed his belief that the US Constitution is a living document (subject to reinterpretation and change) and states that, as president, he would not appoint a strict constructionist (a justice who seeks to apply the text as it is written and without further inference) to the Supreme Court.

Labor unions: Obama has extremely close ties to the Service Employees International Union (SEIU). At a September 2007 SEIU event, he shouted:

> I've spent my entire adult life working with SEIU. I'm not a newcomer to this. I didn't just suddenly discover SEIU...Your

agenda's been my agenda in the United States Senate. Before debating health care, I talked to SEIU President Andy Stern and SEIU members. Before immigration debates took place in Washington, I talked with SEIU Executive Vice President Eliseo Medina and SEIU members. Before the EFCA (Employee Free Choice Act), I talked to SEIU!

Foreign aid: Obama supports an initiative known as the Global Poverty Act (GPA), which, if signed into law, would compel the US president to develop "and implement" a policy to "cut extreme global poverty in half by 2015 through aid, trade, debt relief," and other means. Hey, I'm all for cutting global poverty in half, but we've got a heck of a lot of financial problems of our own right here at home right now to make poverty outside of this country a priority. I mean, there are innocent women and children who were gassed to death in Syria, and there is genocide in Africa, and the United States isn't doing anything about any of that right now, either. Liberals need to get their priorities straight about the extent of US foreign aid. I would say that there are a lot of really great charitable organizations that can do a heck of a lot better job reducing extreme global poverty around the world than the US government, and a heck of a lot more efficiently, no doubt.

Foreign policy: During a July 2007 Democratic primary debate, Obama was asked, "Would you be willing to meet separately, without preconditions, during the first year of your administration, with the leaders of Iran, Syria, Venezuela, Cuba, and North Korea in order to bridge the gap that divides our countries?" Obama replied, "I would. And the reason is this, that the notion that somehow not talking to countries is punishment to them—which has been the guiding diplomatic principle of this administration (the Bush administration)—is ridiculous." Notwithstanding subsequent criticism from Hillary Clinton, Joe Biden, and numerous other Democrats as well as political commentators, all of whom contended that some preconditions were essential, Obama initially did not change his position; however, over time, he and his campaign staffers sought to quietly, incrementally reframe Obama's position.

Obama's overall record: In January 2008, the *National Journal* published its rankings of all US senators based on how they voted on a host of foreign and domestic policy bills. Barack Obama was rated "the most liberal senator of 2007." Obama's foreign policy liberal score of 92 (out of 100) and conservative score of 7 indicate that he was more liberal in that issue area than 92 percent of the senators and more conservative than 7 percent, the researchers explained. In the area of domestic policy voting, the study found that "Obama voted the liberal position sixty-five out of sixty-six of the key votes on which he voted, and garnered perfect liberal scores in both the economic and social categories."

After declaring his presidential candidacy in early 2007, Obama clearly became far more focused on campaigning for his White House run than on performing the legislative duties for which he had been elected to the US Senate. From January 2007 through September 2008, Obama missed 303 votes (a total of 46 percent of all votes that came before the Senate.

So where did Barack Obama get his progressive ideology? Why is it that Barack Obama embraces more of a socialist progressive ideology and scorns capitalism? Let's take a closer look at who influenced Barack Obama prior to his election to the highest office in the land. Two characters who've had a great deal of influence on Barack Obama were a) his pastor of over twenty years, Jeremiah Wright, and b) his friends who launched his political career at a fund raiser in their home in 1995, Weather Underground domestic terrorist Bill Ayers and his wife, Bernadine Dohrn.

Candidate Barack Obama quickly disassociated himself with Jeremiah Wright, head pastor of the Trinity United Church of Christ, and described his association with Bill Ayers by saying, "He was just some guy who lived in my neighborhood." That statement as well as his disassociation with Pastor Wright for obvious political reasons is very telling of Obama's character.

So who is the Reverend Jeremiah Wright? Reverend Wright served as the head pastor of the Trinity United Church of Christ (TUCC) in Chicago from March 1971 to March 2008, taking the church from a small congregation of fewer than 250 members to a megachurch with approximately eight-five hundred members. The church practices a form of Christianity that it calls black liberation theology, which is to say that the life of Jesus Christ is a metaphor for the struggle of the African and African American people. The church expresses an adherence to the "black value system" and describes itself in the following manner:

> We are a congregation which is Unashamedly Black and Unapologetically Christian...Our roots in the Black religious experience and tradition are deep, lasting, and permanent. We are an African people, and remain "true to our native land," the mother continent, the cradle of civilization. God has superintended our pilgrimage through the days of slavery, the days of segregation, and the long night of racism. It is God who gives us the strength and courage to continuously address injustice as a people, and as a congregation. We constantly affirm our trust in God through cultural expression of Black worship service and ministries which address the Black Community.

Barack Obama began attending the Trinity United Church of Christ (TUCC) in 1988 after moving to Chicago to become a community organizer. After graduating from Harvard Law School and returning to Chicago, Barack became a member of Trinity in 1992. In Obama's 1995 memoir *Dreams from My Father*, Barack states that Reverend Wright impressed him as he spoke of "the audacity of hope" in times of suffering. Over the next decade, Reverend Wright would officiate at the marriage of Barack and Michelle Obama, bless their children, and provide spiritual support for Senator Obama, while Senator Obama would draw on the phrase *The Audacity of Hope* as the title to his next book.

While running for president, then Senator Obama gave a speech at the TUCC, and when questioned by MNBC in an interview about what his relationship with Reverend Wright was, Obama replied, "I have known him seventeen years. He helped bring me to Jesus and helped bring me to church. He and I have a relationship; he's like an uncle who talked to me not about political things and social views, but faith and God and family."

A few days after the attacks of September 11, 2001, Reverend Wright gave a sermon titled "The Day of Jerusalem's Fall," effectively blaming the terrorist attacks on America: "We bombed Hiroshima, we bombed Nagasaki, and we nuked far more than the thousands in New York and the Pentagon, and we never batted an eye...and now we are indignant, because the stuff we have done oversees is now brought back into our own front yards. America's chickens are coming home to roost."

In another sermon, titled "Confusing God and Government," Reverend Wright preached:

> The government lied about Pearl Harbor, too. They knew the Japanese were going to attack. Governments lie. The government lied about the Gulf of Tonkin incident. They wanted that resolution to get us in the Vietnam War. Governments lie. The

government lied about Nelson Mandela and our CIA helped put him in prison and keep him there for twenty-seven years...The government lied about the Tuskegee experiment. They purposely infected African American men with syphilis. Governments lie. The government lied about bombing Cambodia and Richard Nixon stood in front of the camera, "Let me make myself perfectly clear..." Governments lie. The government lied about the drugs-for-arms Contra scheme orchestrated by Oliver North, and then the government proposed all the perpetrators so they could get better jobs in the government. Governments lie...The government lied about inventing the HIV virus as a means of genocide against people of color.

Wright effectively accusing the government of infecting African Americans with syphilis and inventing the AIDS virus as a means of committing genocide against people of color.

In one of Reverend Wright's even more explosive sermons, he preached, "God damn America!" More and more excerpts from Reverend Wright's racist, bigoted sermons continued to surface. In an April 2008 fund-raising dinner for the Detroit chapter of the National Association for the Advancement of Colored People, Reverend Wright gave the keynote speech made several overtly racist comments, and at times mocked the behavior of various ethnicities and previous presidents. Criticism continued to mount about the close relationship between Obama and Wright. Two days after the NAACP speech, with Obama's candidacy in jeopardy, candidate Obama gave a press conference and said, "Our relations with Trinity have been strained by the divisive statements of Reverend Wright, which sharply conflict with our own views."

It's important to point out that Reverend Wright had been Barack and Michelle Obama's pastor for the previous twenty years. He officiated at the marriage of Barack and Michelle. Reverend Wright didn't just become a fanatical racist with a deep hatred toward America and white people on the day Barack Obama decided to run for president. If you watch any of the videos of Reverend Wright's sermons over several years, his anti-white, anti-American, bigoted profanity is clear in every single sermon. Moreover, it's obvious by the reaction of the congregation that they all have the same racist beliefs as are clearly evidenced in each of the videos of his sermons. Barack and Michelle Obama were a part of that congregation for two decades. Any decent American wouldn't listen to ten minutes of one of Reverend Wright's sermons without immediately getting up and walking out!

Barack Obama initially claimed that he had never heard Reverend Wright make statements which were controversial in nature and stated that he didn't think his church is actually particularly controversial. I believe that he meant that, because I think the views of his pastor and his church are the views of Barack Obama. After the tapes surfaced, Obama admitted that he had heard Reverend Wright make remarks that could be considered controversial, but in an interview with Bill O'Reilly he specifically denied that he had ever heard Wright say that white people were bad. However, in his *Dreams of My Father*, Obama had quoted Reverend Wright as saying in a sermon, "It's this world, where cruise ships throw away more food in a day than most residents of Port-au-Prince see in a year, where white folks' greed runs a world in need." I'd say that kind of contradicts what Mr. Obama told Bill O'Reilly.

A 2012 article in the *Washington Times* by Jeffrey Kuhner, president of the Edmund Burke Institute, outlines a recorded interview Edward Klein was granted with Reverend Wright, on the record. In the interview Reverend Wright claims that Dr. Erik Whitaker, a close friend of Obama, contacted him (Wright) and offered him $150,000 if Wright would put a muzzle on about his relationship with the Obamas.

(Ironically the Obama administration recently gave a $6 million grant to the University of Chicago Medical Center's Urban Initiative, run by Dr. Whitaker). Wright declined the offer. Reverend Wright went on to claim that Barack Obama personally visited him, urging the pastor to remain silent and do nothing that would cripple his candidacy for president.

According to Mr. Klein, Mr. Wright directly contradicts Mr. Obama's narrative of having little contact with the Trinity United Church. Instead, Mr. Wright alleges that he was Mr. Obama's close spiritual and political advisor, someone who for more than twenty years shaped the future president's world view. In fact, the pastor claims that he was like "a second father" to Obama. Furthermore, Mr. Wright says Mr. Obama possessed an "Islamic background" and, despite his conversion to Christianity, has never abandoned his Muslim roots. In short, Mr. Wright appears to confirm that Barack Obama is a cultural Muslim whose Christianity is deeply tied to black liberation theology—the belief that America and the West have an evil, imperialist civilization bent on oppressing the Third World.

So why is Reverend Wright speaking out against President Obama now? Wright admits that he feels burned by Obama, Saying, "He threw me under the bus to win the 2008 election." No doubt these allegations should be investigated—at the very least the allegation of the $150,000 bribe from Dr. Whitaker. What else did Dr. Whitaker do for Mr. Obama to deserve a $6 million grant? If these allegations are true, this is no doubt a crime.

Obama's father and stepfather were both Muslim. Obama attended a madrassa in Indonesia as a boy, and he studied the Koran. He has openly admitted that the "most beautiful sound" is the Muslim call for evening prayer, frequently refers to Islam as a "revealed religion," and further claims that America is a "post-Christian" nation.

Barack Obama is the true protégé of the radical leftist, anti-American Reverend Jeremiah Wright. And America elected him president.

So who is Bill Ayers? Bill Ayers is the founder of the 1960s and early 1970s radical antiwar activist group the Weather Underground, which was responsible for bombings of the New York City Police head-quarters in 1970, the US Capitol in 1971, and the Pentagon in 1972. Ayers participated in the Days of Rage riot in Chicago in October 1969, and in December of that year was at the "War Council" meeting in Flint, Michigan, where the group proclaimed that it would immedi-ately begin a violent, armed struggle, including bombings and armed robberies, against the state. In 1970, fellow Weatherman members and close friends of Ayers Ted Gold and Terry Robbins, along with Ayers's then girlfriend Diana Oughton, were all killed when a nail bomb they were assembling exploded. The FBI filed charges against Ayers for his planning and involvement in the bombings of the New York City Police Department, the Pentagon, and the Capitol. However, due to the illegal tactics of some of the FBI agents involved with the covert operation against the Weather Underground and Ayers, the US attorney was forced to drop all weapons and bomb-related charges against the Weather Underground and Bill Ayers. In a 2001 *New York Times* interview, Ayers said, "I don't regret setting bombs; I feel we didn't do enough."

After Bill Ayers's reign of domestic terrorism, he went on to found the Chicago Annenberg Challenge, or CAC, an education reform group dedicated to the radicalization of school teachers. Ayers also served as co-chairman of the Chicago School Reform Collaborative, one of the two operational arms of the CAC from its formation in 1995 until 2000.

Obama's initial claims that Bill Ayers was "just a guy from the neighborhood" were less than forthright. Barack Obama was appointed the chairman of the CAC in 1995. Several 1994 and 1995 articles in the Chicago *Tribune* detail Ayers's extensive work to secure the original grant for the CAC from a national education initiative by Ambassador Walter Annenberg, as well as Ayers's molding of the CAC guidelines. In response to an inquiry by *National Review* writer Stanley Kurtz, the Obama 2008 presidential campaign issued a statement claiming that Ayers was not involved with Obama's "recruitment" to the CAC board. The statement said Deborah Leff and Patricia Albjerg Graham, who served as presidents of other foundations, recruited Obama. Stanley Kurtz is a senior fellow at the Ethics and Public Policy Center.

You might be saying, "Who cares what board Barack Obama chaired while he was a state senator and remained involved with just five years before he ran for president?" Well, I care, and here's why: The CAC agenda flows directly from the educational philosophy, according to Kurtz, that called for infusing students and their parents with a radical political commitment and that downplayed achievement tests in favor of activism. CAC translated Mr. Ayers's radicalism into practice. Instead of funding schools directly, it required schools to affiliate with external partners who actually got the money. Proposals from groups focused on math and science achievements were turned down. Instead, CAC disbursed money through various Far-Left community organizers, such as the Association of Community Organizations for Reform Now (ACORN). Surely you remember ACORN, the voter registration community organizer group that filed for Chapter 7 liquidation after losing government funding and donors due to controversial videos that surfaced showing ACORN employees engaging in and encouraging criminal activity. According to Kurtz, Obama once conducted "leadership training" seminars with ACORN, and ACORN members also served as volunteers in Obama's early campaigns. External partners like the South Shore African Village Collaborative and the Dual Language Exchange focused more on political consciousness, Afrocentricity, and bilingualism than traditional education. CAC's in-house evaluators comprehensively studied the effects of its grants on the test scores of Chicago public school students. They found no evidence of educational improvement.

Kurtz wrote in a *Wall Street Journal* opinion piece, "Ayers founded the CAC and was its guiding spirit. No one would have been appointed the CAC chairman without Ayers approval". Kurtz reviewed the CAC archives at the Richard J. Daley Library at the University of Illinois at Chicago, which houses the CAC board meeting minutes and other documents from the education foundation. He found that along with Leff and Graham, Ayers was in a working group of five people who assembled the initial board of the CAC that hired Obama. Kurtz went on to report that the CAC archives demonstrated Obama and Ayers worked as a team to further the foundation's agenda. The documents showed Ayers served as a member of the board that Obama chaired through the CAC's first year. Ayers also served on the board's governance committee with Obama and worked with him to craft the CAC bylaws, according to the documents.

While we are on the subject, let's talk about Deborah Leff, one of the individuals who the '08 Obama campaign indicated recruited Obama to serve as the chairman of the Chicago Annenberg Challenge (CAC), founded by Bill Ayers. Deborah Leff served as the president of the Joyce Foundation in the 1990s. The Joyce Foundation is an education reform and anti-gun activist group of which Barack Obama was a board member from 1994 through 2002. Obama was named to that board by Leff. While Leff served as president of the Joyce Foundation, it provided critical start-up capital to the CAC. So what is Deborah Leff doing today? She's a senior advisor to Attorney General Eric Holder and the new head of the US Pardon Office, the official in charge of vetting federal inmates' applications for presidential grants of clemency. Keep in mind that Deborah Leff was the key point person in connecting Barack Obama with the domestic terrorist Bill Ayers.

So, where did Barack Obama chose to start his political career? You guessed it; in the living room of terrorists Bill Ayers and his wife and co-terrorist, Bernadine Dohrn. Kurtz reports that Barack Obama's first run for the Illinois state senate was launched at a famous fund raiser and kickoff for the campaign at a 1995 gathering at the house of Bill Ayers and his wife, Bernadine Dohrn.

This 1995 fund raiser launching Barack Obama's political career in the living room of Bill Ayers was confirmed by Ayers in an April 2013 interview with the Daily Beast. In an October 2008 MSNBC interview, Chris Matthews asked then Obama campaign spokesperson Robert Gibbs, "Did Ayers have a fund raiser for Obama or not?" Gibbs, who would become the White House spokesman, replied, "No, he did not have a fund raiser for our candidate," and categorically denied the fund raiser ever took place. However, Ayers disputes that and says of his relationship with Obama, "We were friendly, that was true; we served on a couple of boards together, that was true; he held a fund raiser in our living room, that was true; Michelle Obama and Bernadine (Ayers's wife) were at the law firm together, that was true. Hyde Park in Chicago is a tiny neighborhood, so when he (Obama) said I was 'a guy around the neighborhood,' that was also true."

Ayers went on to explain: "It was at that meeting that New Party member Alice Palmer announced that she wanted Obama as her successor as state senator since she was stepping down to run for Congress." Single-payer activist Quintin Young, who advised Obama on health care when Obama was a state senator, was reportedly present at the meeting and acknowledged that he was one of those present at the Ayers house when Alice Palmer announced she was stepping down to run for Congress and introduced Obama to take her seat. Chicago-based blogger Maria Warren was also present; she wrote that she remembered watching Obama give a "standard, innocuous little talk" in the Ayers home. "They were launching him," Warren wrote, introducing him to the Hyde Park community as the best thing since sliced bread.

It makes sense that the New Party sponsored the event in the Ayers's living room for the announcement. Palmer was the New Party's signed candidate for office. The New Party, which had partnered closely with ACORN, was mobilizing support for Palmer among its constituents and the larger Chicago progressive community. Reportedly at one point ACORN had such a close relationship with the New Party that they shared an office, address, fax lines, and e-mail addresses.

According to Breitbart columnist John Sexton, a neighbor of Bill Ayers's claims that then Senator Barack Obama attended a Fourth of July party at Bill Ayers's house as early as July 2005. It's also worth noting the financial connection between Obama and Ayers; various boards on which Obama sat in the late '90s granted nearly $2 million to the Bill Ayers Small School Workshop, and over $1 million was granted to Ayers's project by the CAC, but the Woods Fund and Joyce Foundation (on whose boards Obama also sat) granted nearly an additional million in donations to Ayers's group during the same time period. Additionally, the same foundations donated $761,100 to a related group run by Ayers's brother, John Ayers. In fact, in 2001 Obama would join John Ayers on the "leadership council," a successor group to the CAC called the Chicago Public Education Fund.

So what is the New Party? Good question. And even more importantly, what was Barack Obama's relationship to the New Party? The New Party was founded by Marxist activist Carl Davidson and was strong in the mid- to late 1990s as an electoral alliance dedicated to electing leftist candidates to office through the Democratic Party. Two organizations formed the backbone of the New Party: the Democratic Socialists of America and the Association of Community Organizations for Reform Now (ACORN). Labor union SEIU also had considerable input, as did members of the Communist Party USA breakaway group Committees of Correspondence. Another very strong influence was the Far Left Washington, DC-based think tank the Institute for Policy Studies. In Chicago, the New Party founded an equally radical sister organization called Progressive Chicago.

In Chicago, the New Party consisted mainly of members of ACORN, the Democratic Socialists of America, the Service Employees International Union (SEIU), and the Committees of Correspondence (CoC). A breakaway from the Communist Party USA, CoC worked closely with DSA, and many activists were members of both organizations. The New Party's intent was to move the Democratic Party to the Far Left and, ultimately, form a new political party with a socialist agenda.

The socialist goals of the New Party, established in 1992, took advantage of what was known as electoral "fusion," which enabled candidates to run on two tickets simultaneously, attracting voters from both parties. But the New Party disbanded in 1998, one year after fusion was halted by the Supreme Court. The socialist-oriented goals of the New Party were enumerated on its old website.

Among the New Party's stated objectives are "full employment, a shorter work week and a guaranteed minimum income for all adults; a universal 'social wage' to include such basic benefits as health care, child care, vacation time, and lifelong access to education and training; a systematic phase-in of comparable worth; and like programs to ensure gender equality."

The New Party stated it also sought "the democratization of our banking and financial system—including popular election of those charged with public stewardship of our banking system, worker-owned control over their pension assets and community-controlled alternative financial institutions."

In 2008 the Obama campaign adamantly denied that Barack Obama was ever a member of the New Party, amid reports citing the New Party's own literature listing Obama as a member. Six years later, I'd say it's pretty obvious that Barack Obama holds the same socialist views of these radical groups.

On January 11, 1996, Obama did formally join the New Party, which is deeply hostile to the mainstream of even the Democratic Party and American capitalism. Fight the Smears, an official Obama campaign website, staunchly maintained that "Barack Obama has been a member of only one party: the Democratic Party. *National Review*'s Stanley Kurtz has repeatedly rebuffed this claim; however, the so-called mainstream media have refused to take up the issue.

Evidence obtained from the records of Illinois ACORN at the Wisconsin Historical Society now definitively establishes that Obama was a member of the New Party. He also signed a "contract" promising to publicly support and associate himself with the New Party while in office. The minutes of the meeting on January 11, 1996, of the New Party's Chicago chapter read as follows: "Barack Obama, candidate for state senate in the Thirteenth Legislative District, gave a statement to the membership and answered questions. He signed the New Party "Candidate Contract" and requested an endorsement from the New Party. He also joined the New Party. Consistent with this, a roster of the Chicago chapter of the New Party from early 1997 lists Obama as a member, with January 11, 1996, indicated as the date he joined.

Knowing that Obama later disguised or denied his New Party membership for obvious political reasons explains his questionable handling of the 2008 controversy over his ties to ACORN. During a 2007 debate with John McCain, Obama said that the "only" involvement with ACORN was to represent the group in a lawsuit seeking to compel Illinois to implement the National Voter Registration Act, or motor-voter law. The records of Illinois ACORN and its associated union clearly contradict that assertion. So why did Obama deny his close ties to ACORN? Because they were notorious in 2008 for using thug tactics and fraudulent voter registrations, not to mention ACORN's support of risky subprime lending, which was a major contributor to the housing bubble and the economic collapse. No, the real reason Obama deceived the American people about his ties to ACORN is because he knew that it would have exposed his New Party affiliation and his other socialist organization ties.

Barack Obama has spent his entire presidency implementing the New Party progressive ideology that he and his leftist friends such as Bill Ayers have professed all along, and it is bringing our country to its knees.

So how did Barack Obama get a pass on all of this? How did he get by without being completely scrutinized by the press and the public about his close ties to such radicals as Jeremiah Wright and Bill Ayers? You tell me; the answer's not politically correct.

One other note; for Barack Obama being a guy who claims to have been a constitutional law professor, he sure doesn't know the constitution. In fact, by mid-2014, the US Supreme Court had voted unanimously on thirteen separate rulings, that President Obama had exceeded his constitutional authority. Mind you, that at least four of the nine justices are very liberal, and two of them were appointed by Barack Obama himself. Maybe that has something to do with why Barack Obama doesn't want his college grade transcripts to be released, because he obviously doesn't know much about constitutional law.

CHAPTER SIX

Progressive Government: A Failed Ideology Reborn

"A free people (claim) their rights as derived from the laws of nature, and not as the gift of their chief magistrate." —Thomas Jefferson, 1774

You would think that Thomas Jefferson was talking directly to the first progressive and is proclaiming that as a free people, our rights are derived from the laws of nature and are not a gift from the government or any politicians.

From FDR's New Deal to Obama's Hope and Change, it's all the same old failed, big government, progressive policy. Progressive big government ideology certainly didn't work throughout the Great Depression era, and it certainly hasn't worked throughout the Great Recession. Another "lost decade at the hands of progressivism.

Franklin D. Roosevelt's New Deal claiming credit for ending the Great Depression is nothing short of folklore! Unfortunately all too often, the facts seem to take a back seat to rhetoric. Whole generations have been "educated" to believe that Franklin D. Roosevelt and his New Deal are what saved this country from the Great Depression. Nothing could be further from the truth. Like President Obama, FDR continuously blamed his predecessor, Herbert Hoover. The Great Depression lasted more than ten long years, longer than any other recession in US history. Unemployment never fell below 20 percent, and, contrary to what desperate defenders of big government would have you believe, World War II had much more to do with ending the Great Depression than the New Deal.

Guess who said this:

"We have tried spending money. We are spending more than we have ever spent before and it does not work."

Are you thinking it sounds like Speaker Boehner or Rush Limbaugh? Not even close. Listen to some more;

"I want to see this country prosperous. I want to see people get a job. I want to see people get enough to eat. We have never made good on our promises."

"I say after eight years of this administration we have just as much unemployment as when we started…and an enormous amount of debt to boot!"

"We are just sitting here and fiddling and I am just wearing myself out and getting sick. Because why? I can't see any daylight, I want for my people, for my children and your children. I want to see some daylight and I don't see it."

The words are those of none other than Henry Morgenthau Jr., a close friend and the loyal secretary of the Treasury to President Franklin D. Roosevelt, and the key architect of FDR's New Deal, which was intended to try to end the Great Depression. These words were part of an address during Morgenthau's appearance in Washington before Democrats on the House Ways and Means Committee on May 9, 1939. This quote was from the FDR Presidential Library.

Morgenthau made this startling confession during the seventh year of FDR's New Deal programs to combat the rampant unemployment of the Great Depression. In these words, Morgenthau summarized a decade of disaster, especially during the years Roosevelt was in power. Indeed average unemployment for the whole year in 1939 would be higher than that in 1931, the year before Roosevelt captured the presidency from Herbert Hoover.

Indeed, with those words, Morgenthau confessed what so many keepers of FDR's flame won't admit today: the New Deal was failed public policy. Massive spending on public works programs didn't erase historic unemployment. It didn't produce any recovery. The New Deal represented the first "Lost Decade", a failed experiment in progressive government. Unfortunately history hasn't taught us much of anything.

If you read most history books or writings about the Great Depression, you might easily be misled into thinking that Franklin D. Roosevelt was the coming of the Messiah. Many historians consider FDR the third best president in history, behind only George Washington and Abraham Lincoln. Nothing could be further from the truth. No doubt Roosevelt was a brilliant politician, but he was an economic illiterate. Both Roosevelt's opponents and even his friends referred to him as a "feather duster"—a lightweight, and a clever dig at his blueblood heritage. Supreme Court Justice Oliver Wendell Holmes Jr. described FDR as a "second-rate intellect, but a first-rate temperament."

In the 1930s, the conventional wisdom was that capitalism had failed. As expressed by Scott Reeves in his 2008 *Minyanville* report, FDR apparently never challenged that assumption. But the failure of government—not the free market—created the Great Depression. The economic collapse could have been avoided. The money supply dropped about 33 percent from 1929 to 1933, in large part due to the Federal Reserve's incompetence.

FDR's temperament saved the nation—not his failed economic policy. Despite endless cheerleading from those with a vested interest in making big government bigger, FDR's New Deal did nothing to restart the nation's economic engine. What did restart the nation's economic engine was America's rearmament for World War II. You might say that WWII saved FDR's from himself!

The median annual unemployment rate during the New Deal was about 17 percent and never dropped below 14 percent during the 1930s. The hard times almost certainly would have continued for years if US industry hadn't hired millions to produce the endless supply of armaments needed to defeat Nazi Germany and imperial Japan. In many cases, FDR's policies deepened the Depression and created needless hardship for those he sought to help.

FDR nearly tripled the tax burden between 1933 and 1940, boosting excise, income, inheritance, corporate, and dividend taxes and slapping a tax on "excess profits." The highest individual tax rate soared to 79 percent. High taxes sucked money out of the private sector, smothered entrepreneurship, and killed incentives to work and invest. By contrast, Treasury Secretary Andrew Mellon helped spark an economic boom in the 1920s (the Roaring Twenties) by backing a plan to slash the top individual tax rate from 73 percent to 25 percent.

The New Deal raised the cost of employment, making it expensive to hire new workers and contributing to the nation's high unemployment rate. The National Industrial Recovery Act and the Davis-Bacon Act mandated artificially high wages, further crimping private employment. It's worth pointing out that the Davis-Bacon Act, still mandates artificially high wages, and still adversely impacts our economic growth, and our tax burden.

The new minimum wage cut the demand for unskilled workers. The new Social Security tax raised compensation costs. Compulsory union membership often fostered violent tactics, and the goal wasn't increased efficiency or innovative products to grab market share. The WPA and other agencies "created" jobs, but at great cost—private sector employment was lower in 1940 than it was in 1929.

Is any of this sounding very familiar? Read on.

FDR railed against "economic royalists" and "privileged princes" who sought to establish an "industrial dictatorship". Roosevelt issued about thirty-seven hundred executive orders, many limiting business activity, and let loose a plague of antitrust lawyers on American industry. New securities laws made it difficult to raise capital. FDR ordered the breakup of the nation's strongest banks, including those with the lowest failure rates. This created an uncertain business climate that stifled investment and killed private-sector jobs creation.

The National Industrial Recovery Act of 1933, struck down by the US Supreme Court two years later, created "codes"—cartels—in about five hundred industries and limited competition in an effort to maintain high prices and, it was thought, wages. Business owners who responded to the market by cutting prices received a stiff warning from the federal government, followed by a fine. The Agricultural Adjustment

Act of 1933 also sought to keep prices high by limiting production. "Excess" food was destroyed or sold below cost overseas as millions of Americans went hungry. In 1937, marketing orders limited production of milk and fruit. Roosevelt apparently thought it was government's role to protect established high-cost producers from entrepreneurs who could beat them on price. Roosevelt's policies stifled job creation and raised prices for families already struggling to make ends meet.

FDR used tax money to build the Tennessee Valley Authority, TVA, a power-generating monopoly. He then exempted the TVA from state and federal taxes and regulations. But the massive project failed to produce an economic boom. In a report for the Cato Institute, Jim Powell, author of *FDR's Folly": How Roosevelt and His New Deal Prolonged the Great Depression*, says non-TVA Southern states such as North Carolina and Georgia posted stronger growth than TVA states because there was a faster transition from farming to higher-paying jobs in manufacturing and services.

Roosevelt did get one thing right: the Securities and Exchange Act of 1933. Think of it as a recognition of "efficient markets" long before economists developed the idea. The SEC is unlike most New Deal legislation because it required full disclosure of relevant information and it didn't attempt to pick and choose or mandate the winners and losers. The keys to success on Wall Street are brain wattage and hard work. This creates intense competition among brokerage houses as well as providers of market information, such as Moody's (MCO) and Standard & Poor's. Investors benefit because everyone starts with the same basic information and therefore competes on quality of research, not the number of cronies that analysts can buttonhole in Congress.

If the New Deal were a product in a competitive market, Roosevelt would have been bankrupt. But politicians have different goals, different means of achieving them, and a different scale for measuring success that has little to do with a market economy. Most of FDR's "make work" government jobs created little of value and therefore didn't give the economy a long-term boost. No matter; Harry Hopkins, one of FDR's closest advisors, summed up the political philosophy of the New Deal: "We shall tax and tax, spend and spend, elect and elect."

Voters might want to keep this in mind the next time a presidential candidate carries on about giving you some big benefit (buying your vote with taxpayer money) or "investing" in a new program, which will obviously eat up more of your money and raise your taxes.

Historian David M. Kennedy won the 1999 Pulitzer Prize for his book *Freedom from Fear: A Review of the Economic Consequences of the New Deal*. Whatever it was, he wrote, FDR's New Deal "was not a recovery program."

While we're talking about the great Franklin D. Roosevelt, we would be remiss if we didn't take note of a few other facts about FDR's character or moral compass. Let's move past the fact that when FDR died, he was with his mistress, Lucy Page Mercer Rutherford. Rutherford was the former social secretary of FDR's wife, Eleanor Roosevelt. Lucy was hustled away before the First Lady was notified of her husband's death. FDR's infidelities were pretty trivial in the scheme of things. At the beginning of World War II, seventy-five years after Abraham Lincoln abolished slavery and successfully amended the Constitution to outlaw slavery, Franklin D. Roosevelt thought it appropriate to enslave over a hundred thousand American citizens and immigrants who were one sixteenth or more of Japanese heritage. FDR's own attorney general, Frances Biddle, ridiculed the idea as "armchair strategists and junior G-men" pushing for internment with no evidence of sabotage. Even FBI Director J. Edgar Hoover, who was no big defender of civil liberties, criticized the move as being caused by public and political pressure without any factual data. FDR sided with his assistant secretary of war,

John J. McCloy, who argued that "we can cover the legal situation... in spite of the Constitution." Even as late as 1945, when the war was clearly decided and thousands of young Japanese men had served with distinction on the European front, FDR did not back off, reconsider, apologize, or offer any compensation. Those tasks would be left to successors Harry Truman, Gerald Ford, and Ronald Reagan.

Our country's first president, George Washington, to whom some misguided historians try to compare Roosevelt, spoke incessantly of how America must offer refuge for those suffering religious persecution. FDR certainly didn't adhere to that philosophy; but then again, Roosevelt, contrary to what some historians may write, was no George Washington. As if FDR's immoral acts of enslaving American citizens who had any trace of Japanese heritage wasn't bad enough, FDR's lack of leadership turned a blind eye to Germany's acts of genocide and failed to take any real steps to end or mitigate the Holocaust. FDR was silent in the thirties as Hitler began his anti-Semitic policies. FDR was silent in 1940 as the ship *St. Louis* hovered off the coast of Florida with almost a thousand German Jews unsuccessfully seeking refuge. FDR was again silent in 1941 when his State Department refused to apply unused quotas to Jewish refugees seeking entrance to the United States. And again in 1942, FDR remained silent as it was made public that millions of Jews had been gassed to death in Nazi death camps. Roosevelt refused to meet with Jewish leaders who professed for action, and he even personally refused to consider a request from his interior secretary, Harold Ickes, to use the Virgin Islands as a refuge for Jews fleeing Europe.

FDR's undersecretary Henry Morgenthau Jr. pushed hard for the rescue of Jews through Switzerland. One treasury lawyer, Randolph Paul, commented: "I don't know how we can blame the Germans for killing them when we are doing this." The law calls it *in pari delicto*, which means "of equal guilt." In a public rally honoring the far greater efforts of Sweden and Denmark to rescue Jews, the former head of the Office of Price Administration, Leon Henderson, called the allied governments and their leaders guilty of "moral cowardice" for failing to offer refuge from the Nazi extermination efforts. The problem, said Henderson, has been "avoided, submerged, postponed, played down, and resisted with all the forms of political force available to powerful governments. Many newspapers editorialized, demanding action. The Hearst papers repeated the refrain 'This is not a Christian or Jewish question; it is a human question and concerns men and women of all creeds.' But until way too late, all these pleas were to no avail. Roosevelt's inaction was capped by his refusal in 1944 to order the bombing of the Auschwitz gas chambers and railroads leading there, despite the pleas of the Slovak Jewish underground leaders, the Polish and Czech governments in exile, and the Emergency Committee to Save the Jewish People.

So, the next time you hear a historian or a schoolteacher proclaim Franklin D. Roosevelt as one of the great presidents, please give him or her a reality check and a bit of a history lesson. When you hear progressive Democrats try to proclaim that it was the big government progressive policies of the New Deal that ended the Great Depression, again give them a bit of an economics lesson. Barack Obama has referred to FDR as a hero; no wonder. Like FDR, Obama has relied on the misery of our country to blast through his grandiose agenda, embracing one radical scheme after another. The parallels between Roosevelt and Obama are extraordinary; both presidents have so divided and unsettled our country, expanded the power of the government over the people, and lacked real moral courage, and neither was able to foster a robust economic recovery.

I would say however, that FDR and Barack Obama are completely different on one respect; FDR was at least a strong, and decisive leader, no matter how wrong or misguided his policies and ideology was, or how questionable his character was. Barack Obama on the other hand, reacts to every crisis by retrieving to a golf course or a fund raiser.

Franklin D. Roosevelt and Barack Obama and their big government policies are, without a doubt, the best or most accurate way to describe progressive government. Both FDR's New Deal as well as Obama's Hope and Change turned America upside down in their determination to remake American society. Both presidents failed miserably, and each of them gave America a lost decade.

In general terms, progressivism in the United States could be described as a broadly based reform movement that reached its height early in the twentieth century and is generally considered to be middle class and reformist in nature. It arose as a response to the vast changes that were brought on by modernization, such as the growth of large corporations and railroads and fears of corruption in American politics. In the twenty-first century, progressives continue to embrace concepts such as environmentalism and social justice. Social progressivism, the view that governmental practices ought to be adjusted as society evolves, forms the ideological basis for many American progressives. One historian defined progressivism as the "political movement that addresses ideas, impulses, and issues stemming from modernization of American society." Emerging at the end of the nineteenth century, it established much of the tone of American politics throughout the first half of the century.

Many of the core principles of the progressive movement focused on the need for efficiency in all areas of society. Purification to eliminate waste and corruption was a powerful element, according to historian William Leuchtenburg:

> The Progressives believed in the Hamiltonian concept of positive government, of a national government directing the destinies of

the nation at home and abroad. They had nothing but contempt for the strict construction of the Constitution by conservative judges, who would restrict the power of the national government to act against social evils and to extend the blessings of democracy to less favored lands. The real enemy was particularism, state rights, and limited government.

Pay attention to that statement: "Progressives have nothing but contempt for the strict construction of the Constitution by conservative judges, who would restrict the power of the national government to act against social evils...The real enemy was... state rights and limited government." In other words, progressives didn't want a limited government, they didn't want the states to have rights, and they didn't want the government to be restrained by that pesky Constitution! And who's to say what social evils are? Progressives' idea of how things should be is that there should be one all-powerful government, unrestrained by our Constitution and with complete power over the people, commerce, and the individual states. They believe that the federal government should be able to dictate what constitutes a "social evil" and what doesn't.

In the United States there have been several periods where progressive political parties have developed. The first of these was around the start of the twentieth century. This period notably included the emergence of the Progressive Party, founded in 1912 by then former President Theodore Roosevelt. Ironically, Theodore Roosevelt was a Republican; that's right, the Progressive Party in America was founded by a Republican. It's important to point out however, that when Theodore Roosevelt founded the party, it was three years after he left the office of President, and founded the party to launch what became a failed attempt at defeating his successor, William Howard Taft as president, in Roosevelt's run at a third term. Make no mistake; FDR was no Theodore Roosevelt, and FDR's New Deal was no Square Deal. Contrary to what some might think regarding any family relationship between FDR and TR, they were only distant fifth cousins. FDR's wife, Eleanor, however, was Theodore Roosevelt's niece (the daughter of Theodore's brother Elliot).

As president, Theodore Roosevelt took on the captains of industry and argued for greater government control over the economy, pursuing a two-pronged strategy of anti-trust prosecutions and regulatory control. He pushed through legislation that gave the Interstate Commerce Commission (ICC) new powers to set railroad rates, laying the foundation for the modern administrative state. Roosevelt cast himself as the steward of the nation's natural resources, he presided over the birth of the conservation movement. Convinced that a strong national defense was the best guarantee of peace, he built up the Navy and sent it around the world. Theodore Roosevelt thought that no one had ever enjoyed being President as much as he had.

Teddy Roosevelt's successor, William Howard Taft, greatly disappointed Roosevelt when he used the Sherman Anti-Trust Act to break up J.P Morgan owned US Steel. Roosevelt as president had approved U.S. Steel as a "good" trust. Roosevelt and Taft became openly hostile, and Roosevelt decided to seek a third term. Although Roosevelt failed in his attempt to regain the presidency, his Progressive Party was the most successful third party in modern American history. After the peak of the Progressive Party after Roosevelt's failed run in 2012, the party detoured into disastrous third-party status as it adopted Far Left ideology. Most Progressives later joined FDR's New Deal philosophy. Later Progressive parties were far less successful than the 1912 version. There are also two notable state Progressive parties: the Wisconsin Progressive Party and the Vermont Progressive Party. The latter is still in operation and currently has several positions in state government.

Today, members of the Green Party of the United States are considered most likely to self-identify as liberal progressives. In the

US Congress, the congressional Progressive caucus is the most liberal wing of the Democratic Party, and it is often in opposition to the more centrist or conservative Democrats, who form the "blue dog" caucus. It is also in continuous opposition to the Republican Party.

The term "progressive" is today often used in place of "liberal." Although the two are related in some ways, they are separate and distinct political ideologies. In the United States in particular, the term "progressive" tends to have the same value as the European term "social democrat," which is scarcely used in American political language.

The reason for this confusion in the United States might partly be rooted in the political spectrum being two dimensional; social liberalism is a tenet of modern progressivism, whereas economic liberalism (and its associated deregulation) is not. According to John Halpin, senior advisor on the staff of the center-left Center for American Progress, "Progressivism is an orientation toward politics. It's not a longstanding ideology like liberalism, but a historically grounded concept that accepts the world as dynamic.

During President Obama's first presidential press conference, Barack Obama defended federal economic intervention, stating: "There are several who have suggested that FDR was wrong to intervene back in the New Deal. They are fighting battles that I thought were resolved a pretty long time ago." Historian Anita Folsom responded to Obama's assertions: "We were just amazed to hear him say that. While this idea is taught in colleges all over the country, we have to come to the realization that these big government ideas do not lead to prosperity."

Roosevelt's big government approach has, unfortunately, been instrumental in shaping the modern world. Everything from Obamacare to the Community Reinvestment Act draws a direct line from FDR's actions to the worst public policies of today, along with the general view that government programs are the solution to economic and political problems. Obamacare has stifled our current recovery, and the Community Reinvestment Act was instrumental in causing the Great Recession.

Fortunately we have since amended the US Constitution to limit a president's time in office to two terms. At the time of the Great Depression there was no such limit, and Franklin D. Roosevelt was elected to office four times. He passed away a few weeks into his fourth term. FDR served as president of the United States for twelve years and forty days; in that time he and the big government he had created had become so powerful and America had been in such turmoil with the Great Depression and World War II that Americans were fearful of changing presidents at a time of such crisis. The last two years of President Obama's term can't get over with soon enough; I can't imagine the thought of another term.

"We the people" need to set the record straight about the disaster that the New Deal caused America if we ever plan to learn from our own history. As we discussed in chapter 1, "Sleight of Hand," politicians are expert "spin masters"; they can take almost any issue and fool people into believing whatever they say. No question, the Great Depression did eventually come to an end; damn few people are economists, so if their elected officials tell them it was because of how great FDR was and credit his New Deal policies, most people just accept that explanation and move on. People are all too happy to simply move on with their lives and are glad that the worst is now behind them; they don't care to give it much more thought than that. That is a very dangerous mentality! As citizens of this country, and as taxpayers; we have an obligation not only to find the facts, but to carefully evaluate them with an open mind and come to an informed and educated conclusion.

Politicians, however, seldom want the public to ask the hard questions; I mean, in the words of Secretary Hillary Clinton, "What difference does it really make?" They (politicians) would have Americans simply accept whatever line they try to shove down our throats, regardless of whether there is any truth to it or not. Kind of like blaming some stupid Internet video for a terrorist attack on our American embassy, which killed our ambassador and three other brave Americans! OK, we'll leave that conversation for another chapter, but the parallel still applies. If "we the people" fail to ask the tough questions and demand the truth, or if our press is asleep at the wheel and we fail to learn the truth, we are destined to repeat the mistakes of our past. It's incumbent on us to know our history, understand it, and learn from it.

It's pretty simple: if we're not dealing in reality, we're living in fantasy.

Whatever you call it, no matter how you parse it, progressive government is a disastrous ideology that held America in peril for more than a decade during the Great Depression and is causing the same misery in America today that it did eighty years ago.

Another lost decade at the hands of progressive government.

"The problem with socialism, is sooner or later, you run out of other people's money" – Margret Thatcher

CHAPTER SEVEN

Buy the Votes:
Never Let a Good Crisis Go to Waste

"But a Constitution of Government once changed from Freedom, can never be restored. Liberty, once lost, is lost forever." —John Adams, 1775

In a time of crisis, Americans are at the highest risk of losing their freedoms and their liberty. Slick politicians all too often take advantage of a crisis. Society is looking for quick answers to the crisis, and people are all too often willing to accept what they are being told, even at the risk of their liberties and freedoms.

Let's keep in mind, that for the full first two years of Barack Obama's presidency, he had one hundred percent complete control of the government. Obama was in the White House, Nancy Pelosi controlled the House of Representatives, and Harry Reid controlled the US Senate. Republicans had virtually zero say for two long miserable years. And now Barack Obama, Nancy Pelosi, and Harry Reid complain that the Republicans are to blame for our economy not recovering? They complain that Republicans aren't going along and giving them what they want. They had two full years in complete power, and they could have passed as much of their agenda as they wished, and boy did they ever! The Republicans simply refuse to let matters get any worse than they already are; until "we the people" are able to hire a new commander in chief.

In the words of then Obama Chief of Staff Rahm Emanuel, "You never let a serious crisis go to waste. And what I mean by that, it's an opportunity to do things you think you couldn't do before." Emanuel was commenting about the economy to a *Wall Street Journal* conference of top corporate chief executives shortly after Obama was elected.

You should really burn that message into your brain. Never let a serious crisis go to waste. Remember talking in chapter 1 about how politicians can be great magicians? Get people focusing on one distraction or another and a slick politician can get away with just about anything. A huge economic crash, such as the Great Depression or the more recent Great Recession, hit everyone in America hard, and they immediately wanted action. Americans weren't exactly sure what action they wanted, but they expected "Big Brother" to do something to fix the problem. There's an old saying, "Do something, even if it's wrong." The problem is, doing the wrong thing is usually worse than doing nothing at all.

The economic collapse certainly brought about a serious crisis, and the Obama administration certainly didn't let it go to waste! It would have been far better for our recovery had they let it go to waste. But they didn't. They were quick to jam their liberal, progressive ideology down America's throat, and, having control of all three branches of government, nothing was going to slow them down or put on the brakes.

A serious crisis creates a sense of urgency and opens up a big opportunity for whomever is in power to make sweeping and often radical changes in policy and legislation. Obama walked into the White House and was afforded the same opportunity to fulfill his desire to completely transform America as Franklin D. Roosevelt was at the time of the Great Depression.

Barack Obama, along with his co-conspirators Speaker Nancy Pelosi and Senate Majority Leader Harry Reid, found himself with the keys to the kingdom (Washington, DC), and unfettered access to the vault (the US Treasury). Like kids turned loose in a candy store; they started spending like drunken sailors, charging up everything under the sun, and putting it all on the American Express!

It took all of the previous forty-three presidents, from George Washington to George W. Bush, 220 years to run up a $9 trillion debt, and Barack Obama was able to double it in just six years! Obama didn't waste any time, either; less than thirty days after his inauguration, he signed the $787 billion stimulus bill into law. The bill was later revised and increased to $831 billion. Not a single House Republican voted for the bill, and only three Senate Republicans voted for it.

On January 28, 2009, a full-page advertisement with the names of approximately two hundred economists who were against the stimulus plan appeared in the *New York Times* and the *Wall Street Journal*. Among these economists were Nobel Memorial Prize in Economic Sciences laureates Edward C. Prescott, Vernon L. Smith, Gary Becker, and James M. Buchanan. The economists denied the quoted statement by President Obama that there was "no disagreement that we need action by our government, a recovery plan that will help to jump-start our economy." Instead, the signers believed that "to improve the economy, policy makers should focus on reforms that remove impediments to work, savings, investment, and production. Lower tax rates and a reduction in the burden of government are the best ways of using fiscal policy to boost growth".

Americans were paralyzed with plenty of problems of their own and certainly too busy to pay much attention to the heist going on right under their noses. What was sold to the public as an economic stimulus intended for infrastructure and "shovel-ready projects" never really materialized the way it was sold to the American public, to garner support for the largest economic stimulus package in American history, the American Recovery and Reinvestment Act of 2009.

Shovel-ready jobs were supposed to be a staple of Obama's recovery act. It was a big justification for spending the money involved in the legislation, and it was what he used to sell his big government spending stimulus plan to the American people. Pretty soon word started leaking out that there was no such thing as a shovel-ready project.

In June 2011, more than two years after the passage of Obama's recovery act, Obama himself was addressing his Council on Jobs and Competitiveness in Durham, North Carolina, at Cree Inc., a company that manufactures energy-efficient LED lighting. One of the council's recommendations to President Obama was to streamline the federal permit process for construction and infrastructure projects. It was explained to Obama that the permitting process can delay projects for months and even years and, in some cases, can even cause projects to be canceled or abandoned. "I'm sure that when you implemented the recovery act, your staff briefed you on many of these challenges," the council expressed to President Obama. At which point Obama smiled and interjected, "Shovel-ready was not as…uh…shovel-ready as we expected." The council, led by General Electric's Jeffrey Immelt, erupted in laughter.

Let's pause for a second and really give that some thought. Not the fact that this so-called jobs council were laughing over the fact that President Obama didn't have a clue about "shovel-ready projects" or have any concept as to how much his big government regulations were stifling any chance of progress, to the point that we can't even get a simple permit approved. Think about the fact that 51 percent of American voters elected someone so incompetent to the highest office in the land! If there is anything funny about his statement, it was how ridiculous he looked in making it, not to mention the fact that it was true! I guess you have to laugh just to keep from crying.

How could he know about shovel-ready projects; he's never had to manage anything. Heck, the Keystone Pipeline project has been "shovel-ready" for over five years, and that project still hasn't been permitted. To put that into perspective; America entered, fought, and won World War II in less time than it's now taken the federal government to approve a permit on a project that will create thousands of jobs and make America less dependent on foreign oil.

Not to get off point here, but while we're mentioning the Keystone Pipeline, I don't get the environmentalists' argument on this issue; the environment certainly isn't safer without the pipeline than what it is with the pipeline. Transporting oil through a sophisticated pipeline is certainly much safer than it is to truck it across our highways. It's not like Americans are going to use any more or less oil with the pipeline than without it. Not to mention that the pipeline is going to be built one way or the other, regardless of whether it runs across America or through Canada, and if, God forbid, there was some catastrophic event that caused a leak in the pipeline, it would damage the environment the same in Canada as it would in America. I would assume that environmentalists care about the environment equally across the globe. Maybe not.

I'm not so sure whether it really made much difference to Obama one way or the other if there were projects that were "shovel-ready." I mean, the way he sold the recovery act to America, you would think that most, if not all, of the $800 billion stimulus was slated for infrastructure-type projects, such as highways and bridges. You might be surprised to find out, however, that of the $831.0 billion (plus) recovery act; only about 12.5 percent ($105.3 billion) of that amount was intended for infrastructure-type projects. So where did the other $726.0 billion get spent? Good question. In rough numbers, there were about $288.0 billion in tax incentives (primarily for low- and middle-income tax payers, and renewable energy), $155.1 billion for health care (primarily entitlements), $100.0 billion for education (teachers unions), $82.2 billion for aid to low-income workers and the unemployed, $27.2 billion for renewable energy, $14.7 billion for housing (primarily HUD and low income), $7.6 billion for science and research, and $140.3 billion for "other." You can go to www.recovery.gov or www.recovery.org to see for yourself and get a more detailed breakdown of what our treasure is going toward.

When you take a closer look at where all those billions went, it's pretty obvious that the vast majority went to unions and other supporters of Obama and the Democrats, and also to a number of troubled states that live beyond their means and tend to vote Democratic—states looking for their own "bailout" because they can't get their own houses in order. States such as California, New York, and Michigan, for example. As you start to read through each detailed line item, it soon becomes pretty obvious that Obama's union supporters across the board made out like bandits and certainly got their fair share of the pie.

Let's take another look at Obama's pro-union affiliation. In Obama's mind, not all workers are equal, and, by design, the vast majority of his stimulus package funded only union workers and union projects even though union workers represent only a small part of the American work force. You need only look at Obama's union-friendly executive order EO 13502, an executive order President Obama signed his first weeks in office, which forces any contractors who bid on large-scale public construction projects in excess of $25 million to submit to union representation for their employees.

The pro-union instrument that gives unions a huge advantage is the Project Labor Agreement (PLA), which in theory appears to set reasonable work terms and conditions, but in practice requires contractors to hand over exclusive bargaining control and to pay above-market and inflated wages and benefits and exorbitant dues money and pension funding to corrupt, cash-starved labor organizations. These anti-competitive agreements undermine a fair bidding process on projects that locked out nonunion laborers and were funded with our own tax dollars.

The Project Labor Agreement (PLA) benefits only the privileged few at the expense of the vast majority. Eighty-five percent of all construction workers in this country are nonunion by choice.

So how many jobs did the "stimulus" create or save? That number gets into some fuzzy math and depends on which side of the smoke-and-mirrors you look at. In January 2009, President Obama claimed that if we passed the stimulus bill, unemployment wouldn't exceed 8 percent. It's no secret that unemployment skyrocketed to over 10 percent and didn't ever drop to just barely below 8 percent until, ironically, just prior to the 2012 presidential election, or about the same time our embassy was attacked on September 11, 2012, in Benghazi. If you'd asked the Obama administration at that time, they would have claimed that the recovery act saved or created four and a half million private-sector jobs. However, the Obama administration forgot, or neglected to include, all of 2009 in that figure, citing that they shouldn't have to include 2009 because those job losses were beyond their control because the recession began the year prior. Keep in mind, these are the same folks that spent $830 billion their first month in office proclaiming it would fix the economy and keep unemployment from ever exceeding 8 percent. They pick and choose their numbers, because if you calculate Obama's first four years in office, there were six hundred thousand fewer jobs at the end of his first term than there were the day he took office. Obama tries to skirt this issue by claiming that the economy was worse than they thought; maybe it's because Obama's policies made it worse than it needed to be.

What else happened in 2009 that affected the unemployment rate? Increased regulation, antibusiness policies, and the inevitable drumbeat of Obamacare made businesses in this country very nervous, and the uncertainty definitely stifled job creation. So, regardless of the unemployment trajectory when Obama took office, Obama certainly can't be exonerated from his participation in the dismal job numbers in 2009.

In July 2011, two years after the recession "officially" ended, the seventh quarterly report on the economic impact of the stimulus was released and provided further evidence that the stimulus had done little, if anything, to stimulate the economy but had greatly increased our debt. The report was written by the White House's Council of Economic Advisors, a group of three economists all handpicked by Obama, and it outlined the alleged success of the stimulus in adding or saving jobs. The council reported that "using mainstream estimates" of economic multipliers for the effects of fiscal stimulus, the stimulus had added or saved just under 2.4 million jobs, whether private or public, at a cost (as of July 1, 2011) of $666 billion. Keep in mind that the Obama administration excluded 2009 numbers from their calculations. But accepting their numbers at face value that would be a cost to taxpayers of $278,000 per job. If the government had just written all those same people a check for $100,000, it would have saved the taxpayers $427 billion.

Let's take a closer look at the unemployment rate and how it's calculated, because it definitely gets into some "fuzzy math." States calculate their unemployment rate simply by the number of people who are collecting unemployment checks. This is obviously flawed because of a number of reasons, namely, a) not everyone who's unemployed qualifies for unemployment, b) not everyone whose unemployed files for unemployment benefits, and c) unemployment benefits expire, often before workers have found a job. This methodology can easily skew the accurate unemployment rate in a given state, especially when the economy is in poor condition, because some people are often unemployed after their benefits expire.

The Bureau of Labor Statistics (BLS) takes the same state data into consideration; however, they do take the calculation one step further, and unfortunately that additional step is equally as flawed. Surveyors from the BLS visit sixty thousand households every month and ask a number of questions to determine someone's employment status. If someone works full time or is self-employed, he or she is considered employed. If someone does not have a job of any kind but has been looking for one for the past four weeks, he or she is considered unemployed. If someone does not have a job and isn't looking for one, he or she is considered outside the labor force (meaning that he or she isn't included in the unemployment number). The rate is then calculated as the number of people who are actively looking for jobs (i.e., the "unemployed") divided by the number of people who have jobs plus those actively looking (i.e., the "labor force"). Anyone who is not looking is not considered part of the calculation.

There are a great number of flaws in the way the unemployment rates are calculated by the BLS, whose methods are equally as flawed as the states' calculations. The number of people left out of the calculation because they are considered "out of the work force" are staggering. These flaws include:

a) The household survey uses only a small sample of households and represents only a small fraction of the 115 million households in the country.

b) People who work only part time or even a few hours a week are considered employed and not included in the un-employment rate.

c) People who work more than one job are counted multiple times; for example, if someone works three part-time jobs, he or she is considered three employed persons in the calculation.

d) Students not in search of a job, disabled people who've recently lost their job, and people on temporary leave are all left out of the calculation. People who've given up on looking for a job or are living off of Mom and Dad and not looking for a job also are not calculated into the unemployment rate.

Understanding how the unemployment rate is calculated is important, because not understanding it allows slick politicians to play some tricky games with the numbers. You may recall Obama touting how the unemployment rate had finally dropped to just below 8 percent just prior to his reelection in 2012, as if his policies had something to do with that. Unemployment benefits started ending in droves all over the country by late summer to early fall of 2012, which gave the president two gifts for his reelection campaign: a) because hundreds of thousands of people had recently lost their unemployment benefits, they were no longer included in the calculation, which caused the unemployment rate to drop just prior to Obama's reelection, and b) it gave Obama something to beat up on Republicans with about further extending benefits.

We all know just how careful our government is with spending our treasure, right? Not! No one can waste money as much or as quickly as the US government. Let's take a quick review of how upward of a $100 million of our treasure, via the stimulus Recovery Act, was spent:

- $54.00 million to a politically connected Mohegan Indian tribe in Connecticut that runs one of the highest grossing casinos in the country.

- $219,000 to a Syracuse professor of psychology, Michael Carey, to study the sex patterns of college women.

- $1.15 million to install a new guard rail around the nonexistent Optima Lake in Oklahoma.

- $389,000 for Buffalo (New York) State University study to record how much malt liquor residents drink and how much pot they smoke.

- $100,000 for a martini bar and a Brazilian steakhouse.

- $1.00 million to a dinner cruise company in Chicago to combat terrorism.

- $325,000 to the University of Florida to study the mating decisions of cactus bugs.

- $13.00 million in tax credits to a Denver developer to build a senior housing complex; however, the developer is being sued as a slum lord for running a rodent-infested apartment building in San Francisco.

- $22.30 million to Sheltering Arms Senior Services to weatherize homes for poor families in Houston; however, the work was so poor that thirty-three of the fifty-three homes needed to be redone.

- $100,000 to a liberal theater in Minnesota named "In the Heart of the Beast" for a socially conscious puppet show.

- $489,000 to Landon Cox, a Duke University assistant professor of computer science, to study Facebook.

- $578,000 to Union, New York, for a homelessness problem it claims it doesn't have.

- $1.00 million to California for youth summer jobs; however, the funds were used for rent and utility bills.

- $3.40 million to help turtles cross a highway in Tallahassee, Florida.

Don't get me wrong; I don't have anything against turtles in Tallahassee or Indian casinos in Connecticut, and I'm sure that understanding the sex patterns of Syracuse college girls may be a "stimulus" to someone, but, call me crazy, I fail to see how any of that $100 million stimulated our economy one little bit at all. I don't know, maybe I'm just a little slower than your average duck.

And then there are Obama's pet "green energy" projects that all too often have left the American taxpayer holding the bag. Denver's News 9 reporter Kyle Clark asked Barack Obama in an interview,

"How do you answer critics who see Abound Solar as Colorado's Solyndra—a politically connected clean energy company that went under and took our money with it?" Obama chuckled, saying only "4 percent" of green energy loans went to companies like Abound Solar and Solyndra. Since those decisions are made by the Department of Energy, he reasoned, "They have nothing to do with politics." Obama then claimed just "some of the companies that benefited from stimulus funds have failed, and the vast majority of them are pushing us forward into a clean energy direction; and that's good for Colorado, and good for the country," he concluded.

Except that it's not. Pat Stryker, an Obama supporter who, according to the Center for Responsive Politics, has donated $500,000 to Democrats over the last five years, including $50,000 to President Obama's inaugural fund and $35,800 to his victory fund in 2008, was an original investor in Abound and visited the White House three times around the time the Department of Energy (DOE) loan was approved. Abound subsequently filed for bankruptcy, and the government is refusing to release the company's trade secrets for fear that they will reveal that Abound's solar panels were not up to par. Todd Sheperd, an investigative reporter at a Libertarian think tank, told Fox News that former employees have told him the panels had "catastrophic" defects, such as a tendency to catch fire and much lower output than promised. Sheperd went on to say, "Either people at Abound knew they couldn't produce a good product and they misled the DOE, or the DOE knew how bad the product was and they were willing to overlook it simply because the politics of green energy is such a feel-good political movement." Weld County Attorney General Ken Buck is investigating Abound separately from the US House Energy and Commerce Committee investigation for potential securities fraud and consumer fraud.

President Obama's "Green Initiative" promised that investments in green energy would take the country forward. However, time after time that promise hasn't panned out; the companies our tax dollars have invested in are going belly up and taking jobs and our dollars with them.

In July 2011, President Obama touted A123 Systems as a job-creating company with soaring demand for its vehicle components. "There's A123, a clean-energy manufacturer in Michigan that just hired its one thousandth worker as demand has soared for its vehicle components. Companies like these are taking root and putting people to work in every corner of the country," Obama remarked in a speech on fuel efficiency standards. A123 filed bankruptcy after posting at least fourteen straight quarterly losses, with shares falling 85 percent (*Bloomberg Businessweek*, October 16, 2012). The company filed bankruptcy after failing to make a debt payment. The company listed a debt of $376.0 million. A123 received a $249.1 million federal grant and had been struggling with the cost of their recalled batteries, which had been supplied to Fisker Automotive, another Obama green energy blunder. The company was purchased by Wanxiang Group Corporation, China's largest auto parts maker. So much for our tax dollars going to products "made in America."

Speaking of Fisker, a Fisker Karma plug-in hybrid with an A123 battery failed during testing by *Consumer Reports* magazine. The repairs will cost nearly $67 million and force A123 to rebuild its inventory. One of Fisker's Karmas broke down in the middle of a *Consumer Reports* test, spawning a battery recall. Fisker Automotive also announced a strange, spontaneous combustion of a Karma plug-in hybrid due to the A123 battery defect. Fisker had drawn $193 million of $529 million from an Obama administration energy loan. The remaining funds were frozen, and it's doubtful the Fisker will ever be built in the United States (ABC News, May 30, 2012).

The American Taxpayer has gotten precious little for the administration's investment in battery-powered vehicles, in terms of permanent jobs or lower carbon dioxide emissions. "No matter how you slice it, the American taxpayer has gotten precious little for the administration's investment in battery-powered vehicles, in terms of permanent jobs or lower carbon dioxide emissions. There is no market, or not much of one, for vehicles that are less convenient and cost thousands of dollars more than similar-sized gas-powered alternatives—but do not save enough fuel to compensate. The basic theory of the Obama push for electric vehicles—if you build them, customers will come—was a myth. And an expensive one, at that. (Editorial, "GM's Vaunted Volt Is on the Road to Nowhere Fast," *Washington Post*, September 14, 2012)

Despite the commitment of hundreds of millions of taxpayer dollars, it is very clear that Obama's 2008 campaign promise to get one million all-electric, plug-in hybrid vehicles on the road by 2015 will not happen. In February 2011 the Obama administration's Energy Department issued an analysis purporting to show that, with the help of subsidies and tax credits, "the goal is achievable." To begin with, one million cars is nothing in the scheme of things and doesn't even represent 1 percent of all the cars in the United States. Since President Obama's photo op at GM's Hamtramck, Michigan, plant, when the Volt was rolled out, and his pledge that a million plug-in cars would be on the road by 2015, the Volt has thus far sold only sixty thousand vehicles in the United States as of April 2014.

Everyone surely remembers Solyndra, the solar panel company that received a $535 million government loan that will never be repaid. To add insult to injury, the Obama Department of Energy agreed to take a second position on the failed loan to George Kaiser's Argonaut

Investments. Kaiser, of course, is a campaign donor to Obama, and, according to the Center for Responsive Politics, Kaiser bundled between $50,000 and $100,000 for Obama's 2008 campaign. Not only did the American taxpayers take a second position on a $535 million loan; Solyndra investors may be able to take advantage of about a $350 million tax benefit (editorial, "The Solyndra Memorial Tax Break," October 15, 2012).

The list of Obama's failed green energy investments goes on and on: Solar Trust of America, Bright Source, LSP Energy, Energy Conversions Devices, SunPower, Beacon Power, Ecotality, and so on. The American government should not be in the business of picking winners and losers. That's what the free capitalist market is for.

If the government could spend its way to prosperity, good times would have been rolling back a long time ago!

"Never let a good crisis go to waste, and if there is no good crisis, make one up!" That's not actually a quote from someone, but it might as well be a quote from the Obama administration, because they are masters of creating a crisis that doesn't even exist to rile up the voters.

In April 2014 Obama met at the White House for a Holy Week prayer breakfast with the controversial activist and former FBI informant turned MSNBC host Al Sharpton. Obama used the Sharpton event to accuse Republicans of trying to reverse the 1965 Voting Rights Act to intentionally suppress black voters with state laws requiring voters to show identification. "The real voter fraud is those that try to deny our rights by making arguments about voter fraud." Obama compared the ID laws to the Jim Crow restrictions of the segregated South and cast himself as a modern-day civil rights leader. It may not wash with most voters, but will likely be enough to frighten the Democratic base.

What possible reason could there be to not require an ID when voting? The only possible reason is so people can vote multiple times, or to use someone else's name when casting a vote. You can't get married without an ID, you can't collect any Social Security benefits without an ID, you can't cash a check without an ID, you can't purchase cigarettes or alcohol without an ID, you can't even enter any federal building without an ID. All states will provide a state ID at no cost. That kind of "thug" politics is terrible, and the president ought to be ashamed of himself for accusing Republicans of being racists for supporting a very reasonable requirement to have an ID to vote.

Attorney General Eric holder played the same "race card" when he suggested at a forum on civil rights that "the past five years in Washington have been marked by unprecedented, unwarranted, ugly, and divisive adversity," insinuating that when he testified before the House Judiciary Committee the previous day, House Republicans were asking him tough questions just because he's black.

If it's not playing the race card, it's the war on women, or income inequality, or the rich aren't paying their fair share. The Obama political machine has mastered the art of inventing a good crisis to rile up his liberal base, regardless of whether there is any truth to it or not.

CHAPTER EIGHT

Pass the Bill to See What's in It? "You Can Keep Your Doctor?"

"All men having power ought to be distrusted to a certain degree."—James Madison, 1787

Boy, how right Madison was. Nancy Pelosi said, "We have to pass the bill so you can find out what's in it," and Barack Obama said, "If you like your health care plan, you can keep it." The American people never should have trusted those in power, especially on something as enormous as our health care.

"We have to pass the bill so that you can find out what is in it, away from the fog of the controversy," said then Speaker Nancy Pelosi as she promoted the pending passage of the Affordable Care Act/Obamacare.

Really? On what planet does that even sound like a good idea? Pelosi suggested that the US Congress should pass a twenty-five-hundred-page bill that turned our entire health care system upside down, affecting every man, woman, and child in America and impacting one sixth of our entire economy—and she thought it was a good idea to pass the bill before everyone found out what was in it? I swear, you couldn't make this stuff up! But pass it they did. The Democratic-controlled Senate passed the bill late in the evening on Christmas Eve 2009 without one single Republican vote.

The bill still had to go on to the House and, under normal circumstances, the House would be able to make their changes to the bill and then send it back to the Senate for final approval before sending it on to the president's desk. When the Senate passed the bill on Christmas Eve, they had a filibuster-proof supermajority (sixty Democrats, forty Republicans); however, with the passing of the late Ted Kennedy of Massachusetts, their filibuster-proof supermajority was in jeopardy. Republican Scott Brown won a special election for Kennedy's seat, running on "giving Republicans forty-one votes" and preventing Obamacare from becoming law. This forced the Democratic-controlled House to pass the Senate bill without making any substantive changes, to prevent it from having to go back to the Senate for approval. With the Democrats losing their supermajority due to Scott Brown's election, it forced the House to abandon their own health reform bill and pass the Senate bill, which had already been approved prior to Brown's special election. President Obama signed the Affordable Care Act into law on March 23, 2010.

The Affordable Care act is the largest, most expensive piece of legislation ever passed into law. The law impacts every man, woman, and child in America, and it impacts 20 percent of our entire US economy. This law was passed on a completely partisan basis, notably without even one single Republican vote. The following day,

Republicans introduced legislation to repeal the bill, and the House has since passed a number of bills to repeal the Affordable Care Act, none of which, however, has been taken up by Senate Majority Leader Harry Reid and the Democratic-controlled Senate.

Republicans are all for health care reform and have circulated a number of their own plans that primarily involve repeal of the existing Affordable Care Act and replacing it or making some substantial amendments to the bill. Obama actually made a symbolic gesture to Republicans while the reform bill was being debated; however, that "symbolic gesture" turned out to be nothing more than a photo op to make it appear to voters that he was seeking bipartisan support. Instead, any Republican input was quickly dismissed and ridiculed by the president and his supports.

Eight months after President Obama passed the Affordable Care Act into law; Nancy Pelosi lost her speakership to John Boehner after the Republicans delivered the Dems what Obama himself described as a "shellacking" in the 2010 midterm elections.

The Affordable Care Act has been riddled with controversy and has been generally not well received by the American public. In poll after poll since the passage of the law in March 2010, the majority of Americans have not had a favorable opinion of the law. Americans are for health care reform, and there are a number of basic provisions under the law that Americans do favor—primarily that insurers can't deny or increase premiums due to preexisting health conditions.

Early implementation efforts for the health care exchanges, especially the exchanges operated by the federal government, have received nearly universally negative reactions in the media and from politicians. HealthCare.gov, the website that allows people to apply for insurance through the exchanges operated by the federal government, crashed on opening and suffered from a rash of problems throughout the first few months. Many users have also found the available plans to be unattractive. Ongoing problems with the website have prompted the development of Health Sherpa, an independently produced alternative to HealthCare.gov that contains consumer information. Various committees in both chambers of Congress have conducted hearings where cybersecurity concerns related to HealthCare.gov have been discussed.

No one can deny the complete and utter failure of the initial rollout of Obamacare. The planners and architects of Obamacare were all pointing fingers in every direction of the globe as to who was to blame for such a disastrous rollout. In the few weeks leading up to the October website roll out, then Secretary of Health and Human Services Kathleen Sibelius and Barack Obama were reassuring the public that everything was right on track and moving full steam ahead. A few weeks later, when HealthCare.gov went live, it crashed! After continued promises that the website would quickly be repaired and up and running, one debacle led to another, and Obama's signature legislation left nothing short of egg all over the president's face. Two months passed, and the administration and its Department of Health and Human Services continued to be embarrassed and humiliated by their obvious inability to launch something as simple as a website.

Government officials repeatedly tried to deny that the price tag on the failed Obamacare website is as big as $634 million, as has been widely reported. Nevertheless, a close look at the cost of the website and the overall design of this enormous federal program, proves it to be really big waste of money for the American taxpayer. Obama administration officials, repeatedly denied that the cost of the website was anywhere close to $600 million, however by July 2014, the Government Accountability Office (GAO) confirmed that thus far, the website had already cost $840 million dollars! These costs are attributed to a combination of inconsistent oversight and constantly changing requirements, according to testimony prepared by GAO's Director of Acquisition and Sourcing Management, William Woods.

Speaker of the House John Boehner expressed his frustration: "What a train wreck. How can we tax people for not buying a product from a website that doesn't work?" Boehner demanded as report after report continued to indicate that the software problems experienced by the online portal were nowhere near being resolved. Computer experts who spoke with news outlets said that bad code and lack of testing could be the culprit, though more complicated problems could mean issues for months to come.

The website Digital Trends reported in early October 2013 that, based on government documents displaying contracts awarded to CGI Federal Inc., the Canadian company which in 2011 won a $93 million contract to build the federal health care exchange, the cost of HealthCare.gov was actually about $634 million. Officials claim that the contract figures cited by Digital Trends dated back to 2008, before the Affordable Care Act was passed into law, and included other CGI federal projects not associates with the new Obamacare exchange.

Digital Trends later revised its numbers down, settling on an estimated amount of $500 million, taking into account a figure of $398 million in obligated contracts for building the website and the entire technology portion, which includes everything from the massive data hub and call centers to network security, training and support, financial management systems, and all other information technology that supports the new online and offline marketplace, as reported by the Government Accountability Office (GAO) in June 2013.

Regardless of what the actual cost of the website is once you calculate in all costs over and above the contract amount, there is no dispute that the contract amount to build the original website was $93 million. That number alone is mind boggling, just to build a website to enable Americans to sign up for health care. Granted, it's a website that could experience high traffic at times; however, there isn't any time that it would experience anywhere close to the traffic that is regularly on private-sector sites such as Amazon or Facebook. Not only did the site not work, but when they finally did get it to stop crashing every other day, it still had no way to allow users to pay for their insurance. Kind of like putting something in your checkout cart and not actually being able to order it. Not much good if you're trying to sell a product and there is no way to accept payment for it.

So, who exactly built this disastrous website? I mean, you would think that if you were going to hire a firm to build a website responsible for accessing health care insurance to the entire population who is now required to purchase it by law, you would chose a highly experienced contractor and recruit the expertise and experience of what you expect from Facebook or Amazon. Don't you think? No, the Obama administration thought it best to entrust the task of developing the HealthCare.gov site to GSI Federal, who has a questionable track record and earned a "no-bid" contract as the lead contractor to design the disastrous website. But hey, the GSI company officers are at least Obama contributors. ("No bid" means that there was no competitive bid process and the contract was simply given to GSI Federal).

Oh, yeah, one more thing; I forgot to mention one other little detail about the company who earned (was given) the "no-bid" contract to design the failed website: the executive vice president of CGI Federal, Toni Towns-Whitley, was a Princeton classmate of first lady Michelle Obama. Both Towns-Whitley and the first lady are members of the Association of Black Princeton Alumni. Towns-Whitley and her husband even enjoyed Christmas with the Obamas at the White House in December 2010, according to a Facebook album created by Towns-Whitley. I'm guessing, however, that Towns Whitley and her husband probably won't be back to the White House for any Christmas celebration this year; CGI Federal was fired in February 2014 after the complete incompetence of those involved with the development of HealthCare.gov became a huge political liability to Obama and his administration.

So, between wasting somewhere between $93 million and $500 million, depending on how you slice, dice, and parse the costs, that ship has sailed, and since the Obama administration hasn't demonstrated any stomach to hold any incompetence within his administration accountable, whatever we lost is certainly spilled milk at this point. But that still doesn't fix the site; no, as previously pointed out, that number has already reached an incredible $840 Million dollars, more than eight times the amount originally estimated.

Ironically one of the reasons the site had a lot of its early troubles was because of the Obama administration's insistence that users of the site had to put in their income information before the site would show them the cost of their insurance options. Why? Again, smoke and mirrors; the Obama administration didn't want the average Joe signing up for the program to see what the true cost was, and wanted him to see what his cost was only after the government subsidy (entitlement) had been applied. This caused excessive wait time, which added to the number of users on the system at any given time. But again, there certainly weren't any more users on the site than what Amazon or Facebook has every single day.

In an effort to try and minimize his complete embarrassment over the failed rollout of his signature legislation, Obama took it upon himself to unilaterally make sweeping changes to the law via executive order, regardless of whether or not he had any clear constitutional authority to do so. Ironically, Republicans offered Obama a huge face-saving gift just prior to the website's disastrous rollout when they threatened to defund the law unless Obama agreed to delay its implementation. Unfortunately for Obama, however, the Republicans didn't have enough votes to defund the law; but if Obama had agreed to the delay, it would have gotten him past the 2014 midterms, and the Dems wouldn't find themselves headed into the next midterm elections with such an albatross as Obamacare hanging around their necks. In an effort to lessen the pain of the implementation, which by now was obvious to everyone, Obama delayed the employer mandate and later pushed back the individual mandate—two of the very issues that the Republicans were fighting for that resulted in a short-term government shutdown.

Not only did President Obama take it upon himself to make sweeping changes to the law; he further took it upon himself for purely political purposes to delay until after the midterm elections much of the law that was obviously poised to send shock waves throughout America. As if that wasn't bad enough, Obama was soon to grant exemptions right and left for his union supporters, among others, who didn't want to have to accept the same health care plan that the rest of the American public had shoved down their throats. It's also worth pointing out, in case you aren't aware, that neither Congress nor the president got stuck with Obamacare themselves. No, the plan "we the people" get stuck with isn't good enough for our elected officials. Let's not forget that they are supposed to be working for us.

For months on end, the Obama administration and the Department of Health and Human Services refused to provide the American public any data or information about how many people had actually signed up, how many people had paid, and how many people who may have signed up were being subsidized. All very important information. The administration's goal was to sign up seven million people by the end of March 2014, and at the twelfth hour they claimed that they had successfully surpassed that objective, notably still not disclosing how many of the people they claimed to have signed up actually did sign up and pay for their insurance. They also didn't disclose how many of the people signed up were on Medicare or any other pertinent information.

One thing was for sure: over six million people who had previously had their own insurance coverage, coverage they were happy with; lost their policies due to Obamacare by the end of 2013. So it's pretty clear that nearly as many, or as many people who had gained any insurance on Obamacare, had lost the care they previously had and were paying for without the government subsidy.

In a press conference on March 13, 2014, House Speaker John Boehner claimed "there are less people today with health insurance than there were before this law went into effect." A reporter later asked him if he really meant that. Boehner doubled down. "I believe that to be the case," Boehner said. "When you look at the 6.0 million American who've lost their policies, and (government officials) claim 4.2 million who've signed up—I don't know how many have actually paid for it—that would indicate to me a net loss of people with health insurance. And I actually do believe that to be the case." There are a lot of holes in the administration's data for signups.

Further clouding the stats are fluctuations in the existing insurance market caused when insurance companies canceled plans that didn't meet Obamacare's coverage standards. Whether that resulted in a net loss one way or another isn't really the question; one way or the other, it is at best a very close trade-off whether there are more or fewer insured Americans as a result of Obamacare. The point is that we are spending trillions of dollars and have completely turned our country and our economy upside down, all for a result that is minimal at best! And we may well be much worse off once all of the true data comes to life—granted, however, that is likely not to be while Mr. Obama is still in office or while the Dems still control two thirds of the government.

The one thing that President Obama had going for him through-out his first term is that; a) the American people generally liked him and b) they trusted him. I think a lot of people had their heads in the sands about that; but there isn't any dispute that President Obama enjoyed that sentiment from most of the American people throughout his first term. No doubt, I firmly believe that if voters had been pay-ing any attention at all in the weeks that followed September 11, 2012 (the Benghazi terrorist attacks) or if the biased media had done their jobs, the curtains would have been pulled back and the wizard of Oz (Obama) would have been exposed for who we now know he is. Unfortunately for our country, most people weren't paying attention, and the so-called mainstream media weren't doing their jobs, and Obama's character and integrity wouldn't be exposed for another year. His character and integrity, or lack thereof, was finally exposed when his signature legislation (Obamacare) was rolled out. The American people realized that they had been lied to and the wool had been pulled over their eyes while their heads were buried in the sand.

Obama spent nearly all of 2009 campaigning all around the country promoting his health care plan, which was still being written, in an effort to try to sell the American public on his signature legis-lation, the Affordable Care Act. As he made his rounds around the country, he made a number of promises, starting with his claims that if "we the people" would convince Congress to pass this overwhelming piece of legislation, it would, among other things, save our economy and cut the costs of health insurance for every family in America by at least $2,500 a year. America has since given Obama a pass on that lie. OK, maybe it's because he can't add and we've since learned that his economists are incompetent, so we can cut him some slack on that. And then there's the fact that there have been so many other lies that one now seem fairly insignificant by comparison:

"That means that no matter how we reform health care, we will keep this promise to the American people: If you like your doctor, you will be able to keep your doctor, period. If you like your health care plan, you'll be able to keep your health care plan, period. No one will take it away, no matter what" (June 15, 2009, speech to the American Medical Association).

Now, forgive me for my apparent lack of intellect—I admit that I'm not an English scholar—but there isn't anything in that statement that is at all ambiguous. Or maybe it's just my lack of ability to adequately parse words. You see, I'm a pretty simple guy; a country boy who appreciates straightforward, honest talk. Say what you mean, and mean what you say. I realize that he was giving a speech to a group of doctors, so I guess that Obama just assumed they all knew that what he really meant was that no one's health care would change one little bit at all if and only if every insurance company in the country and every single doctor and every single hospital in the county all agreed to completely transform the way they treat patients and accept whatever compensation Obama the "almighty" dictated to them that they would have to accept. I understand that President Obama has a socialist ideology; but we are still a democracy, and a capitalist democracy at that. Maybe not for long, however.

"And if you like your insurance plan, you will keep it. No one will be able to take that away from you. It hasn't happened yet. It won't happen in the future" (from Obama's remarks in Portland, Oregon, after the Affordable Care Act was signed into law).

As with every other "mistruth," lie, scandal, or just blunder, President Obama and his administration's cronies never take ownership of anything. Unable to blame Bush for this whopper, the administration first tried to put the blame on the insurers:

"Fact: Nothing in Obamacare forces people out of their health plans. No change is required unless insurance companies change existing plans"—Obama aide Valerie Jarrett on October 28, 2013, after NBC News aired a report that the Obama administration knew "millions" could not keep their health insurance.

Really? "Unless insurance companies change existing plans"? What happened to "That means that no matter how we reform health care, we will keep this promise to the American people: If you like your doctor, you will be able to keep your doctor, period. If you like your health care plan, you'll be able to keep your health care plan, period. No one will take it away, no matter what"?

When a president says words like "no matter how we reform" and "no one will take it away, no matter what," and then he actually says the word "period" after a sentence, most people accept that as meaning that there are no ifs, ands, or buts; "period" means without exception!

Obama then really put his foot in his mouth when he tried to rewrite his slogan, telling political supporters on November 4, 2013, "Now, if you have ever had one of these plans before the Affordable Care Act came into law, and you really liked that plan, what we said was you can keep it if it hasn't changed since the law passed." Unbelievable! Like Obama forgot that every news outlet had dozens of pieces of video footage with him making the promise to people over and over: "You can keep it no matter what, period!" "No one will take it away, no matter what."

On November 6, 2013, columnist Clarence Page of the *Chicago Tribune* wrote that the public "was entitled to hear the unvarnished truth, not spin, from their president about what they were about to face. I don't feel good about calling out Obama's whopper, because

I support most of his policies and programs. But in this instance, he would have to be delusional to think he was telling the truth."

PolitiFact, the Washington fact checker, called Obama's promises "the Lie of the Year" (2013). In fact, four of the past five years (2008–2013) PolitiFact's Lie of the Year has involved the Affordable Care Act. PolitiFact counted at least thirty-seven times that Obama made that promise in various speeches. The lie was so blatant and so completely obvious that even his staunchest allies had to cry foul.

The worst part of the lie is that Obama and his administration knew that the promises couldn't be kept. On August 24, 2009, Rep. Tom Price (R-GA), a doctor, made this point: "On the stump, the president regularly tells Americans that 'if you like your plan, you can keep your plan.' But if you read the bill, that just isn't so. For starters, within five years, every health care plan will have to meet a new federal definition for coverage—one that your current plan might not match, even if you like it." Which meant that as of 2014, the time when Obamacare was implemented, everyone's health care is subject to change.

On November 7, 2013, the day after the *Chicago Tribune*'s article saying the president "would have to be delusional to think he was telling the truth," Obama was forced to apologize during a lengthy interview with NBC News's Chuck Todd: "We weren't as clear as we needed to be in terms of the changes that were taking place, and I want to do everything we can to make sure that people are finding themselves in a good position, a better position than they were before this law happened. And I am sorry that they are finding themselves in this situation based on assurances they got from me," he said.

Kind of reminds you of Richard Nixon's "I'm not a crook" statement, or "Bill Clinton's "I did not have sexual relations with that woman." Both of those lies led to the impeachment of both presidents.

Nixon's and Clinton's lies, however, were minor by comparison. Nixon lied about his knowledge of someone breaking into an office to get information, which had minimal if any direct impact on the American people. Bill Clinton's lie to Congress was about his consensual affair with a twenty-two-year-old intern; again, minimal direct impact on the American people. Obama's lies, however, were made numerous times directly to the American people about something that directly impacts every single American citizen. President Obama has told lie after lie to the American people, and neither he nor anyone in his administration is ever held accountable.

I don't mean to minimize the Watergate scandal or the Lewinsky scandal. Both scandals and impeachment trials cost American tax payers tens of millions of dollars and disrupted Congress from doing the American peoples business. Nixon was a crook, and did more than just lie, and he definitely did deserved to be impeached, and probably should have gone to prison. Clinton lying to Congress about his affair with a 22 year old intern, certainly didn't rise to the level of Watergate, which is why Clinton wasn't forced out of office after his impeachment. I would add, that some might compare Clinton's impeachment to Al Capone being convicted only of tax evasion, because that is all that could be proved; but it was understood that there were a lot of other skeletons in the closet that couldn't be proved.

Fortunately for Barack Obama, it's not a crime for the President of the United States to out-right lie to the American people. That said, Obama's lies have completely upended the US economy, and have cost American tax payers ten times the amount of the Nixon and Clinton impeachments. I'm not suggesting that President Obama's lies about the Affordable Care Act, rise to the level of impeachment; certainly not on their own. There are however, numerous other things that are detailed throughout this book, that collectively do rise to the level of impeachment. I'm not suggesting that Barack Obama be impeached at this point either, because I think that would only further divide the country, and leave us with Joe Biden as President. I do however think that there is a strong argument for his impeachment. The best course is for the Republicans to take control of the Senate in the 2014 midterms, and keep Barack Obama from doing any further damage.

The new health care law is now forcing insurers to offer what they refer to as an "essential health benefits" package, which provides multiple categories that your old plan may not have covered, which will obviously cause changes in premiums, changes in doctors, and likely cancellation of an existing policy. The categories that all policies must now include are ambulatory services, emergency service, hospitalization, maternity and newborn care, mental health and substance use or disorders, behavioral health, prescription drugs, rehabilitative services, laboratory services, preventative care and wellness, chronic disease management, pediatric services, and oral and vision care.

Not that many of these newly required health care services wouldn't be nice to have; but don't we live in a country where we have freedom of choice? Oh, I keep forgetting, progressives only want freedom of choice when it comes to abortion rights.

The health care law did include some "grandfathering" provisions into the bill that in theory might have allowed some people to "keep their plan." (A "grandfather clause" means that if you were doing something prior to a law being changed, you can continue to do so after the law is changed; for example, if you are legally driving when you are sixteen, and the law changes to say you now have to be eighteen, you would be "grandfathered" so you could continue to drive even though you weren't eighteen.) This, however, caused a nightmare for insurers. And the way the bill was written, Democrats who passed the law purposely made the language in the health care bill so stringent that if you choose to make any changes to your plan, the grandfather clause ceases to exist. Things as small as changing your co-pay at all will void your ability to grandfather your plan. If your insurance carrier chooses to change or amend your policy for whatever reason, your grandfather status is void. What insurance policy have you ever heard of that doesn't change almost every year? The president knew that people would lose their plans, regardless of any grandfather provisions.

Insurance carriers are as frustrated as everyone else. Aetna's chief executive officer blasted the Obamacare tech debacle, giving it a harshly critical review in October 2013, saying, "There's so much wrong, you just don't know what's broken until you get a lot more of it fixed." Asked on CNBC's *Squawk Box* if he knew that the rollout of HealthCare.gov would be problematic, the insurer's CEO, Mark Bertolini, said his giant company's role as an alpha tester for the system gave it a sense of how many problems the health insurance marketplace faced on the eve of its launch. "We were pretty nervous as we got further along. As they started missing deadlines, we were pretty convinced it was going to be a difficult launch." Bertolini went on to say, "It's nothing you ever like to repeat…it's career-ending in a lot of cases." In addition, "it's all been on the fly," Bertolini said of the construction of the marketplace and the integration of insurers such as Aetna, whose plans are being offered to up to forty million customers. "We didn't get code drops until the last month before the system went live," he said. Bertolini was asked if the rollout should have been delayed, and he replied; "I would have if I'd been in their seat." But, he added, "the politics got in the way of a good business decision." Bertolini went on to say that it could be three years or so before the marketplaces problems are fully sorted out.

"The politics got in the way of a good business decision"… Unfortunately for the American people, politics gets in the way of every decision the Obama administration makes. Besides, how could

Obama be expected to make a "good business decision"? He's a bureaucrat and has never run a business, so he wouldn't have any idea what a good business decision looks like.

I think Republicans, and the American people, for that matter, are missing the point about the Obamacare debate. Let's look past the incompetence and complete inefficiency of the federal government. Let's talk a little more about the subsidy that the government applies to the health insurance cost of lower income earners. Let's consider this: What about the hardworking, lower income earners who don't want a subsidy or a government handout? Why does the Obama administration assume that everyone would want a handout or a health care subsidy? It seems to me that the Affordable Care Act is forcing someone to take a handout whether one wants to or not. What kind of a country do you think that is making America?

Why didn't they from the beginning have the website show everyone what the normal cost of each plan is without requesting one's income information, and then direct the user to another section of the site in the event the user chooses to apply for the subsidy and believes that he or she will qualify? Don't get me wrong, I'm not contending that we shouldn't provide people a helping hand if they really need it; but what on earth is the point in not being honest with everyone and saying, "Here is the full cost of your insurance coverage"? Then, if it's more than they are able to afford, follow it up with, "Let's see if we can help you out, if you would like us to," and then see if they qualify.

Whatever happened to the American spirit of self-reliance? It seems to me that something has gotten lost in all of this that smacks in the face of living the American dream. Our government dictates to us that we *must* purchase a product (health care); but then they justify that it's OK for them to do so, because they follow it up by saying that if for some reason we can't afford it, they will subsidize whatever it is that we can't afford. But what if I don't want our government's charity? What if I was raised to be an American who stands on my own two feet? What if taking charity or a handout is morally repugnant to me, whatever the reason or good intent?

OK, my ears are ringing; I know that some are thinking that I'm being judgmental or insensitive to honest people struggling to get by. That is not at all what I'm saying. I do believe that there are lots of people in our society that, as a nation, we need to look after: certainly the children, the elderly, and the disabled. That said, I am probably a little more callous about subsidizing able-bodied persons. But, OK, let's agree that we will provide the assistance as outlined in the Affordable Care Act and subsidize those who need it. Why not be honest with them that they are being subsidized and give them every incentive to work their way off of that subsidy so they can stand on their own two feet? It seems to me that Obamacare wants to let people pretend that they aren't being subsidized. And that is the absolute surest way in the world to keep a population down.

Imagine if you never taught your children the value of a dollar or what it actually costs to get by in life and pay your own way. Kids would become adults unable and unprepared to fend for themselves, and they would be dependent on their parents indefinitely. The Obama government is making our vast population dependent on the government! Why? Because it buys votes! You give people subsidies and entitlements and they are not going to vote for anyone who will take those entitlements away.

I'm going to tell you a quick personal story that I think is on point here. My two eldest children were born when I was in my early twenties. I had been a carpenter making a decent wage, but things were tight, and I had a growing family and a lot of responsibility for a young guy. Unfortunately we didn't have any health insurance when my eldest child was born, and by the time I was able to afford health insurance, I had just found out that my wife (ex-wife now) was already pregnant with our second child. So I didn't have any health insurance to cover any maternity expenses for either of my two oldest children. Anyone whose familiar with how much it costs to have a baby can easily imagine just how completely stressed out I was.

My ex-wife had two children from a previous marriage, and we had decided that she would quit working to be a stay-at-home mom for a while. So with a fairly large family and a limited income, we would have most likely qualified for government assistance that might have covered the cost of the pregnancy and delivery. I have to tell you, however, that the very thought of that made me ill. I was a grown man, a young man, for sure, but a grown man. I had always been raised that I am responsible for myself and my family. I and I alone, not society, and not my parents. My decision in starting a family surely wasn't society's problem. The one thing I did have on my side, however, was a little time; not much, mind you, but about eight months. So I started inquiring what my options might be; I mean, what do people do when something like this happens and they don't have any insurance? Surely I wasn't the first person on the planet to have this happen to him. The one thing I was determined about, however, was that no one but me was going to be financially responsible for bringing my kids into the world. What kind of message or lesson would that have sent to my kids? How would I ever be able to look at my wife, or my dad, or my then father-in-law in the face and still have any sense of pride? I wouldn't have been able to, and it would have demoralized me.

I started checking out the hospitals to see what my options were; surely a hospital would try and work out some sort of payment plan with me. I mean, if we just showed up at a hospital the day the baby was coming, no hospital could turn us away, and they would have to work out some sort of payment arrangements with me; right? So, knowing that I wasn't the only soon to be parent that ever faced this challenge, it seemed pretty obvious to me that most hospitals had to have some sort of a reasonable program worked out for people in my situation. After talking to a couple of hospitals, I found one that had two options that were something along these lines; option a) if you could pay the entire amount prior to the day the baby was born, the cost was $5,000, and option b) if you couldn't pay up front, then the cost was $10,000, but they would spread it out over as much as four years.

OK, $5,000; ouch...that was a big chunk of change for me twenty-five years ago. But starting a family was my decision and my choice, and it certainly wasn't society's responsibility. Like I said, I had about an eight-month advance warning, which definitely helped. I had a small amount in savings and picked up extra side jobs working nights and weekends for the next eight months to make sure I had the $5,000 and to make sure I paid my own way.

I'm not saying that there is anything wrong with giving or receiving a "hand up," and obviously, if I or someone in my family had a catastrophic need for assistance that I absolutely could not first provide for myself, I would reluctantly accept it. The problem, however, with the way our new health care system is, and for that matter, a lot of other entitlement programs, is that there is no great incentive for self-reliance, and far too often people are more and more becoming dependent on Uncle Obama.

If there is any good to come out of Obamacare, it's the fact that it has shed light on the fact that "big government" and progressive policies don't work. Its failures have been exposed, and the American people have been forced to open their eyes and take notice.

I would advise Republicans to take note of the number one rule in politics: "when your opponents are screwing up, don't interrupt them."

The Democrats created this nightmare without one single Republican vote; I suspect the public will hold them accountable.

What was once called the president's "signature achievement" has turned out to be the albatross that endangers his own party and his legacy.

NOTICE

INTOLERANCE
WILL NOT BE
TOLERATED.

CHAPTER NINE

Tolerance?
Only If You Agree with
the Liberal Left

"Freedom of speech is a principal pillar of a free government; when this support is taken away, the constitution of a free society is dissolved and tyranny is erected on its ruins."—Benjamin Franklin, 1737

Freedom of speech is embraced by the Progressive Left in America only if it's speech that they agree with. If they don't agree with what someone is saying, they will make every effort to silence that speech.

You might find this chapter a little off point, and I certainly do not intend to offend anyone. I do however think that it is very important that if we are going to overcome the progressive mindset that has infected so much of our country, that we try and understand the way progressives think, and how they operate on the political and social stage. So

I think it's good for us to have an open and honest conversation about some polarizing issues that highlight the hypocrisy of the progressive left.

From the Progressive Left's playbook, "Politics 101":

a) When you can't make any intelligent argument with someone who has a different opinion than you, call him a racist, a bigot, a liar, a homophobe, or an "Uncle Tom." If that doesn't work, lie, lie, lie!

b) When you're caught in a blunder, blame someone else.

c) When your bad ideas are exposed, spin them, blame someone else, and then change the subject.

d) When you have no good ideas, accuse your opponents of being responsible for everyone's troubles.

e) If you're in power, use it to silence and punish your adversaries.

f) If you're exposed in a scandal, proclaim your outrage, vow to get to the bottom of it, and launch an investigation until it all gets swept under the rug and goes away.

g) The liberal's credo: "we take credit, not responsibility."

I have little doubt that Barack Obama and his campaign team, and his administration have mastered that play book, like no politician to have ever come before him.

Liberal Progressives have long considered themselves the champions of tolerance, and probably still do. Hey, it's their story, so I suppose they can tell it however they choose. Their tolerance, however, extends only to those who agree with them. Those who disagree, they want silenced and will go to any extent to do so!

It perplexes me; why is it that anyone who disagrees with President Obama is automatically dismissed as a racist by the Left? I don't have a racist bone in my body, but I completely disagree with President Obama on just about every single issue, precisely the same as I disagree with Nancy Pelosi or Harry Reid. My disagreement with all three of those politicians has nothing to do with race or the color of their skin! Harry Reid and Nancy Pelosi took control of the House and the Senate two years before Barack Obama took office, and my feelings toward both Harry Reid and Nancy Pelosi were precisely the same then as they are now. And the color of their skin and their gender do not play into that disagreement whatsoever!

While President Obama himself, is usually smart enough of a politician to navigate between the ditches of playing the race card himself, he has absolutely no problem having everyone else around him do it for him. From Nancy Pelosi and Harry Reid, to the Attorney General of the United States, Eric Holder. Even the Obama campaign when he was running for President in 2008, used the race card against their former opponent, Hillary Clinton.

The point is that progressives can't give any reasonable defense for their failed policies, so they immediately attack their opponents as racists. Why? Because of a number of reasons, one of which is the fact that it's an effective weapon because it immediately puts their opponents on the defense, and it changes the subject; now, instead of a legitimate debate on the issues, you're forced to defend yourself as not being a racist. It also works as an effective silencer of those who disagree with their policies, because no one wants to be referred to as a racist. Hillary Clinton often uses the "gender card" in the same fashion.

The most despised human beings in America today are conservative African Americans. And female conservative African Americans are even more despised. They are also the bravest human beings in America today, and they have my complete and absolute respect! Black conservatives basically have to "come out of the closet," so to speak, to be able to express their conservative thoughts or beliefs, often at great risk and under tremendous ridicule from friends, family, and coworkers. Liberals have great disdain for black conservatives and call them everything from traitors to "Uncle Toms" or worse. And I thought liberals were supposed to be the party of tolerance. No such luck.

So why are Progressives so afraid of black conservatives? Because it makes it much harder to support their false narrative of conservatives being racists. Liberals are scared to death of being exposed, and, worse yet, they are scared to death of their failed ideas being exposed. The more black conservatives, Hispanic conservatives, gay conservatives, and female conservatives "come out," the more it diminishes the liberal propaganda that conservatives are racist bigots. Liberals hate conservative blacks, especially those who are elected to high office or become celebrities, because it jeopardizes their base, as the vast majority of blacks are registered Democrats.

Ironically, conservative values and principles are very much in line with the historically traditional values of both African Americans and Hispanics when it comes to self-reliance, family, and religion. Somewhere along the line, however, Democrats have done a better job of courting that constituency.

The Democratic Party has long touted itself as being the accepting party and being tolerant of others; yet it is the quickest to attack anyone with differing views.

If anyone believes that the Democrats are the party of tolerance or even a free press, I might suggest that they speak with Sharyl Attkisson, a hard-hitting, tough investigative journalist who after twenty years was forced to resign from CBS News in March of 2014. Attkisson provided hard-hitting and breaking news reporting on important scandals such as Operation Fast and Furious and Benghazi. Her reporting on the Fast and Furious gunrunning scandal won *CBS Evening News* an Edward R. Murrow Award in 2012. This straightforward and honest reporting on extremely important matters, however, flew in the face of the CBS News organization's liberal media bias. Attkisson had grown frustrated with what she saw as the network's liberal bias and increasingly felt like her work was no longer supported and that it was a struggle to get her reporting on the air. Since leaving CBS, Attkisson's been writing a book, tentatively titled *Stonewalled: One Reporter's Fight for Truth in Obama's Washington*. The book addresses the challenges of reporting critically on the Obama administration.

Senator Tim Scott was attacked in early 2014 by the increasingly liberal National Association for the Advancement of Colored People simply for being a politically conservative African American politician. This is a group that supposedly is for the advancement of colored people, but their Far Left hypocrisy only cares about advancing colored people so long as they agree with them. They even went so far as to call Scott a "ventriloquist dummy" for not following a liberal agenda. This is a sad misuse of authority by this organization, and it's nothing short of racism.

Stacy Dash, a conservative black actress, joined the Fox News team in June 2014. Fox News Executive Vice President of Programing Bill Shine released a statement accompanying the announcement that read, "Stacy is an engaging conversationalist whose distinctive viewpoints amongst her Hollywood peers have spawned national debates.

We're pleased to have her join Fox News." Immediately after the announcement was made, the forty-seven-year-old actress faced a relentless barrage of hateful commentary from every direction, accusing her of being a "turncoat" for being a black female with conservative leanings.

There is probably no place in the world less tolerant than many of our universities around the country. You would really think that a college or university would be a place that embraces tolerance and acceptance of all different viewpoints. Sure, that's what they would have one believe, but viewpoints at most universities are generally embraced only if they are liberal progressive viewpoints. Liberals preach the values of diversity and inclusion; unfortunately, that is only rhetoric, because the closer you examine the reality, the more it seems that liberals hate diversity!

It seems like just about every year around the time when school gets out in late May or so, you hear a plethora of unbelievable evidence of liberal intolerance. Most recently I'm reminded of the disturbing activities of Rutgers University. When former Secretary of State and National Security Advisor Condoleezza Rice was invited to give the commencement address, liberals went absolutely crazy! In February 2014, the faculty council passed a resolution demanding that the university withdraw its invitation to Dr. Rice. Thereafter, student protestors stormed the office of the Rutgers president to express their disapproval of the selection and to condemn Rice as a war criminal.

Regardless of whether you agree with Condoleezza Rice's politics or not, she certainly is no war criminal (let's not forget that Congress overwhelmingly approved military action in both Iraq and Afghanistan). Putting that ridiculous excuse aside, Condoleezza Rice is without question one of the most accomplished women in the world. That is a fact that is undisputable. Her academic and professional credentials are extraordinary, and Rutgers students should have been extremely grateful to have someone of her caliber address them at their graduation.

Liberals are scared to death of the likes of Condoleezza Rice, a highly educated and exceptionally accomplished African American female with conservative principles. Liberals absolutely hate that reality. And the last thing they want is to have her addressing college graduates that have already been brainwashed with progressive ideology. Oh, no; they can't have that. Impressionable students hearing from someone as accomplished as Dr. Rice, who has risen to the highest levels of education and politics and did it on her own, might just completely unravel what a liberal faculty had just spent the past four years trying to instill in the naïve and impressionable minds of their students.

In 2013, retired CIA Director and four-star General David Petraeus was berated, protested, and harassed in New York City while teaching a once-a-week college course titled "Are We on the Threshold of the North American Decade?" at Macaulay Honors College. The protests were organized by the City University of New York students and faculty and their then recently formed Ad Hoc Committee against the Militarization of CUNY. A flier from the committee lists several student groups and professors who support banning "this mass murderer" from teaching at the CUNY school. The group also vowed to make Petraeus's life a living hell while he was in New York. Hunter College adjunct professor Sandor John, who teaches Latin American history and helped organize the protest, says it should come as no surprise that so many diverse groups support the committee's effort to oust Petraeus.

My question is, if Progressives are right about their ideology, or have better ideas, what are they afraid of? They are all too quick to silence, vilify, and demagogue conservatives because they know that their ideas won't hold up to the scrutiny of an open-minded person who thinks for himself or herself.

Unfortunately, only negative protests were heard from both faculty and students, so Dr. Rice gracefully declined. In her letter to the university she noted, "I have defended America's belief in free speech and the exchange of ideas. These values are essential to the health of our democracy." She was gracefully acknowledging the students and faculty's right to express themselves. Sadly, however, it's apparent that our universities today are no longer committed to free speech or open debate; only liberalism is allowed. This has been going on in our universities across the country for years. I ask, aren't our educational institutions supposed to be laboratories for free discussion, embracing all ideological viewpoints? It appears upon closer examination that liberalism is not only the dominant viewpoint of our academia, it's allowed to go unchallenged. That is very dangerous.

The issue of intolerance in our universities has become so blatantly obvious that even former New York Mayor Michel Bloomberg thought it appropriate for him to address it in his 2014 commencement speech at Harvard University. It's worth noting that Michael Bloomberg is a fairly liberal independent, and certainly no conservative. Bloomberg criticized what he described as a disturbing trend of liberals silencing voices "deemed politically objectionable."

"This spring, it has been disturbing to see a number of college commencement speakers withdraw—or have their invitations rescinded—after protests from students and—to me, shockingly—from senior faculty and administrators who should know better," Bloomberg said. Bloomberg went on to cite a speech given the previous October by his ex-police commissioner, Ray Kelly, during which he was shouted down by students at Brown University. The university canceled Kelly's speech when protesters opposed to the police department's stop-and-frisk policy shouted down and interrupted Kelly.

Bloomberg further noted the Rutgers clash with Dr. Rice previously mentioned and also cited a similar protest at Smith College, where International Monetary Fund Chief Christine Lagarde withdrew after a student petition.

"In each case, liberal Progressives silenced a voice—and denied an honorary degree—to individuals they deemed politically objectionable. This is an outrage," Bloomberg said. He went on to advocate the role of universities as places where people of all backgrounds and beliefs can freely debate ideas without that "sacred trust" being threatened by the "tyrannical tendencies of monarchs, mobs, and majorities."

"If you want the freedom to worship as you wish, to speak as you wish, and to marry whom you wish, you must tolerate my freedom to do so—or not do so—too. What I do may offend you. You may find my actions immoral or unjust. But attempting to restrict my freedoms in ways that you would not restrict your own leads only to injustice," Bloomberg said. "Today, on many college campuses, it is liberals trying to repress conservative ideas, even as conservative faculty members are at risk of becoming an endangered species," Bloomberg concluded.

The speech was generally very well received by the graduating students, and many commented afterward that it was a refreshing, eye-opening viewpoint, according to CNN.

Prior to Bloomberg's speech, Cary Williams, president of the Association of Black Harvard Women, questioned why Bloomberg was selected as speaker, because, she said, the NYPD's stop-and-frisk program "disproportionately has targeted people of color in New York" (CNN).

"It's basically racial profiling," Harvard junior Keyanna Wigglesworth said of the New York policing policy under Bloomberg, "and so it's unsettling to me for someone to speak who advocates a racist policy when you want students of color on campus to feel comfortable. It's confusing and I don't think it is what Harvard stands for" (CNN).

Our colleges and universities have become an intolerant, "politically correct" sponge for liberalism. This is how the youth of America's minds are being molded. If it's not startling to you, it should be. If you ever ask yourself the same question as I do—"how on earth did Obama get reelected?"—now you know the answer.

All of these liberal college students and faculty protestors at universities from coast to coast solidify the charge that they are in fact intolerant. How can they possibly consider themselves tolerant of others when the only objective of their protests is to silence those with different views? You never hear of conservative students, faculty, or others protesting and causing such a ruckus over any liberals giving commencement speeches. That's because conservatives are tolerant, and we are all too happy to have the debate. Liberals want to shut up those with opposing views because they are afraid of the debate, because their ideology doesn't hold up under scrutiny.

OK, now let's tackle the liberal Progressives intolerance of the "gay marriage" activists. There is no denying that the gay rights sentiment in America has evolved full circle in the past ten years, and Americans are generally much more accepting and open minded about the issue than they were a decade ago.

If there is anyone more intolerant than a liberal college professor, it would definitely be a liberal same-sex marriage activist.

Let's clear the air; I'm a traditional guy who firmly believes that the institution of marriage is between a man and a woman, period. That said, the issue of same-sex marriage is at the absolute bottom of my list of issues of importance to me; in fact, it probably doesn't even make the list. I don't think that it's my business or the government's business to have any say whatsoever on what two consenting adults do in the privacy of their own bedrooms, "period." I do believe that gay couples should have legal protections similar to those of heterosexual married couples. I also have little doubt that regardless of whether you call it mar-riage or civil union or whatever, it will soon be legal across the country. The majority of Americans have evolved to accept same-sex marriage. The only threat that jeopardizes that clock from ever being turned back-ward is the intolerant, liberal, gay rights activists themselves.

What do I mean? Gay Americans have won their plight for accep-tance and equal rights in American society. I'm happy for them. They should feel good about what they've accomplished and make every effort to champion the rights and acceptance of every other group that is subjected to the same "intolerance" that they themselves have overcome. Unfortunately, all too many gay rights or same-sex marriage activists aren't happy that they've won the battle, I guess, possibly, because that might just mean that they are now out of a cause?

No, it's not enough for them that they've overcome the sins of bigotry; they aren't going to be satisfied until everyone in America completely agrees with them. And if everyone doesn't agree, they are going to silence people with differing opinions. Yes, they are all too happy to discriminate against people with differing views in the same ugly, bigoted manner that they themselves endured and overcame. My point is that attitude and that lack of tolerance for people with whom they disagree may just backfire in their faces and derail the progress they've made.

What am I talking about? I can go on and on with example after example, but let's just focus on a few. In the spring of 2014, Brendan Eich, chief executive of Mozilla, the maker of the web browser Firefox, was forced to resign when he came under fire and harsh criticism when it was revealed that he had made a donation six years earlier to a campaign that supported Proposition Eight, a California constitutional amendment that disallowed the marriage of same-sex couples in the state.

Eich had been working at Mozilla for years, had been interim CEO for more than a year, and is credited as the founder of JavaScript, a popular programming language. Numerous Mozilla staffers took to Twitter to call for his resignation. A popular dating site for same-sex couples, OKCupid, displayed a message on its website asking Firefox users to access the web using a different browser. Mozilla chairwoman Mitchell Baker commented, "While painful, the events of the last week show exactly why we need the web—so all of us can engage freely in the tough conversations we need to make the world better. We need to put our focus back on protecting that web and doing so in a way that will make you proud to support Mozilla."

Really? OK, regardless of your position on same-sex marriage, surely you see the blaring hypocrisy in all of this. I for one can say that I would not be proud to support any business in America where someone gets fired for his or her personal beliefs on a controversial social issue or for contributing money to support a piece of legislation with which not everyone agrees.

Let me take this one step further: Eich donated to a campaign that supported Proposition Eight six years prior to losing his job for it. This was back in 2008, the same time that Barack Obama ran for president, at which time he professed that he did not support same-sex marriage. Obviously his position has since flipped on the issue, but under the same logic that Eich was fired, Obama should be impeached. I would also remind everyone that both Bill and Hillary Clinton were not supportive of same-sex marriage and strongly supported traditional marriage. Does anyone remember the "Defense of Marriage Act"? And at least the Clintons were OK with homosexuals in the military, just so long as they stayed in the closet. Does anyone remember the Clintons' policy of "don't ask, don't tell"? But of course, the Clintons have politically correctly flipped on their position, or, as Hillary Clinton says, we've "evolved." Hey, I'm glad they've evolved. Good for them. But just as Mozilla CEO Brendan Eich was harshly criticized and forced to resign, Hillary Clinton surely should be held to that same standard for her past feelings on the subject, and the left should scorn her in her attempts to reach higher office.

No, I'm *not* suggesting that because of Hillary Clinton's past position on same-sex marriage she should be disqualified as a candidate for higher office. I am merely pointing out the hypocrisy and intolerance of the intolerant left.

There is something dreadfully wrong with our society when a group of people can dictate to a company that they must fire one of their employees, especially their CEO, simply because they don't agree with that person's position on a social or political issue.

Again, the intolerant Left; if you don't agree with them, they will make every effort to silence you, harm you, and destroy your life. Kind of like what the IRS has been doing to conservative groups and conservative donors.

No doubt everyone remembers the *Duck Dynasty* brouhaha, which exposed and highlighted some more of the intolerant Left.

Regardless of whether or not you are a *Duck Dynasty* fan, you had to have appreciated the drama at the end of 2013 when GLAAD (formerly the Gay and Lesbian Alliance Against Defamation—now LGBT to include bisexuals and transgenders) pressured A&E to suspend the hit show's family patriarch, Phil Robertson, for his remarks on homosexual behavior in an interview with *GQ* magazine. The issue, however, has little to do with gay rights and everything to do with speech control and the Left's intolerance. Regardless of whether you like, dislike, agree, or disagree with Phil Roberts, he is a "reality TV" personality. The whole point of reality TV is to highlight the oddities, lifestyles, and characters of the differing personalities.

Robertson is an old Southern hillbilly who makes few bones about his Christian faith and his incredulity that some men find other men more attractive than women. Fine, call him insensitive, but it isn't any big secret that heterosexuals don't quite understand the allure of homosexuality. Granted, Robertson went a little further than that statement, which is where the real rub is, when he identified that homosexual behavior is a sin, citing the New Testament book of First Corinthians as including homosexuality in a list of sins. At that point, ol' Phil had stepped past the point of no return. You would have thought that he robbed a bank on national television. Maybe it was a bigoted thing for him to say; certainly it was an insensitive thing for him to say; and probably even a very stupid thing for him to say. That said, that is what the New Testament says; and he was doing nothing more than voicing his religious beliefs and his opinion.

What the Progressive Left and GLAAD hate about *Duck Dynasty* is that it is a pro-family, pro-Christian, pro-traditional family values program that smacks in the face of everything they believe. Plus the fact that *Duck Dynasty* is the number-one-rated reality TV show of all time. They despise Phil Robertson and everyone who thinks the way he believes, and they find his speech contemptible. GLAAD spokesman

Wilson Cruz said, "What's clear is that such hateful anti-gay comments are unacceptable to fans, viewers, and networks alike. Robertson's removal has sent a strong message that discrimination is neither a Christian nor an American value."

My question is, who discriminated against who? Robertson didn't call for any action against homosexuals, and he didn't discriminate in any way toward homosexuals; he simply voiced his beliefs. On the other hand, Robertson was subject to discriminatory action; he was suspended for voicing his Christian beliefs.

My previous point mentioning that the only threat of turning the clock back on gay rights is from the intolerant, liberal gay rights activists themselves is highlighted by the suspension of Phil Robertson. The intolerance of GLAAD and their calls for his suspension because of his beliefs has backfired in their faces. The Robertson family certainly didn't abandon their patriarch, and neither did their fans. Quite the contrary; they pushed back, and pushed back hard, forcing A&E to reverse their decision and reinstate Robertson. This intolerance displayed by GLAAD overplayed their hand and weakened their cause. If GLAAD and the gay community want tolerance and acceptance of their points of view, they had better figure out that they need to extend the same courtesy and tolerance to those with opposing views.

While we're talking about tolerance, we can't get past this chapter without touching on tolerance of ignorance or bigotry that some people were born into or grew up in through no fault of their own, but have since evolved to understand the ignorance of their past and to become a better human being.

I'm going to jump off the cliff here and directly into the fire and try to have a conversation about bigotry, racism, and intolerance.

Americans are typically a forgiving people by nature. Hell, they say the only thing that will kill a politician's career is if he gets caught with a live boy or a dead girl. Everything else is forgivable. The one exception, however, is if anyone has ever said a racially derogative word at any time in their entire life. Don't get me wrong; I think it is an extremely despicable thing for anyone to ever use any type of bigoted, racist, or hurtful language for any reason whatsoever. But we also do have to accept that this is a whole different world than what it was forty or fifty years ago. Some older Americans grew up in a different time, and often a different culture, than what's prevalent today. There's no question that America has a very ugly past. In order for our country to ever heal from the divisive sins of our past, we have to learn to forgive. Not forget, but forgive.

Here's what I'm talking about: A basketball superstar, the immortal Michael Jordan, published his new book in May 2014, authored by Roland Lazenby. In his book Lazenby shares some surprising revelations about Jordan, and some courageous admissions. As it turns out, in a 1992 interview with *Playboy* magazine, Jordan acknowledged growing up "hating white people." Jordan recalled his upbringing in North Carolina and dealing with a culture that was still largely openly hostile toward people of color. "The tipping point came in 1977 when a girl at my school called me the N word. So I threw a soda at her," Jordan said. "I was really rebelling. I considered myself a racist at the time. Basically, I was against all white people."

I greatly respect Jordan for sharing that. His past racist feelings have obviously evolved and overcome his bigotry, and he's grown into a fine person. No one can blame Jordan for his feelings as a young person growing up in the late seventies. It was a very different time. I recall very well that time in my life; Jordan and I are about the same age and grew up in a very different time than what our kids have grown up in today. There was a lot of confusion and racial tension in the country.

No doubt, Jordan's admitted racist behavior toward white people only escalated the tensions and deepened the divide. It's easy to understand Jordan's behavior, and it's easy to forgive and excuse because of the sins of our history. I have little doubt that Jordan's admitted racial hatred and anger toward white people at the time may have incited bigoted behavior in response back to him by people who might not have ordinarily reacted that way otherwise. My point is not that any of it was right; it wasn't. My point is that it all created a vicious cycle. Some ignorant, adolescent fool calls Jordan the *N* word, and he responds with similar racist behavior and holds all white people accountable and in contempt. I would hope that Jordan has found it within his heart to forgive the terrible and bigoted behavior of the people he encountered early in life; as well, I would hope that the people toward whom he admittedly was a racist would forgive him for his bad behavior. Let's all keep in mind that we can't justify one person's bad behavior because of the bad behavior of another. We can understand it, but we can't justify it.

I would bet that the thought of Jordan ever apologizing for his racist feelings and behavior has never entered his mind. I'm not suggesting that he owes anyone any apology; only he knows that. My point is that if Larry Bird had given the same interview and had acknowledged that he hated black people at one point in his life, people would scream from the rooftops, and he would never be admitted to the NBA Hall of Fame. It's a double standard; we can accept Jordan's admitted racist behavior because he was young and we all recognize the sins of our history. But if we have truly healed as a country with an ugly past and we embrace Jordan's acknowledgement of his bad behavior, we then too need to forgive and move past the bad behavior of others, especially others who have realized the ignorance of their past.

I really do appreciate Jordan's story and acknowledgment of his past feelings. That kind of honesty and openness and willingness to have a tough conversation is likely the very best medicine to heal America's racist past. However, I was surprised that Jordan didn't take a more cautious and tolerant position when he condemned fellow NBA team owner Donald Sterling, owner/former owner of the Los Angeles Clippers. Jordan's comments about Sterling: "As an owner, I'm obviously disgusted that a fellow team owner could hold such sickening and offensive views. As a former player I'm completely outraged. There is no room in the NBA—or anywhere else—for the kind of racism and hatred that Mr. Sterling allegedly expressed. I am appalled that this type of ignorance still exists within our country and at the highest levels of our sport. In a league where the majority of players are African American, we cannot and must not tolerate discrimination."

Sterling did make some stupid, bigoted comments in a private, and in person conversation that was recorded without his knowledge or consent; but he didn't discriminate against anyone. The NBA banned Sterling for life and is forcing him to sell his team. Sterling's scorned mistress had released a recorded conversation between herself and Sterling following their split in which Sterling jealously told her that he didn't want her to bring any black fans, including Magic Johnson, to Clippers games.

No doubt Sterling's comments were bigoted and stupid things to say; even reprehensible things to say. Don't get me wrong, I'm not defending Donald Sterling and certainly not saying that what he said was at all defensible. It isn't. But let's keep in mind that he was having a "private conversation" with his ex-lover and expressing some obviously jealous bigotry for sure. That said, it is alarming to me that an eighty-one-year-old man can be forced out of his business, banned from his industry for life, fined $2 million, and scorned and ridiculed by millions of people all because of a stupid, even racist comment that he made in a jealous rant in a private conversation he was having with his ex-girlfriend.

Sterling's comments weren't intended to hurt anyone, other than possibly his mistress; and he didn't discriminate against anyone. Jealousy is a terrible thing, and it can bring out the very worst in most people. He's an eighty-one-year-old man who said something extremely stupid, and in doing so may have exposed some racial feelings he may have, but he certainly didn't commit any crime. The free market would have punished him and his business without a doubt. I understand the NBA's necessity to protect their brand; I would, however, ask every other owner of an NBA basketball team, or any other professional sports team, for that matter, if he or she has ever had a private conversation with anyone at any time in their life; and said something so stupid (racial or otherwise) that he or she would be mortified if that conversation was recorded and made public. I have little doubt that there would be a whole heck of a lot of team owners in a world of trouble. Probably not a good idea for people to live in glass houses. Sterling has since expressed that he is going to hire a private investigator to investigate all of the NBA owners who have condemned him. Like I said, probably not a good idea to throw stones at glass houses.

Barack Obama couldn't help but weigh in, and pile on the criticism of the eighty one year old Sterling. "When ignorant folks want to advertise their ignorance, you don't really have to do anything, you just let them talk. And that's what happened here", Obama said at a news conference with Malaysian Prime Minister Najib Razak, reported by Sports Illustrated. Obama continued; "the NBA is a league that is beloved by fans all across the country. It's got an awful lot of African-American players. It's steeped in African-American culture. And I suspect that the NBA is going to be deeply concerned in resolving this."

I think it might have been more appropriate for President Obama to not weigh in on this, due to the fact that he has put his foot in his mouth several other times on issues of race. That said, if he needed to comment, I think a more appropriate response should have been something more along the lines of this; "Mr. Sterling's comments were unfortunate, and I imagine he regrets what he said; I'm confident that the NBA will address this matter with him."

Southern celebrity chef Paula Deen found herself in a similar situation as Donald Sterling when the *National Enquirer* reported that she had once used the *N* word. The controversy came from a deposition Deen gave pursuant to a lawsuit. The following is an excerpt of the transcript that was obtained by the *Huffington Post*:

Lawyer: Have you ever used the *N* word yourself?

Deen: Yes, of course.

Lawyer: OK. In what context?

Deen: Well, it was probably when a black man burst into the bank that I was working at and put a gun to my head.

Lawyer: OK. And what did you say?

Deen: Well, I don't remember, but the gun was dancing all around my temple...I didn't—I didn't feel real favorable toward him.

Lawyer: OK, well, did you use the *N* word to him as he pointed a gun in your head at your face?

Deen: Absolutely not.

Lawyer: Well, then, when did you use it?

Deen: Probably when telling my husband.

Lawyer: OK. Have you used it since then?

Deen: I'm sure I have, but it's been a very long time.

Lawyer: Can you remember the context in which you have used the N word?

Deen: No.

Lawyer: Has it occurred with sufficient frequency that you cannot recall all of the various context in which you've used it?

Deen: No.

Lawyer: Well, then tell me the other context in which you've used the N word.

Deen: I don't know, maybe in repeating something that was said to me.

Lawyer: Like a joke?

Deen: No, probably a conversation between blacks. I don't know. But that's just not a word that we use as time has gone on. Things have changed since the sixties in the South. And my children and my brother object to that word being used in any cruel or mean behavior. As well as I do.

Paula Dean's spokesperson later released the following statement;

During a deposition where she swore to tell the truth, Ms. Deen recounted having used a racial epithet in the past, speaking largely about a time in American history which was quite different than today. She was born sixty years ago when America's South had schools that were segregated, different bathrooms, different restaurants, and Americans rode in different parts of the bus. This is not today. To be clear, Ms. Deen does not find acceptable the use of this term under any circumstances by anyone nor condone any form of racism or discrimination.

Paula Deen was asked under oath in a deposition if she'd ever used the N word, and she answered honestly that she had used that word many years ago. She also said that she didn't use the word anymore and objected to its use. She also told of a time she once had a black man put a gun to her head during a bank robbery, which likely caused some harsh racial sentiments—similar to the girl in school that called Michael Jordan the N word, resulting in his hatred of white people at that time of his life.

When the content of Deen's deposition went public, she was crucified in all directions. The Food Network dropped her show, and she lost most of her other sponsors. Hey, that's the free market. My question is, was anyone really surprised to find out that someone growing up in the South in the sixties had ever used that word?

It is worth pointing out, that Paula Deen, did in-fact campaign heavily for Barack Obama when he ran for President in 2008, and was a big supporter. After Barack Obama was elected, First Lady Michelle Obama was a guest on Paula Deen's hit cooking show on the Food Network.

I'm certainly no big fan of Donald Sterling or Paula Deen, and I find their racial comments despicable. The free market has certainly punished both of them severely. The overwhelming public outrage toward both Sterling and Deen, however, is somewhat troubling because it highlights just how unforgiving and intolerant many of us really are as a society. I'm troubled that Michael Jordan can admit being a racist at one time in his life and be applauded and hailed a hero for his candor. However, it's a clear double standard when Paula Deen acknowledges the very same thing and she is destroyed for it. Jordan and Deen both grew up in a tumultuous time in American history; Deen even more so than Jordan because of her age. They both grew and acknowledged the ignorance of their past. They have both publically condemned racism and discrimination in any form. The double standard of Jordan being embraced and Deen being completely condemned seems very hypocritical.

Racism or discrimination in any form should never be tolerated by anyone for any reason, period. I would, however, ask: If society can pick and choose who can be crucified for a terrible word someone admits saying or ignorant thoughts he or she may have harbored at any point in his or her distant past, then who among us would answer such a question with complete honesty?

Racism is a terribly ugly thing, but it is unfortunately a part of America's dark history, and we have to accept the fact that there is a segment of our older population who grew up in that era of ugliness through no fault of their own. If you're born into ignorance and hatred, it may take a few days or more to find your way. I mean, we can't pick our parents or the circumstances, times, or place in which we are born. Like it or not, that is our history, and there is no getting around it. Thank God our country has grown and evolved, and with every new generation the darkness of our ugly past gets further and further behind us. Please don't get me wrong; there is absolutely no excuse for racism now, then, or ever. My point is that two wrongs don't make a right. If we are ever going to rid racism from our history for good, we have got to be able to have an open and honest conversation about it without demonizing those who have grown out of the bigotry they may have inherited and changed the errors of their ways. If we aren't able to do so, what does that make us? Intolerant bigots.

Are we sure we want a society where anyone can be vilified by all of society and have our businesses and our livelihood taken from us because of a stupid and bigoted comment made in a private conversation with a lover and in a rage of jealousy? That standard is a very slippery slope, and if that's our idea of tolerance and forgiveness, then we are all in a world of trouble! Be careful what you wish for, because I'm not sure that's a world we want. So much for freedom of speech, but might I at least suggest a little tolerance and forgiveness?

While we are on the topic of race in America, I have correctly pointed out that racism is a sin of Americas past, and there is no doubt about that fact. Racism however was not just an American sin, it was a sin of the entire world's past that started thousands of years before Christopher Columbus ever even got here. America led the way to ending slavery a hundred and fifty years ago, not just in our own country, but throughout the world. My point is, as much as it's important for us to recognize the sins of our history, it's also important for us to acknowledge that America was a strong enough nation to put an end to that ugly history, and has championed equal rights for all human beings, in our own country and around the world. No doubt there is still a lot of work to do around the world, and America still has some healing to do, but as a country we also have a lot to be proud of as well. Contrary to what the likes of progressive black activists like Al Sharpton and Jesse Jackson would have you believe, as they profit off of keeping racial tensions alive in America.

Political correctness has run amok in America. If one person or a small but vocal minority group of individuals takes issue with anything, you are vilified if you have an opposing view. Let's take the Washington Redskins NFL football team. Here you have a professional football team that's been around for more than three quarters of a century and that was originally named in honor of its first coach, who was an American Indian. The NFL and the Washington Redskins point to a past survey showing that as many as 90 percent of Native Americans are not offended and support the name. NFL Commissioner Roger Goodell and Redskins owner Daniel Snyder have dug their heels in and have staunchly rejected any name change.

Politicians such as Senate Majority Leader Harry Reid have been hounding the NFL and Snyder about changing the name. I guess if you are as completely ineffective as a lawmaker as Harry Reid is, you have plenty of time to be the PC police. PC pressure unbelievably led a division of the federal government to rule that the Redskins name was disparaging, and it stripped the team of federal protections for six of its trademarks. Other professional sports teams such as the Cleveland Indians and even my hometown team, the Kansas City Chiefs, have also been criticized for not changing their names.

The next thing the PC activists will be demanding is that the state of Oklahoma change their name. Why? The word "Oklahoma" is a Choctaw Indian word that is translation for; "Red People". Where would it ever end?

Freedom of religion? Maybe if you are anything other than a Christian. The one thing the liberal Left will not tolerate is Christianity. While many liberals may call themselves Christians, they are tolerant only of other Christians who share their same liberal beliefs. Christians traditionally support the biblical view of marriage as being between a man and a woman. Christians value the sanctity of life and consider abortion a sin. Christians also support and promote strong family values and self-reliance. Therein lies a big part of the wedge. Christianity represents just about everything liberal ideology opposes.

Liberals can't get around the fact that Christianity stands for a specific set of values with which they, for the most part, disagree. They can't rewrite scripture to fit their narrative. Christians have been in an all-out, full-fledged culture war with the so-called tolerant liberals, who want nothing more than to silence them. Why? Christianity is a powerful force that has been around for centuries. It's far more than a simple ideology; it's a faith. Faith in something bigger than all of us. That faith poses a tremendous hurdle for progressive liberalism to overcome. If Christianity is true, if it's real, then liberal ideology is wrong, and there is no way for the Left to spin around that fact. America is a Christian nation; our Founding Fathers were Christians. Even though our Founding Fathers were wise to ensure that there would always be a separation between the church and the state, that was as much to protect the church from the government as it was to ensure the freedom of religion. God is referenced five times in the Declaration of Independence.

Whether it's trying to force retailers to abandon Christmas as a celebration of the birth of Jesus Christ or screaming bloody murder about when and where citizens are allowed to pray, make no mistake, the intolerant progressive Left is on the warpath!

Take the Chick-fil-A controversy. The company has long held conservative Christian values and has never made any secret about it. Chick-fil-A Chief Operating Officer Dan Cathy told the Baptist Press that his company was "guilty as charged" for taking a "traditionalist" view of marriage, and the statement turned into a culture war run rampant. Those comments led to huge protests at a new Orange County, California, Chick-fil-A, with kids protesting and gay rights activists rallying in favor of same-sex marriage and calling for a boycott against the fast-food chicken restaurant. Former Arkansas Governor and presidential candidate Mike Huckabee responded to that "intolerant" move by declaring a national day of appreciation for Chick-fil-A, who reported that all of its stores nationwide had record turnouts.

It is one thing for liberals to be intolerant of those with whom they disagree, but it's certainly another when you dictate to a private company that it must provide abortion inducing contraceptives to its employees, in direct violation of its religious beliefs. That's exactly what the Obama administration has done with the Affordable Care Act. Under one controversial provision of Obamacare, businesses are required to offer health insurance plans that include all forms of contraception including drugs that some feel induce abortion. Hobby Lobby and Conestoga Woods are family-owned companies and hold deep religious beliefs, and would rather close their doors before being complicit in causing an abortion. Hobby Lobby has long had a great insurance plan that is provided to their employees, that does cover more than a dozen different types of contraception, however they do not want to cover drugs that they feel induce abortion such as the morning after pill. These businesses have a First Amendment right of freedom of religion, and took their case to the Supreme Court.

It's a very sad day when our government tries to argue the legality of infringing on First Amendment rights, forcing business owners to violate their religious convictions. It's wrong and unconstitutional. Fortunately the Supreme Court agreed, and ruled in favor of Hobby Lobby and Conestoga Woods, delivering a big blow to the Affordable Care Act.

Obama vs. Little Sisters of the Poor: If this isn't proof positive of just how far progressive liberals will go to be intolerant! How on earth does a US president get into a tangle with nuns who provide hospice care for the indigent? Well, that's what progressive liberals do; you either agree with them or they come after you, even if you are the Little Sisters of the Poor. The Obamacare conscience-trampling contraception mandate was destined to have this kind of logical consequence.

The Little Sisters of the Poor are Catholic nuns who follow the doctrinal teachings of the church and therefore oppose contraceptive and abortive drugs and sterilization, all of which Obamacare mandates that employers cover in their insurance plans. Yes, even Catholic hospitals, and yes, even for nuns.

You would think that this would be an issue that Obama would simply walk away from and let the nuns get back to their business of taking care of the sick and dying. I mean, with all the waivers he gave all of his union buddies, you would think this one is a no-brainer.

No, not the Obama administration; they want to stand on their beliefs that the almighty government trumps the convictions of people with deeply held religious beliefs. So the Obama administration thought that they would be cute; they came up with a document that requires a group to register its moral objection to contraceptives and abortions, but also authorizes the insurer to cover them for the group's employees. So, in other words, what the accommodation gives with one hand, it takes away with the other.

The Little Sisters refused to sign such a document. They happen to be in an unusual situation because they get their insurance from another religiously affiliated organization which is also opposed to contraceptives and abortions. The nuns stand on their religious convictions and refuse to sign the document. Supporters of the mandate criticize the nuns and argue that it's only a piece of paper! So is a mortgage, so is a contract; they are just pieces of paper.

Kathleen Sibelius, former Health and Human Services secretary, notoriously declared in 2011 that anyone who opposed the mandate would want to roll back the last fifty years of progress that women have made in comprehensive health care in America. "We've come a long way in women's health over the last few decades, but we are in a war," she said. Pretty ironic that a small congregation of nuns who care for the most vulnerable could somehow now be complicit in the war on women's health. Instead of accepting and respecting the moral views of the Little Sisters, the administration chooses to grind them into the ground by force of law. Tolerance? I think not.

We certainly can't end this chapter without addressing the motley crew of Progressive liberals who continuously wage war on Christmas, using every tactic possible to ruin the holiday season for everyone. American atheists describe themselves as a group of "free thinkers" who seem to spend all of their time attacking the free thinking of others with everything from posting billboards in cities across America mocking the birth of Christ to suing municipalities for supporting public display of mangers. That list goes on and on. Christians certainly tolerate atheists' rights not to believe in God, so it perplexes me why atheists have such a distain for those who do.

For most progressive liberals the word "tolerance" is merely a politically correct punch line. Liberals tolerate everything except that with which they disagree, and that isn't tolerance at all.

So why was the information in this chapter important to "the Lost Decade"? Because this is the kind of craziness or nonsense that we Americans are subjected too, when the progressive liberals are in control of our government.

CHAPTER TEN

A Force to Be Reckoned With: Rise of the Tea Party

"Government is instituted for the common good; for the protection, safety, prosperity, and happiness of the people: and not for profit; honor, or private interest of any one man, family, or class of men: therefore, the people alone have an incontestable, unalienable, and indefeasible right to institute government; and to reform, alter, or totally change the same, when their protection, safety, prosperity, and happiness require it."—John Adams, *Thoughts on Government*, 1776

I can't think of a stronger argument in favor of the need for the Tea Party than those words of John Adams.

The political winds were brewing for a significant change in 2008, and the winds were blowing to the Left. A young and energetic generation of voters showed up at the polls, catapulted Barack Obama into the presidency, and increased the Democrats' control of both houses of Congress, even giving the Democrats a "supermajority" in the Senate.

A few short months later, the Democrats went on a major spending spree and started passing a series of mega-bailouts for the financial sector, and the tide started to turn. Conservatives were dumbfounded about the dramatic changes taking place right in front of them, and a grassroots movement was born. The tea party movement has grown quickly as an American grassroots movement, aided by social networking sites such as Twitter and Facebook as well as viral videos. The loyal following grew to include many who felt taxes and spending were excessive and leading to the country's demise.

The *tea* in tea party stands for "taxed enough already." Although the term tea party has been loosely used as far back as the 1990s and before, anti-tax protesters have been known to use the theme of the 1773 Boston Tea Party as a rallying point for Tax Day protests on April 15. The basic tea party platform is pretty self-evident in its name: "taxed enough already," which in and of itself represents that the group is for lowering taxes and, in turn, smaller government, reducing the US national debt, and eliminating the budget deficit. In addition, the tea party is for less government regulation and intervention and staunchly supports civil liberties, the Constitution, and the Bill of Rights. How can you not support that kind of a platform? I agree, however, that the tea party has been going through some major growing pains and has taken a lot of hits. Next to the IRS, Barack Obama, and the left-wing media, the tea party has been its own worst enemy. That said, if supporters ever really get organized and get their act together, they may prove to be the saviors of our democracy.

I want to clarify that although most tea party members identify themselves as conservatives or as members of the Republican Party, the tea party is not the Republican Party, even though the left-wing media tries to always to tie the two together. Those on the more moderate side of the Republican Party recognize the benefits of the tea party and hold a similar ideology but often distance themselves from the tea party. The tea party's primary focus is on fiscal responsibility, lower taxes, and smaller government, and that often flies in the face of politicians who've been in Washington too long. The tea party is a staunch watchdog of how every politician votes, especially the Republicans, and when the Republicans vote in a manner the tea party feels is irresponsible, supporters don't hesitate to hold that politician accountable and put up a candidate to try to take that person's seat in the next primary. The rub, however, is that the tea party's "our way or the highway" attitude, while well intended, doesn't necessarily take into consideration the reality of politics. This often creates friction between the tea party and the Republican establishment.

It's interesting to go through a synopsis of the way this grassroots political movement quickly grew and took hold in American politics.

In December 2007, Republican Congressman and former presidential candidate Ron Paul commemorated the 234th anniversary of the Boston Tea Party as part of a fund-raising event for the presidential primaries. One of the issues Paul advocated was an end to the Federal Reserve System and fiat money. The following timeline of events was acquired from the tea party movement platform.

Regardless of your opinions of the tea party, it is undeniable that they proved to be a force to be reckoned with in the 2010 midterms—so much so that the Internal Revenue Service, under President Barack Obama, targeted tea party groups and supporters. This targeting began in March 2010 and wasn't revealed until three years later, on May 10, 2013, when former IRS administrator Lois Lerner reluctantly admitted that the IRS had been targeting conservative groups. By then, however, the damage to the grassroots conservative movement had already been done. Barack Obama had already been reelected.

The Democrats originally dismissed the tea party as a bunch of fanatics; however, they would soon be forced to pay attention to the power of the tea party when supporters handed the Democrats what even Barack Obama had to admit was a "shellacking" in the 2010 midterms. Obama and fellow Democrats, in collusion with the so-called mainstream media, immediately went to the liberal playbook and lobbied with a vile campaign of accusing tea party members as racists. Yes, if you disagree with Barack Obama, you must be a racist.

The tea party movement as a powerful political force in America can be dated to February 19, 2009, when CNBC reporter Rick Santelli was reporting live from the floor of the Chicago Mercantile Exchange. Sentelli began expressing his disgust for a government proposal to assist homeowners who were facing home foreclosures to refinance their home mortgages. Sentelli claimed that the government was promoting bad behavior by subsidizing mortgages.

"Do we really want to subsidize the loser's mortgages?" Santelli asked, adding, "This is America! How many of you people want to pay for your neighbor's mortgage that has an extra bathroom and can't pay their bills?" Santelli then said he wanted to organize, in July of 2009, a Chicago tea party so that capitalists could dump "some derivative securities into Lake Michigan." The traders who were near Santelli on the trading floor cheered when they heard his comments, and the show's hosts in the CNBC studio also displayed amusement at his comments. A video of Santelli's rant was shown on the Drudge Report website and then went viral on the Internet on YouTube, and within weeks the era of tea party protests all around the United States had begun.

Within a day, a website called ChicagoTeaParty.com was live on the Internet. The site was originally registered in August 2008 by Zack Christenson, a radio producer in Chicago, and the website reTeaParty.com was purchased with the goal of coordinating tea party protests and demonstrations that were being organized for July 4, 2009.

Santelli's comments on the trading floor and the resulting publicity are believed by most to be the primary event that led to the rapid rise of the modern-day tea party movement and the coalescing of many people around the term "tea party" to signify a distaste for particular government actions.

On February 20, 2009, a Facebook page was set up to rally people to organize tea party protests nationally. The result was the coordination of a nationwide tea party protest in forty different cities on February 27. That was the first day that the modern-day tea party movement appeared on a national scale. Less than a week later, the website reTeaParty.com was receiving substantial traffic and reported up to eleven thousand visits per day.

Not that Sentelli is completely credited with the birth of the modern-day tea party; many others had already been conducting similar protests, laying the groundwork for the grassroots movement to really take hold. A few weeks before Sentelli's rant on the floor of the Chicago Mercantile, the Young Americans for Liberty in New York, chaired by Trevor Leach, held a tea party protest against the government's overspending, as well as more than one hundred taxes being proposed by the state's governor, David Paterson. Some of the protesters wore traditional colonists' headdresses of the original Boston Tea Party era, when colonists threw tea in the Boston Harbor to protest British taxation.

At about the same time Santelli's YouTube video was going viral, conservative Seattle blogger Keli Carender organized a protest that didn't use the term "tea party" but carried a similar theme. This protest took place the day before President Obama signed the stimulus bill. With only four days' notice, 120 people showed up at the protest. Eleven days later Carender held another protest and the attendance doubled.

On April 15, 2009, former Speaker of the House Newt Gingrich talked to a crowd at a New York City tea party rally.

On January 19, the tea party had its first victorious election when it helped Scott Brown, a tea party supporter, fill the Senate seat of the late Ted Kennedy in a special election.

Three months after the Scott Brown victory, Charles Perry was victorious in the GOP primary against an established Republican opponent, the incumbent, Delwin Jones. Perry went on to win unopposed in the general election on November 2, 2010.

The following month, Rand Paul, backed by the tea party, won the Super Tuesday GOP Senate primary in Kentucky against established Republican Tray Grayson. Paul got about 60 percent of the vote and stated that the tea party movement is about "saving our country from a mountain of debt." Rand went on to win the Senate seat. The same month Paul defeated Grayson (May 2009), tea party candidate Mike Lee, an attorney from Utah, beat the Republican establishment candidate, Bob Bennett.

The following month Anna C Littleton beat establishment Republican candidate Diane Gooch in the New Jersey primary.

In July 2010, Michele Bachman, a US representative from Minnesota, formed and chaired the House Congressional Tea Party

Caucus, which focuses on the principles of the tea party movement, including limited government, adhering to the US Constitution, and insisting on fiscal responsibility. By August the tea party caucus was comprised of forty-nine Republican representatives.

In the 2010 midterm elections, the tea party supported nine senatorial candidates and 129 House candidates after upsetting numerous Republican establishment candidates in primaries. The tea party was greatly credited for the Republicans taking back the US House of Representatives in the 2010 midterms, effectively dethroning her majesty, Nancy Pelosi.

The targeting of tea party groups by the IRS certainly delivered a blow to the tea party; I mean, it's kind of hard to be very effective grassroots organizers when you have the IRS and the Justice Department breathing down your neck, auditing you, and not approving your application for 501(c) (4) tax-exempt status.

The tea party has also had its share of problems and setbacks. A number of candidates the party supported turned out to be pretty much off the mainstream reservation, so to speak. In some cases the tea party didn't do a very good job of vetting candidates, which not only cost the Republicans some seats, it also tarnished their brand. The old rule of thumb, "nominate and support the most conservative candidate that can get elected," didn't always completely resonate in their vetting process. It's kind of hard to make any substantive changes in Washington if you don't control at least two of the three branches of government. All too often the tea party lost track of that fundamental political reality.

One other significant problem with the Tea Party is that it doesn't really have one centralized organization. It consists of a number of local and regional "chapters," if you will, but you can't really call them chapters, either, because they don't necessarily always have a constant platform.

A third major political party is not seen as a viable option, so the only alternative for the tea party is to keep increasing its influence in the Republican Party. A third party would only splinter and fracture the conservative vote, and liberals would win every election from then on out. The tea party supporters are much more in line with Republicans than they are with Democrats, so the Republican Party is the only home for them. However, many tea partiers despise many establishment Republicans, whom they often refer to as RINOs (Republicans in name only), accusing them of being "the country club elite." Tea party candidates often challenge establishment Republicans in the primaries and have picked a good number of them off.

As much as the tea party is credited for booting Nancy Pelosi out of office and handing the House of Representatives back to the Republicans in the 2010 midterm elections, they are equally blamed for Harry Reid still being the Senate majority leader and certainly have some culpability in Barack Obama being reelected. Why? Fringe candidates such as Sharron Angle, who lost the 2010 senatorial race in Nevada against Harry Reid. Then there was Christine O'Donnell in the 2010 Delaware race for Senate. In 2012, Democratic Senator Claire McCaskill should have been easy picking for Republicans to pick up the seat from Missouri, but tea party candidate Todd Akin definitely stubbed his toe on some pretty stupid comments involving rape and abortion.

So, did the tea party cost Mitt Romney the election in 2012? I'm not going to say that they cost Republicans the presidency, but they didn't help either. Some of their choices of fringe candidates, such as Todd Akin, made it very easy for the liberal Left to paint all conservatives as part of the same fringe, out of the mainstream ideology. Not fair, but who ever said politics was fair? Nobody.

Because the modern-day tea party movement is a grassroots movement of local as well as national groups, there is no one central leadership of the tea party movement. Each tea party group determines its own priorities and sets its own agenda, though there are loose affiliations between groups and communication for the purpose of organizing particular tea party events. This lack of a general direction and consensus may be one of the obstacles that the tea party needs to overcome if they ever plan to reinvigorate themselves and really make a difference in American politics. The fact that they don't all fall under one central leadership tent, so to speak, prevents them from establishing a unified message and platform. It also puts each of the tea party affiliated groups at risk of the misfortunes or mistakes of other tea party groups with whom they don't really have any direct association.

The tea party would be wise to coalesce around one centralized leadership, establish a unified message, establish a strong criteria for the candidates they support, identify their brand, and protect their brand. Food for thought.

While I'm giving my unsolicited advice, I'm sure a lot of my conservative colleagues won't agree with this, but I'm going to put it out there anyway. We can't win the war to take our country back if we don't focus first on winning the battles. I understand the very real and heartfelt concerns about most all of the social issues that conservatives care deeply about. That said, many of those issues need to be put on the back burner for the time being so we can focus first and foremost on getting our fiscal house in order and repairing America's standing on the world stage. As a country we are now in grave danger, and if we don't quickly get our act together and take our country back from the liberals who are trying to drive us off the cliff, we are going to hit the bottom and crash hard! At which point, all of the social issues we're fretting over now will be moot. My point is, when your house is burning down the way our country is now, you focus all of your attention on putting the fire out, and you don't stand around watering the lawn.

Those in the Republican establishment who think that they can take the Tea Party for granted, do so at their own peril, as was evident in the 2014 GOP primary challenge of Majority Leader Eric Cantor in his race to keep his Virginia congressional seat when he was challenged by newcomer and tea party candidate Dave Brat, a college professor who took the media by storm when he challenged the House majority leader and beat him. This race has historical impact because it is the very first time in history that a sitting majority leader has been beaten in a primary. It's worth noting that Cantor spent about $5 million to Dave Brat's mere $125,000. Cantor had miscalculated the tea party sentiment and had taken more of a pro-establishment and anti-tea-party position, and, as we now know, he did so at his own peril.

Tea party supporters do have their hearts in the right place, and if their brains and hearts ever do get lined up, they do have a real opportunity to make a positive difference in America. I thought I would share with you the vision and principles of the Tea Party Patriots as described on their website:

Our Vision:

We envision a nation where personal freedom is cherished and where all Americans are treated equally, assuring our ability to pursue the American dream. Pursue your American dream.

Our Core Principles:

Tea Party Patriots stands for every American and is home to millions who have come together to pursue the American dream and to keep that dream alive for their children and grandchildren.

What unites the tea party movement is the same set of core principles that brought America together at its founding, that kindled the American dream in the hearts of those who struggled to build our nation, and made the United States of America the greatest, most successful country in world history.

At its root the American dream is about freedom. Freedom to work hard and the freedom to keep the fruits of your labor to use as you see fit without harming others and without hindering their freedom. Very simply, three guiding principles give rise to the freedom necessary to pursue and live the American dream:

- Constitutionally limited government, or your personal freedom and your rights

- Free market economics, or economic freedom to grow jobs and your opportunities

- Fiscal responsibility, or, very simply, a debt-free future for you and generations to come

I ask you, how can you possibly not agree with all of that?

CHAPTER ELEVEN

Lead from Behind?
Failure of Leadership

"Against the insidious wiles of foreign influence, (I conjure you to believe me fellow citizens) the jealousy of a free people ought to be constantly awake; since history and experience prove that foreign influence is one of the most baneful foes of Republican Government."— George Washington, Farewell Address, September 19, 1796

The father of our country couldn't have been any clearer in warning America to not get complacent—that as a free people there would be foreign aggressors who would stop at nothing to do us harm and would attack us for what we hold most dear: our freedom. Make no mistake, there are vultures at the gate and radical enemies who hate what America stands for and despise our very existence. George Washington spoke those words nearly 220 years ago, and our elected officials would be wise to heed those words today.

Where on earth to start; obviously the Benghazi scandal is a glaring example of Obama's complete and utter failure as a leader, but we'll save that conversation for its own chapter. The complete collapse of all the gains the US military made in Iraq, have now been lost to radical Islamic terrorists calling themselves ISIS, can leave no other conclusion than that of Barack Obama being derelict of his duties as commander in chief. But we will save that topic for its own chapter as well.

Because of Obama's failed foreign policies, the world has never been a more dangerous place. The entire Middle East is in worse chaos now than it ever has been, Iraq is on the verge of an all-out civil war with radical Muslim terrorists taking over half of the country, Russia has invaded and taken over its sovereign neighbor, and, as Obama is about to cut and run from Afghanistan, he decides it's a good idea to release five of the top Taliban leaders so they can undo all of the gains we've made. While we are talking about the blunders of giving up terrorists who were taken into custody on the battlefield—and notice that I don't consider these terrorists "prisoners of war"; to the contrary, they are guilty of war crimes and crimes against humanity—my question is, why weren't these guys tried, prosecuted, and sentenced to life in prison or, better yet, sentenced to death? Why on earth is the Obama administration releasing any of these terrorists? You may recall John Walker Lindh, the American Taliban who was captured on the battlefield in Afghanistan. Lindh was sentenced to twenty years in federal prison after pleading guilty to two counts that basically amounted to providing material support to our enemy and taking up arms against Americans. Lindh was certainly no Taliban leader, so why was he tried and imprisoned and these notorious terrorist leaders simply let go? Hey, I'm glad that Lindh was convicted, and as far as I'm concerned he got off way too easily; my point is that terrorists much worse than he is were let off scot free.

Ironically, as I'm editing this chapter in June, 2014, President Obama is giving another sermon in the Rose Garden alongside the parents of Sgt. Bowe Bergdahl while patting himself on the back for a prisoner exchange that garnered Bergdahl's release from the Taliban in Afghanistan. I'm thinking it's really great that we've brought our only missing prisoner of war home, but I'm also thinking that our giving up five of the most ruthless Taliban leaders in exchange for one guy is a pretty heavy price to pay. I'm also asking myself: I thought America's long standing policy was to never negotiate with terrorists. Admittedly, my lack of any confidence in President Obama's judgment or leadership is sounding alarm bells in my head.

Then, the very next day, good ol' Susan Rice is back out on the Sunday news programs (notably, Fox was excluded from her rounds). I immediately smelled a rat. When Susan Rice shows up on a Sunday morning news program, you know that the Obama administration is trying to spin something and lie to the American people. You surely recall Susan Rice telling the world that the terrorist attacks in Benghazi, Libya, were nothing more than a protest gone awry, and all because of some stupid anti-Muslim Internet video. In any event, I'm not sure why, but President Obama must think Susan Rice looks like an honest forthright person. Not that I care to give President Obama any advice, but he should really keep her as far away from television cameras or news reporters as possible.

Anyway, Susan Rice proclaimed that Bergdahl a) was captured on the field of battle and b) had served with honor and distinction. When questioned why the administration didn't give Congress thirty days' notice as required by law, she claimed it was because he was in such bad health that they needed to act immediately.

The one person in the Obama administration who lies more than Susan Rice is his former spokesperson Jay Carney. Amazingly even the so-called mainstream media weren't able to keep looking past his carnage of lies and deceit, by the end of his tenure, but not before Carney weighing in on the latest Obama scandal and backing up Susan Rice's claims that Bergdahl served with honor.

And as everyone has come to realize, Senate Majority Leader Harry Reid is without question the biggest liar in Washington, so he certainly couldn't pass up the opportunity to jump on the Obama team bandwagon and was all too happy to continue the Obama propaganda, supporting Obama's decision for the prisoner exchange.

As we've come to expect, when Susan Rice, Jay Carney, and Harry Reid open their mouths in harmony, you know the jig is up; you know we are being lied to. As it turned out, everything they were claiming about Sergeant Bergdahl was a lie. It didn't take more than another day for other soldiers who had served with Sergeant Bergdahl—and who, it's worth noting, are now retired and out of the service, so they can speak candidly—to claim that he was no prisoner of war! In fact, as it turns out he was a deserter! He took off his uniform, left a note on his cot saying that he was leaving the military to start another life, then walked off of a secured military base to join up with the Taliban.

To add insult to injury, soldiers who had served with Bergdahl have claimed that as many as six soldiers may have been killed in action trying to locate and retrieve Bergdahl.

It didn't take long for what the Obama administration had calculated as being a good story that would tamp down the Veterans Administration scandal, which had been dominating the media, to blow up in Obama's face! The Obama machine immediately grabbed the liberals' playbook and attempted to spin, spin, spin, claiming that what Susan Rice and Jay Carney and Harry Reid really meant was that Bergdahl volunteered to join the military, and he voluntarily "put on the uniform," so that in and of itself was with "distinction."

The problem is that, while at war, he "took off" his uniform, left all of his gear, and abandoned his platoon. Realizing that their spin wasn't being swallowed, the Obama machine went right back to the liberal playbook and started calling those who served with Bergdahl liars, claiming that they were "swift boating" him. When John Kerry sought the presidency in 2004, that term was effectively pinned on him by those who served with him in Vietnam; Kerry's fellow soldiers who served with Kerry on a swift boat in Vietnam, had little if any respect for Kerry, and publically criticized him; thus the term; swift boated him.

Obama doubled down on his bad decision, claiming, "America has always had a long-standing policy of leaving no man behind on the battlefield." First off, I certainly wouldn't call a guy who takes his uniform off and deserts his team and seeks out the Taliban a guy who America would have "left behind." But here's the blaring hypocrisy in Obama's comments of "no man left behind": What about our four Americans who were under attack in Benghazi and who were left behind?

Before the fact that Bergdahl was a deserter came completely to light, there was bipartisan outrage on Capitol Hill because Obama failed to give lawmakers thirty days' notice of any prisoner transfer as outlined in the National Defense Authorization Act (NDAA). Obama responded by telling reporters that "we saw an opportunity and we were concerned about his health and had cooperation from the Qataris, and we seized that. It was truncated to make sure we didn't miss that opportunity."

The problem with that claim, other than the fact that Obama clearly violated the law and did so for obviously calculated political reasons, is that when the Taliban released a propaganda video showing Bergdahl being turned over to the United States, Bergdahl was obviously in relatively good health. The Taliban, of course, celebrated their huge victory over Obama and the United States. The Taliban returned an enemy sympathizer who had deserted in exchange for five notorious Taliban leaders. Terrorists, I might add, that will no doubt rejoin the fight against America and will in all likelihood cause the deaths of Americans.

Talk about America getting played; reports continue to circulate, and by the time this book is published, my guess is that it will have all come to light: Sergeant Bergdahl was not only a deserter, he was a collaborator with the Taliban. In other words, the Taliban gave up nothing and in return received five of their high-level leaders.

There is no question that negotiating with terrorists is never a good idea. Negotiating a prisoner swap with terrorists only puts every American in danger, and certainly every American serving in harm's way. Now that terrorists have come to realize that American leadership will return five notorious terrorists in exchange for one American, even one deserter, well, it doesn't take a rocket scientist to realize that our enemies will go to great lengths to capture or kidnap Americans serving in the military or otherwise.

Mr. Obama claimed in a press conference that he had assurances from officials in Qatar that they would keep an eye on these five terrorists, and make sure that they remained in Qatar for one year. He went on to say that "we" would also be keeping an eye on them as well. I'm not sure who he is referring to as "we." I can't figure out if the president is really that naïve, or if he thinks that "we the people" are naïve enough to believe that five terrorists are really going to stick around Qatar and are really going to behave themselves. In 2008, a Pentagon dossier put all five of these men at a "high risk" to launch attacks against the United States if they were ever released. This was a terrible decision and will undoubtedly come back to haunt us at some point in the future.

So why did President Obama do something so foolish? First of all, he certainly didn't expect the tremendous backlash he's received. He completely misread the way that this would be received. He actually thought that this was going to be a "feel-good" moment, and help his tanking poll numbers. However, there's an even bigger reason as to why he did this: he had just announced that America was set to leave Afghanistan (cut and run), claiming that the war in Afghanistan was wrapping up. Obama's campaign promise of 2008 was to shut down Gitmo (the Guantanamo Bay, Cuba, military base and terrorist detention camp and prison). Obama soon learned that shutting Gitmo down may have sounded good on the campaign trail, but once in office he was forced to accept the reality that we had to keep these terrorist prisoners some place, and bringing them to the United States would not have been a good idea. So, the only way Obama can see to ever close Gitmo is to start releasing the terrorist prisoners.

A few days after the release of Bergdahl, *Time* magazine had an interview with Taliban leaders in which they boasted about the prisoner swap, saying that it reinvigorated them and that the deal encouraged them to kidnap more soldiers or any Americans in general. High-level military officials and former administration officials, including Leon Panetta, who was Obama's director of the Central Intelligence Agency and defense secretary, have since said that in previous discussions they had adamantly argued against the deal to release five Taliban leaders for one deserter.

According to Pentagon reports, one in every three Taliban fighters who have ever been released has been recaptured in battle. If one in three has actually been recaptured, that's a pretty good indicator that a very high percent that have ever been released do return to battle. According to reports from Qatar, where the five released prisoners are supposed to remain for one year before returning to Afghanistan, the five Taliban leaders who were released have been received by the Taliban as "rock stars." It shouldn't be any surprise that all of them have already vowed to return to the fight against America at their first chance.

Megan Kelly on Fox News interviewed six of Bergdahl's fellow soldiers who served with him at the time he deserted. All six of his platoon members, including his team leader, Evan Buetow, unanimously were certain that he deserted. They all indicated that there was never any question whether he deserted; it was a known fact by his entire platoon and military leadership. Buetow and his teammates explained that when Bergdahl deserted, it changed the whole mission for their platoon, as well as several other platoons. They explained that their entire focus shifted to trying to locate Bergdahl. They went on to indicate that as many as six soldiers were killed in battle in the area where they were subsequent to Bergdahl's desertion, and they speculated that since it was everyone's mission to find Bergdahl, that change in the mission may have led to those six deaths. Kelly asked if there was anything he or anyone else could say that might change their minds that he was a deserter. They all responded absolutely not.

No doubt, it's a good thing that we did get Sgt. Bowe Bergdahl back, and I do think that it's important for America not to leave any one behind who's served in war. I do, however, think that we paid way too high a price, even if Bergdahl had served with honor and distinction. That said, Bergdahl should now be held accountable and stand trial for desertion, possibly even collaborating with the enemy, and whatever else applies.

Oh, yes, it is also worth noting that after the release of these five Taliban generals, it was reported that one of the five played a role in Al-Qaeda's strategy for the 9/11 terrorist attacks in New York. Mohammad Fazl, who served as the Taliban's army chief of staff and deputy defense minister, worked with one of Osama bin Laden's chief lieutenants to execute a military offensive against the Northern Alliance on September 10, 2001, according to the *Weekly Standard*. The successful operation was a key part of the strategy to ensure that opposition to the Taliban in Afghanistan was weakened. The Taliban was preparing for an anticipated American retaliation immediately following 9/11. A leaked Joint Task Force Guantanamo threat assessment of Fazl said that he met with Abdul Hadi al Iraqi to "immediately coordinate an attack with the Taliban against the Northern Alliance." In other words, this was a preemptive move to limit America's retaliatory response after the attacks, as the Taliban knew that the Northern Alliance would assist in America's response against the Taliban and Al-Qaeda.

It's also worth noting that former Secretary of State Hillary Clinton didn't believe that the release of these five Taliban leaders caused any threat to the United States. I would just about bet that she didn't think those Taliban leaders caused much a threat to America when her husband was president, either. Yet eight short months after she and her husband left the White House, the Taliban supported Al-Qaeda and did launch an attack on our homeland.

I must say, I can't help but ponder the irony of President Obama giving up five terrorists in exchange for a deserter, considering another story that's been in the news lately. Sgt. Andrew Tahmooressi, a US Marine reservist and Afghan war veteran, accidentally found himself at the US–Mexico border, trying to get turned around back into America. You might question how on earth you accidentally get into Mexico, but if you've ever been to that border, you soon realize just how easily it could happen. There are several lanes with barriers on each side that don't allow any lane change or deviation, and the U turn that would allow you to turn around and head back into the United States is not only very poorly identified, but if you aren't in the far left lane to begin with, it's difficult if not impossible to maneuver over to it. In any event, Sergeant Tahmooressi found himself at the border; however, unfortunately for him, he also had three weapons in his vehicle. All three were legally registered to him in the United States.

Tahmooressi immediately acknowledged to the border guards that he did have three weapons in his vehicle, explaining that he was just wanting to get turned around. They immediately arrested him and threw him into prison. According to the *San Diego Union-Tribune*, Sergeant Tahmooressi has been held at La Mesa State Penitentiary in Tijuana, Mexico, for allegedly trying to bring weapons over the US–Mexican border. He faces federal weapons charges. Bail is not permitted, and if convicted he faces up to twenty-one years in a Mexican prison. He's been held since March 31, 2014, and hopefully by the time you are reading this book he will have been released. My point in going a little off course here is to point out the irony of President Obama giving up five terrorists in exchange for one deserter, but he can't pick up the phone and call the president of Mexico, our neighboring ally to the south, and get a war veteran released who's being held on what's obviously a trumped-up charge.

I'm not even sure where to begin when laying out all of the compounding evidence of President Obama's complete incompetence and lack of leadership. I guess we could start with the Obama doctrine of leading from behind. How do you lead from behind? You can't; you either "lead, follow, or get out of the way"! Obama's naïve idea of leadership certainly hasn't worked out for us.

If you are at all interested in statistics, here's an interesting… scratch that, here's a horrifying statistic regarding casualties of the Afghanistan war. The Afghan war went on for eighty-seven months under President Bush as commander in chief, and in that time, which was undoubtedly the hardest, most dangerous time, we lost 630 military personnel. That's an average of 7.2 fatalities every month. In contrast, as of the end of February 2014, under President Obama as commander in chief, in sixty-two months of war, we've suffered 1,681 fatalities, or an average of 27.1 per month. That is a staggering statistic! Under President Obama, our fighting men and women are suffering nearly four times the number of casualties every month that were experienced under President Bush.

The fact is that 73 percent of all Afghan war casualties have occurred under Barack Obama! And those casualties occurred in two years less time than the 27 percent of casualties under Bush. Let's look at this one step closer: in the first seven-plus years of the Afghan war under Bush, 2,638 soldiers were wounded in action. The first forty-five months under Obama, our soldiers suffered 15,036 wounded in action. Let's do that math real quick: under Barack Obama as commander in chief, the United States suffered nearly *six* times the number of soldiers wounded in battle, and in almost half the time! So, 82 percent of all soldiers wounded in Afghanistan were wounded under Barack Obama, and in half the amount of time that President Bush was the commander in chief. Don't take my word for it, check it out for yourself: http://icasualties.org/oef/.

You may be asking yourself, how on earth can you hold Obama accountable for such a thing? I mean, war is war, right? Well, let's examine why Obama is accountable. Let's get past the obvious fact that he is the commander in chief, which certainly in and of itself makes him accountable. However, there are some much more specific reasons as to why our military has suffered nearly four times the number of deaths and six times more injuries under Obama than under his predecessor. The very simple answer is the rules of engagement (ROE). If you have any military background or a close friend of relative with a military background, you probably have a very good understanding of what "rules of engagement" means. If not, ROE is the rules that a soldier must obey when engaging the enemy. In early 2009, shortly after President Obama took office, the Obama administration immediately started to incessantly tighten our rules of engagement and authorized the implementation of the COIN (counterinsurgent) strategy, which focused on "winning the hearts and minds" of our enemy rather than winning the war. Over the next five years our soldiers would suffer gravely for Obama's failure of leadership.

Under President Obama, the rules of engagement in Afghanistan are nothing more than extreme political correctness. Our fighting men and women have paid for Obama's failure of leadership with life and limb, and their blood will forever be on his hands. The rules of engagement under Obama are dangerously overly restrictive.

Major General Robert Scales, former Commandant of the US Army War College, criticized Obama's prosecution of the war and his rules of engagement in a Fox News interview:

> Imagine if you're a marine in Afghanistan, charged with fighting terrorists, yet you can't shoot at Taliban terrorists unless you see them actually holding weapons in their hands! If the Taliban terrorists only temporarily put their arms down, marines are forbidden from shooting at them! Imagine that you also can't treat the captured terrorists "roughly"—as in using "harsh" language against them that may hurt their feelings—and that you must release your terrorist foe after ninety-six hours if you don't hand them over to the Afghan police. Think this is a bad dream, a cruel joke, or simply a liberal's wildest fantasy come true? Think again, for this is actual war policy going on in Afghanistan right now under Obama."

We should have expected this kind of political correctness from Mr. Obama, as he's gone so far out of his way to apologize to the Arab world and has put the all-important sensibilities of the Muslim world ahead of the welfare of our men and women in battle.

The Taliban learned pretty quickly when our rules of engagement changed and have found it to be an extremely effective weapon against us. When you know what your enemy can and can't do, it's an incredible advantage! Our enemies, however, don't have any rules of engagement! Their only rule is to kill or maim as many of our soldiers as they can.

Lt. Col and former US Senator Allen West said, "As a former combat commander, I can tell you that fear is difficult to avoid on the battlefield. But on today's battlefields, a new fear haunts our troops: the fear of persecution by their own government. That fear leads to internal hesitation. And that leads to death."

US soldiers in Afghanistan have been forced to fight a two-front war. These soldiers understand before each deployment that day after day, they will have to do battle against a vicious and relentless enemy, terrorists with unspeakable hatred toward them, and will stop at nothing to kill them. Our brave men and women face our enemy head on with honor, but the enemy that they couldn't have foreseen was the killing field they would endure at the hands of their commander in chief.

OK, I can feel my blood pressure skyrocketing as I'm typing...so I'm going to move on from this topic for now. I can tell you firsthand that as a parent who has a son proudly serving in the military, the thought of knowing that our president calculates all of his decisions based on politics or political correctness outrages me. Knowing that Barack Obama is the commander in chief scares the hell out of me.

In September 2009, President Obama scrapped the missile-defense agreement former President Bush had negotiated with Poland and the Czech Republic. Both governments took huge political risks in going along with America, including the threat from their former Russian overlords, who were dead set against America having a missile defense system in such close proximity. The Bush administration negoti-ated the deal to put a missile defense system in the Czech Republic and Poland in order to defend against a possible missile attack from Iran. Obama's move to scrap the missile defense system left our allies with a lot of egg on their faces and a very bad taste in their mouths about America reneging on our commitments at their expense.

Hillary Clinton's "reset with Russia" has turned out to be one of the most disastrous foreign policies of modern times. America's weak-ness under Barack Obama, has allowed Russia to invade its sovereign neighbor, Ukraine. So how is Hillary Clinton's, Russian reset working out for us? Better yet, how is it working out for the people of Ukraine?

Obama's decision to scrap the missile defense system also under-mines the credibility of the US nuclear defense umbrella. The Bush administration sought to develop a global defense posture in part to reassure our allies that they don't need their own nuclear deterrent, even as rogue regimes seek nuclear arms and the missiles to deliver them. America's Europe reversal tells other countries that they can't rely on the United States, so it's best to follow the Israeli path and develop their own weapons and defenses. For that matter, this also makes the US East Coast far less safe. The ground-based system in Alaska and California covers the East, but just barely. The Polish and Czech sites would have provided us that added protection.

So, the next time you hear Barack Obama's supporters try to say that there was nothing Obama could have done to have prevented Russia from invading Ukraine; please remind them that he scrapped the missile defense agreement in a naïve effort to try and play nice with Russian President Putin. While we are on that subject; what is it that he could do now? Obama should immediately re-implement the missile defense agreement with Poland and the Czech Republic. He should also implement much tougher sanctions, and ramp up the production of US oil so we can supply it to our European allies whom are currently dependent on Russia for their oil. Obama should also demand that all credit card companies immediately discontinue accepting any transactions from Russia. That would certainly get Putin's attention and it would stifle the Russian economy.

It's absolutely undeniable that President Obama has gone out of his way to court adversaries while turning his back on our allies. Obama has tried to garner warmer relations with Iran, Burma, North Korea, Russia, and even Venezuela, all while picking trade fights with our friends such as Canada and Mexico, and sat on treaties with Colombia and South Korea. He ignored Japan in deciding to talk with North Korea and sanctioned Honduras for resisting the encroachments of Venezuela's Hugo Chavez. Oh, and let's not forget about Obama's battle with Israel over the West Bank settlements. As scholar Bernard Lewis said, the problem with becoming friends with the United States is that you never know when it will shoot itself in the foot.

Israel is undoubtedly our one true ally in the Middle East, but is the Obama administration and the Democrats really a true ally to Israel? The evidence doesn't support that. Yes the Obama administration "painfully" acknowledges Israel's right to defend itself against rockets being launched on Israel by the Palestine and the terrorist organization Hamas. But the Obama administration has been very meek in their support of Israel's right to defend itself. And for anyone to criticize the Israeli retaliatory response is absurd. Hamas purposely store their rockets and rocket launchers in residential areas and schools, knowing that when Israel strikes, that there will be Palestinian women and children casualties, and they do so to enable them to use the photos and videos of dead women and children as a propaganda against Israel. Israel has taken painstaking efforts to warn the Palestinian people by dropping leaflets and making endless announcements that they will be targeting the areas where the Hamas missiles are stored and being launched from, to give the Palestinians ample time to move away from the dangerous areas. However Hamas, encourages them to stay in harm's way.

If you haven't been paying attention to world events, you may not be aware that in July, 2014, Hamas launched thousands of missiles into Israel, maliciously targeting Israelis citizens. Nearly eighty percent of the Israeli population was forced to live in bomb shelters for weeks on end. Fortunately Israel is mostly protected by an "Iron Dome" missile defense system (Similar to the defense system Obama scratched in Poland and the Czech Republic). This defense system has proved to be extremely effective at shooting down the vast majority of the missiles coming into Israel. This defense system was established through a joint US and Israeli partnership, and was effective in shooting down thousands of Hamas rockets, and has certainly saved thousands of lives. In late July, 2014 while Israel, still engaged in a ground offense to stop the Hamas rockets from their continued barrage, and in an effort to close down tunnels that Hamas had dug into Israel; Israel requested an emergency two hundred million dollars from America, to re-arm their missile defense system. How did Democrats respond? They added it to a ridiculous $2.7 billion spending bill to deal with the border crisis. Our allies are at war, fighting for their lives, and Democrats are playing politics?

Let's think about this for a second; Liberals are criticizing Israel for defending themselves, and playing games, with a serious and emergency request from one of our staunchest allies. What do you suppose America's response would be if Canada shot missiles into New York City? Or if Mexico shot missiles into Dallas Texas? Do you think America would have a temped response? Who knows, with Barack Obama as commander in chief, I suppose doing nothing might really be an option. But no other American president in the history of our democracy would allow that to happen without an immediate and deadly retaliatory response. And I would say that even if Obama chose a temped response; Americans would demand an immediate impeachment, and an immediate military response. When Japan attacked our Navy ships in Pearl Harbor, President Truman dropped two nuclear bombs on Japan. When Al-Qaeda hijacked four air planes and flew two of them into the world trade center, and another into the Pentagon, America responded with an all-out war for more than a decade against those who attacked us. Israel has every right to protect itself, in the same manner the US or any other country would for that matter.

In March 2012, President Obama sat with Russian President Dmitry Medvedev (Putin's puppet) in Seoul. While discussing the touchy issue of missile defense, Obama assured Medvedev that he (Obama) would have more "flexibility" after the November elections. Obama urged Moscow to give him "space" until after the elections; "This is my last election. After my election, I have more flexibility," Obama told Medvedev, "on all these issues, but particularly missile defense...this can be solved but it's important for him to give me space," Obama said. Medvedev told the president he understood the "message about space. Space for you..." After Obama noted he'd have more flexibility in the future, Medvedev told him: "I understand. I will transmit this information to Vladimir." The two men apparently didn't realize that they were being recorded; the conversation was relayed by a TV pool producer who listened to the recording from a Russian journalist.

It's now no secret to anyone in the world how Obama and Clinton's feckless foreign policy and lack of any leadership have turned into a huge black eye for America and have only emboldened Russia, not to mention our enemies around the world. During the 2012 presidential debates, Mitt Romney told Obama he was being naïve about Russia and referred to Russia as our geopolitical foe. Obama scoffed at Romney, saying that the Cold War was long over. I would say that Obama's lack of leadership, may have actually reignited the Cold War.

Obama's "flexibility" with Putin and scrapping our missile defense system only emboldened Putin to invade his sovereign neighbor, Ukraine, and Russian military forces seized Crimea—a political move by Russian President Vladimir Putin that was best summed up by Representative and Chairman of the House Select Committee on Intelligence Mike Rogers as "I think Putin is playing chess, and I think Obama is playing marbles."

So what was Obama's reaction to his calls to take swift and stern action to Russia's annexation of Crimea? President Obama whipped his ink pen out of his pocket and wielded another executive order, slapping seven in Vladimir Putin's inner circle—but not Putin himself—with sanctions freezing their US assets and restricting any travel of the seven cronies into the United States. As if these seven friends hadn't already moved any of their assets out of the United States when Obama telegraphed his intent before actually doing so? Crimea provided Putin with a very strategic peninsula on the Black Sea that Russia previously had to lease from Ukraine. So, all in all, a pretty good trade for Putin, even if a couple of his buddies had some US assets frozen.

Obama: "We're making it clear that there are consequences for their actions."

In Russia, one of the Russian officials Obama supposedly sanctioned appeared to mock President Obama and the US sanctions, reportedly saying on Twitter: "Comrade Obama, and what will you do with those who have neither accounts nor property abroad? Or didn't you think of that?"

"We'll continue to make clear to Russia that further provocations will achieve nothing except to further isolate Russia and diminish its place in the world," Obama said. "The international community will continue to stand together to oppose any violations of Ukrainian sovereignty and territorial integrity, and continued Russian military intervention in Ukraine will only deepen Russia's diplomatic isolation and exact a greater toll on the Russian economy."

Sen. John McCain had just returned from a weekend trip to Kiev and told MSNBC, "I think Vladimir Putin must be encouraged by the absolute timidity. I don't know how it could have been weaker, besides doing nothing—seven people being sanctioned after naked aggression has taken place."

At this point, no amount of sanctions is going to make a bit of difference. Crimea is now under the control of Putin and Russia, and there is no practical response that will ever change that. The time to act was gone a long time ago. Obama's weakness completely emboldened Putin, and America looked not only weak, we looked ridiculous.

Lack of American leadership in the world ever since Barack Obama was sworn in has opened up the floodgates of bad behavior all around the world. While the reset with Russia may have started out as an embarrassment, it's now resulted in Russia invading its neighbor while the rest of the world just sat back and watched it happen. Sitting back and watching the world crumble around us and only making some meaningless comments or speeches has been the Obama mode of operation since day one.

In June 2009, President Obama chose a position of passiveness when the Iranian people tried to stand up against the regime after the widely disputed reelection of Iranian President Mahmoud Ahmadinejad despite several reported irregularities, and claims that the votes were manipulated and the election was rigged. Police started to suppress the protesters, and opposition groups were accusing the Iranian Revolutionary Guards of torturing and raping men, women, and children in prisons around the country. According to the *New*

York Times, Iranian authorities closed universities in Tehran, blocked websites, blocked cell phone transmissions and text messaging, and banned all rallies. The Iranian uprising has been called the Iranian Green Movement. Iranian officials and Russian media have accused the Western media of unfair coverage and have contended that the protests were planned by the CIA.

Syndicated columnist, Charles Krauthammer critiqued the president's remarks about the uprising:

> Flaccid words. Meaningless words. This is a revolution in the streets. Revolutions happen quickly. There is a moment here in which if the thugs in the streets who are shooting in the crowds stop shooting, it's over and the regime will fall. The courage of the demonstrators and the boldness isn't only a demonstration of courage, it is an indication of a shift in the balance of power. The regime is weakening, this is a hinge of history. Everything in the region will change if the regime is to change. Obama ought to be strong out there and saying to the illegitimate government, we stand shoulder to shoulder with the people in the street. He talks about diplomacy. He should be urging our Western allies who have relations to cut them off, isolate the regime, to ostracize it. He ought to be going in the U.N., every forum, denouncing it. This is a moment in history and he's missing it. Maybe the president's problem is that he can see only himself as the Lever of History. He is The One. This is his time. Not only is it inconceivable to him that other people might be changing history, it's a damn nuisance to hear about these things while he's on vacation.

President Obama passed up on a big opportunity to stand with the Iranian people and potentially make substantial strides in Iran and the Middle East. Iran has been hell bent on obtaining a nuclear weapon for some time, and a weak American president may very likely assist in that becoming a reality.

The year 2011 brought us the Arab Spring and uprising in the streets of Libya and Egypt. The Obama administration didn't know which end was up, nor how to react. This is how the Obama doctrine of leading from behind began. In Egypt, Obama didn't know whether to support the Egyptian president, Hosni Mubarak, who had been a US ally for many years, or the Egyptian people, who had taken to the streets in protest of police brutality, corruption, high unemployment, and a lack of free and open elections. The Egyptian military brought the protests to a relative calm, and Mubarak was ousted, tried, found guilty of complicity in the murders of the protesters, and sentenced to life in prison. Not really knowing what to do, Obama basically did nothing. He did, however, succeed in creating serious doubts around the world about America's leadership. Doubts about America's policies and goals in Egypt fueled fears in Israel and painted the Obama administration into a no-win policy position, resulting in America being seen as a paper tiger.

The Obama administration touted their leading-from-behind strategy in Libya as a huge success. What was touted and hailed by the Obama administration and supporters as a model of measured interventionism has turned out to be a very large mistake. Obama's failed leadership in Libya set in motion a chain of events that aren't good for Libya, the United States, or the world in general. Shortly after the Benghazi attack on September 11, 2012, *Washington Post* reporter Abigail Hauslohner wrote from Darna, Libya, of a chilling picture of the armed Islamist extremists who were terrorizing that eastern Libyan city with bombings and death threats designed to push an Islamist culture guided by Sharia law. "What is unfolding here may be the most extreme example of the confrontation underway across Libya, underscoring just how deeply the fundamentalists have sown their seeds in the security vacuum that has defined Libya since the fall of Moammar Qadafi."

The question is, with that kind of unrest in Libya in the fall of 2012, why wasn't our embassy much better protected? Or, if we weren't going to effectively protect our embassy, why was our ambassador still there? The answer is politics, pure and simple. Obama had just had his Democratic convention and was strongly pushing the narrative that Osama bin Laden was dead and Al-Qaeda was on the run. With Obama's reelection just a few short weeks away, Obama didn't want his failed policies in Libya or with Al-Qaeda to be exposed. A strong military presence in Libya would have smacked in the face of that narrative.

The Obama administration continued to cling to their false narrative despite every available bit of evidence to the contrary, maintaining that their Libya strategy of leading from behind was a success. In reality, the US involvement in Libya was a victory for the terrorists and not a success story for the United States or the Obama administration.

Probably the most glaring lack of leadership that emboldened Russian President Putin was the red lines Obama kept drawing and the fact that he never responded when the Assad (Syrian President/Dictator) regime crossed those lines with impunity. In August 2012 Obama said the following: "We have been very clear to the Assad regime, but also to the other players on the ground, that a red line for us is we start seeing a whole bunch of chemical weapons moving around or being utilized. That would change my calculus. That would change my equation."

The *New York Times* later reported that Obama had stunned his aides with this "unscripted" language. The times said that his comments were made "to the surprise of some of the advisers who had attended the weekend meetings and wondered where the red line came from.

With such an evocative phrase, the president had defined his policy in a way some advisers wish they could take back."

But the administration didn't walk it back. The very next day, when asked about the "red line," White House spokesman Josh Earnest said, "As the president said yesterday in terms of Syria, we're watching very closely the stockpile of Syrian chemical weapons, that any use or proliferation of efforts related to those chemical weapons is something that would be very serious and it would be a grave mistake. There are important international obligations that the Syrian regime must live up to in terms of the handling of their chemical weapons. And the officials who have that responsibility will be held accountable for their actions and will be held accountable for living up to those international obligations." So, for better or worse, the red line was in place.

In a letter from the Obama administration to lawmakers saying there was evidence that chemical weapons had been used in Syria, White House legislative affairs director Miguel E. Rodriguez asserted:

> Because of our concerns about the deteriorating situation in Syria, the president has made it clear that the use of chemical weapons—or transfer of chemical weapons to terrorists groups—is a red line for the United States of America. The Obama administration has communicated that message publicly and privately to governments around the world, including the Assad regime.

The claim of ownership of the "red line" was also restated in a conference call that White House officials held with reporters when the letter was made public:

> We go on to reaffirm that the president has set a clear red line as it relates to the United States that the use of chemical

weapons or the transfer of chemical weapons to terrorist groups is a red line that is not acceptable to us, nor should it be to the international community. It's precisely because we take this red line so seriously that we believe there is an obligation to fully investigate any and all evidence of chemical weapons used within Syria."

Of course, in true Obama fashion, he later denied the "red line" statement and spun it to say that the world had drawn a red line, not him. Obama was intent on sending some air strikes into Syria, just a few pinpricks. The administration unexpectedly decided to seek congressional approval for a military strike, and officials clearly faced a conundrum. Obama sent Secretary of State John Kerry out to garner support for air strikes in Syria, but his efforts bore little fruit. Realizing the Republican distrust of his leadership, the White House apparently decided it would not be helpful to ask for support for an Obama red line air strike. So, the rhetoric shifted, and Obama claimed that it was the world's red line.

The Obama administration's incoherent if not strange reactions to the Syrian chemical weapons crisis created confusion around the world about the US president's policy and position on the Syrian crisis.

Except for Jimmy Carter, all American presidents for the past century have been very careful in not committing themselves or the US military to any action by drawing such a red line. In all past global diplomacy, the phrase "America has spoken" carried a lot of special weight around the globe. America's word was its bond. Obama has now diminished that capital of trust, and once it's lost it is damn difficult to earn back.

In a *New York Times* op-ed in September 2013, Russian President Vladimir Putin made it clear that his "veto" goes beyond foreign policy to include cultural topics such as the "specialness" of the United States. That is a very dangerous perception that Russia may have gained a veto on aspects of US foreign policy.

In the blink of an eye, Obama has diminished the American presidency's respect around the globe to a place where it takes a back seat to the Russian presidency. Russian Foreign Minister Sergei Lavrov was quick to make the point of who's running the show and announce that a new round of talks on Syria would start soon, with Iran and Saudi Arabia invited to discuss the transition plans for Syria. The deal concocted by Moscow, with Obama having little if any say, gives Bashar Al-Assad a free hand to kill Syrians as long as he wishes, so long as he doesn't use chemical weapons. So, in short, Russia made the United States agree to abandon Obama's stated "Assad must go" policy in exchange for a Russian-led policy.

The fact that Assad is a war criminal, has used chemical weapons on his own population, including women and children, and can now continue to operate with impunity sends a big message across the world to all other ruthless regimes that American might and influence are no longer! Whatever happens in Syria, the United States is likely to lose.

There is little question that Obama's invisible red line in the sand has turned to a red stain of blood throughout the Middle East. Obama showed the world that he didn't mean any of his rhetoric and gave all the bad guys around the world the green light that they had at least two more years to deliver their reign of terror on the world and make as many gains as possible in their quest for a caliphate. Lack of American leadership around the world has turned the tides of hell, and those chickens will no doubt be coming home to roost.

A recent study from the Rand Corporation spells out the aftermath of the Obama doctrine of leading from behind. The study identifies that from 2010 through mid-2014, there has been a 58 percent increase in the number of jihadist groups, a doubling of jihadist fighters, and a tripling of attacks by Al-Qaeda affiliates. The most significant threat to the United States, the report concludes, comes from terrorist groups operating in Yemen, Syria, Afghanistan, and Pakistan.

"Based on these threats, the United States cannot afford to withdraw or remain disengaged from key parts of North Africa, the Middle East, and South Asia," said Seth Jones, author of the study and associate director of the International Security and Defense Policy Center at Rand a nonprofit research organization. "After more than a decade of war in Afghanistan and Iraq, it may be tempting for the United States to turn its attention elsewhere and scale back on counterterrorism efforts. But this research indicates that the struggle is far from over," Jones said.

The world is in total chaos, and Islamic extremists calling themselves ISIS or ISIL, have established a Caliphate throughout Syria and Iraq, and are threatening to fly their flag over the White House. What is Barack Obama doing? Playing golf!

Obama would have done well taking a lesson from Ronald Reagan: "peace through strength." It doesn't work any other way.

Eric H. Holder Jr

CHAPTER TWELVE

Holder's Contempt: The Justice Department Scandal

"Human nature itself is evermore an advocate for liberty. There is also in human nature a resentment of injury, and indignation against wrong. A love of truth and a veneration of virtue. These amiable passions, are the 'latent spark'...If the people are capable of understanding, seeing and feeling the differences between true and false, right and wrong, virtue and vice, to what better principal can the friends of mankind apply than to the sense of this difference?"—John Adams, 1775

John Adams eloquently describes how human nature is an advocate of liberty and drives mankind to seek out the truth—that friends of mankind know the difference between right and wrong, hold those accountable who would cause injury, and hold indignation against those who would do wrong.

I would contend that Eric Holder's tenure as the attorney general of the United States smacks squarely in the face of what John Adams professes.

When Barack Obama campaigned for president of the United States, he vowed to have the most transparent administration ever! Nothing could have turned out to be further from the truth.

In scandal after scandal, Barack Obama and his comrade in arms, Attorney General Eric Holder, have stonewalled, claimed executive privilege, classified documents under the ruse of national security, and outright deceived Congress and the American people. OK, I'm not a PC (politically correct) guy; *deceived* is way too weak a word— they've out and out lied!

Lie is a pretty serious word, so let's get that out of the way right now. As outlined in previous areas throughout this book, it is a matter of fact that Barack Obama has lied several times. Even the Politico Fact Checker called Barack Obama's promises about Obamacare the lies of the year: "If you like your doctor, you can keep your doctor, period. If you like your health care plan, you can keep it, period. No one's going to take it away from you, no matter what!" That's just the tip of the iceberg.

I would add that there are a multitude of other mistruths that Obama perpetrated that any reasonable person's own deductive reasoning would conclude. But let's face it; it's damn hard to actually pin a lie on politicians because—and Obama is a master at this—they talk in circles and out of both sides of their mouth. And when they do get caught, they spin, spin, spin, and say, "What I really said…" or "What I really meant was…." In any event, every once in a while a politician says something over and over on tape, so that when the lie does come to light, it's hard for him to backpedal his way out of it.

The reality is, if you actually catch a politician in a lie "red handed," how many other times has he or she lied to you that he or she didn't get caught or was able to spin his or her way out of it?

OK, now that we've established the "trustworthiness," or lack thereof, rather, of our commander in chief, let's establish the same for Attorney General Holder. Let's keep in mind that both Barack Obama and Eric Holder are very skilled lawyers, and catching a skilled lawyer red-handed in a lie is really difficult to do.

You don't have to look very far to find that Eric Holder has faced a number of difficulties that bring his honesty and character into serious question. Again, it's darn tough to catch experienced lawyers in an outright lie, so when they do get caught with their foot in their mouth, it's pretty clear it's been there all along. Eric Holder has earned his share of controversy, and a lot of that controversy was rekindled during his congressional confirmation hearings in 2009.

In 2001 the House Government Reform Committee questioned the accuracy of Mr. Holder's depiction of what he did as the deputy attorney general in the twelfth-hour pardon by then President Bill Clinton of fugitive financier Marc Rich, whose former wife, Denise Rich, had donated $1.3 million to Democrats. Holder had come under fire two years prior for refusing to tell a Senate committee whether the Justice Department had recommended against Clinton's offer of clemency to a number of Puerto Rican nationalists after then Attorney General Janet Reno said that their release posed a national security threat.

The first Obama/Holder scandal pretty much got swept under the rug by the mainstream media while much of the country was still experiencing euphoria, having just elected Barack Obama. It was inconceivable that early on in the Obama administration that the president who promised to bring the country together and be an American president for all would tolerate a racist Justice Department. America was in for a rude awakening.

Maybe we shouldn't have been so surprised. Obama's own racial tendencies soon slipped out and were revealed; you may recall the Obama "beer summit" when President Obama had to play politics after Cambridge, Massachusetts, Police Sgt. James Crowley arrested Harvard University Professor Henry Louis Gates Jr. for disorderly conduct in front of Gates's own house. Mr. Gates is African American, and Sergeant Crowley is a white police officer, so President Obama immediately took Gates's side. He weighed in criticizing the Cambridge police and said that Sergeant Crowley had acted "stupidly." This was, of course, before Mr. Obama knew the details of the altercation. As it turns out, Gates had just returned from a trip and was having difficulties getting his key to work in his door, so he had the driver who was dropping him off at his residence help him jimmy the door open. A neighbor, Lucia Whalen, witnessed the two men doing what appeared to her as trying to break into the residence. She called the police and Sergeant Crowley responded. By then Professor Gates had already gotten into his house. Sergeant Crowley knocked on the door, identified himself, and informed Mr. Gates that he was responding to a 911 call of a reported breaking and entering, and he asked if Mr. Gates would step out on the porch. Mr. Gates immediately became belligerent with Sergeant Crowley and shouted, "Why, because I'm a black man in America?" Crowley's report states that he did believe that Mr. Gates was probably the resident and merely needed to confirm that. Sergeant Crowley was surprised, however, and confused by Mr. Gates's behavior, which included a threat that Crowley didn't know who he was "messing with." Gates initially refused to provide any identification, and when he finally did he kept repeatedly shouting at Sergeant Crowley, so much that the 911 dispatcher audio recordings picked it up. Gates yelled, "Yeah, I'll speak with your mama," and continued to accuse Sergeant Crowley of racial profiling and threaten that Crowley had not heard the last of him. Sergeant Crowley informed Gates that he was being disorderly and that if he persisted he would be arrested. Gates did persist and was arrested for disorderly conduct. Sgt. Leon Lashley, a black police sergeant, was also present at Gates's arrest and said that he completely supported Sergeant Crowley and the arrest 100 percent, noting that Professor Gates was completely belligerent and way out of line.

Ironically Sergeant Crowley had been chosen by a black police commissioner to serve as a police academy instructor of a course entitled "Racial Profiling," which Crowley had taught for the previous five years. Crowley received widespread public support from the Cambridge Police Department. Gates was only held for a couple of hours, and five days after the arrest the Middlesex County district attorney's office dropped the charges after consultation with the Cambridge Police Department. In a joint press release by the authorities and Professor Gates, all parties agreed that this was a just resolution to an unfortunate set of circumstances and that the incident "should not be viewed as one that demeans the character and reputation of Professor Gates or the character of the Cambridge Police Department."

The altercation made news, and without knowing what actually happened, good ol' Reverend Al Sharpton weighed in with his rhetoric, preaching from the sidelines and calling Sergeant Crowley a racist and calling for his head. Sharpton gravely criticized the Cambridge Police Department. President Obama picked up on it and joined Sharpton's rant before knowing the facts of the case. Once the facts of the arrest came out, both Sharpton and Obama looked pretty stupid. Not only did Obama look stupid, it exposed his racial tendencies.

Law enforcement across the country expressed outrage over the president of the United States weighing in on something he knew nothing about, and the fact that he immediately jumped to the conclusion that because Mr. Gates was a black professor arrested at his home and Sergeant Crowley was a white cop, then Sergeant Crowley was automatically in the wrong. When all of the facts came to light, Obama realized the egg of hypocrisy on his face. By the following day, Obama was forced to admit he had jumped to conclusions, and he announced that he regretted his comments and hoped that the situation could become a "teachable moment." Realizing that his own stupidity had created something of his own "teachable moment," Obama thought it was a good PR (public relations) opportunity for him to invite Sergeant Crowley and Professor Gates to the White House for what was referred to as a "beer summit" so the two could kiss and make up. Forgive and forget, right? No doubt, both Crowley and Gates could have and definitely should have handled the situation much better. If you ask me, they both looked pretty foolish. Not nearly as foolish as President Obama, but foolish nonetheless.

I thought it was a good idea to discuss the "beer summit" story because it did give us some early insight about Barack Obama and the kind of president he would be. It told us that as much as he may have promised to be a president for all Americans and wanted to bring the country together, he either had no intention of living up to that commitment or no ability because of his biased ideology. It showed us who he really is: a divisive person with obvious racial overtones. It also gave us a lot of insight into how he would govern—without learning or even caring about all the facts, or educating himself on the other side of the story. It showed us that he would jump to all conclusions, and always as they align with his own ideology. Obama was a black professor, and Gates is a black professor, so Obama immediately concluded that he and Mr. Gates were of the same ideology and of the same cloth, and a white cop was always in the wrong when dealing with any racial issues. It also showed us just how completely incompetent Obama is. I mean, you have to question the intellect of a man who's risen to high office but still doesn't have the intelligence to know how stupid it was for him to interject himself in something as inconsequential as a misdemeanor disorderly conduct arrest. This was one of the first big red flags for me; but you can point to countless of other similarly stupid moves throughout the rest of his presidency.

The August 2014 riots in Ferguson Missouri following the shooting death of Michael Brown, an unarmed eighteen year old black male, by a white twenty eight year old Ferguson police officer, dominated the news cycle, and brought out the same "race baiters" as usual; Jesse Jackson and Al Sharpton. The event was tragic for sure, and my heart goes out to the parents and family of Michael Brown. The shooting occurred shortly after Brown was involved in a strong armed robbery at a Ferguson convenience store that was caught on video tape. There were conflicting eye witness testimony, and the Ferguson community was protesting and demanding that the police officer be arrested, and put in jail, before any facts were determined. The protests turned into riots, and for the first time since World War II, the Missouri Governor had to call in the National Guard.

President Obama took a brief break from his Martha's Vineyard vacation to weigh in on the situation, and sent Attorney General Eric Holder, along with fifty federal agents to Ferguson, to conduct their own investigation. Jim Pasco, director of the Fraternal Order of Police, said Obama's response to the Ferguson Missouri, riots isn't helping. "I would contend that discussing the police tactics from Martha's Vineyard is not helpful to ultimately calming the situation. I think what he has to do as president and as a constitutional lawyer is remind that there is a process in the United States and the process is being followed, for good or for ill, by the police and by the county and by the city and by the prosecutors' office. When Obama weighs in with an opinion he formed during a vacation briefing, he hurts more than he helps."

I don't have a problem with the President weighing in on an important matter, or the Justice department providing some oversight. That said, it is concerning that both Obama and Holder go at any matters that might involve race, with a completely biased point of view, before they know of any of the facts. This only escalates racial tensions, and does nothing to bring calm to a tenuous situation. It's worth noting that both President Obama and Attorney General Holder, are both from Chicago. Chicago has one of the highest murder rates in the country, and it's especially high among black youth. Where is their attention to that travesty? Where is the outrage from Obama, Holder, Sharpton and Jackson over the violence and out of control murder rate against young African American's in Obama's very own home town?

I have little doubt that if the Ferguson police officer who shot and killed Michael Brown, did so with any malice of intent, that he will spend the rest of his life in prison, and rightfully so. But he may very well have simply been defending himself. Jumping to conclusions without all of the facts, is reckless, and not the way our criminal justice system is supposed to work. Regardless of what the outcome of this tragedy is, there is no excuse for the reckless violence, looting and vandalism that went on for days on end.

The day of the 2008 presidential election, the New Black Panther Party took to the streets armed with batons and brandishing weapons to harass and intimidate white voters at various voting stations across the country. Shortly after the elections and prior to Obama's inauguration, the Justice Department brought a case against the New Black Panther Party for voter intimidation at a Philadelphia voting station. According to multiple witnesses, members of the New Black Panther Party blocked access to polling stations, harassed voters, and hurled racial epithets. The Justice Department was confident that their case against the New Black Panther Party (NBPP) was extremely strong. Then Eric Holder came into the picture, and with Holder now in control of the Justice Department, the case was dismissed over the objections of the Justice Department's staff and attorneys, who had put the case together against the black civil action group.

Current and former Department of Justice attorneys have alleged in sworn testimony before the US Commission on Civil Rights that under Eric Holder, the Department of Justice has mishandled the New Black Panther Party and other civil rights related decisions, and have charged that all decisions on who to prosecute and who not to prosecute are made on the basis of race and political affiliation.

Eric Holder, and his assistant attorney generals Messer and Perez denied that they had a hand in the decision not to prosecute the NBPP and testified to Congress that the decision to dismiss the case was made by low-level attorneys at Justice, shaking it off as if Holder or any of the higher ups at Justice didn't have a hand in siding with the New Black Panther Party. Documents later turned up by Judicial Watch through the Freedom of Information Act (FOIA) revealed that the Holder team had not been truthful in their testimony or in their written communications denying any involvement.

"It is becoming increasingly clear that the leadership of the Justice Department, including Attorney General Holder, has a problem with the truth. There needs to be an independent investigation into whether Messer, Holder, and Perez committed perjury in testifying under oath about the Black Panther controversy. We are pleased that the court has already seen through the false narrative presented to it by the Justice Department. We can't have our nation's top law enforcement officers playing fast and loose with the truth," stated Judicial Watch President, Tom Fitton.

The thought that the chief law enforcement agent in the United States would not hold some thugs responsible for voter intimidation is unbelievable to me. This is the same attorney general who professes that the Republicans are trying to repress people's right to vote because they believe that it's a good idea for someone to have to prove who they are when they vote. I have little question that Holder dismissed the charges against the New Black Panther Party because of race.

So why did Holder and his Justice Department dismiss the case against the Black Panthers? It's pretty obvious; Holder and his motley crew do not believe that voting rights laws equally apply to all races, including whites. If you look at Holder's attitude and record on racial issues, it's pretty clear that he also doesn't think that civil rights apply to anyone other than blacks. You may recall a bunch of thugs that were playing the "knockout" game, in which some thug walks up behind some unsuspecting bystander and beats him or her in the back of the head, knocking them out. There were thousands of reported cases of these vicious attacks, and in the vast majority of cases the perpetrator was black and the victim was white. However, the only person the Justice Department prosecuted under "hate crimes" laws was a white man who had victimized a black man. When George Zimmerman was acquitted by a Florida jury of his peers for killing Trayvon Martin, Holder was intent on having the Justice Department take up the case as a race crime and recharging Zimmerman with violating Martin's civil rights. The death of Trayvon Martin was a tragedy for sure, and Zimmerman may have possibly been guilty of manslaughter or even second-degree murder, but, contrary to what Holder and others were accusing him of, it was not a hate crime.

Let's go back for a second and talk about voter ID cards again, because it does have a lot to do with Holder's decision not to prosecute the NBPP for voter intimidation. The Obama administration and the Holder Justice Department have continued to try to make this an issue. On what planet does it not make sense for someone who is voting to have to produce a picture ID? These IDs can be driver's licenses or state IDs, which are provided free of charge. The only possible reason Holder and Obama could think that it's OK for the New Black Panther Party to intimidate voters but it's a bad idea for someone to have to show some sort of ID when they vote is to promote voter fraud! Who among us don't have to have a valid photo ID to get by in life? You can't drive without an ID, you can't purchase liquor or cigarettes without an ID, you can't enter a secure government building without an ID, you can't open a bank account or even cash a check without a valid ID.

Since our "right to vote" is probably our most important fundamental right, as voters we shouldn't be disenfranchised. The arguments that Holder and Obama are making is that no one should have to show any form of identification in order to vote. Their argument is that no one should be "disenfranchised" and that somehow requiring someone to show a photo ID disenfranchises that individual because of some ridiculous argument that some folks might not have a photo ID. The reality is that by not requiring a photo ID, you are disenfranchising every honest vote in America. Why? Because by not having to show a photo ID, there is *nothing* to stop voter fraud! Without a photo ID, what on earth would stop one party or another from loading a bus up with people and taking them from one voting station to another, and claiming that they are someone who they aren't? If one person is allowed to vote twice, it immediately disenfranchises another person's vote.

The New Black Panther Party scandal was just the first scandal that came to light under Holders tenure as Attorney General, but many more would follow. Mr. Holder's trustworthiness once again came into serious question in telling what he knew about the Bureau of Alcohol, Tobacco, Firearms, and Explosives' Operation Fast and Furious probe. According to House Oversight and Government Reform Committee Chairman Rep. Darrell Issa, statements made under oath by General Holder about the operation have "proven to be untrue." ("Proven to be untrue" sounds an awful lot like a lie to me). Issa added that his failure to "come clean" with the American public called his credibility to serve as attorney general into question.

Operation Fast and Furious was a gunrunning operation launched in 2009 by DOJ officials in collaboration with the FBI, the Drug Enforcement Agency, and the Bureau of Alcohol, Tobacco, and Firearms (ATF) as part of a strategy to identify and eliminate arms trafficking networks. Instead of prosecuting the individual "straw purchasers" who buy weapons for the Mexican cartels, ATF agents would track the guns to the top bosses of Mexico's powerful cartels. It's notable that the "gun walking" strategy was actually started by the Bush administration in 2006 under a different operation altogether. The difference being that prior to 2009, the ATF actually tracked and knew where the guns were once they crossed the border and actually accounted for the weapons, whereas the Holder Justice Department hasn't tracked nor has it accounted for the vast majority of weapons they let walk.

Between 2009 and 2011, ATF agents allowed more than two thousand firearms to "walk" across the border. As many as seventeen hundred of those guns have been lost and never recovered. Over a hundred of those guns have been found at bloody crime scenes on both the Mexican side and the American side of the border, including two that were found in December 2010 at the murder site of US Border Patrol Agent Brian Terry.

OK, I realize that it's easy to get lost in the details of any scandal, but that's the problem; the ones guilty of a scandal are often able to get away with it because either people aren't paying attention or because it gets too cumbersome to follow along. I need for you to follow this course of events as you would if you were a juror in an important case. Make no mistake, the attorney general is lying to the American people and to Congress. I've tried to summarize the chain of events as briefly as possible to keep your interest without completely watering it down enough to present the facts for you to come to your own conclusion. I've also added in a few one-line notes to make it a little easier to follow.

Shortly after the death of Border Patrol Agent Brian Terry, ATF whistle blowers blew the lid off of Operation Fast and Furious. The border agent's murder prompted a House investigation into who knew what about the gun-smuggling operation.

In a letter dated February 4, 2011, to Chairman Issa and Senator Charles Grassley, the Senate Judiciary Committee's ranking Republican, the Justice Department denied any existence of Operation Fast and Furious, writing, "The ATF makes every effort to interdict weapons that have been purchased illegally and prevent their transportation into Mexico."

Note: In the February 4 letter, the Justice Department is denying to Congress that there is any gunrunning program. This was soon proven undeniably to be a lie.

It didn't take long for evidence to be revealed that in fact senior Justice Department officials did know about Operation Fast and Furious months prior to sending the February 4 letter. In December of 2011, the Justice Department finally did acknowledge that the letter sent earlier that year was inaccurate, and they turned over about fourteen hundred pages of documents that they claimed proved that there was no intent to mislead Congress.

Note: the gunrunning scandal was boiling, which forced Justice to admit to the lie.

In May 2011, Holder claimed to the Oversight Committee that he had only heard about Fast and Furious "over the last few weeks."

Internal DOJ memos related to Fast and Furious that were addressed to Holder dated all the way back to September 2010. These memos clearly evidenced that Holder was less than forthcoming (lied) when he told the committee in February 2011 that he had no knowledge of the operation, as the memos addressed to Holder clearly evidenced that he had known about it for at least the previous five months.

Note: this is clear and indisputable evidence that Holder lied to Congress.

The Committee demanded internal DOJ documents after the February 4, 2011, letter to Congress. In a letter to Holder, Issa explained that the House Oversight Committee needed those documents to "understand what the Department knew about Fast and Furious, including when and how it discovered its February 4 letter was false, and the Department's efforts to conceal that information from Congress and the public".

Note: Congress was demanding answers about Holder's lies.

So, in order to make an end run around congressional oversight of the Justice Department, President Obama issued an executive order claiming executive privilege. Holder's argument basically boiled down to his assertion that the House Oversight Committee can't have oversight over how the executive branch responds to an investigation.

Note: Holder stonewalls, and Obama provides executive privilege cover.

In June 2012, the US House of Representatives voted to hold Attorney General Eric Holder in contempt for refusing to turn over documents tied to the botched Fast and Furious gunrunning operation.

The House approved both criminal and civil measures against the attorney general, making it the first time in all of American history that the head of the Justice Department has been held in contempt by Congress. The criminal contempt was approved in a 255 to 67 vote, which included seventeen Democrats.

Note: for the first time in American history; the attorney general was held in contempt of Congress!

A number of Democrats, including members of the Black Caucus and House minority leader Pelosi, walked off the floor in protest and refused to participate in the criminal contempt vote.

After Holder was held in contempt, he spoke in New Orleans and dismissed the House actions as "the regrettable culmination of what became a misguided, politically motivated investigation during an election year." In a written statement the White House communication director, Dan Pfeifer, blasted congressional Republicans for pushing "political theater rather than legitimate congressional oversight."

It's unlikely, however, that the contempt charge will actually have any real consequences for the attorney general. The criminal contempt charge refers the dispute to District of Columbia US Attorney Ronald Machen, who will decide whether to file charges against Holder. Most legal analysts, however, do not expect Machen, an Obama appointee who ultimately answers to Holder, to take any action. Despite being technically required by law to bring forth criminal charges against Holder, under orders from Holder's Justice Department of Justice, Machen chose to ignore the resolution. The civil contempt allows the House Committee on Oversight and Government Reform to file a lawsuit asking the courts to examine the Justice Department's failure to produce certain subpoenaed documents, as well as the validity of the administration's assertion of executive privilege over the documents requested.

Note: the wagons circled around Holder; no accountability for contempt.

CNN spoke with legal experts that have indicated that based on precedent, it could take years for the courts to reach any final decision in the civil case.

It's unclear what's in the documents that Obama asserted privilege over, but the president's use of the extraordinary power appears weak at best. There are two types of presidential executive privilege: the presidential communications privilege and the deliberative process privilege. Use of the presidential communications privilege would require that the president himself or his most senior advisors were involved in the discussions.

The president and his cabinet-level officials continually claimed that they had no knowledge of Operation Fast and Furious until early 2011, when the information became public—and Holder claims he didn't read the briefing documents he was sent that outlined the scandal and how guns were walking while the operation was going on. Efforts to get to the whole truth have been blocked by President Obama, exerting executive privilege. Obama would have to be involved in Fast and Furious on some level or his executive privilege claim is not a justified privilege; but both he and Holder are claiming they knew nothing about it. Obama's argument is weak at best, because the Supreme Court has held that such an executive privilege assertion is invalidated by even the suspicion of government wrongdoing. Obama, Holder, the Department of Justice, the Bureau of Alcohol, Tobacco, Firearms, and Explosives, and virtually everyone else involved in this scandal have admitted that government wrongdoing actually took place in the operation. So unless Holder and Obama do have blood on their hands, why not put all of the facts on the table?

House Speaker John Boehner said, "The House needs to know how this happened, and it's our constitutional duty to find out. No Justice Department is above the law, and no Justice Department is above the Constitution."

Some gun rights advocates, including the National Rifle Association (NRA), contend that the gunrunning program allowed for hundreds of weapons, including assault rifles, to end up in the hands of Mexican drug lords and cartels in order for the Obama administration to press for new gun control laws. The NRA heavily pressured House members, most notably moderate and conservative Democrats, to back the contempt of Congress charges.

Judicial Watch filed, on June 22, 2012, a Freedom of Information Act (FOIA) request seeking all documents relating to Operation Fast and Furious and specifically all records subject to the claim of executive privilege invoked by President Barack Obama on or about June 20, 2012." According to Judicial Watch, the administration has refused to comply with Judicial Watch's FOIA request, and in mid-September 2012 the group filed a lawsuit challenging Holder's denial. President Barack Obama's administration filed in response what's called a "motion to stay" the suit. If the judge grants such a motion, it would delay the lawsuit indefinitely.

Judicial Watch President Tom Fitton responded that Holder's and Obama's desire to continually hide the Fast and Furious documents is "ironic" since they are so gung-ho on gun control. "It's beyond ironic that the Obama administration has initiated an anti-gun-violence push as it seeks to keep secret key documents about its very own Fast and Furious gun walking scandal. Getting beyond the Obama administration's smokescreen, this lawsuit is about a very simple principle: the public's right to know the full truth about an egregious political scandal that led to the death of at least one American and countless others in Mexico. The American people are sick and tired of the Obama administration trying to rewrite FOIA law to protect this president and his appointees. Americans want answers about Fast and Furious killings and lies," Fitton said.

Note the Obama administration continued to stonewall as Judicial Watch tried to hold their feet to the fire.

In May 2013, the Justice Department inspector general released a report blasting a government leak intended to smear a key ATF whistleblower in the Fast and Furious gunrunning operation. The leaked memorandum was apparently aimed at discrediting Special Agent John Dodson and contradicting his explosive testimony before Congress, which blew the lid off of the federal gunrunning program that put thousands of high-powered assault weapons into the hands of deadly criminals in Mexico. This twist in the scandal surrounds disgraced former US Attorney Dennis Burke, one of the officials at the center of the administration's lawless gun-trafficking scheme. The ex-prosecutor, who resigned in August of 2011 along with acting ATF boss Kenneth Melson, was furious after learning that the brave whistle blowers had gone to Congress and the media, documents show. He was particularly upset because Dodson, one of the crucial figures in exposing Fast and Furious had written a memo outlining a plot to let guns "walk" across the border into Mexico and into the hands of known criminals.

Note: US Attorney Burke was basically trying to imply that because Dodson (the whistle blower) had written a memo outlining the plot, he was somehow culpable in the scandal. Burke was mad at being exposed by Dodson, so he tried to retaliate against Dodson, insinuating that Dodson was also part of the scandal.

Special Agent Dodson, however, said he had been alarmed about the idea from the start, only putting the plot down on paper in an effort to show superiors how preposterous it really was. When the ATF agent went to Senator Charles Grassley and CBS News to blow the whistle, Burke wanted desperately to protect his reputation. The then US attorney, who worked in Arizona, learned that Fox News reporter Mike Levine was working on a story about the issue. Burke then leaked the Dodson memo to Levine in an obvious attempt to smear Agent Dodson, implying that the Dodson memo somehow made him equally complicit in the scandal.

"We (the inspector general) also concluded that Burke's disclosure of the Dodson memorandum to Levine was likely motivated by a desire to undermine Dodson's public criticism of Operation Fast and Furious. Although Burke denied to congressional investigators that he had any retaliatory motive for his actions, we found substantial evidence to the contrary." Burke refused to be interviewed for the investigation.

Among the most interesting findings in the inspector general investigation was Burke's sense that he was being sacrificed by the administration. Quoted in the OIG report, Burke explained that several US attorneys commented to him that "the Department was throwing my office under the bus."

Evidence has continued to trickle out about Operation Fast and Furious, which indicates the fact that the scandal was much bigger than the press and the administration have admitted. Mexican drug lords, for example, have said that the US government was shipping weapons to their cartels and allowing them to bring drugs across the border in exchange for information. The possible CIA involvement has also continued to be largely concealed. Unfortunately, with all of the other more newsworthy scandals that Eric Holder and the Obama administration have been in, this scandal has seemed to have taken a back seat. We should all remember that one of our brave Border Patrol agents lost his life to a weapon that our government allowed to walk into the hands of dangerous drug cartels. Someone should be held accountable for that.

Note: Holder's Justice Department sent two thousand automatic weapons to Mexican drug cartels, one of which killed a US Border Patrol agent, and Holder and Obama have dodged any accountability.

So what about Border Agent Brian Terry? What about him? Who in our government is accountable for allowing two thousand automatic assault rifles to be provided to notorious Mexican drug cartels? That's a damn good question, and a question that Brian Terry's family has been asking since the day their son was murdered by one of those assault rifles. In June 2012, Terry's parents told Fox News's Sean Hannity that they think Attorney General Eric Holder and other Justice Department officials are "hiding something" in their response to the botched gun-running operation Fast and Furious.

Two of the ATF weapons were found at the murder scene of Brian Terry. Terry's parents, Kent and Josephine Terry, told Hannity, "They're lying...They're passing the buck. I just know that they're hiding something big. Something happened out there."

The real question about the documents Holder has refused to turn over to Congress is whether the documents contain information so damaging that the president was willing to risk the bad PR by moving to exert executive privilege. Lawmakers questioned whether Obama's assertion was even legitimate and later voted in committee that it was not appropriate in this case. Republicans argue that Obama has now tipped his hand, because the only way executive privilege could apply is if the White House was somehow involved in Fast and Furious.

In December 2012, the family of murdered Border Patrol Agent Brian Terry filed suit against seven government employees and a gun shop in Texas that was involved with the ATF and the Fast and Furious gunrunning program. The seventy-two-page lawsuit claims the defendants "created, organized, implemented, and/or participated in a plan code named "Operation Fast and Furious" to facilitate the distribution of dangerous firearms to violent criminals, and that they knew or should have known that their actions would cause substantial injuries, significant harm, and even death to Mexican and American civilians and law enforcement, but were recklessly indifferent to the consequences of their actions." Agent Terry was gunned down in Arizona on December 15, 2010, by illegal immigrants who used at least two rifles bought in Fast and Furious. The lawsuit claims that more ATF agents could be liable, as well as other Justice Department attorneys and administrators, but, because of actions to cover up their wrongdoing and hide their misconduct, their names are not currently known and could be added at a later date.

Lengthy investigations by Congress and the inspector general have faulted at least seventeen ATF and the Justice Department officials for alleged mismanagement and other violations of conduct.

As a parent, wouldn't you want to know what happened to your murdered loved one? Attorney General Eric Holder's refusal to fully disclose the documents associated with Operation Fast and Furious and President Obama's assertion of executive privilege serve to compound this tragedy. It denies the Terry family and the American people the truth.

I would ask, what kind of a world is it when we have elected officials and appointed officials who are above the law? How can there be justice in America when the chief law enforcement officer of the land doesn't have to comply with Congress or answer to a subpoena? That is certainly not "justice."

It seems that in every instance of a scandal that comes to light, the Obama administration and virtually every government department under the Obama administration, including the Justice Department, always seem to tout when they are under investigation that they've already turned over thousands of documents or undergone a number of investigations. When you hear a politician or an attorney saying that, you know that he or she is hiding something. If someone turns over ten thousand pages of documents and keeps only the one that is the smoking gun, the other ten thousand are meaningless now, aren't they?

When politicians or attorneys or government departments try claiming that there have already been a number of investigations clearing them of this or that, so now this matter should be put behind them, you know there is a cover-up in the works. What the Obama administration would have the public believe is that Obama appointees are somehow impartial or independent. What good does it do for Eric Holder to investigate his boss, the guy who put him in power, especially knowing that when Holder didn't want to turn documents over to the House Oversight Committee, all he had to do was give Obama a call and ask him to exert executive privilege? Holder has Obama's unconditional loyalty, and Obama has Holder's unconditional loyalty, no matter what either of them is doing, no matter what lies they tell, no matter how many laws they break, and no matter the number of times they trash the US Constitution. That's a recipe for disaster for America. When we have a government that has no accountability, a government where officials aren't answerable to Congress or the people and have proven time and time again that they believe they are above the law that is a real travesty of justice.

There was an interesting article in the November 2, 2013, Daily Caller that I wanted to share some excerpts from to give us some insight from a former Secret Service agent, Dan Bongino, author of *Life Inside the Bubble: Why a Top-Ranked Secret Service Agent Walked Away from It All*. Bongino left his post after a twelve-year Secret Service career to get away from the "fog of scandals" he believes have enveloped the Obama administration.

Bongino sat down with the Daily Caller and expressed his disgust on the politicized state of the Department of Justice:

Question: "What's your opinion of the Obama administration's Department of Justice and Eric Holder's tenure, and the difference between finding actual criminal cases and cases that are just neatly packaged?"

Bongino: "It's a travesty, what's happening to the Department of Justice. It's an actual travesty. It's political malpractice at its worst. I don't think its coincidence that Lady Justice has got a blindfold on. That has not been the case for this administration. Think about the things they've wasted their time on. Political statements about the voter intimidation, Fast and Furious, hiding documents from Congress, the most recent scandal, and I think the most egregious is going after Louisiana for the school voucher program...This Department of Justice is a Department of Injustice. It's just sad what has happened; I'm stunned that more people have not come forward. Because I get phone calls, e-mails, texts from people all the time who, I cannot express to you the level of frustration among federal agents and administrative employees. People are really fed up with this administration and the way they politicize things. I think the DOJ is just the tip of the spear."

Note: The Louisiana school voucher program Bongino is referring to is part of a lawsuit Holder filed against the State of Louisiana asking the court to permanently enjoin the State of Louisiana from awarding any school vouchers. (School vouchers are something that the teachers union despises, because they give students the option of using a voucher to attend nonunion charter schools.)

From my perspective and what I've learned, Agent Bongino's comments are spot on. It is, however, very interesting to get some insight from a federal agent who's actually been inside the Justice Department and can give us his insight as to what is actually going on in the belly of the beast.

I realize that trying to follow along with the details and chain of events is difficult for most of us to do, but that's what the ones we need to hold accountable are counting on—that we will lose track of what's going on or forget about it altogether. When those in power investigate themselves or refuse to cooperate in an independent investigation, which is a monumental problem. As Americans we cannot allow ourselves to be so gullible. We have to pay attention, and we have to pay close attention to the details of what is going on in our country and hold those we've trusted accountable when they've violated the office we've entrusted to them. No one is above the law, and it's incumbent upon us to hold our government accountable. I understand that "we the people" are able to hold our elected representatives accountable at the polls when we vote, but we have to do better than that. Time is not our friend; while members of the House serve only two-year terms, presidents serve four-year terms, and senators serve six-year terms. My point is that two years, four years, and six years can be an awfully long time to subject our country to corruption or incompetence.

Nothing could be worse than to have our own government using its power to retaliate against those who voice disagreement with the government. It's against everything America stands for, and it shreds our Constitution, and America's confidence in our government. You have the IRS targeting conservatives, but you may not be aware of the Justice Departments targeting of a number of businesses with whom they disagree. Operation Choke Point is a Department of Justice operation which used its power to threat and strong-arm banks into denying financial services to business for political reasons.

Operation Choke Point works as a partnership between the Department of Justice and various other federal agencies which deal with bank regulations, specifically the Treasury and the Securities and Exchange Commission (SEC). The objective of the project is to choke-off fraudulent business from accessing financial services, in an effort to protect consumers. The rub however is over allegations that the DOJ is pressuring financial institutions to decline doing business with so-called "high risk" industries which line up squarely against the political leanings of the current administration. These institutions include ammunition sales, payday loans and fireworks companies and several others; 24 industries in total, as listed by the Federal Deposit Insurance Corporation (FDIC).

Former Chairman of the FDIC, William M. Isaac responded to Operation Choke Point; "Operation Choke Point is one of the most dangerous programs I have ever experienced in my 45 years of service as a bank regulator, bank attorney and consultant, and bank board member. Operating without legal authority and guided by a political agenda, unelected officials at the DOJ are discouraging banks from providing basic banking services...to lawful businesses simply because they don't like them."

The DOJ has reportedly directly strong-armed banks into dropping clients not engaging in fraud. According to an article in *The Daily Caller;* the DOJ reportedly told a bank that provided financial services to a payday loan company that; "I don't like this product, and I don't believe it should have a place in our financial system. And if you don't agree, there will be an immediate, unplanned audit of your entire bank."

The Justice Department has now served over 50 subpoenas on banks, and Alabama Republican Representative Spencer Bachus expressed considerable concern that dragging banks into a long and expensive process is just an underhanded way of encouraging banks to drop clients as an easy-out. "Subpoenas are expensive to comply with and can bring unwarranted scrutiny. The natural reaction from a financial institution might be to sever relations with the merchant and be done with it", Bachus said in a July 2014 hearing at the Subcommittee on Regulatory Reform, Commercial and Antitrust Law.

Missouri Republican Representative Blaine Luetkemeyer brought forward the End Operation Choke Point Act in July 2014 to curb the DOJ's activities in this area. The act would provide financial institutions with safe harbor to serve customers engaged in legal activities, so as to cut out politically motivated attacks on businesses deemed undesirable by the Justice Department.

We all have a voice, and when we know our government is on the obtrusive and disastrous course it obviously is, we must as citizens use that voice to do everything in our power to hold those responsible for our pending demise as a country, accountable.

CHAPTER THIRTEEN

Most Transparent Presidency?
Free Press Scandal

"A popular Government, without popular information, or the means of acquiring it, is but a Prologue to a Farce or a Tragedy: or, perhaps both. Knowledge will forever govern ignorance. And a people who mean to be their own Governors, must arm themselves with the power which knowledge gives." —James Madison, 1822

Madison clearly lays out the why a free press was so important to our republic that our Founding Fathers sought to defend it at every turn. The ultra-liberally biased "so called" main stream media, would be well advised to study the insightfulness of our Founding Fathers, because they have been asleep at the wheel throughout the entire Obama presidency, and were complicit in his re-election.

When President Obama campaigned for his job, and even after the American people entrusted him with his office, he promised to deliver to us the most transparent presidency in history! What he's delivered, however, is anything but a transparent presidency or a transparent government. In fact, no other presidency in history has been as cloaked and nontransparent as the Obama administration is. Not even the Nixon administration, which has long been accepted as the most secretive. Most would also agree that before Mr. Obama took office, the Nixon presidency was the most corrupt. President Obama has certainly taken both of those titles from former President Nixon.

There is so much to talk about on this topic, it's difficult to know where to begin. Let's first narrow it down to the heart of how the Obama administration has been so successful at hiding things from the media and the American public and not being transparent. The best way to describe this is the Obama–Holder tag team. What do I mean by that? The very best way to cover something up if you have the power of the government at your disposal is to pretend to "investigate it."

President Obama and Attorney General Holder have become masters at using so-called investigations as a very clever tool to cloak their incompetence or corruption. At every turn, when any potential scandal comes about, there is a standard operating procedure for the Obama administration: Obama takes to the podium and says, "We are going to investigate this serious accusation, and if there is any truth to it, those responsible will be held accountable."

Obama never acknowledges anything and promises only that an investigation will be conducted to get to the bottom of things. All the while knowing that his comrade in arms, Mr. Holder, and his Justice Department will control any inspector general or other inves-tigation. He then assures the public that "if" there is any findings of wrongdoing, those responsible will be held accountable. Other than an occasional sacrificial resignation, no one has ever been held accountable.

The investigation then becomes the Obama administration's weapon of choice! It provides him all the cover in the world to not have to say or do anything, and allows him not to take any meaningful action whatsoever. He simply answers from that day forward that "it wouldn't be appropriate for me to comment while the investigation is still underway." The investigation is never concluded, or, if it ever is, the issue is so far in the past that everyone's forgotten about it, and the corrupt or incompetent people are never made accountable. Or, if he does need a political conclusion to the scandal, Comrade Holder concludes the investigation with a "there wasn't a smidgen of corruption" statement. Or, if they really need to, they will throw some low-level government employee under the bus and say that that person has been disciplined and held accountable and the problem has been rectified. For the first five and a half years of the Obama presidency, the mainstream media have let him get away with that over and over.

It is worth pointing out that when the IRS scandal broke, Mr. Obama took to the podium and recited his usual lines about "if" there is any truth to it (even though the IRS had already admitted to targeting conservatives, so there wasn't any question of if it was true or not), heads would roll...yada, yada, yada...

A short time after President Obama had promised the American people, that the IRS scandal would be swiftly investigated, Attorney General Eric Holder was called before Congress, and was asked which assistant attorney general was put in charge of the investigation. Pretty simple question that one would think Holder should have been prepared for? Nope. Holder couldn't identify who he had put in charge of investigating such a huge scandal. An investigation, mind you, that should have risen to the level of Mr. Holder himself being involved in the probe. Mr. Holder couldn't point to someone being put in charge of the investigation because he obviously hadn't put anyone in charge of the investigation. That fact is very telling, because it suggests that the Obama administration and the Justice Department had no intention of investigating the IRS scandal because they knew what was going on, and they knew that the administration was complicit in the scandal.

We'll talk a lot more about the IRS scandal later in this book, because it is obviously a scandal of monumental proportion; however, how the administration handles every scandal is relevant to our conversation.

One last thing about the IRS scandal worth pointing out: In an interview President Obama had with Bill O'Reilly just prior to the Super Bowl in February 2014, O'Reilly asked Obama if there was any corruption in the IRS scandal, and Obama famously replied, "There's not a smidgen of corruption." The president of the United States makes this statement of fact, mind you, while the investigation is still ongoing! Not to mention the glaring fact that there was a mountain of corruption already completely and undisputedly exposed! Sure, it may have at the time only been blamed on a few "low-level" perpetrators, but let's not forget that a very high-level IRS official, Lois Lerner, had already "pled the Fifth" to avoid testifying to Congress. Her problem with pleading the Fifth is that she gave a long statement of factual assertions prior to pleading the Fifth that waived her Fifth Amendment rights. It's also worth pointing out that since the president made the "not a smidgen of corruption in the IRS" remark, the IRS has "claimed" that all of the e-mails between Lois Lerner and the White House have somehow disappeared. How convenient.

My point in all of this is that for the president of the United States to make such a statement—"there's not a smidgen of corruption"—is very telling about just how completely delusional or detached he is from the reality around him.

Why pretend to have just one investigation? Why not two, three, or four investigations? The more, the better, right? I mean, if you're the attorney general or the president of the United States, you can put some of your "appointees" in charge of an investigation, give them a little wink and a nod, and hey, they know the deal. So now you not only have one investigation clearing those in power; you have several investigations coming to the same conclusions. The question is, what earthly good is any investigation that wasn't thoroughly conducted or was strictly biased?

OK, you can criticize me and call me cynical for not buying into the naïve thought that all government employees—career, appointed, or elected—are of impeccable character. I can accept that government employees are as honest as everyone else. But using that standard tells us unequivocally that there are a lot of people in our government who are of very questionable character or who may feel pressured or beholden to those in power, or both. Take character out of the equation; I have little doubt that like-minded people tend to look out for one another. If someone shares the same ideology as those in power, he or she would certainly start any investigation with that bias—a bias that may start the investigation looking for any reason to exonerate someone rather than convict someone. It's like if you take a defense attorney and a prosecuting attorney; they can both argue the same case from differing perspectives. They might even both convince themselves that their perspective is the right one. The point is that you get the facts out and present them to a jury.

"We the people" are the jury of our government. President Obama and Attorney General Holder are their own defense attorneys and want "we the people," the jury, so to speak, to see only their version of the facts, and nothing else. Any investigation that the Justice Department has any hand in whatsoever is damned likely to produce only whatever facts they want us to see that will support whatever false narrative they are pushing. It would be precisely like going to court for a felony and not having a prosecutor to present the evidence; while that might be a great thing for whoever is getting prosecuted, it would be a terrible thing for "we the people" and a travesty of justice. There would be no justice if we had a system that didn't dispose of all of the facts.

This is not a partisan position that I'm arguing. Both parties have used tactics similar to those the Obama–Holder tag team is using. Nixon, a Republican, used very similar tactics; the difference, however, is back then the American press didn't let him get away with it and he was held accountable, as he should have been. Barack Obama and Eric Holder, however, are not being held accountable by the so-called mainstream press. And "we the people" are paying the price for this dereliction of duty.

My question is to Mr. Obama and Mr. Holder and their motley crew of followers: What are you afraid of? If you have nothing to hide, if you have done nothing wrong, why do you persist in refusing to turn over documents? Why do you make every effort to prevent an independent investigation at every turn? Why not cooperate and put all the facts forth and let the chips fall where they may?

Facts are a funny critter; they are what they are. If you've done nothing wrong, the facts aren't going to say that you did. To the contrary, if you've done nothing wrong the facts will bear that out. The facts may embarrass someone, but if that's the price of getting down to the facts, and if the facts exonerate someone, I would think it would be worth it. No, the reason for not wanting the facts to come to light is because there is something to hide.

I guess the Obama–Holder tag team approach is the quintessential "Chicago style of politics." Certainly I would respect Mr. Obama's and Mr. Holder's rights to remain silent if they choose to exercise that privilege. I'm not so sure how well that would go over with the American public, but hey, I'm sure they realize that they don't have our vote to lose anymore. Remaining silent is one thing; but lying and refusing to turn over evidence or destroying evidence is a whole other ball game, as is intimidating witnesses or retaliating against your adversaries. You know, like using the IRS to go after those with opposing political views.

It's pretty scary knowing what the Obama administration and the Holder Justice Department will do now that it's come to light just what the National Security Agency's (NSA) capabilities really are. On March 12, 2013, Democratic Senator Ron Wyden asked NSA Intelligence Chief James Clapper during an open Senate Intelligence Committee hearing, "Does the NSA collect any type of data at all on millions or hundreds of millions of Americans?" Director Clapper paused and then answered, "No, sir...Not wittingly."

Leaks to the news media later that summer by Edward Snowden revealed that the NSA was in fact collecting huge amounts of cell phone metadata from US citizens as well as data on their Internet activity. This revelation smacked in the face of Clapper's testimony and proved that Director Clapper had in fact lied to Congress. Clapper later apologized for his answer and said he gave "the least untruthful answer" to a question that could not be answered in an open, unclassified hearing. Clapper described Senator Wyden's query as a "how long have you been beating your wife" question. Clapper also offered to resign after the Snowden leaks appeared to contradict his answers to Wyden.

Congressman Jim Sensenbrenner, who coauthored the Patriot Act, called for Clapper to be prosecuted for lying to Congress and rejected Clapper's apology, telling *The Hill*, "Lying to Congress is a federal offense, and Clapper ought to be fired and prosecuted for it."

I'm not going to completely jump on the prosecute-Clapper band-wagon just yet, and he certainly shouldn't have lied to Congress. What he should have said is that he would address that question in a closed-door, classified session. Moreover, he should have been prepared for that question and had ready an answer; it wasn't like he didn't know it would likely be asked.

I understand the importance of our government having to use what many might not consider as conventional methods to gain intelligence. I also understand that what the NSA does is legal, and I do understand the processes they are required to go through to protect Americans' privacy. The problem is that we are at the mercy of our government to act responsibly, not overstep its authority, and not use its power against those with whom they disagree or who dare question or criticize them.

Therein lies the problem. I don't trust our government anymore, not one little iota! The evidence is already in; there isn't any question that the Obama–Holder tag team will use whatever means necessary to silence and even destroy those with whom they disagree, all the while giving a free rein and turning a blind eye to those who support them. So, yes, because of what I know for certain, it scares the hell out of me that these characters have control of this kind of power.

The Obama–Holder tag team doesn't just stop at going after conservative groups and their donors. No, they have no tolerance of the freedom of the press, either. They haven't given a second thought to infringing on journalists' rights to shed light on the truth. That, of course, is despite the assertion of their party that they are the "tolerant" ones and champions of free speech. But, then again, we have already effectively rebutted that folklore. The Obama–Holder tag team has been well documented in the contempt they have for any media outlets or reporters with whom they disagree. It's no secret that the Obama administration despises Fox News and has demonized them at every opportunity.

Regardless of your opinions about Fox News, it is one of the few television news organization that does give the conservative point of view. If you do watch Fox News, as I do, you know that Fox does give both points of view (thus their slogan, "fair & balanced"). Fox does not have any primetime news programs that don't include panels with both respected liberals and conservatives debating both sides of the issue. Even if you are of the opinion that Fox News leans more conservative, there is little question that all other news organizations either lean left or are completely left with no diversity at all. In almost every single instance, at least during the first five and a half years of the Obama presidency, the only news organization that did its job was Fox News. OK, if you are no fan of Fox News, you surely understand that a news organization's primary responsibility is to ask the tough questions and investigate the facts. Barack Obama despises Fox News and has made every effort to try and delegitimize Fox, because it has been the only news outlet who hasn't given him a pass. Sure, Barack Obama has on very few occasions gave a limited interview with Fox, like the one he gave on Super Bowl Sunday, 2014; but that is only because he realizes that Fox has the largest audience. Ironically, everything that the Obama administration and the so-called mainstream media was mocking Fox News for over the past couple of years, saying they were focusing on "old news" or trumped-up political scandals, has come to light. Most of it would never have come to light without the aggressive reporting and investigation of Fox News.

For the Obama administration there is no such thing anymore as the war on terror; however, there is a war on Fox News. Over and over, President Obama is complaining about the one television news outlet in America that won't fall in line and treat him as king. He hates

Fox because they haven't toed the Obama line. You would think that he would recognize that at least one news organization should be asking the hard questions. Isn't it a journalist's job to ask difficult questions, get to the facts, and hold people accountable?

Even liberal columnist Kirsten Powers, a Fox News contributor whom I rarely agree with, has great concerns with how the Obama administration has gone to great lengths to try to delegitimize an entire news organization of hardworking reporters just because the administration doesn't like what they have to say.

"Whether you are liberal or conservative, libertarian, moderate, or politically agnostic, everyone should be concerned when leaders of our government believe they can intentionally try to delegitimize a news organization they don't like. If you are a liberal, as I am," Powers said, "you should be the most offended, as liberalism is founded on the idea of cherishing dissent and an inviolable right to freedom of expression. That more liberals aren't calling out the White House for this outrageous behavior tells you something about the state of liberalism in America today." Sounds to me like Kirsten Powers is starting to have an epiphany about the tolerance or lack thereof of her liberal ideology. Good for her. Powers goes on to express her thoughts on Media Matters' (a liberal media activist organization) intent to destroy Fox News: "Can someone explain to me how it's 'liberal' to try and shut down a media organization? What the Obama administration is doing and what liberals are funding at Media Matters is beyond chilling; it's a deep freeze."

Kirsten Powers is a self-identified liberal, and if you have ever listened to her, you know she's definitely a liberal, but on this topic she has hit the nail on the head about what lengths the White House and Media Matters will go to, to silence those who disagree with their progressive ideology. Powers goes on to say:

Point of order: Who put Media Matters in charge of determining what is and isn't a news operation? A Media Matters memo found its way into the public domain, and if you care at all about decency and freedom of the press, it will make you throw up. If you like McCarthyism, it's right up your alley. It details to liberal donors how they have plans to assemble opposition research on Fox News employees. It complains of the "pervasive unwillingness among members of the media to officially kick Fox News to the curb of the press club" and outlines how they are going to change that through targeting elite media figures and turning them against Fox. They say they want to set up a legal fund to sue (harass) conservatives for any "slanderous" comments they make about progressives on air. They actually cite one of the best journalists around, Jake Tapper, as a problem because he questioned the White House about calling a news outlet "illegitimate." Tapper can see the obvious: If the White House can call one news outlet illegitimate for asking tough questions, then guess who is next? Anyone."

In a news correspondence conference call to journalists about Benghazi, the Obama White House intentionally excluded Fox News from the conversation despite Fox News being the only outlet that was regularly reporting on Benghazi. Senior Obama advisor David Axelrod told ABC that the Fox News Channel isn't really a news station and that their news programing isn't really news, despite the fact that Fox is the largest news outlet in the world, with more listenership than all of their competition combined. President Obama has said himself that he doesn't think he gets a fair shake from Fox, and even admitted as much in his Bill O'Reilly Super Bowl interview. White House Communications Director Anita Dunn told the *New York Times* that no one need pretend that Fox News was a legitimate news organization. On CNN she declared Fox as a wing of the Republican Party. The White House cronies, early in the administration, even tried to officially kick Fox News out of the Washington press corps. Fortunately the majority of the press corps cried foul, realizing that they wouldn't want a different administration to have the ability to do that to them. For a party who professes to be the party of tolerance and the champion of free speech, the Democrats sure do spend a lot of time attacking and trying to delegitimize a news organization.

It's one thing for a president or his administration not to appreciate the press or to have problems with one news outlet or another. Richard Nixon had a terrible relationship with the news media. But, then again, Richard Nixon, like Barack Obama, had a lot to hide, so it's not at all surprising that Nixon complained about the press the way Obama complains about Fox News, the only news outlet that's consistently held him accountable. The Obama–Holder tag team, however, has taken their dislike of Fox beyond the pale. To be fair, they didn't target only Fox in their disdain for journalists; believe it or not, the Associated Press (AP) has been in their sights as well.

This is extremely important, because when any president or his administration goes after the press for simply doing their job, it should be an eye-opening moment for "we the people." That is exactly what the Obama administration has been doing. Not only did Eric Holder target Fox News and the Associated Press, he lied about it (again) to Congress.

The Justice Department secretly obtained two months of telephone records of reporters and editors for the Associated Press in what the news agency's top executive called a "massive and unprecedented intrusion" into how the news organization gathers the news.

The records obtained by the Justice Department listed outgoing calls for the work and personal phone numbers of individual reporters for general Associated Press office numbers in New York, Washington, and Hartford, Connecticut, and for the main numbers for the AP in the House of Representatives press gallery, according to attorneys for AP.

The Justice Department seized the records for more than twenty separate telephone lines assigned to the AP and its journalists in April and May of 2012. More than one hundred journalists use the phone lines that the DOJ targeted, on a wide array of stories about government and other matters.

In a letter of protest sent to Attorney General Holder, AP President and CEO Gary Pruitt said the government sought and obtained information far beyond anything that could be justified by any specific investigation. He demanded the return of the phone records and destruction of all copies. "There can be no possible justification for such an overbroad collection of the telephone communications of the Associated Press and its reporters. These records potentially reveal communications with confidential sources across all of the newsgathering activities undertaken by the AP during a two-month period, provide a road map to AP's newsgathering operations, and disclose information about the AP's activities and operations that the government has no conceivable right to know."

The government would not say why it sought the records. In a letter to the AP from the Justice Department, the government offered no explanation for the seizure.

In order to get a search warrant that allowed the FBI to secure a subpoena to secure the private e-mails and phone records of Fox News Chief Washington Correspondent James Rosen, Holder personally approved the search warrant and did so by telling a judge that Rosen was a suspected co-conspirator of espionage. News of the DOJ probe into Rosen came on the heels of revelations about the Justice Department's secret subpoena of the Associated Press.

After having targeted both the Associated Press and Fox News, Eric Holder testified before a House Judiciary Committee on May 15, 2013. Holder was asked by Congressman Hank Johnson, "We have an old law that would allow for prosecution of anyone who published classified information, isn't that correct?" Holder replied with a rambling answer: "You've got a long way to go to try and prosecute people, the press, for the publication of that material. This has...not fared well in American history." Holder went on and proclaimed, "With regard to the potential prosecution of the press for the disclosure of material that is not something I've ever been involved in, heard of, or would think would be a wise policy." Holder testified to this, all the while knowing full well that he was investigating the press. I'm not sure how you could call that testimony anything other than an outright lie!

Chapter 20 of this book includes the first ten amendments to the US Constitution, but I will point to the First Amendment here: "Congress shall make no law respecting an establishment of religion, or prohibiting the free exercise thereof; or abridging the freedom of speech, or the press, or the rights of the people peaceably to assemble, and to petition the Government for a redress of grievances."

It's pretty clear that in the targeting of a Fox News reporter and the Associated Press, Attorney General Eric Holder finds himself to be above the law and has complete contempt for the Constitution of the United States. His actions clearly violate the Constitution, and no one has held him accountable.

According to NBC News, Eric Holder personally signed the warrant in the Rosen case, and then later told Congress (again, lied to Congress) that he didn't know anything about it and didn't think it would be a good idea.

Roger Ailes, Fox News president, charged: "The administration's attempt to intimidate Fox News and its employees will not succeed, and their excuses will stand neither the test of law, the test of decency, nor the test of time. We will not allow a climate of press intimidation unseen since the McCarthy era, to frighten any of us away from the truth."

The House Judiciary Committee openly charged Attorney General Eric Holder over his testimony, in which he claimed to be unaware of any "potential prosecution" of the press, despite his knowing about the investigations that targeted Fox News's chief Washington correspondent, James Rosen. President Obama, again, stood by his embattled attorney general.

House Judiciary Chairman Bob Goodlatte and Representative James Sensenbrenner voiced grave concern in a letter to Holder that asked many questions about the Justice Department's dealings with the press, and pointed out that the Rosen case certainly contradicts his testimony to Congress on May 15, 2013, where he claimed that he wasn't aware of any "potential prosecution" of any reporters. "It is imperative that the committee, the Congress, and the American people be provided a full and accurate account of your involvement," they wrote. In Holder's testimony before the House Judiciary Committee on May 15, he insisted that "the potential prosecution of the press for the disclosure of material" is not something that he was involved in or knew about. That statement was clearly exposed as a lie when it was revealed that Holder had himself lied to a judge in order to get a subpoena claiming that James Rosen might be guilty of espionage. That would certainly rise to the "potential prosecution" of the press.

Fox News Executive Vice President Michael Clements said in a statement, "The network is outraged to learn that James Rosen was named a criminal coconspirator for simply doing his job as a reporter. In fact, it is downright chilling, we will unequivocally defend his right to operate as a member of what up until now has always been a free press."

Glenn Greenwald, a *Guardian* columnist and former constitutional lawyer, wrote, "It is not illegal to publish classified information under US law. The DOJ appears to now be arguing that a journalist can be guilty of crimes for soliciting the disclosure of classified information as a way to criminalize the act of investigative journalism itself."

Senator Lindsey Graham called for a special counsel to investigate the Justice Department's subpoena of Rosen's phone records, saying the attorney general cannot impartially review or investigate a decision that he personally approved. "This is clearly an overreach. James Rosen is a lot of things, but a criminal coconspirator he is not. We're beginning to criminalize journalism, and I think that should worry us all," Graham contended.

Standard Department of Justice guidelines require that a news organization receive a subpoena if any of its reporters or employees are under investigation. Fox News said it never received a notification from the government that it was investigating Rosen.

Even Democrats have started to question Holder's actions against the First Amendment. Even a prominent liberal legal scholar has called for Holder to be fired. Jonathan Turley, an attorney and law professor at George Washington University, hammered Holder in a *USA Today* column. He charged that Holder has "supervised a comprehensive erosion of privacy rights, press freedom, and due process," aided by Democrats who looked the other way. Turley added, "I am neither a Republican nor a conservative, and I believe Holder should be fired."

The Obama administration and the Holder Justice Department are going to all lengths to silence whistle blowers or anyone who would expose them. Holder's actions united journalists who seldom agree on anything. Fox News's Brit Hume said, "The Obama–Holder Justice Department is not prepared to treat the ordinary newsgathering activities of reporters trying to seek information from government officials as a possible crime. I can't think of a case where that has ever happened before."

In true Obama–Holder tag team fashion, Obama took to the podium and said, "I am troubled by the possibility that leak investigations may chill the investigative journalism that holds government accountable. Journalists should not be at legal risk for doing their jobs." You think? Then why in the heck is Eric Holder still the attorney general of the United States?

Good question.

LIVE
7:19 am PT

MS. LERNER

IRS TARGETING OF CONSERVATIVE GROUPS
House Oversight & Government Reform Committee   C-SPAN 3
Rayburn Office Building

ALERT   LOIS LERNER, IRS DIR. OF EXEMPT ORGANIZATIONS INVOKES 5TH AMENDMENT

CHAPTER FOURTEEN

Not a Smidgen of Corruption? The IRS Scandal

"Facts are stubborn things: and whatever may be our wishes, our inclination, or the dictates of our passions, they cannot alter the state of facts and evidence." —John Adams, in defense of the British soldiers on trial for the Boston Massacre, December 4, 1770

Need I say more? But yet our government continues to lie to us, withhold the facts, hide them under executive privilege, or outright destroy evidence, as in the IRS scandal and the loss of two years of e-mails and the destroyed hard drives of the people at the center of the scandal.

In an interview with Bill O'Reilly just prior to the Super Bowl in February of 2014, President Obama infamously proclaimed, "There's not a smidgen of corruption in the IRS." I beg to differ. I would add that it was a remarkably stupid thing for the president to proclaim, given a number of facts:

a) The IRS had already admitted to the corruption on May 10, 2013, during an American Bar Association meeting, when Lois Lerner admitted that organizations were targeted because of their titles or beliefs, calling it "absolutely incorrect, insensitive, and inappropriate."

b) The supposed investigation that the Justice Department was pretending to conduct was still ongoing.

c) Several lawsuits had already been filed by a number of conservative groups against the IRS, all of which were still ongoing.

d) Lois Lerner was placed on administrative leave and has refused to testify to Congress, which begs the question, why? And regardless of whether she has anything to hide or not, it certainly leaves the question of corruption wide open. I'm not sure if President Obama was intentionally being dishonest about the obvious corruption in the IRS or if he is really just that obtuse.

So let's start with what caused the big brouhaha with the IRS and their targeting of conservative groups and conservative donors. In July 2008 in the run-up to the presidential elections, Citizens United, a conservative lobbying group, wanted to air a series of commercials promoting a film targeting Hillary Clinton. The US District Court for the District of Columbia ruled that they couldn't, finding that it was a violation of the Bipartisan Campaign Reform Act of 2002 (also known as the McCain–Feingold Act). The group appealed and in August 2008, the US Supreme Court agreed to hear the matter and put it on the docket. In March 2009, the high court heard oral arguments in the case *Citizens United v. Federal Election Commission*.

In September 2009 more briefs were filed, and on January 21, 2010, the Supreme Court issued an opinion in part affirming the matter and remanding it back to the lower court. The court found that it was unconstitutional to ban all free speech by corporations, unions, and other organizations, even as it applied to political campaigns.

Specifically, the court found that the "government may not suppress political speech on the basis of the speaker's corporate identity. No sufficient governmental interest justifies limits on the political speech of nonprofit or for profit corporations." As a result of the ruling, the number of nonprofit organizations applying for tax-exempt status increased dramatically.

Note: You may recall the president's 2010 State of the Union speech, in which he called out the Supreme Court. This was the decision Barack Obama was criticizing the court for. He obviously didn't agree with the ruling because, as we've previously outlined, he desires to silence those who disagree with him.

As a result of the Supreme Court's decision, at least ten powerful Democratic leaders, including Carl Levin and Max Baucus, began pressuring the IRS to harshly scrutinize conservative groups applying for tax-exempt status. Letters from ten high-profile Democrats were sent to then IRS commissioner Doug Shulman pressuring the IRS to investigate nonprofit groups involved in political action, and even threatening legislation to change IRS standards if the IRS didn't act. The IRS was specifically targeting any groups with "tea party" or "patriot" in their name, and any group that was calling for smaller government or less spending.

In August 2012, Shulman testified that there was absolutely no special targeting of conservative groups going on, Saying, "At no time, to the best of my memory, was I ever given the impression that these IRS employees were only looking closely at conservative groups." IRS official Lois Lerner, however, had already apologized for the IRS's targeting of tax-exempt applications by using keywords such as "tea party" or "patriots."

It was later revealed that letters to Shulman from Democrats date from September 2010 through August 2012, and are from Democratic senators such as Max Baucus, Carl Levin, Charles Schumer, Al Franken, and Peter Welch. Senator Levin specifically asked Shulman to look into a dozen groups, including Americans for Prosperity, the 60 Plus Association, Patriot Majority USA, and the Club for Growth.

The Democrats' complaint was that these nonprofit organizations were engaging in political activity, and the Dems argued that a 501(c)(4) was limited to social welfare organizations (groups that provide some sort of social welfare, but heavily favor and support Democrats). However, the Dems' arguments or complaints had no merit. A tax exempt 501(c)(4) is allowed to engage in limited political campaign activities. And it can engage in unlimited lobbying and advocacy on the issues, in effect giving it unlimited ability to raise and spend money on political advertisements. Again, the Democrats wanted to limit the free speech of those with whom they disagree.

The report from the Treasury inspector general for tax administration (TIGTA) indicated that the intense pressure from Democrats likely led to the IRS breaking the rules and caused them to selectively target the conservative groups. Specifically, the IRS developed and used inappropriate criteria to identify nonprofit applications with the words "tea party," "patriots," and "9/12," or groups that had a focus on "government spending," "debt," or "taxes" or said they wanted to "make America a better place to live," or had any statements that "criticize how the country is being run," the report concluded, instead of focusing on all applications with indications of potential political campaign activities.

Note: 9/12 groups are basically tea party groups, only using 9/12 as their name in reference to the day after 9/11.

NOT A SMIDGEN OF CORRUPTION? THE IRS SCANDAL

A nonprofit's focus on "government spending," "debt," "taxes," wanting "to make America a better place to live," or "criticizing how the country is being run" all fall within the social welfare education mission of tax-exempt groups under the law.

In May 2010, the IRS unit responsible for reviewing tax-exempt groups in Cincinnati launched a spreadsheet that would become known inside the IRS as the "Be on the Lookout" (BOLO) computer listing, which included the emerging issue of the tea party applications, the Treasury IG report indicated. In June 2010 the IRS actually began training specialists to be on the lookout for tea party applications.

The IRS officials started the application process by asking the political affiliation of the group's expected speakers and candidates they supported for a list of important issues to the group, its positions on various issues, details about the conversations and discussions the group members had, and other jobs the group's members held outside of the organization, including hours worked. The IRS also demanded these groups fork over lists of names of past and future donors, which would definitely put a major damper on donations. They further requested the applicant's state how they would use the donations and whether their donors have run or would run for public office. Contrary to the fact that by law, applicants for 501(c)(3) and 501(c)(4) do not have to disclose any of this information.

On May 14, 2013, four days after Lois Lerner's admission that conservative groups had in fact been targeted by the IRS, the TIGTA issued a report on the matter to the attorney general, Eric Holder. Holder announces that the FBI would conduct an investigation. The following day acting IRS Commissioner Steven Miller resigned.

It is extremely telling, however, that even though Eric Holder announced the investigation on May 14, 2013, one year later David

O'Neil, the acting deputy US attorney general in charge of overseeing "public integrity" prosecutions testified to Congress and couldn't even answer the simplest of questions about which one of his deputy attorney generals was in charge of the IRS investigation. Congressman Jim Jordan grilled O'Neil, saying that the House had been trying to get answers from Holder as to who is in charge of the IRS and Lois Lerner investigation and how many attorneys were assigned to it.

This in and of itself represents a smoking gun to me about the administration's involvement and complicity in having the IRS target the president's adversaries. One of the top deputy attorney generals in the Holder Justice Department didn't have a clue as to who was in charge of the IRS investigation, and this was a department that O'Neil oversees! How on earth could he not know who's in charge of an investigation that has been ongoing for the past year in a department that he's in charge of? I would submit that he couldn't answer that question because there wasn't any answer, because the Justice Department wasn't actually conducting an investigation because they already knew everything. O'Neil could only answer, "I'm sure that we can provide that information to you," but he didn't know who it was at that time. Keep in mind that, according to Holder, the investigation had begun a whole year earlier. Robert Mueller, then director of the FBI, also testified in 2013 that he didn't have the answers, and couldn't say who was in charge of the IRS investigation. The director of the FBI can't identify who's in charge of the IRS investigation? That simply isn't credible.

We are talking about the IRS, one of the most powerful government agencies in America, and it had been complicit in violating the First Amendment rights of Americans, and our own Justice Department was refusing to ensure that Americans would ever receive that justice. The American people deserve a real investigation that is open, fair, and honest.

It was subsequently announced that Barbara Bosserman, an obvious partisan and Obama contributor, had been assigned as the point person to investigate the IRS and Lois Lerner. Republicans were outraged over the appointment of such a partisan person to investigate such a serious matter. The House has demanded that Holder appoint a special prosecutor, but Holder has refused to do so.

In what we've all become to recognize as Obama's typical "take to the podium response of outrage," Barack Obama took to the podium in May 2013 in response to Lois Lerner's acknowledgment that conservative groups had in fact been targeted, and he vowed to hold the Internal Revenue Service accountable "if reports of political targeting turn out to be the truth." (*Note;* Mr. President, the IRS admitted that they had targeted conservative groups, so what on earth do you mean when you say "if reports of political targeting turn out to be the truth"?)

"If in fact IRS personnel engaged in the kind of practices that have been reported on and were intentionally targeting conservative groups, then that's outrageous. And there's no place for it," Obama told reporters. "And they have to be held fully accountable. Because the IRS as an independent agency requires absolute integrity, and people have to have confidence that they're...applying the laws in a nonpartisan way," Obama added.

Then, the ole' Obama/Holder tag team two-step jumps right into position. The narrative quickly becomes that it was only a couple of rogue IRS agents in the Cincinnati office. None of whom, by the way, have been fired.

That narrative (lie) doesn't hold up to scrutiny, however, in light of a number of facts. To begin with, the letters from at least ten high-level Democratic lawmakers demanding that the IRS target conservative groups came to light. That fact completely eviscerates any argument that this scandal was limited to a few low-level government employees. Let's take a close look at another fact: according to WhiteHouse.gov, records show that during the time period in which the IRS was targeting conservative groups, then IRS Commissioner Douglas Shulman visited the White House 157 times. That number is vastly more than anyone else in the Obama administration visited the White House. In contrast, Shulman's predecessor Mark Everson only visited the White House once during his entire four-year term in the Bush administration. Obama's good friend and comrade in arms Eric Holder logged only sixty-two visits. The administration commented that not all visits are necessarily logged in to the public record, which may skew the numbers of visits by officials; but no matter how you add it up, the IRS was in constant communication with the White House while the IRS targeting was going on. It's inconceivable that the White House didn't have the ear of the IRS about conducting the targeting of conservative groups.

In the latest bombshell, as if this scandal couldn't possibly get any bigger or any worse, in June 2014 the IRS told Congress that the agency had somehow lost two years of Lois Lerner's e-mails between her and the White House! The House Ways and Means Committee released a statement saying that the IRS informed members that they lost Lerner's e-mails from January 2009 through April 2011; "due to a supposed computer crash, the agency only has Lerner e-mails to and from other IRS employees during this time frame," the statement read. "The IRS claims it cannot produce e-mails written only to or from Lerner and outside agencies or groups, such as the White House, Treasury, Department of Justice, FEC, or Democrat offices." How convenient!

In response to the IRS's claim of losing Lerner's e-mails, Committee Chairman Rep. Dave Camp (R-MI) said, "The fact that I am just learning about this, over a year into the investigation, is completely unacceptable and now calls into question the credibility of the IRS's response to Congressional inquiries. There needs to be an immediate investigation and forensic audit by Department of Justice as well as the inspector general. Just a short time ago, Commissioner John Koskinen promised to produce all Lerner documents. It appears now that was an empty promise. Frankly, these are the critical years of the targeting of conservative groups that could explain who knew what when, and what, if any, coordination there was between agencies. Instead, because of this loss of documents, we are conveniently left to believe that Lois Lerner acted alone. This failure of the IRS requires the White House, which promised to get to the bottom of this, to do an administration wide search and production of any e-mails to or from Lois Lerner. The administration has repeatedly referred us back to the IRS for production of materials. It is clear that is wholly insufficient when it comes to determining the full scope of the violation of taxpayer rights."

So it looks like our government is above the law. Destroying evidence is a felony, and if the IRS and the White House think that the American people are going to stand for that kind of blatant corruption, I think they are going to be in for a rude awakening.

I would remind you that President Obama took to the podium on May 13, 2013, and proclaimed his outrage. The next day Eric Holder announced an investigation, and on the same day the inspector general released a report confirming the corruption, saying, "IRS standards are inappropriate criteria for targeting conservative groups for the past three years." The following week, on May 22, Lois Lerner refused to testify and pleaded the Fifth. President Obama took to the podium and expressed outrage and promised to get to the bottom of the matter.

A month after President Obama expressed outrage and Attorney General Holder announced an investigation into the IRS corruption, then Director of the FBI Robert Muller looked befuddled when asked in a hearing about the IRS investigation. He was at the hearing to discuss the NSA scandal, so he apparently wasn't prepared to have to answer anything concerning the IRS. He was in the dark when pressed to provide any details of the IRS investigation. Director Mueller was obviously rattled when pressed by Congressman Jim Jordan. "You've had a month now to investigate," Jordan said. "This has been the biggest story in the country and you can't even tell me who the lead investigator is. You can't tell me the actions the inspector general took, which are not typically how investigations are done. You can't tell me if that's appropriate or not. This is not speculation. This is what happened." Mueller repeatedly declined to answer Jordan's questions, saying he couldn't and that he'd have to get back to the lawmakers with the answers. Jorden asked Mueller again, "Can you tell me who the lead investigator is?" Mueller responded, "Off the top of my head, no." Mueller stepped down a few months later.

Fast forward to the Super Bowl in February 2014, and Barack Obama in an interview with Bill O'Reilly proclaims that there isn't a smidgen of corruption in the IRS. This is as the investigation is still "supposedly" ongoing; it's unclear who if anyone is even in charge of the investigation. Lois Lerner, the IRS point person involved, has refused to testify, the inspector general has issued a report of inappropriate conduct. Two years of IRS e-mails have somehow miraculously disappeared, and yet the president can say with a straight face that there isn't a "smidgen of corruption in the IRS." Three months later, Lois Lerner was held in contempt of Congress for refusing to comply with a subpoena duly issued by the Committee on Oversight and Government Reform.

After the attempts to try to blame the scandal on a few low-level government employees in one office didn't hold water, the IRS was able to point to six progressive groups that had been scrutinized as well. The problem with that "six" number is that if there was no concerted effort to target one group or another, you would expect there to be a relatively similar number of groups targeted on both sides of the aisle. The fact, however, is that no fewer than 292 tea party groups were targeted, compared to only six progressive groups that only received some scrutiny (probably because the IRS wasn't sure if they were progressive groups or not). In other words, a whopping 98 percent of all groups that received additional scrutiny were tea party groups.

According to Sarah Swinehart, a spokeswoman for the House Ways and Means Committee, "At this point, the evidence shows us that conservative groups were not only flagged, but targeted and abused by the IRS." In a letter to congressional Democrats, the inspector general also said that 100 percent of all tea party groups seeking special tax status were put under IRS review, while less than a third of progressive groups received any look at all.

According to documents obtained by Judicial Watch, Lois Lerner was key in providing tax information about certain groups to the Federal Election Commission. This information includes tax-exempt applications and supporting information such as articles, correspondences, meeting minutes, questionnaires, and other supporting information that, according to Judicial Watch, is supposed to be confidential.

"Once the IRS assembles a file on a group or individual, that body of information is considered taxpayer information," Chris Farrell, director of research and investigations for Judicial Watch, said in an interview with the Blaze. "The IRS was giving out taxpayer information in these documents." Federal law prohibits the IRS from sharing confidential taxpayer information (including sharing it with other government agencies) under USC Section 6013, Farrell said. Some of the forms the IRS provided the FEC are public, including the tax-exempt application itself. However, Farrell said, supporting information, such as meeting minutes and correspondence, qualifies as confidential taxpayer information, potentially violating the law.

As the scandal continued to unravel, it wasn't just conservative groups that had been targeted by the IRS; conservative donors started sounding the alarms that they had been the targets of IRS audits themselves, part of a wave of mistrust on the part of prominent conservatives responding to a report by the IRS inspector general's office about the IRS scandal.

"It makes you wonder," said Charlie Moncrief, a Texas oil executive who raised more than a million dollars for Mitt Romney's 2012 presidential bid. "You just don't know. But given what's out there now, you have to ask the question."

Frank VanderSloot, an Idaho businessman who donated more than a million dollars to groups supporting Romney, told ABC News he believes he may have been targeted for an audit after his opposition to the Obama administration. So did Hal Scherz, a physician who started the group Docs4PatientCare to lobby against President Obama's health care initiative and became a vocal critic of the president on cable news programs. Franklin Graham, the son of evangelist Billy Graham, said he believes his father was a target of unusual IRS scrutiny as well.

The IRS, of course, denies that donors have been targeted. But many conservatives, including me, are extremely skeptical. Cleta Mitchell represents several of the conservative groups that were audited, indicated the following: "I happen to believe there are people inside the IRS who feel emboldened. I've heard of several instances of donors to conservative causes who were audited. We need to find out if this is just random or if it's more than that." Mitchell went on to say that she was hearing from a range of high-profile Republicans who want to know if their politics motivated the government's decision to audit them.

If there is nothing to hide, why is the IRS missing at least two years of Lois Lerner's e-mails to and from the White House, as well as the e-mails of at least six other high-level IRS staffers? And now the IRS conveniently tells us that these specific hard drives had crashed and were then destroyed.

House Ways and Means Chairman Dave Camp (R-MI) accused the IRS of "lying" to the American people and attempting to hide the disappearance of two years of e-mails from Lois Lerner, former head of the agency's tax-exempt division. "It looks like the American people were lied to and the IRS tried to cover up the fact it conveniently lost key documents in this investigation," Camp and Rep. Charles Boustany, (R-LA), chairman of the Oversight Subcommittee, said in a joint statement. "The White House promised full cooperation, the IRS commissioner promised full access to Lois Lerner e-mails, and now the agency claims it cannot produce those materials and they've known for months they couldn't do this." Camp went on to call for an independent prosecutor, saying "plot lines in Hollywood are more believable than what we are getting from this White House and the IRS."

On June 20, 2014, Rep. Paul Ryan (R-WI) dueled it out with IRS Commissioner John Koskinen in what CNN called a "knife fight" of a congressional hearing. Koskinen caused an uproar from Republicans by admitting the IRS destroyed a key hard drive wanted in an investigation, and he did not apologize for the data loss. Koskinen went on to tell Congress, "I don't think an apology is owed; not a single e-mail has been lost since the start of this investigation," Koskinen told a dais full of skeptical GOP members. Paul Ryan told the IRS commissioner, "No one believes you. I don't believe you." Dave Camp added, "The American people have no reason to trust the IRS...on this issue."

Koskinen, who was defensive at times, responded to Ryan's accusations that he has been in public service for a long time, "and that is the first time anybody has said they do not believe me." Ryan repeated, "I don't believe you."

Well, Congressman Ryan, neither do I, and I don't think that any of the American public that are actually paying attention to this huge scandal find Koskinen believable either. It is a disgrace of epic proportions, and there isn't a court in the land that would believe it or accept it either.

US District Judge Emmet G Sullivan gave the IRS thirty days to file a declaration by an "appropriate official" to address the computer issues with ex-official Lois Lerner. The decision came on July 10th, 2014 as part of a Freedom of Information Act lawsuit by the watchdog group Judicial Watch, which has continued to question along with GOP lawmakers on Capitol Hill on how the IRS could have possibly lost the emails and in some cases had no apparent way to retrieve them.

"In our view, there has been a cover-up that has been going on," expressed Judicial Watch President Tom Fitton. "The Department of Justice, the IRS, had an obligation, an absolute obligation...to alert the court and alert Judicial Watch as soon as they knew when these records were supposedly lost."

Judge Sullivan indicated during the court hearing, that he wanted the portion of the declaration on the computer issues to be wide-ranging, saying "that's about as broad as I can make it." Of course the IRS attorney Geoffrey Klimas argued that any further discovery in this case might impede the IG's (Inspector General) investigation. Sullivan seemed leery of that argument and also asked that the IRS official speak to that subject in the explanation the agency submits. Sullivan further ordered that the IRS official explain how Lerner's files may be recovered through "other sources."

In typical Obama administration fashion, they avoid all responsibility under the cover of proclaiming on "ongoing investigation". The 'ole Obama Holder tag-team two step.

There is a growing sentiment out there that the whole point of the IRS targeting of conservative groups is to scare the hell out of their individual donors and to have conservative groups and their supporters embroiled in being harassed by the IRS to stifle their grassroots efforts to rally their members to get out the vote. There isn't any question that the IRS was very successful in pulling that objective off in the 2012 presidential elections.

We need to also keep in mind that whenever an individual or a business donates money to a candidate or a political party or a political group, that information is disclosed and can easily be discovered with a simple Internet search. This would make it very simple for a party or administration or government agency to find out who their political adversaries are and target them.

I can speak on this topic firsthand. I too went through a grueling IRS audit shortly after Barack Obama came into office. I've always donated to conservative candidates and groups. I also used to write a business column for a local business journal publication. My column more times than not advanced a conservative viewpoint, and while Barack Obama was campaigning against John McCain, I was very critical of Obama's relationship with Jeremiah Wright and Bill Ayers. At one point during 2009, I found myself undergoing a horrific IRS audit that lasted the better part of two years. Incidentally, I recall the auditor mentioning that she had read my column, and she even inquired where I accounted for any income I received for writing the column. I thought it was an extremely odd comment, seeing as how I was being audited for a three-year period in which my various businesses collectively had upward of $100 million of revenue run through them. In any event, I didn't give it another thought until after the revelations about the IRS scandal came to light.

It's certainly bad enough going through any type of an audit, especially an IRS audit. Going through an audit is one thing, but when the person auditing you has an agenda, compounded with the fact that he or she is less than competent enough to be looking at any type of a complicated return, as mine was, that only adds insult to injury. At first I didn't give it much consideration. I had been through an audit about ten years prior to that and came out fine. But about a year into the audit, it became painfully obvious that not only was the auditor incompetent, she was out to make a name for herself on my back.

About two years after my audit began, I received a letter from the IRS indicating that I owed them $987,000 in back taxes. Needless to say, I nearly had a stroke. I immediately spoke with my accountant, who was a close friend and had been my certified public accountant for the previous twenty-five years. He not only agreed that the auditor was wrong, but he was also as confident as I was that I didn't owe a single penny in taxes. The problem, however, was that I had only a few days in which to file an appeal, and my CPA said that I really needed to hire a tax attorney to do the appeal for me. By that time I was about $100,000 into the costs I'd already incurred in the two-year period. Now I had to hire a tax attorney. Fortunately I knew a tax attorney that I had some confidence in, and he filed the appeal for me a few days later. The one good thing is that when you file an appeal, your case gets kicked up to a more senior and more experienced auditor.

We battled the appeal out for another year, so I was three years into something that threatened to really cause me a lot of damages, not to mention the fact that by this time I was pushing over $150,000 in incurred costs. In any event, at the conclusion of the audit; it turned out that I had slightly overpaid my taxes in each of the three years they had audited. The IRS wrote me three checks that totaled about $62,000 collectively. I'll tell you, what scares the hell out of me with that experience is, what if I hadn't had the wherewithal to be able to afford paying my CPA, not to mention my in-house bookkeeper, or if I hadn't been able to hire a skilled tax attorney? The IRS would have attacked whatever assets they could get ahold of. It's worth also pointing out that their mistake was much greater than $1 million; in order for me to have owed $1 million in taxes, I would have had to underreport my income by somewhere between $3 million and $4 million. That's a pretty monumental mistake, and a glaring example of government incompetence.

When our government takes the power that "we the people" have entrusted to it and uses that power against us because of our political beliefs, and for standing on our principles, that is a real travesty of justice. When I grew up, I remember learning the importance of being involved in the world around me and respectfully stating my opinions on the things that are important to me. That is not just our right as American citizens, it is our responsibility! The thought that any political party would use the power of the government against its own people should be very alarming to everyone from all parties. I think it's much more than just a travesty; it's immoral and criminal! Those responsible have not only not been fired; our government has refused to disclose the details of who, what, when, and where. We must demand accountability of our government.

I would end this chapter with this thought:

"He has, acting personally and through his subordinates and agents, endeavored to cause, in violation of the constitutional rights of citizens, income tax audits or other income tax investigations to be initiated or conducted in a discriminatory manner."

That is from the article of impeachment against disgraced former President Richard Nixon. Nixon was impeached for doing precisely the same thing that it appears the Obama administration is guilty of.

I would add that Nixon was missing only eighteen minutes of his Oval Office White House tapes, eighteen minutes from his entire presidency that led to his resignation. The IRS is now missing more than two years of e-mails from Lois Lerner and at least six other cohorts involved in the scandal. Destroying evidence is a felony, and someone must be held accountable. Richard Nixon said after his impeachment, that if he'd only took those tapes out into the White House lawn and burned them, he would have finished his term in the White House. He was probably right about that, and it appears that the Obama Administration has heeded Nixon's lesson.

One more thought: The IRS is the government agency tasked with controlling Obamacare. That is really scary when one mega-government agency controls not only our finances, but now our health care. The IRS and its employees, have already proved that they are accountable to no one, not congress, and certainly not the American people. And we're supposed to trust that no special preference will be given in the IRS doling out health care based on who votes one way or another? I wouldn't be so naïve. This is a systemic problem that must be resolved, regardless of which party is in power, no one government agency should ever have such an enormous amount of power over a society. The IRS would soon be more powerful than all three branches of government. The temptation for corruption in that kind of system is too overwhelming, and Americans should never let the IRS, or any other government organization for that matter, control that much of their lives.

CHAPTER FIFTEEN

What Difference Does It Make?
The Benghazi Scandal

"They who would give up essential Liberty, to purchase a little temporary Safety, deserve neither Liberty nor Safety." —Benjamin Franklin, 1755

Those words should go without saying, yet President Obama and his comrades at arms pushed a false narrative on the American public in their run-up for President Obama's reelection in 2012: that America was safe because the terrorists were on the run and Osama bin Laden was dead. That ruse of safety was temporary at best and came at the cost of life and liberty of four brave Americans who died in Benghazi. It was that same false sense of security that President Obama proclaimed when he claimed victory in Iraq and evacuated our troops. That ruse came at the grave cost of forty-five hundred Americans' "lives and liberty" and squandered a trillion dollars of American treasure in bringing liberty to the heart of the Middle East.

On September 11, 2012, the eleven-year anniversary of the 9/11 attacks on our homeland, Al-Qaeda affiliated-terrorists attacked our US Consulate in Benghazi, Libya. This tragic event was just a few weeks before the 2012 presidential elections, and just weeks after the Democratic National Convention, where Obama and his fellow Democrats had been touting the narrative that Al-Qaeda was on their heels, against the ropes, and on the run. The Benghazi terrorist attacks in Libya smacked directly in the face of that narrative. Obama changed his tag team partner for this scandal from Eric Holder to Hillary Clinton. The Obama–Clinton tag team two step went into full dance mode.

According to accounts from congressional investigators and the State Department's Accountability Review Board, the Benghazi attacks came in three waves spread out over at least eight hours at two separate locations. There was a fairly lengthy pause between the first and second assaults. Around 9:40 p.m. (Libyan time) a few attackers scaled the wall of the diplomatic post and opened the front gate, allowing dozens of armed men in. Local Libyan security guards fled. Ambassador Stevens and Sean Smith, a State Department communications specialist, made it to a fortified "safe room" in the main building of the compound. The terrorist attackers set the building and furniture on fire using diesel fuel. Stevens and Smith were overcome by blinding, choking smoke that prevented any security officers from reaching them. Libyan civilians found Stevens in the wreckage hours later and took him to a hospital, where he and Smith both died of smoke inhalation. Stevens was the first US ambassador to be killed in the line of duty in more than thirty years.

A security team from the CIA annex about a mile away arrived about twenty-five minutes into the attack but were armed with only rifles and handguns. The US personnel fled with Smith's body back to the annex in armored vehicles. Hours after the attack on the consulate ended, the terrorists reengaged back at the CIA annex. The annex was twice targeted early the next morning with mortar fire. The second round of mortar fire killed Tyrone Woods and Glen Doherty, two CIA security contractors who were defending the annex from the rooftop. A team of six security officials summoned from Tripoli and a Libyan military unit helped evacuate the remaining US personnel on the site to the airport and out of Benghazi.

When the dust settled, Ambassador Chris Stevens, State Department communications officer Sean Smith, and CIA security contractors Tyrone Woods and Glen Doherty were all four killed in the terrorist attacks.

At the end of the day, we were woefully ill prepared, no military assistance was ordered to help our Americans who were under attack, and the Obama–Clinton tag team two step made every effort to cover up their incompetence and lack of leadership.

In a Senate hearing, Secretary of State Hillary Clinton was questioned by Senator Ron Johnson (R-WI) about why the State Department didn't quickly call the evacuees and people on the ground and ask them whether or not there had been any protesters outside the compound before she started repeating the story that it was because of protesters and an Internet video. "With all due respect, the fact is we had four dead Americans," Clinton said with evident exasperation. "Was it because of a protest or was it because of guys out for a walk one night who decided that they'd go kill some Americans? What difference, at this point, does it make? It is our job to figure out what happened and prevent it from ever happening again, Senator."

What difference does it really make? Really? This happened on your watch, Mrs. Clinton; it was your policies and your lack of leadership that allowed this to happen, and the American public deserves some real answers and not your ranting rhetoric about what difference it makes! I would say it makes all the ever-loving difference in the world. The difference between protesters going out for a stroll one night and getting out of control or a deliberate, concentrated, and military-style terrorist attack amounts to the same difference as whether nineteen terrorists coordinated the hijacking of four airliners and crashed them into Twin Towers, or whether we simply blame that terrorist attack on pilot error!

Can you imagine George W. Bush being questioned after the attacks on the World Trade Center and saying it didn't make any difference whether it was terrorists or pilot error or mechanical failure? Refusing to admit that our country had just been attacked by terrorists, Hillary Clinton said, "What difference does it make?" I have little doubt that her arrogant and brash statement while testifying to the Senate will haunt her in any efforts to further her political career. And rightfully so.

The Benghazi attacks were an all-around blunder by the Obama administration and the State Department and amount to nothing less than dereliction of duty by both President Barack Obama and Secretary of State Hillary Clinton. You may recall Hillary Clinton's campaign commercial when she ran against Barack Obama during the 2008 Democratic primaries; the commercial pondered who you'd rather get the 3:00 a.m. phone call, Hillary Clinton or Obama (basically saying that she had the experience and Obama didn't, so who would the voters prefer get the emergency phone call in the middle of the night). Well, I guess we all know the answer to that question: both Hillary Clinton and Barack Obama received that phone call when our consulate and brave Americans were under attack and seeking leadership and help! As we all know now, that call for leadership and help, fell on deaf ears. What did Clinton and Obama do? They went back to bed. Clinton, however, was sure to send out a tweet before she went to bed to set the false narrative in motion that the attacks were nothing more than some protesters out for a stroll and angry over some stupid

Internet video. The next morning, what does our commander in chief do? He takes Air Force One to Las Vegas to attend a fund raiser.

The attacks on Benghazi represent a glaring insight into the complete and total incompetence, corruption, and lack of leadership at the very highest levels of our government. The attack itself is without question a travesty that cost the lives of our ambassador and three other brave Americans. But the Benghazi scandal is so much worse than simply a tragic event. The lead-up to the event and the complete lack of security or readiness to defend proves nothing short of how completely naïve and incompetent both Secretary Clinton and Barack Obama are. The actual event and lack of any response proves just how inept both Clinton and Obama are and highlights the fact that they have absolutely zero leadership ability in their character, and, even worse yet, it proves that they would jeopardize American lives for political purposes. The ensuing cover-up proves just how completely corrupt both Clinton and Obama really are.

So, why the cover-up, you ask? Simple: politics. Let's begin with the fact that the date of the attacks was just a few short weeks before the 2012 presidential elections. The Obama–Clinton lead-from-behind doctrine was at first touted as a huge success. The action in Libya a few years earlier did allow for the overthrow of Libyan dictator Gadhafi, but what the Obama–Clinton tag team failed to ever acknowledge is that the lack of any leadership or direction on the ground led to an all-out civil war and a vacuum for terrorists to come funneling into Libya. This in and of itself was proof positive that their lead-from-behind doctrine was a complete failure. The administration's narrative at the Democratic convention was that Libya was a success and the era of terrorists was quickly becoming a nonissue. If terrorists were able to launch a military-style attack on our consulate and kill our ambassador and other US personnel, it was proof positive that the Obama–Clinton policies were an utter failure. But if, on the other hand, it was only some protesters getting out of control over a stupid Internet YouTube video, well, who could be responsible for that? So that is the narrative they ran with. It didn't even have to be Obama's idea, and it probably wasn't.

Clinton had every bit as much to lose as Obama did, and she was the first one to put the Internet video narrative out there. The Libyan consulate was under the control of her department of government, the State Department. It's no secret that Hillary Clinton has had aspirations of running for president in 2016. The failures in Benghazi would expose her failed policies and lack of leadership, so the false narrative of the attacks being nothing more than protesters gone out of control over a video was contrived. I have little doubt that Obama told Hillary, "That's a great idea, yes, let's blame it on some protesters and a video. We have the media on our side, and the truth would certainly cost me the election and ruin your chances in four years." So away they went, both of them speaking in unity for weeks. Another fine example of the Obama tag team two step to avoid any accountability for him or his administration, and Hillary Clinton was all too happy to be his dance partner on Benghazi.

Government e-mails showed that the White House and the State Department were both told even as the attack was going on that Ansar al-Sharia, a terrorist group with ties to Al-Qaeda, had already claimed responsibility for the terrorist attacks. Not to mention that the White House and the State Department were watching the attacks unfold in real time via video surveillance at the consulate as well as from drones overhead. There was no doubt in anyone's mind that the assault was a coordinated military-style attack and that there were absolutely no protesters anywhere around the Benghazi consulate at any time prior to or during the attacks.

Libyan President Mohamed Magariaf insisted on September 16, five days after the attack, that it was a preplanned terrorist attack, but yet both Obama and Clinton continued to spread the false narrative of a protest gone-bad. Magariaf said the idea of the attack being a spontaneous protest that just spun out of control is completely unfounded and preposterous. President Obama continued to spread his narrative even on the David Letterman show on September 18, a full week after the attack, and then again on September 24, when he was on *The View*, even though Matt Olsen, director of the National Counterterrorism Center, was the first Obama administration official to finally admit that it was a terrorist attack on September 19 in a congressional hearing, and even Hillary Clinton finally admitted it was a terrorist attack on September 20. Obviously Obama didn't get the memo, because, as I said, he was still blaming it on a spontaneous protest gone-bad over an anti-Muslim video posted on the Internet.

You may recall President Obama's later assertion that he called it a terrorist attack from the beginning, the day after the attack, when he addressed the situation from the White House Rose Garden. He did not call it a terrorist attack; what he said was, "No acts of terror will ever shake the resolve of this great nation, alter that character, or eclipse the light of the values that we stand for." He then made reference to the anti-Muslim video when he said, "Since our founding, the United States has been a nation that respects all faiths. We reject all efforts to denigrate the religious beliefs of others. But there is absolutely no justification to this type of senseless violence. None."

After his Rose Garden speech, Obama taped an interview for *60 Minutes* with Steve Kroft, the show's host.

Kroft: Mr. President, this morning you went out of your way to avoid the use of the word *terrorism* in connection with the Libya attack.

Obama: Right.

Kroft: Do you believe that this was a terrorist attack?

Obama: Well, it's too early to know exactly how this came about, what group was involved, but obviously it was an attack on Americans, and we are going to be working with the Libyan government to make sure that we bring these folks to justice one way or the other.

Kroft: It's been described as a mob action. But there are reports that they were very heavily armed with grenades. That doesn't sound like your normal demonstration.

Obama: As I said, we're still investigating exactly what happened. I don't want to jump the gun on this. But you're right that this is not a situation that was exactly the same as what happened in Egypt. And my suspicion is, is that there are folks involved in this who were looking to target Americans from the start.

In any event, President Obama did not call it a terrorist attack and didn't even come close to finally admitting it was a terrorist attack for the better part of two weeks. The following Sunday, then National Security Advisor Susan Rice was sent out to make the rounds on all the Sunday morning news programs. Rice continued to spread the Obama–Clinton narrative of a protest gone bad all because of an anti-Muslim Internet video.

We know why Obama and Clinton tried to change the narrative and mislead the country. The next question is twofold: Why were we still in Benghazi when all other countries had left because of the deteriorating security, and why were we so completely ill prepared?

In the at least nine months prior to the Benghazi terrorist attacks, there had been an obvious deterioration in security, including numerous thwarted terror plots, beginning back in December 2011. In March 2012 the US Embassy in Tripoli's lead security officer, Regional Security Officer Eric Nordstrom, requested additional security but later testified that he received no response from the State Department. In April 2012 an explosive device was thrown at a convoy carrying UN Envoy Ian Martin. In May 2012 a rocket-propelled grenade hit the offices of the International Red Cross. In June an improvised explosive device exploded outside the Benghazi consulate compound; also in June a rocket-propelled grenade hit a convey carrying the British ambassador, resulting in the United Kingdom closing its consulate. Col. Wood, military Site Security Team (SST) commander, was in Benghazi and helped with emergency response. In July RSO Nordstrom again requested additional security, perhaps in a cable signed by Ambassador Stevens and dated July 9, 2012. Also in July Ambassador Stevens sent a cable requesting continued help from military SST and State Department MSD (the Mobile Security Deployment team) through mid-September 2012, saying that benchmarks for a drawdown had not been met. The teams were not extended to help the deteriorating security situation.

Before his death, Ambassador Stevens warned of the "violent" Libyan landscape, and no additional security was provided by the State Department. In early August, the State Department removed the last of three, six-man State Department security teams and a sixteen-man military assault team (SST) from Libya. Also in August Ambassador Stevens sent a cable to DC requesting "protective detail bodyguard positions," saying the added guards "will fill the vacuum of security personnel currently at post...who will be leaving with the next month and will not be replaced." He called the security condition in Libya "unpredictable, volatile, and violent." In another August cable from Ambassador Stevens to DC, he says "a series of violent incidents has dominated the political landscape" and calls them "targeted and discriminate attacks." On August 27, 2012, just two weeks before the terrorist attacks on our consulate, the State Department issued a travel warning for Libya, citing the threat of assassination and car bombings in Benghazi and Tripoli. On September 10, 2012, the day prior to the attacks, the CIA delivered to the State Department a warning of a possible imminent attack in Libya.

The facts are no longer in question that the State Department is where the protesters and video narrative originated. Further, the CIA's talking points to the State Department adamantly asserted that the attacks in Benghazi were in fact a preplanned terrorist attack and that it had absolutely nothing to do with any protest or video. The State Department took it upon themselves to change the talking points to fit their political narrative. They then fed those talking points to Susan Rice and led her off to the Sunday morning news shows to perpetuate that lie on the American people. It was very suspicious to begin with that Susan Rice, a national security advisor who had no real knowledge of the events that transpired, would be the one to sell this to the public. The entire Benghazi scandal belonged to the State Department, with the White House as a coconspirator. No, Hillary Clinton should have been the one telling the American people what happened; I mean, she is the head of the State Department, and this was an extremely significant event, and it happened on her watch. But she was too slick a politician to put herself in that situation, where she might have had to answer any hard questions. So, Hillary Clinton, knowing this was a lie that might backfire and ruin her political future, sent out Susan Rice as the sacrificial lamb.

It is also worth pointing out that in the ensuing investigation; Thomas Pickering, the former UN ambassador who, along with former Joint Chiefs of Staff Chairman Admiral Mike Mullen, prepared the Accountability Review Board report on the State Department's handling of the Benghazi attacks, says he didn't think it was necessary to interview former Secretary of State Hillary Clinton "because in fact we knew where the responsibility rested." Really? Are you kidding me? We still don't know the complete story; no doubt we do now know that the responsibility lies at the feet of Hillary Clinton and Barack Obama.

Hillary Clinton was the person in charge of the State Department, the first person to perpetrate the protest-because-of-a-video narrative, and the person responsible for the security for Benghazi personnel prior to and during the attacks—but she doesn't need to be investigated, because "we knew where the responsibility rested." That is a ridiculous statement! How on earth could you possibly have a fair investigation without interviewing the person in charge? Clinton did give a brief testimony to Congress about the matter, when she famously said, "What difference does it make?" But if you watch that testimony, she never answered any questions. If you are aware of how congressional hearings go, the Democrats never asked Clinton any questions and only defended her and gave flattering comments about how great she is; meanwhile, the Republicans, who were asking the tough questions, were all limited to a minimal amount of time, and Clinton was allowed to eat up that time by completely dancing around and skirting the issue so that no question ever really got answered.

The Obama–Clinton tag team "cover-up" that pushed the false narrative that the attacks were nothing more than a protest gone awry because of an anti-Muslim Internet video would soon be completely debunked. Unfortunately, however, the truth would not come to light nearly soon enough. Barack Obama was given a pass by the so-called mainstream media, and the majority of the American public turned a blind eye to the scandal and reelected Obama to a second term. Since then, irrefutable evidence has surfaced that clearly proves that Barack Obama and Hillary Clinton knew almost immediately that the attack in Benghazi was not because of any protesters and had absolutely nothing to do with any video.

In June 2014, Fox News Channel's Bret Baier interviewed retired US Air Force Major Eric Stahl, who served as commander and pilot of the C-17 aircraft that was used to transport the corpses of the four casualties from the Benghazi attacks as well as evacuate the surviving

CIA staff members who fled the CIA annex. Stahl said that as soon as they landed at a US military base in Ramstein, Germany, the survivors of the attacks were taken away from the airplane by a senior State Department diplomat, US Ambassador to Germany Philip Murphy, so he could debrief them that evening. This is important because they weren't first debriefed by the FBI or the CIA, which might have been able to conduct a non-biased investigation; instead, the State Department had a huge conflict of interest in conducting the initial interviews, and lacked the ability to be impartial. The State Department conducting the initial interviews and being involved in conducting the investigation in the Benghazi scandal, would amount to the same thing as the Russian Government investigating the recently shot down commercial air-liner flight 17 over Ukraine; which the Russians of course were complicate in shooting down. Just as, the State Department was complicate in the deaths of the four Americans in Benghazi.

Here is another smoking gun that proves that both Barack Obama and Hillary Clinton lied to the American people: Major Stahl told Bret Baier that the passengers he evacuated told him directly that it was a terrorist attack, and they knew that immediately because the terrorists who killed Ambassador Stevens and Sean Smith at the consulate or mission facility had taken some State Department cell phones and were in communication with their higher ups using these cell phones, and the CIA staff, while back at the annex, were able to track and listen to their phone calls in real time. In other words, the CIA and the State Department knew immediately who the terrorists were because of those cell phone calls.

Major Stahl also mentioned that the following morning (September 13), he had the opportunity to talk to all of the passengers he had evacuated, and everyone was confused by the false narrative being promoted by Obama and Clinton. They all indicated to Stahl that there was no protest, and that no video had anything to do with the attacks.

There was no question in any of these CIA staffers' minds about what had happened and the fact that it was a coordinated terrorist attack.

One other point: Major Stahl contended that given his crew's alert status and location, they could have reached Benghazi in time to have played a role in rescuing the victims of the assault and ferrying them to safety in Germany had they been asked to do so. "You would've thought that we would have had a little bit more of an alert posture on 9/11," Stahl added. "A hurried-up timeline probably would take us an hour and a half to get off the ground and three hours and fifteen minutes to get down there. So we could've gone down there and gotten them easily."

The US State Department monitored the attack on the US consulate in Benghazi, Libya, "in almost real time," according to Charlene Lamb, deputy assistant secretary of state for international programs in the Bureau of Diplomatic Security. "A security agent activated a danger-notification system as the attack began, shortly before 10:00 p.m. local time on September 11." "From that point on, I could follow what was happening in almost real time," Lamb said in written testimony prepared for a hearing by the House Oversight and Government Reform Committee, which has been investigating the attack and whether security was adequate. State Department officials said during the hearing that they had never concluded the attack grew out of a protest over a video.

On May 8, 2013, the House Committee on Oversight and Government Reform on Capitol Hill held hearings to investigate the events and response to the Benghazi attacks. Former Acting Deputy Assistant Secretary of State for Counterterrorism Mark Thompson, Foreign Deputy Chief of Mission in Libya Gregory Hicks, and Diplomatic Security Officer and former US State Department Regional Security Officer in Libya Eric Nordstrom testified to lawmakers about the events on the ground during the attack and the political firestorm that ensued after the attacks. Both Hicks and Nordstrom have been identified as "whistle blowers," as their testimony greatly differs from that of the White House and the State Department. This testimony provided perhaps the most detailed public record of what, from their perspectives, happened on the night of September 11, and what might have been done differently.

Hicks recalled Ambassador Stevens telling him "we're under attack" in Benghazi before being cut off. CBS News's Sharyl Attkisson reported more details from Hicks's private testimony in which he claimed a team of Special Forces troops that was prepared to fly from Tripoli to Benghazi during the attacks was forbidden from doing so by US Special Operations Command Africa.

Hicks told congressional investigators that if the United States had quickly sent a military aircraft over Benghazi, it might have saved American lives. The US Souda Bay Naval Base is an hour's flight from Libya. "I think everybody in the mission thought it was a terrorist attack from the beginning," Hicks said. Hicks was the last person to speak with Ambassador Stevens, and Hicks drove his point home that it was no protest by saying, "Chris's last report, if you want to say his final report, is, 'Greg, we are under attack.' "

Gregory Hicks was asked about Susan Rice's appearance on the five Sunday morning news shows and her pushing the administration's narrative that the Benghazi attacks weren't a terrorist attack, but rather some protests gone awry over an Internet video. Hicks replied: "I've never been as embarrassed in my life, in my career, as on that day." Hicks continued in his interview, "The net impact of what has transpired is, Rice, the spokesperson of the most powerful country in the world, has basically said that the president of Libya is either a liar or doesn't know what he's talking about...My jaw hit the floor as I watched this," referring to Susan Rice's assertions. "I have heard from a friend who had dinner with Libyan President Magarif in New York City that he was still angry at Susan Rice well after the incident," Hicks added.

According to Stephen Hays with the *Weekly Standard*, "CIA director David Petraeus was surprised when he read the freshly rewritten talking points an aide had e-mailed him in the early afternoon of Saturday, September 15, 2012; one day earlier, analysts with the CIA's Office of Terrorism Analysis had drafted a set of unclassified talking points policy makers could use to discuss the attacks in Benghazi, Libya. But this new version, produced with input from senior Obama administration policy makers, was a shadow of the original. The original CIA talking points had been blunt: the assault on the US facilities in Benghazi was a terrorist attack conducted by a large group of Islamic extremists, including some with ties to Al-Qaeda."

These were strong claims. The CIA usually qualifies its assessments, providing policy makers a sense of whether the conclusions of its analysis are offered with "high confidence," "moderate confidence," or "low confidence." The first draft signaled confidence, even certainty: "We do know that Islamic extremists with ties to Al-Qaeda participated in the attack."

There was very good reason for this conviction. Within twenty-four hours of the attack, the US government had intercepted communications between two Al-Qaeda-linked terrorists discussing the attacks in Benghazi. One of the jihadists, a member of Ansar al Sharia, reported to the other that he had participated in the assault on the US diplomatic post. Solid evidence. And there was more. Later that same day, the CIA station chief in Libya had sent a memo back to Washington reporting that eyewitnesses to the attack said the participants were known jihadists, with ties to Al-Qaeda.

So the questions that can't be avoided, but have yet to be answered: Why wasn't there much more security as was requested by Ambassador Stevens, and why weren't there military assets in very close proximity, especially given the fact that the CIA issued a warning of a possible attack just the day prior to 9/11, not to mention the obvious fact that 9/11 was the eleven-year anniversary of the 2001 attacks on the US mainland. Hillary Clinton owes the American people an answer to those very simple, but important questions.

It is worth discussing a very real possibility as to why we had a CIA annex and an ambassador at our consulate while there was such violent unrest in Benghazi. When Hillary Clinton testified to the Senate, Sen. Rand Paul asked her about the claims during past hearings over the Benghazi affair if the reason we were in Benghazi had anything to do with reports that had been surfacing about the United States running guns in the region. Paul asked Clinton: "Is the United States involved with any procuring of weapons, transfer of weapons, buying or selling, anyhow transferring weapons to Turkey out of Libya?" Clinton responded: "To Turkey? I will have to take that question for the record. Nobody has ever raised that with me." Paul continued: "It's been in news reports that ships have been leaving from Libya and that may have weapons, and what I'd like to know is, the annex that was close by, were they involved with procuring, buying, selling, obtaining weapons, and were any of these weapons being transferred to other countries, any countries, Turkey included?" Clinton replied: "Well, Senator, you'll have to direct that question to the agency that ran the annex. I will see what information is available." Paul replied: "You're saying you don't know?" Clinton replied: "I don't know. I don't have any information on that."

It's been reported that knowledgeable security sources have reconfirmed the use of the Benghazi mission in aiding the rebels, who are known to be saturated by Al-Qaeda and other Islamic terrorist groups. In November 2012, according to reports, Middle Eastern security sources further described both the US mission and nearby CIA annex in Benghazi as the main intelligence and planning center for US aid to the rebels that were coordinating with Turkey, Saudi Arabia, and Qatar.

It has been further suggested that Ambassador Christopher Stevens played a central role in recruiting jihadists to fight Bashar al-Assad's regime in Syria, according to Egyptian authorities. I'm certainly not criticizing Ambassador Stevens; whatever he was doing, he was obviously doing under orders from his boss, Secretary Clinton. Former Defense Secretary Leon Panetta confirmed in a Senate hearing on Benghazi that he and General Martin Dempsey had supported a plan "that we provide weapons to the resistance in Syria." The White House has been mum on this allegation, and administration officials claim that the White House had rejected the plan to supply arms to the Syrian rebels.

Secretary Clinton's vague answers to Sen. Rand Paul seemed very suspect to me. This could well be another scandal similar to the Iran Contra scandal thirty years ago. You would be very hard pressed to find a more impeachable offense than for the commander in chief to be aiding and abetting an enemy of the United States, such as by providing weapons to vicious militants who have taken up arms against Americans. Fast and Furious was certainly bad enough when the Obama Justice Department provided weapons to Mexican drug cartels. The Benghazi scandal may well be the biggest scandal in American history, rivaling even Watergate and Iran Contra.

The Benghazi facility has often been referred to as an embassy or a consulate. I've even referred to it as such in this book. However, the US government didn't have it identified as either. Rather, it is identified as a "mission." Journalist Aaron Klein has done a considerable amount of reporting on this scandal and suggests that the Benghazi "mission" and CIA annex a few blocks away were used as a staging point to coordinate arms shipments to rebels fighting Assad's forces in Syria, via Turkey. These rebel groups included jihadists, some of whom were Al-Qaeda members among the ranks of the Free Syrian Army and other Syrian opposition groups.

This revelation is contrary to claims from the Obama administration that the United States has supplied only nonlethal aid to the Syrian rebels. According to Klein, his reporting has been confirmed by several major news agencies, including the *New York Times* and *Reuters*. The Obama administration policy of support for the jihadist Libyan and Syrian rebels may have already come back to haunt us in many ways. The United Nations has warned that weapons delivered to Libya during the uprising there are being used to fuel conflicts in Mali, Syria, Gaza, and elsewhere. Besides the questions about the arms used in the coordinated assaults against our facilities in Benghazi and the UN reports on weapons proliferation, there are also claims of ties between the Benghazi attacks and a brazen assault on an Algerian gas complex where foreigners and Americans were employed. This suggests that Ambassador Stevens and the other three Americans killed at the Benghazi mission and CIA annex may well have been killed using weapons that America provided. This may well explain why it took weeks for us to send any US agents in to investigate the site after the attacks.

Now we've identified how and possibly why the Benghazi mission and CIA annex were attacked, and the utter incompetence and the complete lack of readiness or leadership that allowed this tragedy to happen, not to mention the glaring possibility that our government may well have been naively providing weapons to our enemies, thinking that those enemies would use those weapons only to fight enemies we considered worse than the enemies we were arming. The next two

Benghazi scandals that ensued are even worse than the scandal that led up to the attacks.

We've also clearly identified the cover-up of the Obama–Clinton tag team two step, in which both Obama and Clinton perpetuated a ridiculous lie on the American people that the attacks were nothing more than a protest gone-bad that was perpetuated over a stupid anti-Muslim Internet video. The evidence is clear that both the White House and the State Department were watching the events unfold in real time. They knew immediately that there were no protesters in Benghazi and that the attacks were a concentrated, military-style assault. Period. If there is anything that history has taught us about a scandal, it's that the cover-up usually ends up being the biggest part of the scandal, and it's the cover-up that makes the scandal blow up in the face of those who would perpetuate the cover-up. For the life of me, I can't imagine the complete incompetence of an administration that would try to cover up a scandal as big as Benghazi, with a story as ridiculous as the one they peddled upon us. But hey, what the hell do I know; it worked for them just long enough to squeak past the 2012 elections.

Four days after the attacks in Benghazi and a day before Susan Rice made the now infamous Sunday morning news rounds, the CIA chief of staff sent an e-mail to former CIA deputy director Michael Morell and others at the CIA who reported to him that "the attacks were not/not an escalation of protests." This e-mail was obviously sent in response to the false narrative circulating in the press that the attacks started from a protest gone awry. This, combined with the fact that the CIA had already reviewed the closed circuit television video from the mission facility that showed there were no protests prior to the attacks, certainly should have stopped the administration from standing by their false narrative.

After more than a year of the administration's claims that they had turned over any and all documents relative to Benghazi, Judicial

Watch was able to obtain a treasure trove of e-mails from senior White House officials, but only after filing a lawsuit using the Freedom of Information Act (FOIA). In an e-mail from Obama advisor, Ben Rhodes to Susan Rice in which Rhodes preps Rice on the Friday before her Sunday morning media tour, he advises her that her goal is "to underscore that these protests are rooted in an Internet video and not a broader failure of policy." That is unquestionably a "smoking gun" that proves the Obama administration pushed the false narrative for political gain, and, as Rhodes indicated in his e-mail, "not a broader failure of policy." We certainly don't have to look very far around the world today to see just how much of a "broader failure of policy" the Obama administration is responsible for.

There is an old saying that goes back to the Kennedy assassination and probably much longer ago than that: "the bigger the lie, the easier it is to believe." The point is, what reasonable, intelligent person would possibly make up such a ridiculous story if it weren't true? There is a lot of truth to that sentiment; if the lie is so outrageous, it must be true because no one would make such a crazy claim, so the only answer is that it must be true. The protester–video narrative was such a ridiculous lie that just enough of the public gave Obama and Clinton the benefit of the doubt, because who would say something so outrageous unless it's true?

No matter what you understand or believe about the attacks in Benghazi that left our ambassador and three other brave Americans dead, as an American you have got to be completely outraged that President Obama and Secretary Clinton took absolutely zero action to assist, defend, or rescue our Americans under attack. Their argument that they couldn't have gotten there in time to have made a difference is nothing less than a coward's response to their own ineptitude and lack of courage and leadership in a crisis.

Whether we could have gotten there in time or not is completely irrelevant. It's a moot point. The only point worth discussing is the fact that we didn't even try! Obama's claim for trading Sergeant Bergdahl, a defector; for five Taliban leaders was that America has a long-standing tradition that we leave no man behind. I ask you, Mr. President, where was that sentiment when you knew our US ambassador as well as other Americans were under attack, and you did absolutely nothing?

I want you to consider this scenario for just a moment. You are the president of the United States, the commander in chief of the mightiest military force in the world, unquestionably the finest military in all of history. You are watching in real time as Americans serving their country in harm's way come under a heavy military-style assault by well-armed terrorists. I ask you, as commander in chief, how on earth could anyone in that position of authority not immediately order a military response to assist, defend, and rescue our Americans who are in harm's way? That is absolutely unfathomable to me. It is a dereliction of duty as commander in chief!

The administration argues that they couldn't have gotten there in time to have made any difference anyway, so it wouldn't have mattered. First of all, I don't believe that we couldn't have done something to have made some difference and possibly saved some lives. But let's take the Obama administration's position at face value. Maybe knowing what we now know in hindsight, we wouldn't have been able to get there in time. The point is, in order to accept that narrative, you have to accept that they knew in foresight what they may have ultimately discovered in hindsight, and there was no possible way to draw that conclusion from the outset.

No one knew how long the battle would continue! The fact is that the battle went on for at least eight hours, but in foresight neither the president nor anyone else, for that matter, could have possibly had any idea just how long the attacks would last. There are a multitude of real-life, heroic war stories where a very small group of trained soldiers, sailors, airmen, and marines have held off the enemy, sometimes even single handedly, for far more than eight hours. CIA operatives Ty Woods and Glen Doherty weren't just your ordinary CIA agents, either; they were both highly trained navy SEALs, so when you add that to the equation, no one could have possibly been able to accurately assess just how long they might have been able to continue the fight.

Buying into the administration's excuse for not immediately sending a response team in predicates that you accept the narrative that someone happened to have a crystal ball and could somehow see with some clear vision of certainty the precise time that our Americans would die and the fighting would cease. No one could have possibly foreseen any such thing. No one had a crystal ball, and no one had any reasonable idea as to how long the fight would continue. The fact that we didn't immediately launch some sort of effort to assist and defend is extremely troubling to me, and it should be to every American citizen and certainly everyone who has volunteered to serve his or her country.

Secretary of Defense Leon Panetta testified to the Senate that the president "left that up to us." Secretary Panetta said the president was "well informed" about the events and worried about American lives. He and General Dempsey also testified they had no further contact with the president the night of the attack, nor did Secretary of State Hillary Clinton ever communicate with them that evening. Have you noticed that when things get tough or a crisis arises, that President Obama "checks out", and usually falls back into his comfort balloon of campaigning.

Now retired Air Force Brigadier General Robert Lovell, who was a high-ranking officer in the US Africa Command on the night of Benghazi attacks, testified that the US military did not try and was never even ordered to save the Americans under attack at the US diplomatic outpost on September 11, 2012. General Lovell said bluntly when testifying to Congress about the military's response on the night of the Benghazi attack, "The discussion is not in the 'could or could not' in relation to time, space, and capability; the point is, we should have tried." That is pretty telling that our commander in chief isn't completely on point while our Americans are under attack. Nor is Secretary Clinton.

A report from the House Armed Services Committee as well as the State Department's own Accountability Review Board report on the Benghazi incident concluded that no military assets were in place to get US personnel to Benghazi in time. A team from Tripoli did eventually arrive in Benghazi after commandeering an airplane, and for whatever reason they were delayed at the airport, but did finally arrive to evacuate staff personnel at the CIA annex who had not been engaged in the fight. It's worth pointing out that it took six hours just for them to prepare to depart. Not until seventeen hours after Panetta issued any order did the Commanders In-Extremis Force (CIF) finally make it to the staging base in southern Europe. An hour later, one Fleet Antiterrorism Security Team (FAST) platoon arrived in Tripoli. Thirty minutes after that, the Special Ops force from the United States arrived in Europe. It's worth noting that according to the Armed Services report, the FAST platoon was further delayed because they had to stop what they were doing and change out of their military uniforms into civilian clothing because of a supposed request from the Libyan government, which it said apparently feared combat-ready troops would "unduly alarm or inflame Libyans." Do you think things could have been any more inflamed?

You've got to be kidding me. Our military troops that are supposedly on their way to assist Americans in battle are told to stop what they are doing to change out of their military uniforms because we might alarm a few Libyans? I think that there was a political agenda under way, and that the whole idea was for the fight to be over by the time any possible help could arrive. Why, you might ask? Because if it's over, it could then be sold to the American public that it was nothing more than a protest gone awry. If any US military response was issued, that narrative would never fly.

General Lovell, who served as the deputy director for intelligence for Africa Command on the night of the attacks and was in a secure facility monitoring the situation, agreed that military assets were not in place to have gotten to Benghazi in time for the initial attacks. However, he added, "We didn't know how long this would last when we became aware of the distress, nor did we completely understand what we had in front of us, be it a kidnapping, rescue, recovery, protracted hostile engagement, or any or all of the above." He added, "But what we did know quite early on was that this was a hostile action. This was no demonstration gone terribly awry."

Lovell went on to say that the State Department never even asked the military for backup that evening. "Basically, there was a lot of looking to the State Department for what they wanted and the deference to the Libyan people and the sense of deference to the desires of the State Department in terms of what they would like to have," he said when asked why no request was made.

The fact that our commander in chief didn't make every effort to launch an immediate response to help those Americans being attacked has always been the glaring issue to me. No question we were ill prepared, even though every possible sign was out there that our security was not at all up to speed. You can chalk that up to complete and utter incompetence, which anyone who has followed this administration has all too often come to expect. But nothing whatsoever could possibly justify our commander in chief not taking immediate and intentional action to do something. I, like many, have had great difficulty wrapping my head around the assertion that we didn't have any military assets in close enough proximity to Libya to launch any sort of military response to assist those Americans under attack. So, as I began writing this book, I started doing some research as to what military assets might have been available to provide any meaningful assistance. I kept coming back to the conclusion that the excuse the administration made is just simply not credible.

First of all, there were two drones that, according to reports, were flying overhead while the attacks were ongoing and were recording the attacks as they were happening. First one drone, then a second to take its place. Reportedly the drones weren't armed, which I do have serious questions about. I would also question why one of these drones couldn't have been utilized as an offensive weapon even if it weren't armed. Why couldn't it have been crashed into the terrorists? That may have likely caused enough fear and chaos that the attackers may have fled, unsure if or when another might attack. OK, I am admittedly not a military analyst or expert, so maybe that wouldn't have done any good. So then let's look at other viable options.

One question that keeps bothering me is, why weren't we able to respond with a squadron of military fighter jets? There are at least two military bases in very close proximity to Benghazi, Libya: Sigonella, Italy, Naval Air Station is only about 470 miles from Benghazi, and Souda Bay Naval Support Activity Base in Crete, Greece, is a mere 320 miles away from Benghazi. There are two squadrons of F-16 Falcons at Aviona Air Base in Aviano, Italy, which is about a thousand miles from Benghazi and less than an hour's flight for an F-16.

There are literally over two dozen military bases within an hour's flight of Benghazi in an F-16, F-15, F-18, or an F-22 fighter jet. Why wasn't our military, at the very least, ordered to send a squadron of jets to do a flyover, which would have certainly scattered the terrorists? Or why wasn't a squadron of fighter jets sent to either Sigonella or Souda Bay naval stations? Either of those two bases could have been a refueling and forward base to launch an assault. That's assuming that there are no fighter jets at Sigonella or Souda Bay to begin with. I don't think it would be a credible argument that either of those two bases wouldn't have any military assets that could have been used. But if you accept that they do have assets available, it shouldn't take very much time to get them there if an order is given. Worst-case scenario, why not get the fighter jets in the air headed for Crete or Italy, have a game plan worked out by the time they arrive, and launch any offensive from that point?

As I pointed out earlier in this chapter, US Air Force Major Eric Stahl, who piloted the evacuation plane that came from Ramstein Air Force Base in Germany—considerably farther away than a lot of other bases are from Benghazi—indicated that he could have had his C-17 plane in the air from Germany in about an hour and a half and could have arrived in Libya three hours and fifteen minutes later. That is in a plane with a top speed of only 515 miles per hour. In contrast an F-16 Falcon has a top speed of 1,650 miles per hour. US Africa Command (AFRICOM) in Stuttgart, Germany, is even closer to Benghazi than Ramstein Air Base is.

Fox News's Jennifer Griffin and Catherine Herridge should be credited with some incredible investigative journalism on the Benghazi attack. The majority of facts that have come to the surface are because of their efforts to shed some light on this tragedy and scandal. I have relied a great deal on their reporting of facts for this book, and I greatly appreciate their efforts.

General Carter Ham, AFRICOM commander, eventually did send a small response team of twelve Commanders In-Extremis Force troops to a staging area in Sigonella, Italy, but it took them twenty-two hours to get there, and they were never given permission to head to Libya. Defense Secretary Leon Panetta ordered a FAST (Fleet Antiterrorism Security Team) response team to launch from Rota, Spain, to Tripoli the night of the attack on the Benghazi diplomatic mission. However, as previously indicated, the State Department ordered them to deplane and change out of their military uniforms and into civilian clothes before heading to Tripoli, a decision that delayed them from leaving by about ninety minutes, according to senior military officials who briefed Congress. According to Gregory Hicks, once the Special Forces team arrived in Tripoli, the US Special Operations Command Africa refused to authorize them to proceed to Benghazi.

Let's put this in another perspective: During our previous military involvement in Libya, under Obama's lead-from-behind doctrine, the B-2 bomber successfully launched multiple, devastating bombing raids in Libya. The B-2 bomber is kept in my backyard at Whiteman Air Force base just outside of Kansas City, Missouri. The B-2 bomber takes off from Missouri and delivers its "reign of hellfire" anywhere in the world and returns to Missouri without ever landing. The B-2 bomber could fly from here to Benghazi in nine hours, successfully complete its mission, and refuel in air on its way home. I'm not suggesting that the B-2 bomber should have been deployed to Benghazi on September 11, 2012; I'm merely pointing out that we have over two dozen military bases within an hour's flight of Benghazi by jet, far closer than Whiteman Air Force Base is, and Whitman air base is smack dab in the middle of the United States. I would also point out that as incredible an aircraft as the B-2 bomber is, it's much slower than an F-16 or any other comparable fighter jet. In fact an F-16 easily travels twice the speed of the B-2 bomber. The US military has a number of fighter jet squadrons on several bases throughout Europe that could have responded and at the very least conducted a "fast mover" (flyby), which has been used many times in various battles to scare the enemy off.

We may not have been able to save Ambassador Stevens or Sean Smith, but let's not forget that the two CIA operatives and former navy SEALs held the fight for at least eight hours before they were finally overcome by the terrorists. Even a couple of F-16 flyovers may have been enough to make a difference. The point is, we will never know, because we didn't even try!

I would further point out that Ambassador Stevens's body remained missing for eleven hours after the fight began. Former navy SEAL and CIA operative Tyrone Woods was critically wounded during the last mortar attack on the annex, but, according to eyewitnesses at the scene, Woods didn't die right away, but rather bled out over the course of a couple of hours. My point is, again, no one had a crystal ball; no one knew how long the fight would last. No one even knew for sure that Ambassador Stevens had been dead for eleven hours and Tyrone Woods lay bleeding to death for two hours after the last mortar attack ended. That was ten hours after the attack began.

In response to another Freedom of Information Act (FIOA) request from Judicial Watch inquiring about all military assets in any proximity to Benghazi on September 11, 2012, that could have been used to counter the assaults on our facilities and our brave Americans, the navy released a letter revealing that multiple air and naval assets were in the region preceding the deadly attack. "The US military had a multitude of forces in the region surrounding Libya when terrorists attacked the Special Mission in Benghazi and murdered four Americans," according to an unclassified navy map secured by Judicial Watch.

Dozens of vessels were stationed in the region on that day, including two aircraft carriers (*Dwight D. Eisenhower* and *Enterprise*), four amphibious ships, thirteen destroyers, three cruisers, and more than a dozen other smaller navy boats as well as a command ship, the report indicated.

Retired Air Force LTC Randall R. Schmidt, who is investigating the military's response to that terrorist event, insisted that "destroyers could have responded to the attack." He added that unmanned aerial vehicles and manned aircraft were also in the region. "The point is there were enough forces to respond," Schmidt told Judicial Watch.

Regardless of whether you do or don't buy the narrative that we didn't have any military assets in the region that could have responded, the point is that we made little if any real effort to do so. One should further ask the question: Knowing the instability of the region and the multiple security threats in the days and weeks leading up to September 11, 2012, not to mention the fact that the date was the anniversary of September 11, 2001, why on earth didn't we have adequate military in the region to respond to a very real and present danger? That immediate responsibility falls directly at the feet of the State Department and Hillary Clinton. All indications, however, continue to appear that she is looking to get a pass on her dereliction of duty and lack of leadership. Heaven forbid that she has any chance of becoming our next commander in chief.

After the Ben Rhodes e-mails came to light showing a definitive connection from the White House giving Susan Rice the talking points for her Sunday morning news tour the Sunday after the attacks to push the video narrative and not the failure of the Obama policies, John Boehner finally called for a select committee to investigate the scandal. Rep. Trey Gowdy (R-SC), a former federal prosecutor, was named to head up the select committee on Benghazi. "I want to see every single, solitary, relevant, material document regarding the deadly 2011 terrorist attack in Libya!" Gowdy said. "I'm no longer interested in summaries or synopses produced by the Obama administration. I'm interested in access to the document and the witnesses, and I'll decide whether or not I think the appropriate questions were asked in the past," Gowdy said.

John Boehner said after announcing Gowdy to head the select committee, "With four of our countrymen killed at the hands of terrorists, the American people want answers, accountability, and justice. Trey Gowdy is as dogged, focused, and serious minded as they come. Gowdy's courtroom background makes him the ideal person to lead the newly announced investigation." Gowdy said in a statement he was "honored" to serve as chairman. "While people are free to draw different conclusions from the facts, there should be no debate over whether the American public is entitled to have all of the facts," Gowdy said.

Gowdy alleged a coordinated effort to prevent certain documents from being released to Congress. Some documents have likely been classified in a clear effort to stonewall investigators, he said. "There are certain things in our culture that have to transcend politics. And I don't mean to sound naïve, but the murder of four fellow Americans and an attack on a facility that is emblematic of our country should transcend politics, and I know our fellow citizens can handle the truth, but only if they get access to it," Gowdy said.

The very day I was completing my final edits of this book, was September 5th, 2014 which was a significant day because it just so happened to be the same day that Fox News with Bret Baier was to air an interview with three of the surviving security contractors who were engaged in the horrific fight at the CIA annex in Benghazi, and were the first responders to the attack on the diplomatic compound. I postponed sending this book off to print, so I could include the compelling information disclosed in the Fox News interview, in this book. These three men were all engaged in the fight alongside Tyrone Woods and Glen Doherty, and were with them when they died.

Kris ("Tanto") Paronto, Mark ("Oz") Geist, and John ("Tig") Tiegen, spoke with Bret Baier exclusively, and at length for the first time since the Benghazi attacks on September 11, 2012. They have co-wrote a book entitled "13 Hours: The Inside Account of What Really Happened in Benghazi" by Mitchell Zuckoff with the Annex Security Team. I have not had a chance to read the book, but I definitely intend to do so, and if the book is anywhere as compelling as the interview was, I highly recommend you read it.

Bret Baier asked them about one of the most controversial questions arising from the events in Benghazi: Was help delayed?

Word of the attack on the diplomatic compound reached the CIA annex just after 9:30 p.m. Within five minutes, the security team at the annex was geared up for battle, and ready to move to the compound, that was only a mile away.

"Five minutes, we're ready," said Paronto, a former Army Ranger. "It was thumbs up, thumbs up, we're ready to go."

But the team was held back. According to the security operators, they were delayed from responding to the attack by the top CIA officer in Benghazi, whom they refer to only as "Bob".

"It had probably been 15 minutes I think, and... I just said, "Hey, you know, we got to, we need to get over there, we're losing the initiative," said Tiegen. "And Bob just looks straight at me and said, Stand down, you need to wait."

"We're starting to get calls from the State Department, guys saying, hey, we're taking fire, we need you guys here, we need help," said Paronto.

After a delay of nearly 30 minutes, the security team disobeyed the stand down orders, and headed to the besieged consulate. They asked their CIA superiors to send more help, and to call for armed air support, which never came.

Now, looking back the security team said that they believed that if they had not been delayed for a half an hour, or if the air support had come, things might have turned out differently. "Ambassador Stevens and Sean Smith, yeah, they would still be alive, my gut is yes." Paronto said. Tiegen concurred. "I strongly believe if we'd left immediately, they'd still be alive today." He added.

In a statement to Fox News, a senior intelligence official insisted that, "There were no orders to anybody to stand down in providing support."

Baier put that assertion directly to the operators. "You use the words stand down, A number of people now, including the House Intelligence committee insist no one was hindered from responding to the situation at the compound...so what do you say to that?"

"No, it happened," said Tiegen. "It happened on the ground, all I can talk about is what happened on that ground that night, to us." Paronto added. "To myself, twice, and to, to Tig, once. It happened that night. We were told to wait, stand, and stand down. We were delayed three times."

In a statement to Fox News, a senior intelligence official did allow that the security team was delayed from responding while the CIA's top officer in Benghazi tried to rally local support.

Bret Bair also asked them about the infamous You Tube video that was blamed for the violence in Benghazi. Paronto laughed at the suggestion that the video played any role in the events of that night, saying he did not even know of the video until he was out of Libya and on his way home. "I didn't know about the video till I got to Germany, I had no idea about any video, no sir."

The US military has long had a policy of "running toward the sound of gunfire"; it's right up there with "no man left behind." American leadership, or lack thereof, I should say, broke both of those long-held military principles. Not only did we fail to send help toward the sounds of gunfire, we also left our heroic people behind to fend for themselves. It is an absolute travesty of justice. As Americans, we should never allow that to happen again.

CHAPTER SIXTEEN

Big Government Exposed! The VA Scandal

"A dying man can do nothing easy." Benjamin Franklin, 1790

Those words definitely proved to be true in the Veterans Affairs scandal. Here you have the very bravest of all Americans literally dying just while waiting to get to see a doctor. Not just one, but literally dozens of our veterans. And when you listen to the "smugness" of those responsible and their complete lack of accountability, how can any American citizen not be absolutely mortified about it?

America's veterans should all be considered among America's most valued treasures. When we're talking about men and women who have served this country with honor and distinction at considerable risk of the loss of life or limb, and incredible sacrifice, to ensure the safety, security, and rights of all Americans, how can you consider them anything less? If the VA scandal doesn't just make every person in America ill, it damn sure should.

As of June 2014, the US Department of Veterans Affairs concluded after its internal audit of 731 VA facilities that at least fifty-seven thousand veterans had been on a waiting list to see a doctor for over ninety days. That is just the number that they have confirmed; it is likely far short of the real number. Just taking that fifty-seven thousand number, that is an average of seventy-eight veterans at every single VA in the country waiting more than ninety days to see a doctor at any given time! Mind you, that's not fifty-seven thousand vets a year on the list, that is fifty-seven thousand vets on the list at the day and time the investigation was conducted, which means the real number of vets affected could be tenfold or even a hundredfold. That is completely unacceptable!

Thus far, at least thirty-five veterans as of the date of the report have died while waiting to get to see a doctor. That's only the number of vets that have been discovered, because their names were still on a secret list somewhere; that doesn't include the vets that had died at any time in the past while waiting to see a doctor and were subsequently removed from a list once their death was discovered by the VA. That is absolutely reprehensible! This is beyond the pale. People shouldn't just be fired, they should be imprisoned!

According to the Department of Veterans Affairs, an internal audit of hundreds of Veterans Affairs facilities revealed that 63,869 veterans enrolled in the VA health care system in the past ten years have yet to be seen for an appointment.

So, you ask, why would anyone put vets on a secret waiting list? Greed and incompetence. The Obama administration's idea of fixing the VA system was to throw billions of dollars at it and, to fix the wait times; let's just issue a mandate that no veteran will have to wait more than fourteen days to see a doctor. As if just because you mandate something and throw a lot of money at it, it's going to suddenly fix the problem? Definitely not. This proclamation may have sounded good in theory, but in the absence of a new vision and real leadership and the ability to hold people responsible for corruption and incompetence, it only exacerbated the problems.

To make matters worse, VA hospital administrators had bonuses tied into meeting this new fourteen-day mandate. Herein lies the problem. This new mandate, and tying it into bonuses, certainly didn't make these government employees work any harder, smarter, or more efficiently. No, what it did do was create a system-wide incentive for agency officials to "cook the books" and make wait times look much shorter than they actually were.

That's right, cook the books. And that is exactly what VA administration officials across the country did. In fact the VA audit revealed that nearly one in eight of the 3,772 staff members questioned said that their superiors told them to falsify appointment logs. That is 471 VA government employees who actually admitted it! That is a whole heck of a lot of people. My question is, if one in eight government employees questioned actually admitted it, how many weren't questioned, and of those who were, how many chose not to admit it for any number of obvious reasons? This is a national disgrace and a scandal of epic proportions.

You can twist and turn and try to spin this scandal however it fits your political ideology, but there is one unavoidable fact once you get past the politics and rhetoric: after nearly six years under the management of President Barack Obama and his administration, the Veterans Administration remains in shambles and is arguably worse than it ever has been. It continues to fail our veterans in the worst possible way by denying them timely access to doctors and medical care.

So what was Obama's response when this scandal broke? It's not like I need to tell you; it's the same response Obama always gives when a scandal breaks. He takes to the podium and does the ol' Obama tag team two step. Except this time, it hasn't worked. Because when you mess with America's veterans, it is not a partisan issue. Even Obama's own party was justifiably outraged, and the media couldn't give him a pass on it.

Oh, yes; how did Barack Obama find out about this huge scandal, you might ask? No, you wouldn't ask, because you already know. The same way he finds out about every significant scandal his administration is involved in: the very same way the rest of us do, from watching the news. Does Obama have any idea how completely clueless and foolish he looks when he makes that claim? Here you have a guy holding the most powerful office in the world, with immediate access to an unlimited array of intelligence and the head of every single department of government answering directly to him, but yet for some reason the people he's entrusted to these important positions keep him completely in the dark. I'm not sure if it's worse that he did know and just keeps lying about it, or if he is really that obtuse and in the dark.

I think Charles Krauthammer put it best when hammering Obama over his lack of knowledge regarding all of the various scandals engulfing his administration. On May 18, 2014, on Fox News's *Special Report*, Krauthammer slammed Obama: "He acts like he stumbled upon the presidency. As if he stumbled upon the presidency and discovered all this horrible stuff is happening," referring to all of the scandals surrounding the Obama administration. "He's in charge of these departments. At the same point, you have to ask, where has he been, and where is the competence, the elementary competence, he promised when he ran in 2008?" Krauthammer asked. "VA doctors are on salary. They have zero incentive to see a lot of patients. In the

Albuquerque report that you saw in the Daily Beast, they reported the average cardiologist treats alone in one week what the entire eight-person department of cardiology in the Albuquerque facility treated. So that's eight to one, and that's because if you are in private practice, if you want to stay alive, you have to see a lot of patients so you can cover your overhead." Krauthammer is a doctor himself.

The Phoenix VA alone had a secret waiting list with the names of seventeen hundred vets on it who had been waiting several months just to get in to see a doctor. This scandal came to light when Dr. Sam Foote, a sixty-one-year-old doctor working at the Phoenix VA, came forward and blew the whistle in April 2014 about the existence of the secret waiting lists. That opened the floodgates for other doctors at VAs all around the country to come forward and shed light on the systemic government scandal.

The Veterans Administration (VA) scandal that was exposed and brought to light in the spring of 2014, while tragic for sure, should be a big, bright, beaming light that exposes the failures of big government and progressive ideology.

When the Democrats passed the Affordable Care Act, the majority of Democrats wanted it to be a "single payer system," and most have continued to argue that it should be. Single payer means government provided. In other words, the government would provide funds for health insurance rather than insurance companies. The health care services would be paid for by higher taxes. This would mean the total nationalizing or government takeover of health care in America, with the government being the "single payer" for health care and eliminating private insurance companies. Barack Obama, Nancy Pelosi, and Harry Reid all support a single payer nationalized government health care system and lobbied to have the Affordable Care Act be a single payer system. Many Democratic lawmakers wanted the single payer system, but fortunately they couldn't get enough votes from more con-servative Democrats to pass the bill as a single payer system.

Many believe that all of the horrific problems with the current Obamacare system were cooked into the system in hopes that those problems would inevitably result in a single payer system—in other words, that the way the system was designed, it was doomed for fail-ure. One can't help but conclude that the authors of the bill knew that, or at least they should have known it. In any event, the suggestion is that they knew the bill would collapse under its own weight and the public, having gotten used to subsidized health care, would then make it politically more palatable to revert to a single payer health care system.

Medicare and Medicaid are both single payer systems, and while Medicare is relatively popular with current seniors, it is also tril-lions of dollars in debt and is completely unsustainable without some major reforms. Medicaid is not so popular, and more and more doc-tors are refusing to accept Medicare or Medicaid patients. Medicare is not a completely nationalized system because patients, for the time being, are still permitted to go to private practice doctors and private hospitals.

The Veterans Administration, however, is precisely an example of "single payer" nationalized health care, and it is an absolute disas-ter! Granted, there are some VAs in rural areas of America that haven't been subject to the massive incompetence and corruption, so you will find some veterans who are generally happy with the health care they receive at their local VA. That said, the VAs that are servicing any of the more populated areas in America literally have veterans dying while on a waiting list to get any medical care whatsoever! That is the unavoidable consequence of a government-run health care system.

Let's take a closer look at the problem. As we've already laid out in several previous chapters, the government is a huge bureaucracy. It moves very slowly by design and is completely inefficient. Affirmative action requires that preference is given to government employees based on race and gender, rather than hiring the very best candidate regardless of race or gender. By contrast, the private sector and capitalism in general are color and gender blind and typically only hire the very best candidates for whatever position they have. I would add that preference is also often given as political favor, and often to people who aren't at all qualified for a given position to begin with. No matter how you slice it, a government bureaucracy is far more likely by design to end up with a lot of incompetence and corruption.

Private practice doctors and private hospitals have a great deal of incentive to perform to the highest standards of care because patients have a wide variety of choices when it comes to their health care. Private practice doctors and private hospitals have a great deal of incentive to streamline their operations and eliminate waste and corruption because they are responsible for a healthy bottom line. Private practice doctors and private hospitals are completely accountable because they are liable to their patients and their stockholders and are subject to litigation when they make a mistake.

In contrast to private practice doctors and private hospitals, a VA doctor or a VA hospital isn't held to any of the same accountability or standards that the private sector is. In fact, it is actually just the opposite; the more they waste and spend, the more their budget gets increased. There is zero incentive to provide a high quality of service to their patients. There is zero incentive to see as many patients in a day as they are able to. There is zero incentive to prevent mistakes. Patients can't sue a VA doctor, and government employees are more likely to die on the job than to get fired.

That is the same basic fundamental difference between capitalism and socialism. In a capitalistic system, there is all the incentive in the world to excel and deliver the highest level of service while making as few mistakes as possible. In a socialistic society there is zero incentive to do better, and if you can't sue or fire someone there is zero accountability.

Let's look at compensation of VA doctors compared to private sector doctors. According to the Department of Veterans Affairs, there is a four-tier pay scale for doctors based on the time a doctor has worked for the Veterans Administration. These studies are a few years old, so I'm sure the pay scale has increased somewhat, but the comparison would still show the relative difference between doctors' pay in the private sector and in the public sector, which is one of the very few areas in which public sector employees are paid less than their private sector counterparts.

For instance, a primary care physician at tier one earns $96,536, while a tier four primary care doctor takes home $130,000. A specialty doctor at tier one level will earn between $96,536 and $195,000 per year, and a specialty doctor at tier four will earn between $130,000 and a maximum of $245,000. So, the highest paid specialty doctor who works for the VA makes about $245,000. In contrast, a Medical Group Management Association (MGMA) study shows the average private practice family physician earns an annual income of $211,083, and specialty doctors generally average between $400,000 and $500,000, depending on what the specialty is and the area of the country in which he or she practices medicine. So it's pretty clear that the private sector doctors make considerably more than VA doctors do.

If you are a progressive liberal, you are probably saying, "That's the problem! Thanks for pointing that out; let's just throw more money at it and it will be resolved!" No, that certainly isn't the answer to the problem. Let's take a closer look at why. Not that there aren't some really good VA doctors, and I'm sure that there are; however, because of affirmative action, the VA doesn't necessarily draw from the best and the brightest. But it's an even deeper problem than that, and it goes right back to the capitalist vs. socialist argument: there is no incentive to work harder, smarter, and more efficiently in the government, and there is no accountability in an institution where you can't sue or fire anyone.

According to the Daily Beast, a study was done at the Albuquerque VA, which houses eight physicians in the cardiology department, but at any given time only three are working in the clinic, and each doctor on average sees no more than two patients a day. The average weekly number of patients that all the doctors combined saw was thirty-six patients. The study conducted a survey of private practice cardiologists and found that the majority of private practice cardiologists see between fifty and 124 patients per week. In other words, one private practice cardiologist sees far more patients in one week by himself than all eight VA cardiologists see in the same time period. That statistic is glaring, but not at all surprising to me. A private practice doctor sees ten times the number of patients each week as a government VA doctor does. Yet even though private practice doctors make on average more than VA doctors do, the income gap is not that much more given the fact that private practice doctors are seeing ten times more patients on average than a government VA doctor does.

The VA is riddled with many of the same problems as many of our schools in this country. The Connecticut VA commissioner touted that "applicants to her department are screened to minimum qualifications. Applicants who meet the essential level of preparation are not excluded. The human resources administrator must work to bring as many protected members into the system." Her words.

It's obvious that "diversity" trumps talent in government hiring, and once hired it's nearly impossible to fire someone for anything. If cutbacks or layoffs are required, which, let's face it, almost never happens in government, tenure trumps talent. So, in other words, the best and the brightest aren't at all a consideration. So a good health care employee would be terminated before a tenured employee would be. Pretty much the exact same reason many of our school systems across America are failing.

This is how crazy our government is, and it puts a glaring spotlight on why big government bureaucracy doesn't work. Only after public outrage over the VA scandal, which first started in the Phoenix Veterans Affairs facility, where as many as forty gravely ill veterans died while waiting to be treated, did the Congress pass the VA Accountability Bill—just to fire a handful of corrupt VA workers.

Really, are you kidding me? No, that's exactly the way our government works. I can tell you firsthand, I have run a number of businesses in a variety of industries, and if you don't have the ability to hold someone accountable, you are going out of business, and fast!

Let's take a look at Major Nidal Malik Hasan, the jihadi that murdered several of his fellow soldiers at Fort Hood. Believe it or not, he is still on the government's payroll. Hasan worked at Walter Reed Army Medical Center, where he terrified the patients entrusted to his care, but he still kept his job. In contrast, a private hospital would have immediately terminated any such problematic employee.

I'm going to back up for a minute and make sure everyone understands what "affirmative action" means: it refers to laws or policies that give preference to minorities when hiring any employees, accepting students into universities, or even in awarding government contracts to minority contractors. While affirmative action may have been well intended in its inception, its necessity has long since passed, and affirmative action in the twenty-first century is nothing more than reverse discrimination.

What may have started out in only one Phoenix VA hospital, with one whistle blower with enough integrity to say enough is enough, has now turned into a huge nationwide scandal that has impacted VA facilities in nearly every state in the country. It's becoming crystal clear that corruption and incompetence have run rampant across the seventeen hundred hospitals, clinics, and other facilities operated by the federal government. The Daily Beast described the VA scandal as "a common language of bureaucratic corruption."

While soldiers were waiting for care, some found that they were in fact waiting to die. VA staff in hospitals across the country conspired to lie to the auditing VA inspector general, forged appointment records, and kept secret patient lists, and they did so for bonuses and profit. That is nothing short of fraud, and if that fraud, which is a felony, resulted in the death of veterans, that is murder. The definition of *murder* is the act of a felony resulting in a death, regardless of whether the death was the intent of the felony.

But will anyone be held accountable? Not under the Obama administration. President Obama did his usual take-to-the-podium rant and proclaimed, "If these allegations prove to be true, it is dishonorable, it is disgraceful, and I will not tolerate it, period." You may recall the last time Obama said "period" after a sentence—it was preceded by "if you like your doctor, you can keep your doctor," a statement that was labeled the lie of the year by Politico. The House VA Committee chairman, Jeff Miller, said Obama's statements were "too little, too late." After weeks of trying to ignore the scandal, and with dozens of VA facilities under investigation and more and more whistle blowers coming forward all over the country, the VA scandal became too much for even the Democrats to continue overlooking. Calls from both sides of the aisle started mounting for the head of the man who was in charge, VA Secretary General Eric Shinseki. After weeks of supporting Shinseki, Obama was forced to accept his resignation. So there has been at least one sacrificial lamb, and the scandal is way too big for there not to be at least a few more. But will anyone go to jail? They absolutely should, but I seriously doubt anyone will be named, shamed, or jailed.

The Dems did start circling the wagons, however, and have tried their best to blame Bush because the VA has had troubles for years and because of the increased wartime injuries because of the Iraq and Afghanistan wars. But, as previously pointed out in this book, there have been far more wartime injuries under Obama than under Bush, so that argument doesn't hold water. Besides, Obama certainly knew we were a country at war when he ran for president, and those wars continued under his presidency.

If you think I'm being too harsh when using the word "incompetence," let's take a look at just a few of the blunders the VA has been involved in just since Barack Obama took office.

In February 2009, the VA notified more than six thousand patients who went to Alvin C. York VA Medical Center in Murfreesboro, Tennessee, that they may have been exposed to infectious diseases at the clinic due to contaminated endoscopic equipment.

The Charlie Norwood VA Medical Center in Augusta, Georgia, also in February 2009 notified more than twelve hundred veterans that they may have been treated with contaminated equipment.

In March 2009, the VA sent letters to more than three thousand veterans who may have had colonoscopies at VA facilities in Miami, warning that they may have been exposed to hepatitis and HIV. According to hospital officials, a review of safety procedures found that tubing used in endoscope procedures was not disinfected.

In 2010, the VA notified more than eighteen hundred veterans treated at the John Cochran VA hospital in St. Louis that they may have been exposed to infectious diseases during dental procedures.

In 2011, nine Ohio veterans tested positive for hepatitis after routine dental work at a VA clinic in Dayton, Ohio. A dentist working at the VA medical center there acknowledged not washing his hands or even changing gloves between patients for the past eighteen years.

February 2011–November 2012: An outbreak of legionnaire's disease at VA facilities in Pennsylvania killed at least six veterans.

November 2013: A CNN investigation showed that veterans were dying because of long waits and delayed care at US veterans hospitals. The VA confirmed six deaths tied to delays at the Williams Jennings Bryan Dorn Veterans Medical Center in Columbia, South Carolina.

The list of incompetence and corruption goes on and on and has finally blown up in the face of an administration who campaigned promising to fix the problem, yet six years after his taking office, the problem has only gone from bad to worse.

The problems with the Veterans Administration go back decades, so, yes, it is a problem that Obama inherited; however, when he ran for president, he vowed to "build a twenty-first century VA." Obama, touting his very brief membership on the Senate Veterans Affairs committee before groups like the VFW, vowed to fix the broken bureaucracy by slashing the red tape and providing every living vet with electronic medical records. He promised that reforming the VA would be one of his top priorities. We also now know that Obama and his aides were briefed in late 2008 during his transition into the office about the problems with unreliable wait time data at the VA.

Obama's campaign promise to prioritize fixing the broken VA system turned out to be another false promise and another disappointing recurring theme of his administration. Obama does a much better job in speechifying about how to solve a problem than ever actually solving a problem.

Every liberal's answer to any problem is to simply throw more money at it. "The offenders were merely overwhelmed and under-resourced, and encumbered by a lack of funding." That's certainly how Democrats are framing the corruption and incompetency of the VA bureaucracy. That's it, it must be that the VA just isn't getting enough money. Nothing could be further from the truth. When we're talking about the problems of big government, enough funding is never the problem.

Big spender Obama did, however, follow through on his promise to increase funding for the agency, and Congress did agree to supply it. In fact the VA's budget has been exploding, even as the number of veterans steadily declines. From 2000 to 2013 the outlays nearly tripled while the population of veterans declined by 4.3 million. From 2008 to 2012 alone, per-patient spending at the VA climbed 27 percent. To put that in perspective, per-capita health spending nationwide rose only 13 percent during those years. The driving costs, however, are not Iraq and Afghanistan vets, who only account for 7 percent of those treated by the VA and were responsible for only 4 percent of its health care costs. Aging vets from the Vietnam and Korean War eras account for the majority of VA health care costs.

Unfortunately for our veterans, President Obama is incapable of fixing our failed VA system. Let's get past the fact that Obama is completely incompetent and continues to surround himself with people equally as incompetent. Regardless of that fact, Barack Obama wouldn't fix this problem even if he know how to do so. Not that he doesn't want it fixed; I would at least give him that much credit and accept that he wants it fixed. The problem, however, is that his progressive ideology would never allow him to see the problem for what it is: the complete and utter failure of big progressive government bureaucracy. Barack Obama is a big proponent of single payer health care. The Veterans Administration is a prime example of a failed experiment in a single payer health care system. In order for Barack Obama to ever be able to fix the problem, he and his entire party would have to have a complete epiphany that a single payer system can't work.

The VA has had big problems for decades. The VA is a problem that can't be fixed. It is a victim of its own making and a product of its own pending demise. It can't be fixed because no politician has the stomach or the political will to fix it. And if politicians did have the political will, they certainly couldn't muster the political capital (political support) that it would take to make such a sweeping reform. It isn't a matter of money, it's a matter of ideology. The VA can't be fixed because it is fundamentally built on a progressive or socialist ideology, and that has never worked.

A report in June 2014 issued by the office of Senator Tom Coburn, a three time cancer survivor, and himself a physician; finds more than 1,000 veterans may have died in the last decade because of malpractice or lack of care from Department of Veterans Affairs, medical centers. The report aggregates government investigations and media reports to trace a history of fraudulent scheduling practices, budget mis-management, insufficient oversight and lack of accountability that have led to the current controversy plaguing the VA. The VA has admitted that 23 patients have died because of delayed care in recent years, but the report titled "Friendly Fire: Death Delay, and Dismay at the VA", shows many more patient deaths have been linked to systematic issues affecting VA hospitals and clinics throughout the US.

Everyone should be scared to death about any form of government-run health care. The Affordable Care Act is just the "Trojan horse" to a single payer government-run health care. And this Veterans Administration scandal that has been brought to light is a glaring example of what's to come.

Capitalism creates competition, and competition provides the American people so much that they take it for granted. Competition gives us choice. Competition creates innovation, and innovation is what continues to flood our world with new ideas, products, and technology. Competition is what holds people and businesses accountable— accountable to themselves, their employees, their shareholders, and their customers. It does so because if they aren't accountable, the competition will soon run them over. Competition keeps us all on our toes and is the very essence of what makes human beings strive for excellence.

So what needs to be done to fix the broken VA health care system? It needs a good old-fashioned injection of American capitalism. I would suggest that we either privatize all of the veteran's facilities or scrap them altogether and provide the vets an insurance voucher so they can purchase their own private health insurance.

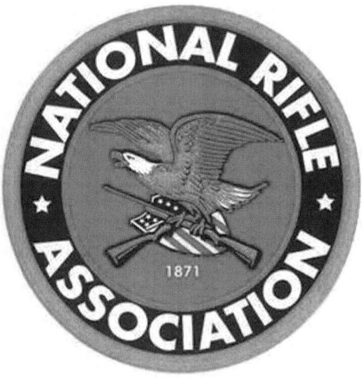

CHAPTER SEVENTEEN

Right to Bear Arms? Progressives assault on the Second Amendment

"Americans have the advantage of being armed – unlike the citizens of other countries where the governments are afraid to trust the people with arms." – James Madison

Progressives hate the second amendment and go to great lengths to try and pass laws limiting American's rights to own and bear arms, claiming that the second amendment doesn't really mean what it says.

Amendment II
"A well regulated Militia, being necessary to the security of a free State, the right of the people to keep and bear Arms, shall not be infringed."

In full disclosure I have been a life member of the NRA (National Rifle Association) for over half of my life, so the second amendment is very important to me as an American. Regardless of how you might personally feel about owning a firearm, this chapter will help you understand why the second amendment is something that every American citizen should defend at all costs.

I completely understand the outrage, anger and fear that most all Americans feel whenever you hear about a tragic event involving firearms. The tragedies at Sandy Hook and Columbine, where troubled youth's obtained firearms and used them to terrorize and murder their classmates and teachers, undoubtedly shake the conscience of all Americans. Progressives immediately try to politicize and take advantage of these tragedies, and quickly beat the drums for restrictive gun control laws.

I know it may be easier to blame tragic events on a firearm, and progressives would have you believe that if only there were stricter gun control laws, that these tragedies wouldn't happen. Nothing could be further from the truth. Guns don't kill people, people kill people, and a firearm is certainly not the only weapon of choice. If someone is intent on harming someone, their inability to obtain a firearm is very likely not going to change that. As tragic as the events at Columbine and Sandy Hook were, they could have just as easily been carried out, and been every bit as deadly, if the assailants would have used any number of other types of weapons.

Let's start by taking a closer look at some revealing statistics. To begin with, the US does have the highest level of gun ownership in the world, however our gun related homicides is only about three per 100,000. The United Nations 2010 chart lists the US as having a murder rate (all murders including those with guns and those without) of 5.22 per 100,000 people. The average gun related homicides in the US are 3 per 100,000. (http://chartsbin.com/view/1454) the average homicide rate for the entire world is 9.63 per 100,000. That is nearly double that of America. In-fact 89 countries in the world have a higher murder rate than that of America, and we have by far the highest gun ownership.

America isn't even in the same league as the worst offenders. Honduras has a murder rate of 60.87 per 100,000. Jamaica has 59.5 per 100,000. El Salvador has 51.83 per 100,000. Guatemala has 45.17 per 100,000. Colombia has 40.1 per 100,000. South Africa has 36.54 per 100,000, and Belize has 34.26 per 100,000.

Gun homicides in the United States are concentrated in major urban areas. And those cities are typically Democratic strongholds with the most stringent gun control laws in the nation, with gun murder rates that rival those of the most violent countries in the world. (http://www.theatlanticcities.com/politics/2013/01/gun-violence-us-cities-compared-deadliest-nations-world/4412/).

If it were a country, New Orleans with a rate of 62.1 gun murders per 100,000 people, would rank second in the world.

Detroit's gun-homicide rate of 35.9 is just less than that of El Salvador's 39.9 per 100,000.

Baltimore's rate of 29.7 per 100,000 people is just shy of Guatemala's 34.8 per 100,000 people.

Gun murders in Newark of 25.4, and Miami's 23.7 are comparable to that of Colombia's 27.1 per 100,000 people.

Atlanta's rate of 17.2 gun murders per 100,000 people is about the same as South Africa's 17 per 100,000 people.

Cleveland's 17.4 is higher than that of the Dominican Republic's 16.3 per 100,000 people.

Buffalo's 16.5 per 100,000 people is about the same as Panama's 16.2 per 100,000 people.

President Obama's home town of Chicago has a higher gun murder rate of 11.6 per 100,000 people than that of Guyana's 11.6 per 100,000 people.

Phoenix's rate of 10.6 per 100,000 people is slightly higher than that of Mexico's 10 per 100,000 people.

Las Angeles, at 9.2 per 100,000 people is higher than that of the Philippines 8.9 per 100,000 people.

Boston's rate of 6.2 per 100,000 people is higher than that of Nicaragua's 5.9 per 100,000 people.

New York is well above the national average at 4 per 100,000 people.

Ironically the cities and states with the most restrictive gun control laws, inevitably have the highest gun murder rates, even rivaling those in some of the most dangerous countries in the world. So why is that? It doesn't take rocket science to understand that strict gun laws are only abided by law abiding citizens, and not by criminals. A criminal is far more likely to commit a crime against someone they know is unarmed, than that of someone who might be armed. Tough gun control laws, only embolden the criminals who aren't going to obey the laws anyway, and put the public in greater danger.

In 1996 Australia banned 60% of all firearms and required registration of all guns and the licensing of gun owners. Police confiscated over 640,000 firearms, going door to door without search warrants. Two years later, the Australian Bureau of Statistics reported that all crime had risen, and armed robberies were up 44%.

Our founding fathers had a pretty good handle on all of this as well, which is why they protected our rights to keep and bear arms with the Second Amendment to the US Constitution. The founding fathers however, also realized that the people's right to keep and bear arms was necessary for far more than simply protecting one's self and property from criminals who would do them harm. The real protection in the Second Amendment, was intended to protect "we the people" from our government, and our elected officials.

Let's look at this a little closer. Progressives would have you believe that the intent of our founding fathers, and the Second Amendment was not somehow literally intended for the average Joe Citizen to be able to own or carry a firearm, but rather it was limited to only apply to police officers, or for hunting purposes. Progressives would also have you believe that the second amendment wasn't literally intended to protect the average Joe Citizen from its own government. I beg to differ. That is exactly what the founding fathers intended, and it is clearly evidenced in many of their writings. Let's look at a few more quotes from our founding fathers, and you can decide for yourself what the intent of our founding fathers was, their language is very unambiguous if you ask me;

"The great objective is that every man be armed... Everyone who is able may have a gun." - Patrick Henry

"To disarm the people is the best and most effectual way to enslave them." - George Mason

"The Constitution shall never be construed... to prevent the people of the United States who are peaceable citizens from keeping their own arms." – Samuel Adams

"The best we can hope for concerning the people at large is that they be properly armed." - Alexander Hamilton

"To preserve liberty, it is essential that the whole body of the people always possess arms, and be taught alike, especially when young, how to use them." – Richard Henry Lee

Our founding fathers knew that in order for "we the people" to truly be a free people, and for our government to be a government "of the people" and "for the people" that the right to keep and bear arms, must be protected, and never infringed upon. Our founding fathers, having already been forced to take up arms against Great Brittan and King George III, to put an end to being governed without representation, knew first hand, all too well the importance of the people being able to take up arms against those who would govern "we the people", if as a last resort, need be.

Read the words of our founding father, George Washington, and tell me that he didn't specifically intend for "we the people" to always be able to keep and bear arms;

"Firearms stand next in importance to the constitution itself. They are the American people's liberty teeth and keystone under independence... from the hour the Pilgrims landed to the present day, events, occurrences and tendencies prove that to ensure peace security and happiness, the rifle and pistol are equally indispensable...the very atmosphere of firearms anywhere restrains evil interference – they deserve a place of honor with all that's good." - George Washington, the first President of the United States.

"The supposed quietude of a good man allures the ruffian; while on the other hand arms, like laws, discourages and keep the invader and plunderer in awe, and preserve order in the world as property. The same balance would be preserved were all the world destitute of arms, for a, for all would be alike; but since some will not, others dare not lay them aside…Horrid mischief would ensue were the law-abiding deprived of the use of them." - Thomas Paine

"Are we at last brought to such humiliating and debasing degradation, that we cannot be trusted with arms for our defense? Where is the difference between having our arms in possession and under our direction and having them under the management of Congress? If our defense be the real object of having those arms, in whose hands can they be rusted with more prosperity, or equal safety to us, as in our own hands?" – Patrick Henry

No doubt, Tyrannical governments kill far more people than private criminals. The Nazis conducted extensive search and seizure operations in 1933 to disarm their political opponents, in 1938 to disarm the Jews, and when they occupied Europe in 1939-41 they proclaimed the death penalty for anyone who failed to surrender all guns within 24 hours.

History teaches us that registration leads to the confiscation of guns and that is the goal of many gun control advocates. Prior to 1958 Cuban dictator Fulgencio Batista had all Cuban citizens register their firearms; after the revolution, Raul and Fidel Castro had their Communist thugs go door to door and, using the registration lists, confiscate all firearms. As soon as the Cubans were disarmed, that was the end of their freedom.

I'm not suggesting that Americans would ever have to take up arms against our government, but I am saying that our founding fathers included the Second Amendment to our constitution to ensure that our government would be kept in check, and would always be "of the people" and "for the people" so that we never would have to take up arms against our government.

I would be the first to admit that owning and using guns, certainly isn't for everyone, and those who do own guns, should do so with great care and extensive training. I do support background checks, and all precautions should be made to prevent anyone with any mental disabilities from owning a firearm. That said, I wouldn't be supportive of restricting any form of gun ownership to law abiding adults, of sound and competent mind.

I think I can speak on this topic with some authority. As I disclosed at the beginning of this chapter, I've been a life member of the NRA for over half of my life. I have had significant firearm training and experience, starting when I was about ten years old. I've held a Conceal Carry permit (CCW – Cary Concealed Weapon) ever since Missouri passed legislation to allow citizens to carry a concealed weapon. Moreover, I understand the gun control debate from a victim's viewpoint. My mother used to manage several rental properties in some fairly rough neighborhoods of Kansas City, Missouri, and in early 1980 my mother was shot twice in the stomach with a 38 caliber pistol. My mother fortunately survived the ordeal without any permanent disability, however it was a very devastating event on my mother, and my entire family. What I didn't do however, was to put the blame of that tragic event, on that of a gun. The blame fell squarely on the person who shot my mother. I only wish my mother would have had a gun to defend herself. A few years later, I was assisting my mother with an eviction, when I was stabbed by some crazy guy with a knife. I can tell you without hesitation, that if I would have had a gun at that time, I wouldn't have been stabbed.

Does anyone really believe that the government can protect all American citizens from those who would do us harm? Does anyone really believe that the police in our local communities will always be able to be there for us when needed? For those who do believe that, I can only say that they are being very naïve.

I'll end this chapter with a true story that should give any anti-gun activists something to ponder. Eighteen year old mother Sarah McKinley was widowed on Christmas Eve in 2011, when she lost her husband to cancer. According to McKinley's account of events, Justin Martin had been prowling around her home in the days following her husband's funeral, and on New Year's Eve, he and accomplice Dustin Stewart aggressively tried to break into McKinley's home. McKinley had barricaded herself into the house and immediately called 911 from her bedroom, with her infant baby by her side. She spoke with the 911 operator for over twenty minutes, awaiting a police response, while the intruders were determined to get into her house. McKinley told the operator that she was armed with a twelve-gauge shotgun and a pistol, and wanted to know if it was OK for her to shoot the intruders if they made it into her bedroom. The operator hesitated with a reply, and McKinley asked a second time. The operator finally replied, "I can't tell you that you can do that, but you do what you have to do to protect your baby." Moments later the intruder Martin kicked the door in, and charged at her with a knife. McKinley didn't hesitate and shot and killed the intruder before he could get to her infant child. Martin's alleged accomplice, Dustin Stewart, fled when he heard the gunshot, and later surrendered to police. He was then charged with burglary, and later charged with Martin's murder, even though he never fired a shot; since his accomplice was killed in the commission of a felony, he was complicit of murder.

I would hate to think of what would have happened to Sarah McKinley and her innocent infant child, had she not been armed with a gun to defend herself, and her baby.

CHAPTER EIGHTEEN

Under Siege; Crisis at the Border

"Are there no inconveniences to be thrown into the scale against the advantage expected by a multiplication of numbers by the importation of foreigners?" - Thomas Jefferson.

Jefferson's concern was that immigrants would come to America from countries that would have given them no experiences of living in a free society, and that they would bring with them the ideas and principals of the government they left behind. Ideas and principals that are often at odds with American liberty.

The founding fathers were generally skeptical of immigration. Our founding fathers were however supportive of attracting immigrants with a particular skillset, when America lacked citizens with that particular skill. They were convinced that mass immigration would bring social turmoil and political confusion in its wake.

You often hear progressives beat the drums that all American's are immigrants, so we shouldn't pay attention to any immigration laws.

While it may be true that most American's are immigrants, with the exception of the American Indians, however the big difference is that when most of our ancestors came to America, they did it on a boat, and landed at Ellis Island, and went through a process to be in America. They didn't illegally climb border walls, and get smuggled through tunnels. So why do progressive democrats want to do away with our immigration laws? Because they believe it increases their voting base, because Hispanics have traditionally voted for democrats.

I spent the majority of my professional career rebuilding disaster struck communities all around America after tornadoes, floods and hurricanes. During that time I had the privilege of working with hundreds if not thousands of Hispanic workers. I can say without hesitation that the vast majority of immigrants that I've known and worked with, were honest, dependable, extremely hard working, and of good character. They were the kind of people that I was proud to work with, and glad to know. America should welcome the kind of immigrants that I've known and worked with, into our country, our communities, and our workforce. But there must first be a legal process that all immigrants must go through before they are able to earn that privilege. Period!

America is a sovereign country, and how could any country be sovereign without securing their borders? America's unsecured borders is an extreme threat to our national security.

America has got to get a handle on immigration reform, and the crisis we're now experiencing at the southern border may be the perfect opportunity for us to do so. No doubt, we must first start with securing the border, and as I said, the current border crisis may well be the best opportunity for us to finally get the country behind a secure border. I certainly am not suggesting nor would I even support amnesty in any manner at all. Amnesty is defined as "A government pardon granted to a number of offenders, especially for political offences." Amnesty in dealing with immigration is basically referring to giving illegal immigrants a pardon for illegally coming to America, and not making them return to their country of origin. I do however believe that we have got to come up with a realistic plan to deal with the twelve-million-plus illegal immigrants in the country. I definitely think that the borders have to be completely secured first and foremost. If that takes building a wall along our southern border where one can be built, then so be it. Where a wall might not be able to be built because of terrain, than sophisticated surveillance, and heavy patrols by the air, ground or however is necessary, needs to be implemented. Any underground tunnels need to be found and shut down permanently.

After the border is secure, there needs to be some incentive to get all illegals to go to any post office in America and register that they are in the country, and give them a path to be here under a legal work status of some sort, with a specified criteria that they would be required to adhere too; including learning the English language. Let's face it, opportunities are much greater for those who speak English in America than for those who do not. All of that said, everything is a nonstarter without first securing the border.

Once the border is secured, I believe that most reasonable people can find some common ground. The problem is that most Americans who support a secure border, have learned a hard lesson that a secure border is always put on the back burner to everything else.

A path to legalization should not be an easy thing, but it should be an attainable thing. It should take considerable time and effort and provide the ability, in fact the mandate, that immigrants are legally and gainfully employed while they are in America, paying taxes, and staying out of trouble; and if they are not gainfully employed for a specific period of time, say six months; than they must be deported. If they are arrested for any felony or otherwise serious crime, they should be immediately deported and not ever allowed the chance for legal-ization or US citizenship. A legal work status would be much different than a legal citizen status, and wouldn't provide for any voting privileges or access to entitlements for adults, without first going through the citizenship process, and actually becoming a US citizen. There should be some provisions and considerations for young children who were brought here by their parents at a very early age and have grown up here through no fault of their own. I don't have all of the answers, and the solution certainly isn't going to be drafted in one chapter of a book. But Americans need to get this figured out, and do it soon.

Let me add that if immigrants came here illegally, I wouldn't be supportive of granting them citizenship without them going back to their country of origin and applying for citizenship through the normal channels that any other immigrant would have to go through, and going to the back of the line in order to do so would be a must. I mean, why should we reward someone for illegally crossing our borders? That said, I do think we should be open to a path to some form of legal immigrant status; without granting citizenship to illegals who are already here. If they want to become a citizen, there is a process, and those who have broken our immigration laws to come here, shouldn't be rewarded by getting any priority over those who have gone thru the painstakingly process to become an American citizen.

American citizenship is an extremely valuable gift and privilege. For those who weren't born here, it should be difficult to obtain, with considerable criteria to accomplish over an extended period of time. If it is easy to become a US citizen, the value of being an American citizen is immediately diminished. That said, citizenship should be attainable for those who are willing to put forth great effort and can display that they have something positive to contribute to America.

The disaster at the US–Mexico border during the summer of 2014 that has unaccompanied children coming to the United States from Honduras, El Salvador, and Guatemala through Mexico is a human tragedy of epic proportions, and a glaring proof positive of the Obama administration's failed immigration policy. As Genevieve Wood, a senior contributor to the Daily Signal, puts it: "You know things aren't going well when the only people using your talking points is you. That is increasingly where the Obama administration finds itself in explaining the massive influx of illegal minors crossing the US southern border." The White House line follows two paths. The first is that there is unrest in Central America and that crime and violence are major reasons these children seek refuge in the United States. The second is that these children have been given incorrect information that they will be allowed to remain in the United States if they successfully cross the border. "Sadly, the first line is true, and the second one is false," Wood said.

The Border crisis is in part due to the 2008 act, the William Wilberforce Trafficking Victims Protection Reauthorization act (TVRPA) of 2008, which forced US officials to inquire into the vulnerability of unaccompanied minors to trafficking and other forms of abuse. US officials were then only allowed to deport the children quickly if they make a voluntary decision to return. Longer processing times created by the 2008 act, meant longer wait times for the minors in immigration detention facilities. As a result, crowding has occurred and the overflow has been moved to military bases. The short-term solution is not to further deprive these children of their rights by deporting them without due process, but to release them quickly into the care of their resident American families or American non-profits charged with their care. In the long term, cheaper and more streamlined family reunification policies should be implemented to move otherwise peaceful and healthy children out of detention as fast as possible.

The fact however, is that few unaccompanied minors have been incentivized to come to America because of the legal change brought about by TVRPA, but rather because of their belief that they will be granted amnesty. In-fact, over ninety percent of the illegals who have come to the United States in 2014 that have been interviewed, said that they came because they had been told that they would receive amnesty once they arrived in America.

The crisis at the border is much bigger than a terrible humanitarian crisis. Consider what is going on with ISIS in Iraq and Syria, in late August of 2014, Judicial Watch President Tom Fitton, claimed that his organization had credible information suggesting that the terror group ISIS is already in Juarez Mexico, just across the US Mexico border, and that they are planning imminent car-bomb attacks in the United States. You may remember Judicial Watch is the organization which has sued the IRS under the freedom of information act, to retrieve IRS e-mails, as well as the State Department to recover e-mails related to the Benghazi scandal. I would consider Judicial Watch to be a very credible source, and Fitton claims that his source on this information is "golden". The Department of Homeland Security quickly denied claims from Judicial Watch, that ISIS has militants stationed in Juarez, Mexico who plan an imminent attack against the United States.

Regardless if ISIS is already setting up in Mexico or not, it is no secret that they intend to do so. Social media chatter shows Islamic State militants are keenly aware of the porous US – Mexico border, and are expressing an increased interest in crossing over to carry out a terrorist attack, according to a Texas law enforcement bulletin entitled "ISIS Interest on the US Southwest Border" dated August 28th, 2014.

Social media account holders believed to be ISIS militants and propagandists have called for unspecified border operations, or they have sought to raise awareness that illegal entry through Mexico is a viable option, states the law enforcement bulletin.

Agents across a number of Homeland Security, Justice and Defense agencies have all been placed on alert and instructed to aggressively work all possible leads and sources concerning any imminent terrorist threat, Judicial Watch stated on its website.

The Texas DPS bulletin comes on the heels of a federal Department of Homeland Security and Department of Justice Joint Intelligence bulletin dated August 22, 2014, a copy of which was also obtained by Fox News. That bulletin, entitled "Online Reaction but No Known Credible Homeland threats from ISIL and its Supporters Following US Air Strikes," addresses potential threats to the Homeland in response to US air strikes on the Islamic State of Iraq and the Levant (ISIL) targets in Iraq and the murder of Journalist James Foley.

Americas porous southern border and the recent surge in illegal immigration is more than just a humanitarian crisis, claims the top US general in charge of Central and South America, it's a threat to the United States, very existence. Marine Corps General John Kelly is commander of the US Southern Command, or SOUTHCOM, charged with responsibility for the Caribbean Sea and all lands south of Mexico.

Particularly in regards to the drug trade, murder rates and terrorist activity brewing in Central America, Kelly says, the waves of Latin Americans sweeping through Mexico and illegally into Texas presents a threat to the US every bit as serious as Iran or North Korea.

"In comparison to other global threats, the near collapse of societies in this hemisphere with the associated drug and illegal immigrant flow are frequently viewed to be of low importance," Kelly said in an interview with Defense One. "Many argue these threats are not existential and do not challenge our national security. I disagree."

In a testimony before the House Armed Services Committee, in February, 2014 Kelly said: "Clearly, criminal networks can move just about anything on these smuggling pipelines. Terrorist organizations

could seek to leverage those same smuggling routes to move operatives with intent to cause grave harm to our citizens or even quite easily
bring weapons of mass destruction into the United States.

SOUTHCOM's intelligence assets reveal the possibility is far
more than just crying wolf.

"Supporters and sympathizers of Lebanese Hezbollah are
involved in both licit and illicit activities in the region," Kelly told
Congress. "Members, supporters, and adherents of Islamic extremist
groups are present in Latin America. Islamic extremists visit the region
to proselytize, recruit, establish business ventures to generate funds,
and expand their radical networks. Some Muslim communities in the
Caribbean and South America are exhibiting increasingly extremist
ideology and activities, mostly as a result from ideologues activities
and external influence from the Middle East, Africa, and South Asia.
Mr. Chairman, we take all these activities seriously."

As America's top military eye on Central America, Kelly is also
warning that the recent spike in illegal immigrants moving from countries like Guatemala, El Salvador and Honduras across the US border
presents another level of threat. Those three countries, he noted, are all
among the Top 5 nations worldwide in homicide rates, in part because
of their rampant gang activity.

"Although there are a number of other countries I work with in
Latin America and the Caribbean that are going in the same direction,"
Kelly told Defense One, "the so-called Northern Triangle (Guatemala,
El Salvador and Honduras) is far and away the worst off."

Since October, tens of thousands of immigrants have made the
dangerous journey north from Latin America to the United States border. Many are children, and statistics show the vast majority of the

immigrants in the recent influx are unaccompanied minors who have traveled from Central America's "Northern Triangle." And between rampant drug trafficking and human trafficking of Central American youngsters, Kelly warned Congress, cartels and gangs that have already spread throughout the US will only grow more dangerous.

"Chairman, gone are the days of the cocaine cowboys," Kelly testified. "Instead, we and our partners are confronted with cocaine corporations that have franchises all over the world, including 1,200 American cities, as well as criminal enterprises like the violent transnational gang Mara Salvatrucha, or MS-13, that specialize in extortion and human trafficking. The FBI has warned that MS-13 has a significant presence in California, North Carolina, New York, and northern Virginia, and is expanding into new areas of the United States, including Indian reservations in South Dakota," Kelly concluded.

Roger Noriega, an American Enterprise Institute fellow and former assistant secretary of state for Western Hemisphere affairs during the George W. Bush administration, was quoted in June 2014 in the Washington Free Beacon, putting a fine point on how gang activity and arms smuggling could create problems not just along the southern border, but anywhere in the country. "There's going to be a time when MS-13 fires an RPG (rocket propelled grenade) into an Alexandria VA police car, and American's are going to say, what the hell happened?" Noriega said. Noriega is pointing out that Americans might not wake up to the very real dangers that of our porous borders, and the Mexican drug cartels, and gangs that sell the cartels drugs, until our police or civilian population are attacked with unconventional weaponry.

Kelly concluded his appeal before the House Armed Services committee by arguing the US needs to call upon and equip the military to protect our southern border, now more than ever. "Some of my counterparts perceive that the United States is disengaging from the region and from the world in general. We should remember that our friends and allies are not the only ones watching our actions closely. And in the meantime, drug traffickers, criminal networks, and other actors, unburdened by budget cuts, cancelled activities, and employee furloughs, will have the opportunity to exploit the partnership vacuum left by reduced US military engagement."

Let's recap all of this. We know for sure that there are thousands of terrorists out there who want nothing more than to murder innocent American citizens. We know that our Border Patrol agents are way over burdened by the crisis at the southern border, and while they are taking care of minor children, there are very few that are able to really pay very close attention to securing the border. We know that Mexican drug cartels have extensive means to smuggle drugs, weapons, and people across the border with relative ease. If anyone actually believes that it is unlikely that sooner or later terrorists are going to be coming across our porous southern borders to kill us, I would submit that is a very naïve point of view.

The border crisis is a tragedy for sure, but as I previously said; the tragedy on the southern US border may well be an opportunity to get something meaningful accomplished on comprehensive immigration reform. In the words of Rahm Emanuel, "Never let a tragedy go to waste." While this event is tragic for sure, politicians be well advised to take advantage of this opportunity to finally do something to secure the border and champion some meaningful immigration reforms. I would add, that the security of our very existence as a country, may well depend on us securing our borders.

CHAPTER NINETEEN

Madame President?
Not! The Hillary Clinton Scandals

"By oft repeating an untruth, men come to believe it themselves."
Thomas Jefferson - 1813

Hillary Clinton certainly has often repeated many untruths, so much so that she may well have convinced herself to believe in the lies she peddles. In the words of Hillary Clinton, "what difference does it really make?" She lied to the American public about the attacks in Benghazi being caused by some U Tube internet video, and then asks "what difference does it make?" It makes a lot of difference to me, and I would hope that it makes a lot of difference to every American citizen.

Madame President? I think not. Mrs. Clinton may be the gift that keeps on giving to conservatives. As much as the mainstream media tout Hillary Clinton as the presumptive Democratic nominee and likely successor to Barack Obama, I'm not buying it. First of all, American voters seldom appreciate a presumptive or anointed politician, and as such Hillary could face the same come-from-behind surprise in the primaries that she faced with Obama. But I for one hope that she is the Democratic nominee for the 2016 presidential elections. I think she is very beatable.

No one can take away from the fact that Mrs. Clinton is an accomplished person, and she will no doubt play up the glass ceiling narrative for all it's worth, hoping that Americans will be ready to elect the first female president in the same manner they were happy to elect America's first African American president in 2008. Mrs. Clinton may have had an accomplished career, but the only thing she has actually accomplished is an impressive resume that was built on her husband's popularity. Hillary Clinton's actual accomplishments as a lawmaker are, however, anything but impressive.

Hillary Clinton's accomplishments, or rather the lack thereof, were so unremarkable that when ABC's Diane Sawyer asked Mrs. Clinton in a June 2014 interview what she considered her top accomplishment as Secretary of State, Mrs. Clinton got a "deer in the headlights" look and couldn't answer the question. That is because there is no answer to the question. Her "reset" with Russia, was a disaster, and, across the board, the world was in much worse of a state the day she left office than it was the day she took office. So how's that reset with Russia working out for America now? That's on Hillary Clinton.

While the attacks in Benghazi were still under the "fog of attack," Mrs. Clinton was lying to the American public and blaming the attacks on some ridiculous YouTube video. The evening of the attacks, she was blaming a YouTube video when she tweeted about it. Even as she stood by as the four dead Americans' flag-draped caskets were taken off the plane, Mrs. Clinton continued to disgrace the honor and dignity of the men who fought and died on her watch as secretary of state.

That was not just a disgrace to the brave Americans who lost their lives; it is a disgrace to the office she was entrusted to serve.

Hillary Clinton has shown just how completely out of touch she is with the average American citizen. In the June 2014 interview with ABC News, Hillary Clinton proclaimed that she and Bill were "dead broke" and saddled with debt when they left the White House. "We came out of the White House not only dead broke, but in debt," Clinton said. "We had no money when we got there, and we struggled to, you know, piece together the resources for mortgages, for houses, for Chelsea's education. You know, it was not easy," Clinton said, as if she was somehow experiencing the same challenges as everyday Americans.

Since leaving the White House both Bill and Hillary Clinton have amassed a fortune in excess of $100 million. When Mrs. Clinton ran for US Senate in 2000—just before Hillary and Bill left the White House and, I would add, the same time she claimed to be dead broke—she claimed in Senate financial disclosure forms filed in 2000 that her assets were between $780,000 and almost $1.8 million. Granted, the Clintons did have some considerable legal bills, but those were quickly paid off. The forms allow senators to report assets in broad ranges. Hillary Clinton now commands speaking fees of up to $300,000 plus expenses, including round-trip transportation on a chartered private jet, specifically a Gulfstream 450 or larger, plus luxury hotel and meal accommodations for her and her staff.

Let's take a quick look at what the US tax payers started paying the Clintons after leaving the White House in 2009. President Clinton's pension was $201,000 annually. Hillary Clinton's salary as a US Senator in 2009 was $169,300. Those two numbers alone are over $370,000 a year. I don't think most American's would think of that as being dead broke. But let's look a little further; when President Clinton turned 55, in 2009, he started collecting $18,000 a year as his pension from his time as Governor of Arkansas. Those numbers are just peanuts in comparison to what the Tax payers are providing the former President and First Lady. Former presidents are also entitled to everything from office staff & benefits, travel, and all office related expenses. In-fact in addition to President Clinton's $201,000 pension, the tax payers are also providing the Clintons an additional $961,000 in other miscellaneous expenses, and that doesn't even include the cost of their secret service detail, which isn't public record. US tax payers provide Bill and Hillary Clinton $516,000 for the cost of rent for their offices. I think Hillary has got some explaining to do, if she thinks that the American people would consider that "dead broke" as she claimed they were when they left the White House, I think she's out of touch with the American people, and reality.

Hey, I'm a die-hard capitalist. I'm not saying that there is anything at all wrong with the Clintons making a lot of money, they certainly have every right to do so, and no one could blame them for doing so. But don't at the same time try to act like you are dealing with the same financial challenges that everyday Americans have to deal with, and be dishonest or at the very least disingenuous about the state of your finances are. If a politician will lie about something as trivial as their financial worth, what more serious issues will they lie about? That is nothing less than proof of just how out of touch Mrs. Clinton is with the American people.

Barack Obama, much like Bill Clinton, was at least cool and likable and could give a really good speech. Hillary Clinton doesn't have any of those characteristics.

If the American people want to see a real war on women, Hillary Clinton may soon be exposed for her long war on women. Let's get past the fact that when her husband, then President Bill Clinton, had an affair with a twenty-two-year-old intern, Monica Lewinsky, Hillary

Clinton called Lewinsky a narcissistic loony-tune, and put the blunt of the blame on her, as if Bill just stood by and said, "Golly, I just couldn't help myself." I know that most Americans have given good ol' Bill a pass on this; after all, it was consensual, right? OK, but let's not forget that Monica Lewinsky was only a few years older than the Clinton's daughter Chelsea Clinton. So OK, maybe it's just me, but there is something kind of creepy about that to me. Monica Lewinsky wasn't the first affair that Hillary Clinton had to defend either, does anyone remember Paula Jones or Gennifer Flowers?

My contention is not with Bill Clinton having an inappropriate yet consensual affair with a woman thirty years younger than he, or the fact that he lied under oath to Congress and was impeached for it. My contention is the fact that Hillary Clinton professes herself as a champion of women's rights, but yet condemns Lewinsky and dismisses the fact that this young girl was seduced by the most powerful man in the world.

I do understand Hillary Clinton standing by and supporting her husband; that is certainly her prerogative. And she certainly has every right to have very hard feelings about Lewinsky, but I do not understand her blaming a naïve twenty-two-year-old young girl, all the while acting as if Bill Clinton was an innocent bystander and had no responsibility. I'm not at all defending Monica Lewinski, either; however, when a fifty-two-year-old man who's the president of the United States, the most powerful man in the world, is entrusted by the people with the highest office in the land, it's pretty hard to blame an affair on a twenty-two-year-old "naïve" intern. I know that President Clinton's supporters gave him a complete pass on this and were all too happy to demonize Lewinski, but doesn't that sound pretty hypocritical coming from the party that pretends to be the champion of women's rights?

One shouldn't be surprised, however, by Hillary Clinton's reaction to all of her husbands affairs. You may not know it, but the

Lewinsky, Jones, and Flowers affairs certainly were not the only time Hillary Clinton came to a man's defense for sexual harassment. No, Mrs. Clinton, in her early days as an attorney, apparently defended a pedophile who beat and raped a twelve-year-old girl.

The rape victim in the 1975 sexual abuse case came forward after hearing about an audio recording that was discovered by the *Washington Free Beacon* and was made public in late June 2014. The recording, which was made some ten years after the rape, has Hillary Clinton callously acknowledging and even laughing on the recordings about knowing of her client's guilt and bragging about how she got him off by discrediting the victim—and all the while Clinton knew the guy she was defending was guilty as hell.

The rape victim, now in her early fifties, told the Daily Beast that Clinton intentionally lied about her in court documents and went to extraordinary lengths to discredit evidence of the rape. The victim went on to say that if she could speak to Clinton, "I would say, you took a case of mine in 1975, you lied on me...I realize the truth now, the heart of what you've done to me. And you are supposed to be for women? You call that being for women, what you done to me? And I hear you on tape laughing."

The victim's claim that Clinton smeared her following her rape is based on a May 1975 court affidavit Clinton wrote on behalf of Thomas Alfred Taylor, who Clinton had agreed to defend, at the request of a friend. Taylor had specifically requested a female attorney, and Hillary Clinton was happy to oblige him.

"I have been informed that the complainant is emotionally unstable with a tendency to seek out older men and engage in fantasizing," Clinton, then named Hillary D. Rodham, wrote in the affidavit. "I have also been informed that she has in the past made false accusations about persons, claiming they had attacked her body. Also that she exhibits an unusual stubbornness and temper when she does not get her way," Hillary Rodham Clinton said. The victim denied Clinton's claim she had ever accused anyone of attacking her before her rape. "I've never said that about anyone. I don't know why she said that. I have never made false allegations. I know she was lying," she said. "I definitely didn't see older men. I don't know why Hillary put that in there and it makes me plumb mad," the victim said.

The newly revealed audio recordings were taped in a series of interviews with a reporter ten years after the rape. The reporter's interview and story were never published but were recently uncovered by the *Free Beacon* at the University of Arkansas in Fayetteville, amid thousands of pieces of Clinton history. On the tapes Clinton seems to acknowledge that she was aware of her client's guilt, boasts about successfully getting the only piece of physical evidence thrown out of court, and laughs about it all whimsically.

Instead of the original charge of first-degree rape, prosecutors let Taylor plead to a lesser charge, unlawful fondling of a child. Taylor was sentenced to only one year, with two months less for time served. "I got him off with time served," Clinton bragged on the recording.

So I guess that no one should be surprised that Hillary Clinton, the self-described "champion of women's rights," would treat Monica Lewinsky in a similar fashion as she treated a twelve-year-old child who was the rape victim of a pedophile. If Hillary Clinton is the type of person America would elect as the president of the United States, we are all in for worse trouble than we already are now.

We haven't even touched on the great number of other scandals that plague Hillary Clinton. Long-time friend and former law partner of Hillary Clinton, Vincent Foster served as an aid to Hillary Clinton when they moved to the White House. Rumors had circulated that there had previously been more than just a close friendship between Foster and

Clinton. Hillary Clinton and Vincent foster, as well as Fosters wife, denied any affair. Vincent soon found it difficult to being ordered around by Hillary, his once equal. Vincent expressed that he was under extreme pressure, and even twice told his wife that he was thinking about returning to Arkansas. Foster confided in a colleague about his dealings with Hillary, he said; "It's not the same." One matter after another, he confided, she would bark "Fix it, Vince!" or "Handle it Vince!" and leave him to pick up the pieces. On July 16th, 1993 he broke down to his wife Lisa at dinner and cried when Lisa asked him; "if he felt trapped?" Four days later he was found dead on a park bench with a bullet through his mouth.

Foster Apparently committed suicide, while trying to make sense of the Clinton's questionable tax returns concerning the Whitewater Land Investment deal and his concerns over the collapse of a bank called Madison Guaranty. Allegations had been made that funds had been illegally diverted to Bill Clinton's campaign for Governor in the mid-Eighties, and that Bill and Hillary had intervened with state regulators to help keep the bank solvent (part of the Savings & Loan scandal in the mid-Eighties). According to White House council Bernie Nussbaum, what may have drove Foster over the edge, was Hillary Clinton's insistence that Foster fire seven staff members of the White House travel office. Foster was asked to help get rid of them. In a meeting on May 13, 1993, Hillary asked him if he was "on top of" the travel office situation. Foster assured her that his team was working on it. Afterwards, Foster noted that Hillary's mood was "general impatience...general frustration." Other White House aides later confirmed that she wanted her own "people" in the office, and that everyone felt "there would be hell to pay" if her wishes were defied. When the seven staff members were fired, there was an immediate uproar of cronyism that hit the headlines when it emerged that a distant cousin of bill was to be put in charge of the office, while a friend of a friend was being promoted to take over some of the White House's air-charter busses.

Although Fosters suicide was described as questionable by many at the time. Robert Fiske was first assigned to investigate the circumstances surrounding Fosters death. "No evidence" made the headlines. But with the Senate Banking Committee no longer under Democratic control, it was soon discovered that such evidence was there all along. Foster, was in a sweat about their claims of loss in Whitewater. "A can of worms you shouldn't open," he noted in a note that was later found in his office in his hand writing. Because the Clinton's explanation during the campaign was deceptive, "Don't want to go back into that box." The Washington Times discovered months later that Whitewater files were secretly spirited out of Foster's White House office by Hillary Clinton's Chief of Staff, immediately after his death.

In another letter found in Foster's brief case on a torn up yellow piece of paper, was a list of grievances and concerns about life in the White House that he had jotted down in the days before his death. Nussbaum went to Hillary's office to tell her he'd found something Vince wrote that may help explain why he did what he did. Hillary "looked startled," Nussbaum recalled. She glanced at the note, said "I can't deal with this,' and abruptly left the room. The contents of Foster's note were tantalizing. At one point, the man who knew so many of the First Couple's secrets had written: "The public will never believe the innocence of the Clinton's and their loyal staff." He also noted; "I was not meant for the job in the spotlight of public life in Washington," Foster had written: "here, ruining people is considered sport."

How about the "Reset with Russia". Hillary Clintons campaign of foreign policy blunders and incompetence while serving as Secretary of State in the Obama administration, can be tracked back to 2009 when Hillary Clinton met with Russian Foreign Minister Sergei Lavrov and presented him with a poorly translated "reset" button. According to journalists Jonathan Allen and Amie Parnes in their book *HRC*, the red and yellow button was apparently swiped from a Jacuzzi or swimming pool in Geneva. The two authors detail the chain of events:

> Philippe Reines (senior advisor to Clinton), a lover of both gim-micky and iconic imagery, had come up with a plan to show the world a symbol of the "reset" mantra. Hillary would give Russian Foreign Minister Sergei Lavrov a gift-wrapped button emblazoned with the English and Russian words for "reset." It seemed like a clever way to draw attention to the message, one sure to be bounced across the globe on television and in news-paper pictures. But Reines had sidestepped traditional protocol by not asking State's team of translators to help with the project from the start. He later said he was unaware of such resources being available to him.

Kind of hard to imagine that Hillary Clinton's senior advisor didn't know that his agency even had translators.

> Reines had asked NSC Russia director Mike McFaul for the word and both McFaul and State Russia expert Bill Burns signed off on the spelling...
>
> Lavrov pointed out that "peregruzka"—printed not in Cyrillic but in Latin script—means "overcharge."
>
> Reins tried to correct the error, asking Russia's ambassador to Switzerland to give the gift back temporarily so that a new label—with the right word—could be printed and affixed to it.
>
> "This is a gift from the United States. I don't think I can give it back to you," the ambassador replied with a smile. "If I did, my minister would be very upset."

"If your minister doesn't give that back, my minister," Reines said, referring to Hillary Clinton, "is going to send me to Siberia."

Reines pleaded his case in good humor, even suggesting they bring a label maker into the room so that the Russian ambassador didn't have to let the gift—an emergency stop button that had been hastily pilfered from a swimming pool or Jacuzzi at the hotel—out of his sight. Nyet, the ambassador said.

I guess that story would be funny if it wasn't so serious. These are the incompetents we've had running our government and in charge of our foreign policy and responsible for the safety and welfare of our country. The "reset with Russia" debacle is a prime example of the Obama administration's and Hillary Clinton's State Departments, feckless foreign policy across the board. Why should we be at all surprised? While on the campaign trail, Obama promised that under an Obama presidency, America would make friends where George W. Bush had been an antagonist. The sad reality of the results of Obama's policies is that we now have more foes than friends, our foes are greatly emboldened by America's lack of leadership, and our friends can no longer count on us.

Ironically that "reset" button Hillary Clinton gave Russian Prime Minister Lavrov, which was intended to say that America wanted to be better friends with Russia, was the start of an era that would leave America and President Obama looking impotent on the world stage. The Russian invasion of Ukraine, is all a part of Hillary Clinton's "reset with Russia". That is a fine example of her diplomatic experiences.

Between the Russian reset, leading from behind in Libya, the debacles in Syria, not to mention the fact that Iran looks to surely obtain a nuclear weapon, and ending with the blood of four brave

Americans who were murdered in Benghazi on September 11th, 2012, that is a sneak preview of the kind of Commander in Chief that Hillary Clinton would make.

While we're taking another look at Hillary Clinton's Benghazi scandal, during my final edit review of this book, there is a new "bomb shell" revelation that Hillary Clinton's top aids may have destroyed documents that may have been very damaging to Hillary Clinton and her culpability in the Benghazi scandal. Raymond Maxwell, former head of the Bureau of Near Eastern Affairs (NEA) informed Rep. Jason Chaffetz, R-Utah and other lawmakers that Clinton's chief of staff and deputy chief of staff were overseeing an operation to scrub any documents that would cast Clinton and senior leaders in a "bad light". This operation allegedly took place one weekend, in the basement of the State Department. "What they were looking for was anything that made them look bad. That's the way it was described to us" Chaffetz said. Chaffetz went on to say that such documents were said to be removed, so that Congress and the Accountability Review Board, the board probing security lapses as well as the attack's aftermath; would not see them.

Sharyl Attkisson originally reported the revelation in the Daily Signal, and Chaffetz only spoke publically about Maxwell's claims, after Maxwell himself went public with them. Chaffetz described Maxwell's account as "consistent" all this time. State Department spokesman Alec Gerlach denied the allegations in a statement to FoxNews.com

According to the Daily Signal report, Maxwell walked in on the weekend session on a Sunday afternoon after hearing about it. He reportedly claims he saw stacks of documents when he arrived as well as an office director who worked for him, but who hadn't told him about the assignment. Maxwell reportedly claimed she told him they were instructed to go through the stacks and pull out items that could put anybody in the NEA "front office" or seventh floor, where Hillary Clinton's office is, in a "bad light". Maxwell said he "didn't feel good about it" and left a short time later. According to Maxwell Clinton's Chief of Staff Cheryl Mills and Deputy Chief of Staff Jake Sullivan were there and overseeing the operation.

"For Hillary Clinton's personal chief of staff and deputy chief of staff to be making a concerted effort to hide documents, make sure that the Accountability Review Board and Congress did not see those documents is unbelievable and absolutely wrong," Chaffetz said.

Requests for comment to representatives for Clinton, Sullivan and Mills have not been returned as of the final edit of this book. The new allegations surfaced just as the House select committee on Benghazi prepared to hold its first open hearing in mid-September. I'm thinking that between this new revelation, and the revelations that came out from the three CIA contractors who were on the ground in Benghazi, that the House select committee will have a lot of new information on a scandal that the progressive left continues to claim is old news.

This isn't the first time that team Clinton has been involved with destroying documents either. You may recall former President Bill Clinton's national security advisor, Sandy Berger plead guilty to a misdemeanor in federal court, acknowledging to US Magistrate Deborah Robinson that he had intentionally took and deliberately destroyed three copies of the same "classified documents" dealing with terror threats during the 2000 millennium celebration from the National Archives. He then lied about it to Archives staff when they told him the documents were missing.

"Guilty your honor," Berger responded when asked how he pleaded. Robinson did not ask Berger why he cut up the materials and threw them away at the Washington office of his Stonebridge International consulting firm. Berger, accompanied by his wife, Susan, did not offer an explanation when he addressed reporters outside the federal courthouse following the hearing. "It was a mistake and it was wrong," he said, and refused to answer any questions.

In any event, I don't believe that Hillary Clinton will be that formidable of a candidate; she's no Bill Clinton, she's not very likable, she's done a terrible job as Secretary of State, has made absolutely no credible contribution by way of any meaningful legislation or achievement, and she has a heck of a lot of skeletons in her closet. I for one, hope she is the Democratic nominee, because I think she is very beatable.

The world cannot afford another weak American President, and Hillary Clinton would only be more of what we've had to endure with Barack Obama. The turmoil around the world, is partially of Hillary Clinton's own making. The reset with Russia was a disaster. The list goes on and on; Libya, Syria, Egypt, Iraq, and the Benghazi terrorist attack. All of those disasters have Hillary Clinton's finger prints all over them.

America needs a very strong Commander in Chief, and a President with character and integrity. Hillary Clinton, isn't it.

CHAPTER TWENTY

ISIS/ISIL Caliphate, JV? Obamas Dereliction of Duty

"How could a readiness for war in time of peace be safely prohibited, unless we could prohibit, in like manner, the preparations and establishments of every hostile nation?" – James Madison, 1788

James Madison was absolutely right on point with that statement 226 years ago, and it is certainly right on point today! Madison clearly points out the necessity of Americas military being ready for war, even in times of peace. Unfortunately Barack Obama has left little doubt, about just how clueless his is on this point. President Obama, is not only diminishing America's war readiness, he's trying to do so when we're not at a "time of peace". Granted, President Obama obviously has created some illusion in his mind that America is currently in a time of peace. Just because he may wish it to be that way, it certainly is not. War is waging across the globe, Russia has invaded neighboring Ukraine, the US is still involved in Afghanistan, and again back in Iraq, China is showing aggression towards Japan, missiles are being launched between Israel and Palestine, and radical Islamic terrorists have established a Caliphate across half of Iraq and Syria and have beheaded two American journalists! Oh yes, let's not forget the fact that Iran, a sworn enemy of America and our ally Israel, are about to develop nuclear weapons. Does this sound like a time of peace? With the world in such disarray does it really sound like a good idea to reduce our military to pre-World War II levels? I think not!

America's military readiness policy for decades, has always been to be ready and able to fight two wars at the same time. That seems like very sound policy to me. I mean a Super Powers military, if not able to fight two wars at one time, would surely be most vulnerable if they were engaged in one war, and unable to defend or engage in another. What better time would there ever be for our enemies to strike us than at that time?

For some reason, President Obama doesn't see the logic or wisdom in that kind of policy. In February 2014, the Obama administration announced its plans to shrink the US Army to its smallest force since before the World War II build up, and eliminate an entire class of Air Force attack jets in a new spending proposal that officials described as the first Pentagon budget to aggressively push the military off of the war footing it adopted after the terror attacks of 2001.

Unfortunately our enemies who want nothing more than to wipe America off of the face of the map, didn't get Barack Obama's memo that we were in a "time of peace". As if, just because Barack Obama speaks the words that the war is over, and pulls our troops off of the battlefield that our enemies are somehow relieved that everything is all better, and the fight is over.

President Obama has kept his campaign promise of ending the war in Iraq, but at what cost? After failing to negotiate a status of forces agreement with Iraqi Prime Minister Nuri Kamal al-Maliki—not that President Obama really tried to negotiate an agreement, but it sure did give him a very convenient way to cut and run—the last American combat troops departed from Iraq on December 18, 2011. It is painfully obvious that Obama had no desire to stay in Iraq and preserve the fragile stability we had fought so hard to achieve. The war was won, and had we left the twenty three thousand troops that were recommended by military commanders on the ground in Iraq, to train and assist the developing Iraqi military, Iraq would surely have been on its way to being a stable ally in the heart of the Middle East. At the time we left Iraq, Obama had touted how much better off the world is than it was when he took office. Well, he sure as heck can't say that today with a straight face.

Let's take two issues off of the table. First, the Obama administration's contention that it was Maliki's fault that America wasn't able to negotiate a status of forces agreement, which would have protected US forces from being prosecuted by an Iraqi court. This is an agreement that the United States requires anywhere in the world where we have troops on foreign soil. The facts of this case, however, do not play out for Obama. Yes, it is true that Maliki was reluctant to agree to a status of forces agreement, which was obviously politically unpopular in Iraq because it would prevent Iraq from prosecuting any soldier for any crime committed on Iraqi soil or against the Iraqi people. It's worth noting, however, that a status of forces agreement doesn't make a soldier immune from prosecution by the US military if he or she commits any crime; it just dictates that the United States and not a foreign nation will hold a soldier accountable. The reality, however, is that Obama made it clear to the Iraqis that he wasn't at all serious about keeping any adequate troop level behind to keep the peace and hold the gains we had made. In fact the military commanders recommended to Obama that the United States keep twenty-three thousand US forces in Iraq for training and command and control assistance. Obama, on the other hand, believed that he knew better than his military commanders and would only agree to three thousand troops staying in Iraq. This was a totally insufficient number of troops to have made any meaningful difference, and Maliki knew that if the United States wasn't willing to make any meaningful commitment to maintain all of the gains we'd made, it wasn't worth the political cost to Maliki. Obama didn't want to stay, so he made a joke of an offer so that he could pull all US forces out of Iraq.

Blame Bush: Right, let's go back to 2003 when George Bush and Dick Cheney got us all into the war in Iraq under the pretense of Saddam Hussein possessing weapons of mass destruction (WMD), and, as history has taught us, very few weapons of mass destruction, at best, were ever discovered. I want to remind everyone that nearly all lawmakers that had the advantage of the same intelligence on Iraq's WMDs as the White House did, supported the war in Iraq and voted for the resolution. Even Bill Clinton and Al Gore supported military action in Iraq, and they certainly had the same intelligence that Bush and Cheney did. Hillary Clinton, John Kerry, and even the ultraliberal Harry Reid and Nancy Pelosi supported and voted for the war in Iraq. Barack Obama had the luxury of not being elected to the Senate when the war resolution was passed, so it's easy for him to play Monday morning quarterback, because he doesn't have a vote to now defend.

Regardless of whether you agreed with US intervention in Iraq or not, and regardless of whether now, in hindsight, you think the United States was right or wrong, it is a moot point. It has absolutely no bearing on the conversation about what is now occurring in Iraq. Why? Because for all of the things Obama blames George Bush for, he has at least begrudgingly acknowledged that the Iraq he inherited from Bush was on its way to being a "sovereign, stable, and self-reliant" Iraq. In fact, even the gaff-riddled Vice President Joe Biden told Larry King in a

February 2010 CNN interview that Iraq was one of Obama's "great achievements." This, mind you, only one year after coming into office.

In a book written by former Defense Secretary Robert Gates, who served under Obama, Gates said that both Hillary Clinton and Barack Obama acknowledged that their opposition to Bush's "surge" in Iraq (increasing US troop levels from 140,000 to 160,000); was political as the two of them (Obama and Clinton) faced off in the 2008 Iowa primaries. "Hillary told the president that her opposition to the 2007 surge in Iraq had been political because she was facing him in the Iowa primary...The president conceded vaguely that his opposition to the Iraq surge had been political. To hear the two of them making these admissions, and in front of me, was surprising as it was dismaying," Gates said.

"Today, I can announce that our review is complete and that the United States will pursue a new strategy to end the war in Iraq through a transition to full Iraqi responsibility," Obama said on February 27, 2009, shortly after he took office.

> This strategy is grounded in a clear and achievable goal shared by the Iraqi people and the American people: an Iraq that is sovereign, stable, and self-reliant. To achieve that goal, we will work to promote an Iraqi government that is just, representative, and accountable, and that provides neither support nor safe haven to terrorists; and under the Status of Forces Agreement with the Iraqi government, I intend to remove all US troops from Iraq by the end of 2011. We will complete this transition to Iraqi responsibility, and we will bring our troops home with the honor that they have earned".

Two years later, on December 14, 2011, when he was removing the last US troops from Iraq, Obama gave a speech at Fort Bragg in

North Carolina. At that time he said his strategy based on building a sovereign, stable, self-reliant Iraq had succeeded.

> "It's harder to end a war than begin one," Obama said. "Indeed, everything that American troops have done in Iraq— all the fighting and the dying, the bleeding and the building, and the training and the partnering—all of it has led to this moment of success. Now, Iraq is not a perfect place. It has many challenges ahead. But we're leaving behind a sovereign, stable, and self-reliant Iraq, with a representative government that was elected by its people. We're building a new partnership between our nations. And we are ending a war not with a final battle, but with a final march toward home. This is an extraordinary achievement, nearly nine years in the making," Obama proclaimed.

Someone needs to have a serious heart to heart with President Obama and let him know that just because *he* says the war is over, doesn't mean that our enemy agrees.

Two and a half years after Obama pulled our troops out of Iraq, Islamic militants calling themselves ISIS (the Islamic State of Iraq) or ISIL (the Islamic State of Iraq and the Levant), a terrorist group that sprang from Al-Qaeda, and captured Fallujah and Mosul, are sweeping through Iraq and Syria, and are intent on taking Baghdad and then advancing on to Jordan to kill King Abdullah and take control of Jordan. This leaves a war-weary America, with a weak commander in chief, at a very dangerous crossroad. Move past the tragedy that forty-five hundred brave Americans gave their lives liberating Iraq and Americans spent a trillion dollars to help Iraq become a stable democracy; America has little if any choice but to go back to Iraq to stop this terrorist group intent on creating a radical Islamist emirate in the Middle East. Unfortunately it may be too late for us to make any meaningful recovery of all that's been lost.

In poll after poll, a very war-weary American people have indicated that they have no confidence in Barack Obama as the commander in chief and have accepted the tragedy in Iraq as merely a civil war brought on by a weak Iraqi prime minister, Nouri al Maliki, and his inability to keep the country together.

The terrorist group ISIS, is not just your run-of-the-mill terrorist organization. Even Al-Qaeda considers the ISIS as too ruthless. There are numerous reports of the ISIS terrorists beheading Iraqis in the streets, and hanging people on crosses. They have already captured the cities of Mosul and Tikrit and have left many Arabs and Muslims in the region worried that their countries may soon be targeted as well.

Iran has already told Iraq that it would be happy to come into Iraq and help fight off the ISIS, but it would be a disaster for America if Iran takes a foothold in Iraq. I realize that many might be thinking America needs to mind its own business and should let Iraq figure out its own problems. It's not that easy. It's not just Iraq. There are numerous US allies in the region, including Jordan, Kuwait, and even Israel, are all in grave jeopardy. Not to mention, America's national interests are front and center and completely at stake. If terrorists are allowed to gain any control in an oil-rich country like Iraq, Jordan, or Kuwait, the repercussions for the world economy and the safety and security of the world are in grave danger. The United States cannot afford to allow these terrorists to succeed, which means that the American military will be back in Iraq. Hopefully we are able to do so without boots on the ground, but without some special forces on the ground gathering intelligence, air strikes alone might not be all that effective. I would add, that the commander in chief of the most powerful military in the world, should never take any options off of the table, including US military "boots on the ground".

In an unbelievable twist of naiveté, President Obama and Secretary of State John Kerry have indicated a possible willingness to work with Iran in the Iraq debacle. Iran would love to vacuum up Iraq, and that would be a disaster for the United States. Iran has been an enemy of the United States and Israel for more than thirty years.

To add insult to injury, Barack Obama announces to the world, and our enemies, that there will be no US military boots on the ground! The stupidity of that statement is unbelievable! Barack Obama draws meaningless redlines in the sand, and takes absolutely zero action when those lines are challenged and crossed, then he back tracks and pretends that he never really drew a red line. Now, he tells our enemies that under no circumstances will America commit troops or "boots on the ground" to fight. It is literally unimaginable that an American President, would announce to the world and our enemies what we are unwilling to do. For goodness sakes, Mr. President, please keep your mouth shut! Even if you are dead set against committing US "boots on the ground", why on earth did you feel so compelled to disclose that to our enemies?

The problem in Iraq was caused when all US troops pulled out without leaving a residual force behind, and Maliki, who's a Shiite, failed to bring the Sunni minority into the political fold. Sunnis are only about 30 percent of Iraq, but they ruled with Saddam Hussein for over eighty years and oppressed the Shiite majority. Iran is almost completely Shiite, so it will have more of a natural alliance with Maliki and the Shiites and will be all too happy to align itself against the Sunnis. This has garnered support for the ISIS from the Sunnis, who are fed up with Maliki. The United States, however, cannot take sides with the Shiites against the Sunnis. This creates a real nightmare, because it may well end up enabling fanatical Muslim extremists to succeed in the creation of a caliphate (the political unity of an Islamic form of government and leadership in the Muslim world). At this point, the only Iraqi's the US can really depend on, are the Kurds.

ISIS has made no secret of their intentions. They intend to control the majority of Iraq and Syria, then move into the Kingdom of Jordan, overthrow King Abdullah, turn the kingdom into an Islamic terrorist state, then go after their primary goals of Israel and the United States.

It's almost unbelievable that the leader of the ISIS, a terrorist named Abu Bakr al-Baghdadi, was in US custody until sometime in 2009, when he was turned over to the Iraqis and subsequently released. According to the commanding officer of Camp Bucca, army Col. Kenneth King, the terrorist's parting words were, "I'll see you guys in New York." King didn't take these words from Abu Bakr al-Baghdadi as an idle threat. Al-Baghdadi knew that many of his captors were from New York, reservists with the 306 Military Police Battalion, a unit based on Long Island that includes numerous members of the New York Police Department and the Fire Department of New York. The camp itself was named after FDNY Fire Marshal Ronald Bucca, who was killed at the World Trade Center in the September 11, 2001, attacks. He said it "like, this is no big thing, I'll see you on the block," King says. "We spent how many missions and how many soldiers were put at risk when we caught this guy, and we just released him," King says.

In a wide-ranging interview with the New Yorker in January 2014, President Barack Obama compared Al-Qaeda-linked militants in Iraq and Syria, ISIS, to junior varsity basketball players, downplaying their threat as small-league. New Yorker editor David Remnick pointed out to the president that the Al Qaeda flag is now seen flying in Fallujah in Iraq and in certain locations in Syria, and thus the terrorist group has not been "decimated" as Obama had claimed during his 2012 reelection campaign. Obama responded;

> "The analogy we use around here sometimes, and I think is accurate, is if a jayvee (JV) team puts on Lakers uniforms that doesn't make them Kobe Bryant. I think there is a distinction

between the capacity and reach of a bin Laden and a network that is actively planning major terrorist plots against the homeland versus jihadists who are engaged in various local power struggles and disputes, often sectarian."

Remnick characterized Obama's analogy as "uncharacteristically flip." Keep in mind that at the time Obama made this very naïve and downright stupid comment, ISIS had already taken control of Fallujah, which was one of the hardest fought battles that the US faced in Iraq.

Less than six months later, it was obvious to anyone paying attention, that these Islamic radicals were certainly no JV team. In-fact Defense Secretary Chuck Hagel addressed the subject at a press conference:

> "They're beyond just a terrorist group. They marry ideology, a sophistication of strategic and tactical military prowess. They are tremendously well-funded. They are beyond anything that we've seen. So we must prepare for everything. And the only way you do that is that you take a cold, steely, hard look at it and get ready."

General Martin Dempsey, the chairman of the Joint Chiefs of Staff, said it would require escalating the conflict and striking targets inside of Syria. Dempsey went on to say that the Islamic terrorist group ISIS, or the Islamic State of Iraq and Syria, has an "apocalyptic end-of-days strategic vision that must be defeated by a coalition of forces." Dempsey was asked if ISIS can be defeated without addressing that part of their organization which resides in Syria: "The answer is no. That will have to be addressed on both sides of what is essentially at this point a nonexistent border. And that will come when we have a coalition in the region that takes on the task of defeating ISIS over time."

Let's take a closer look at what General Dempsey meant when he said that ISIS has an "Apocalyptic End-of-Days Vision. Muslims believe that in the tenth century, the Islamic Mahdi, or redeemer, went into hiding, but will appear again to make all things right with the world. According to the website *Answering Islam*, Muslims also claim that Jesus will return as a follower of Islam and will establish the religion on the earth.

> "Muslims believe that after Allah miraculously delivered Jesus from death, He was assumed into heaven alive in a similar fashion to the Biblical narrative regarding Elijah," the site outlines. "Since then, Muslims believe, Jesus has remained with Allah and has been awaiting His opportunity to return to the earth to finish His ministry and complete His life."

> "While the Mahdi… is clearly seen as being a superior to Jesus, Jesus is still said to be a leader of the Muslim Community upon his return. According to the Islamic traditions, Jesus primary purpose will be to oversee the institution and the enforcement of the Islamic Shariah law all over the world." Nadeem Walayat of the *Market Oracle* echoed these same sentiments.

> "What ISIS and virtually all Muslims anticipate is for Jesus to return on the white Eastern Minaret of Demascus (Syria) gliding in on the wings of two angels and then through much blood and carnage will convert the whole world to Islam including killing of all of the Jews, break all of the crosses and live as a Muslim for 40 years, before dying and thus heralding the final countdown to Judgment Day when Muslims expect to enter paradise."

ISIS specifically seeks to establish an Islamic State in the areas that it conquers, placing the regions under Islamic rule.

In August 2014, VICE News released a video documentary showing Abu Mosa, a spokesman for ISIS threatening to retaliate if the US interferes with its establishment of the Islamic State in Iraq and Syria. "I say to America that the Islamic Caliphate has been established, don't' be cowards and attack us with drones. Instead send your soldiers, the ones we humiliated in Iraq. We will humiliate them everywhere, Allah willing, and we will raise the flag of Allah in the White House." Mosa declared.

One month after releasing the Abu Mosa video, ISIS released a YouTube videos showing a British ISIS terrorist cutting the head off of journalist James Foley. Two weeks later, they released another YouTube video showing the same ISIS terrorist cutting the head off of journalist Steven Sotloff. While these tragedies were horrific for sure, and ISIS used them as propaganda to attract other jihadists and to put the fear in the hearts and minds of the world, ISIS may well have over played their hand, and awoken a sleeping giant. In a matter of days, Americans took note, and American public opinion cried out for action, and a war-weary America, suddenly paid attention, and supported some sort of military action to fight ISIS.

With the ISIS army raging through Iraq and Syria, cutting the heads off of Iraqi citizens and burying alive anyone who didn't immediately submit to them, finally got the world's attention. Barack Obama's "JV" comments about ISIS six months earlier, made President Obama look like quite the "JV" himself. So, White House spokesman Josh Earnest made every effort to walk back Obama's naïve comments claiming that President Obama wasn't referring to ISIS when he made such a ridiculous comment. The Washington Post slammed the White House for its attempts to "spin" Obama's JV comments, and gave the White House 4 Pinocchio's.

Barack Obama has clearly demonstrated that he doesn't have a clue as to what to do. His naïve views of the world are crashing down all around him while the world is on fire! On August 28th, 2014 Barack Obama admitted that his administration does not yet have a strategy to combat the militant Islamic group ISIS that had already seized large chunks of Iraq and Syria. "The options I'm asking for from the Joint Chiefs focuses primarily on making sure that ISIL is not overrunning Iraq." Obama said during a news conference at the White House. Notice his failure to say that America would defeat ISIS, merely to contain them so they are not overrunning Iraq.

My question is how on earth can the commander in chief of the largest military in the world, "not have a strategy"? Worse yet, that he admits it publically to all the world including our enemies! Again, Mr. President, please keep your mouth shut!

It's not like Barack Obama didn't know about the ISIS threat for over a year. In fact, after Barack Obama tried to blame his inaction on the Pentagon, a former Pentagon official told Fox News that President Obama had in-fact been receiving a detailed and specific intelligence about the rise of the Islamic State as part of his daily briefings for at least a year before the group seized large swaths of territory over the summer. The Pentagon official said that the data was "strong and granular in detail." And further indicated that "a policymaker could not come away with any other impression: This is getting bad." The former Pentagon official further said that Obama, unlike his predecessors who traditionally had the document briefed to them, is known to personally read the daily brief, and said that Obama generally was not known to come back to the intelligence community with any further requests for information based on the daily report.

As if Barack Obama's message on strategy couldn't get any more muddled, after a harsh backlash from both Republicans and Democrats for his "We don't have a strategy" comment, Barack Obama tried to clean that mess up, and made it even worse when he commented that he only wanted to degrade ISIS to a "manageable problem". Mr. President, please tell me how on earth you can reduce a fanatical terrorist group with an "Apocalyptic End of Days Vision", to a "manageable problem? The only way to deal with fanatical terrorists is to exterminate them from the face of the planet, and deliver them to the gates of hell!

So how is our President, our commander in chief, spending his time during all of this crisis going on around him? He's either off playing golf with his celebrity pals, or flying off to the democrat's fundraisers. Barack Obama has a strategy all right, it's not a good strategy but it's a strategy; do nothing!

So who is fighting the ISIS army? Well, after months of dithering and pandering, President Obama did finally authorize some limited airstrikes in Iraq, but as of this writing, Obama still hasn't authorized any airstrikes on ISIS strongholds in Syria. But it's the Iraqi Kurds whom are primarily the "boots on the ground" force that is bravely fighting ISIS. However, they are doing it with thirty year old Soviet weaponry. Why? Because the Obama Administration is only sending arms to Iraq through Bagdad, and those arms aren't getting to the Kurds because of Iraqi politics! The Kurds are very pro-America, much more than the other segments of Iraq's Sunni and Shiite population. The fact that the Obama Administration hasn't been able to at the very least get some modern weaponry to our allies the Kurds, to assist them in the fight, is nothing short of incompetence! It's worth noting, that the ISIS army is fighting using modern US military weaponry that they took from the Iraqi military, when the Iraqi's fled the battlefield in fear for their lives.

ISIS might have been destroyed in the fall of 2013 if the United States had bombed Syria because of Syrian President Bashar Assad's use of chemical weapons against his own people. Barack Obama contemplated air raids against Assad, but then decided to punt to Congress. Congress balked at Obama's request for a vote, because it put his fellow Democrats in a position of having to have a vote for military action on their record that they would be afraid to have to defend. So Obama decided to scrap the idea of air strikes, and looked like a fool for ever drawing a red line to Assad about using chemical weapons. Obama used Congress as the excuse for his inaction. History has quickly proved that inaction and his continued dithering about taking any action, has actually led to a much bigger problem that America has to face.

I would contend that had we took decisive action against Syria in 2013, and backed the Free Syrian Army against Assad, that we wouldn't be facing the terrible situation we find ourselves in today with ISIS. I would add, that Russian President Putin, very likely would have given much greater thought to invading Ukraine.

Befuddled and confused, President Obama appears to be at a total loss for what to do. He believes that he was elected as the president who gets America out of wars, and not a president who gets America into wars. He's shocked that the world is often an ugly and messy place, and is faced with a reality that goes totally against the grain of his very being. The fact that the world can quickly become a tinder box, without real American leadership.

Under intense pressure from both Democrats and Republicans, and the American public, President Obama was finally forced to do what he said he wouldn't ever do, get us into another war. Unfortunately it doesn't appear that Obama has a clear mission or any clear objective. What was a small group of terrorists at the beginning of 2014, a group the Obama referred to as a "JV" team of thugs, eight months later had grown into a terrorist army that even Barack Obama finally admitted it would take three to five years to defeat. It's worth noting, that America entered and ended World War II in about that amount of time. It's also worth noting, that Obama was sure to make sure that the American public had no expectation that he would resolve this problem during his presidency. No, President Obama will likely dither around for the next two years, with the US military doing far less than what they could to crush our enemy, and leave the heavy lifting for the next president to inherit. While Obama's "no boots on the ground" policy, may be much more popular and palatable to the American public, it's likely not going to allow us to defeat ISIS during the Obama presidency.

The lesson in all of this is that President Obama should have established a long-term military presence in Iraq and continued to help the Iraqis shore up and train their military the same way we did in Germany and South Korea. I'm not sure what liberals big obsession is with quickly getting all US troops out of a country after a war. America has dozens of military bases throughout Europe, and we have for over seventy years. The result, has been a relatively safe and stable Europe after World War II. What difference does it make if we have twenty five thousand military personnel at a secured US military base in Iraq and Afghanistan, or if those same soldiers are at a military base in Germany? We've already invested over a trillion dollars in both Iraq and Afghanistan, and already have significant military assets in place. If you look at a map, we have bases throughout Europe, and Iraq would have surely been a good strategic location for our military as well as providing us the ability to ensure that all we had accomplished wouldn't be all for not, and to ensure that our brave men and women who sacrificed their lives, would not have died in vain. A prolonged military presence in Iraq with as few as twenty five thousand troops could have been safe for our troops and certainly would have maintained peace in the region; and would have likely prevented the world from crumbling around us.

Hopefully Obama learns a hard lesson from his Iraq blunder and rethinks his naïve plans to leave Afghanistan in the same manner on a date certain without leaving a presence that can maintain all of the gains we've made. You can just bet that the Taliban and Al-Qaeda are sitting back waiting for us to leave. What is it that the Taliban says? "Americans have watches, but we have time."

I suggest that Barack Obama, and all of his progressive, liberal supporters take note of the words of Ronald Reagan;

"A truly successful army is one that, because of its strength and ability and dedication, will not be called upon to fight, for no one will dare provoke it." – Ronald Reagan, May 27th, 1981

CHAPTER TWENTY ONE

The Obama Doctrine, "Don't do Stupid Stuff"

"America will never be destroyed from outside. If we falter and lose our freedoms, it will be because we destroyed ourselves." – Abraham Lincoln

While Abraham Lincoln wasn't one of our founding fathers, he was certainly one of the best presidents that America ever had. Lincoln's insightful words of wisdom, would do Barack Obama good to heed. If America is ever destroyed, it will be because "we the people" allowed it to happen, and "we the people" would be complicate in our demise because we elect weak leaders who tell us what we want to hear.

"Don't do Stupid Stuff", where on earth to begin. I suppose if there were a second choice for the title of this book that would be it. Pretty much every chapter of this book, highlights dozens of examples of "Stupid Stuff" that have been perpetuated on "we the people" by the progressive left, and Barack Obama for the past eight years. Surprisingly the Obama Administration authorized the distillation of President Obama's foreign policy doctrine; "Don't do stupid stuff". That phrase appeared in the New York Times several times as well as in the Los Angeles Times so the White House has effectively got the media to circulate their policy doctrine.

Christi Parsons, Kathleen Hennessey and Paul Richter in the Los Angeles Times and Chicago Tribune of April 29, 2014: "The president's aides have scrambled to put things in simpler terms. 'Don't do stupid stuff' is the polite-company version of a phrase they use to describe the president's foreign policy." The phrase was cleaned up from "don't do stupid sh-t."

Christi Parsons and Kathleen Hennessey in the LA Times and Chicago Tribune on May 25th, 2014: "Privately, White House officials have described the working label for Obama's doctrine as 'Don't do stupid stuff.' Within the tight circle of foreign policy aides in the White House, the shorthand captured Obama's resistance to a rigid catch-all doctrine, as well as his aversion to what he once called the 'dumb war' in Iraq."

Mark Landler, in a June, 2014 lead story of the New York Times; "In private conversations, the president has used a saltier variation of the phrase, 'don't do stupid stuff' – brushing aside as reckless those who say the United States should consider enforcing a no-fly zone in Syria or supplying arms to Ukrainian troops."

Even Obama's former Secretary of State Hillary Clinton, couldn't resist taking a shot across Obama's bow, describing the remark in an interview with the Atlantic magazine as too simplistic. "Great nations need organizing principles, and 'Don't do stupid stuff' is not an organizing principle," Clinton said. Clinton then called Obama to "make sure he knows that nothing she said was an attempt to attack him," her spokesperson Nick Merrill said in a statement. The two later met at a party hosted by Democratic Party adviser Vernon Jordon on Martha's Vineyard, to "kiss and make up".

In an interview with CNN, Deputy National Security Adviser Ben Rhodes insisted that "DDSS" is not the "entire foreign policy" of the Obama administration. But he maintained the expression does have substance. "It means think carefully before you get into military interventions, I think that's a lesson of the last ten years that the American people have internalized – that we have to be very careful when it comes to the application of military force, that we're not putting US troops in harms way without a clear plan and limited objectives for that effort."

"Don't do stupid stuff ought to be emblazoned on the foreheads of all future presidents and secretaries of state," said Aaron David Miller, a former State Department advisor. Miller said "DDSS" is less a doctrine than it is a presidential mission statement that is shaped by more than a decade of war. Stripped to its essence, after protecting the homeland, it should be US foreign policy's second commandment." Miller added.

Obamas "don't do stupid stuff" slogan can be traced back to an anti-Iraq war speech Obama delivered as an Illinois state senator in 2002. "What I am opposed to is a dumb war. What I am opposed to is a rash war," Obama said at the time.

I am dumbfounded as to why the Obama administration would use "don't do stupid stuff" as a slogan for their foreign policy. Are they completely clueless as to the long laundry list of "stupid stuff" that they have done for the past six years, and continue to do today?

Obama's "stupid stuff foreign policy" is what has the world in total chaos today, and the vast majority of Americans in fear of an imminent terrorist attack.

According to New York Times reporter Peter Baker, ten people who were invited to a white house meeting following the beheading of American journalists by ISIS, speaking on condition of anonymity, they gave their impressions of the President's demeanor and his plans for destabilizing the ISIS regime. One note of interest was the president's remarks on how he would have advised ISIS, had he been in a position to do so. If he had been "an advisor to ISIS," Mr. Obama added, he would not have killed the hostages but released them and pinned notes on their chest saying, "Stay out of here: this is none of your business." Such a move he speculated might have undercut support for military intervention. This kind of "stupid stuff" naïve statement from our commander in chief, is likely why in an August, 2014 Rasmussen poll, only 29% of Americans felt that Obama has done a good job in dealing with ISIS.

President Obama has been all over the board with regards to "doing stupid stuff" as it pertains to the ISIS threat. First calling them a JV team in January of 2014. Obama later came out in a press conference and proclaimed that the aim is to "degrade and destroy" the terror group. But then, moments later, claiming that he wants to make it a "manageable problem." Which is it Mr. President? Do you intend to degrade and destroy, or simply manage the ISIS threat? When journalist James Foley was beheaded, Obama took a short break from his vacation, to give condolences and say that the US wouldn't tolerate these horrific acts. He then darted off to the golf course a few minutes later. Pretty "stupid stuff" way for the president of the United States to act if you ask me.

Only after president Obama's poll numbers sank to the lowest rate of any president in over two decades, and out cries from the public and congress on both sides of the isle, did president Obama begin to understand that the world around us has a funny way of determining who will be a "war time" president. Barack Obama, who constantly touted that he was the president who was elected to get America out of wars, and not into wars, found himself being drug into war. Kicking and screaming, but none the less, drug into war. Ironically, America being forced into war, was of Obama's own making, because of his failure of leadership.

Just prior to the 2014 congressional recess, President Obama invited over a dozen Senate and House leaders from both parties to the White House to talk about foreign policy and potential military action against ISIS. According to lawmakers inside the meeting, Obama became visibly agitated when confronted by bipartisan criticism of the White House's policy of slow-rolling moderate Syrian rebel's repeated requests for arms to fight the Assad regime and ISIS. The argument that America should have done more in Syria, made for years by foreign policy leaders in both parties and several members of Obama's senior national security team, was brought back to the forefront, as the debate rolls on as to whether the security and humanitarian catastrophe in Syria could have been avoided if the US had played a larger role starting as far back as 2012.

The meeting included a heated exchange between Barack Obama and Senator Bob Corker (R-Tenn.). "I said, 'I got to tell you something, there's a degree of audacity in you being here today. If you look at your three major initiatives they were almost all done on party-line votes, I feel we're all props here today." Corker told Obama. After the meeting Corker wrote a blistering op-ed for the Washington Post criticizing Obama's handling of foreign policy.

> "Today, after three years of bold rhetoric divorced from reality, 170,000 Syrians are dead, and we are not innocent bystanders. The president encouraged the opposition to swallow deadly risks, then left them mostly hanging, Extremist groups from Syria have surged into Iraq, seizing key territory and resources, and are threatening to completely undo the progress of years of US sacrifice." Corker said.

In a New York Times interview published August 8th, 2014, Obama said that "the idea that arming the rebels would have made a difference had always been a fantasy. This idea that we could provide some light arms or even some more sophisticated arms to what was essentially an opposition made up of former doctors, farmers, pharmacists and so forth, and that they were going to be able to battle not only a well-armed state, but also a well-armed state backed by Russia, backed by Iran, a battle-hardened Hezbollah, that was never in the cards." Obama said.

One month after President Obama called it a fantasy that the Syrian rebels were made up of nothing more than doctors, farmers and pharmacists, could ever battle a well-armed opposition, President Obama announced that he planned to do exactly that. The group that our president referrers to as, merely doctors and farmers, is who he is now entrusting to fight the ISIS army. Obama requested half a billion dollars from congress to equip and train these doctors, farmers and pharmacists. Had President Obama made this decision two years ago, when his national security advisors advised him to do so, it may have made a tremendous difference. Now, unfortunately it is likely far too little and far too late.

> "Because of our failure, the rebels have been so badly harmed and so many killed," said Senator John McCain, a long-time advocate for intervening in the Syrian conflict. "The blood is on their hands, the responsibility for the casualties that they have suffered unnecessarily, the responsibility lies with the president."

Does this all sound like "don't do stupid stuff"? Or does it sound much more like "doing stupid stuff"?

> "We may never know for sure if ISIS's decisions were encouraged by Obama's choices in Syria. What we know for sure is that ISIS

metastasized in Syria and was not deterred because of anything Obama said or did so far." Senator Bob Corker (R-Tenn.)

"The president still feels very strongly that we are deluding ourselves if we think American intervention in Syria early on by assisting these rebels would have made a difference. He still believes that. I disagree, respectfully. They were not looking for US troops they were looking for help and the Syria civil war started with the most noblest of causes." -Representative Eliot Engle, the ranking Democrat on the House Foreign Affairs Committee told the Daily Best in an interview.

Hillary Clinton told the Atlantic in an interview published August 10, 2014 that Obama's "failure to help build up a credible fighting force of the people who were the originators of the protests against Assad – there were Islamists, there were secularists, there was everything in the middle – the failure to do that left a big vacuum, which the jihadists have now filled." In 2012, Clinton revealed that she and then CIA Director David Petraeus had pushed a plan earlier that year to arm the Syrian rebels that was rejected by the White House. Defense Secretary Leon Panetta and Joint chiefs Chairman General martin Dempsey later said they supported the plan at the time. Many lawmakers, including Corker and Engle, still support that plan and they agree that Obama's inaction has left a vacuum that ISIS rushed to fill.

The ISIS threat is definitely tied to inaction in Syria, because the uprising started against Bashar al Assad, it was a movement of people wanting freedom and democracy in Syria, and not a war involving jihadists. The Syrian people desperately needed our help, and Barack Obama did nothing. This allowed ISIS to gain the upper hand, and the world is now paying the consequences of that inaction.

President Obama is definitely no stranger to "doing stupid stuff". You may recall earlier in this book, when just prior to the 2012 presidential elections, that Barack Obama was accidentally caught on a microphone telling Russian President Dmitry Medvedev; "this is my last election. And after my election, I have more flexibility." To which Medvedev responded: "I understand you. I transmit this information to Vladimir", speaking of Vladimir Putin. President Obama was referring to scrapping the European missile defense that Putin was adamantly opposed to. We now know how that "stupid stuff" move turned out. Russia invaded Ukraine, and was subsequently complicate in shooting down a commercial airliner, killing 300 innocent civilians.

Pulling out of Iraq without leaving a residual force to keep the peace and all of the gains that US troops had made in bringing Iraq to the verge of being a stable democracy, has certainly turned out to be very "stupid stuff", and resulted in the ISIS army taking over half of Iraq, and massacring thousands of innocent Iraqi civilians.

Stupid stuff? How about bowing to foreign leaders like Saudi King Abdullah, or Japanese Emperor Akihito, and the Chinese Emperor? How about thinking you can negotiate with countries like Iran on their plight to obtain nuclear weapons, and have vowed to wipe Israel off the map? Or playing nice with the likes of Venezuelan Dictator Hugo Chavez? And this from an administration who claims their foreign policy doctrine is "don't do stupid stuff."

We could obviously go on and on and on and on about all of the "stupid stuff" our president has done over the past six years. And as so much of it is already detailed throughout this book, there is little point to continue pointing out the obvious.

While most past American presidents have cared about their legacy, they dared to be bold and met the challenges America faced head on. Unfortunately President Obama has found that the world is a much different reality than what he fanaticized it was. Mr. Obama appears to be completely disengaged, and looks as if he's counting down the days, where he can retire to the golf course and speaking tours.

Imagine if George Washington's policy was "don't do stupid stuff". I would imagine that America would have never won our independence.

Imagine if Abraham Lincoln's policy would have been "don't do stupid stuff." It may well have taken America another hundred years to abolish slavery.

Imagine if Harry Truman's policy would have been "don't do stupid stuff." American's may well be speaking Japanese.

Imagine if John F. Kennedy's policy would have been "don't do stupid stuff." America may have never explored space or put a man on the moon.

Imagine if Ronald Reagan's policy would have been "don't do stupid stuff." The Berlin wall may have never come down, and America certainly wouldn't be the world's only superpower.

No doubt, every American president needs to be well advised when making any decision, and should avoid doing "stupid stuff" at all costs. However, Barack Obama's "doctrine" of "don't do stupid stuff", has caused him to do the very thing he claims he's trying to prevent doing. His feckless foreign policy has left him nothing short of impotent.

America needs strong presidential leadership, and the world needs strong American leadership. "We the people" expect our president to lead, and be bold. Mr. President, please lead, and be bold, the world can't afford to wait two more years for a strong leader.

**If You Want
Food Stamps
Vote Democrat
If You Want
A Paycheck
Vote
Republican**

CHAPTER TWENTY TWO

Light at the End of the Tunnel: Vote for Change!

"I love the man that can smile in trouble; that can gather strength from distress, and grow brave by reflection. Tis the business of little minds to shrink; but he whose heart is firm, and whose conscience approves his conduct will pursue his principles unto death."—Thomas Paine, 1776

How can you not absolutely admire the intellect and foresight of our Founding Fathers? The inspirational words of Thomas Paine are words that should do us all good as we move forward in our cause to recapture our country. We would all do well to reflect on those words as we garner the strength to pursue our principles.

As I began writing this book, I was obviously aggravated and pretty well worked up about what's been going on in America. These past eight years have definitely been the darkest times in America that

I've witnessed in my fifty years of life. I have to tell you, however, as I've spent the past several months researching all of the facts and the overwhelming amount of material I studied for this book, my emotions went from aggravation to anger, and from anger to fear. But as I finish writing this book, that anger and fear have turned to resolve: resolve to try to effect change, resolve to try to help take our country back. This is not the America I grew up in, and it certainly isn't the America I want my children and grandchildren to inherit.

So what do we do to effectuate any meaningful changes? The very first thing we have to do is start paying attention! Take our blinders off and open our eyes, see things the way they really are, and give the issues we face as a country and as a people some serious debate and deliberation. We need to quit voting for slick-talking politicians who tell us what we want to hear for political gain. We have to understand that we all have got to get our hands dirty, break a sweat, and be willing to do the hard lifting ourselves. We have to suck in our guts, tighten up our belts, decide what sacrifices we can live with, and commit ourselves to the cause: the cause of making the "exceptional" country of America, great once again!

I certainly haven't made any secret of my political ideology, and as much as I've highlighted all of the incompetence and corruption surrounding all of the scandals our country has endured over the past several years, the Republicans aren't going to get a pass from me either. Republicans share plenty of blame for the mess we find ourselves in today. I'm a proud conservative, but I often find myself very aggravated by some of my fellow Republicans who have either lost their way or have taken their eye off the ball. Politicians on both sides of the isle have been going crazy on spending for the past couple decades, and it's got to stop!

I'm a Republican because I firmly believe in limited government, lower taxes, strong national security, and the rule of law as set forth in the US Constitution. I believe in American exceptionalism. I believe in an America that encourages innovation and hard work and allows its citizens to reap the rewards of their labor and innovation. That's pretty much it in a nutshell, or should I say "period." I have a fairly strong conservative viewpoint on social issues as well, but with the current mess our country is in today, social matters seldom figure into my politics. The fact that I truly believe in limited government means that I think government should stay out of most social matters and should certainly stay out of matters involving well-meaning and consenting adults.

Conservatives in general are often not the greatest of orators. Not since "the great communicator," Ronald Reagan, has anyone been able to so eloquently deliver our message. Both President Bush's found their voice at times of crisis, but for whatever reason we often find it difficult to tell our story or explain our positions on the issues in a simple and straightforward message. I've given this a considerable amount of thought, and I often think that the answers to our problems are so glaringly obvious to us that we can't believe the opposition can't see it for what it is. That, however, is far too simple an answer, and it smacks of arrogance. It really comes down to the fact that in order to seriously implement strong conservative ideas, you have to level with the voters and tell them what they all too often don't want to hear. It's damned hard to win an election when you're honest with people and tell them what they don't want to hear. So the opposition has an upper hand while campaigning because their ideas often sound so much better in theory to voters who might not want to make the hard decisions and maybe haven't really thought all of the issues out, or even considered the unintended consequences.

The Republican Party needs to pull their heads out of the sand and get their act together, and they had better get that figured out soon. If Republicans are relying on the ineptness of Democrats to win the next couple of elections, they are going to be in for a very rude awakening.

Yes, the winds are in the Republicans' favor, but the people are not going to put Republicans back in power just because the president is incompetent and his administration is bogged down in scandal after scandal. Barack Obama is never going to be on another ballot, but that certainly doesn't mean the Democrats are just going to roll over and hand Republicans the keys to the store.

Republicans need to find a concerted message on a plethora of issues that they can all rally around. Who can expect Republicans to lead this country and bring this country together when we all too often can't agree on a number of issues within our own party? Don't get me wrong, I think it's good that we have a lot of ideas and a lot of diversity in our party, but we have got to come together and get a unified message. Congress has a pretty pathetic approval rating among the American public because all the voters see is gridlock in Washington. It's one thing to have gridlock between two opposing parties, but when we have gridlock within our one party, that's a problem.

Americans are looking for leadership, real leadership. I don't believe that most Americans want a handout or to be dependent on the government. I believe that Americans want the leadership in their government and their elected officials to create an environment of opportunity and prosperity and to keep our country and our children safe. Certainly Americans expect the government to provide a safety net for older Americans who need a safety net and for those who can't provide for themselves. For everyone else, nothing more than a possible hand up and a fair shake. Americans want real leadership so badly that in the absence of it, they will drink sand in the mirage of a clear stream. If conservatives lead, and I mean truly lead, they are on the brink of a real opportunity to effect real and positive change to get this country back on track. And I, for one, pray God that they find the courage, conviction, and strength to do so.

I'm going to make a few suggestions on a few touchy issues about which the Republicans have failed to find a unified message. I realize that regardless of what side of the aisle you are on, people's view points on the issues are all over the board. I'm going to guess that if you are still reading this book, you either see the world through a similar pair of glasses that I do or you are at least open minded enough to hear out my unsolicited thoughts on the challenges that face our country.

First and foremost, we have got to expand the size and appeal of our Republican tent. The core principles and values of conservatives, I believe, are the true core values in the pit of most Americans' stomachs; but because of our inability all too often to effectively project our message, the Dems have been able to splinter and exploit conservative positions in a manner that keeps some voters from embracing our party and our policies. I'm not suggesting that we don't stand firm on our principles; to the contrary, what I am saying is that we had better iron out our platform and have a unified message when our policies are attacked. Then prioritize what it is that we want to accomplish, stay focused on it like a laser, and don't allow ourselves to get sidetracked or derailed unless an unexpected world event forces us to change course.

What do I mean when I suggest we need to broaden our tent? We need to make sure that our platform and our message is an all-inclusive American message that benefits all Americans from all races, income brackets, genders, and orientations. I truly believe that conservative principals and ideology is the very best course for our country and for all Americans.

Let's start with same-sex marriage. We need to get that issue off the table; that ship has sailed, and like it or not it is a losing argument. I can respect the rights of same-sex couples; I don't have to agree with same-sex marriage or even same-sex lifestyle, no more than a same-sex couple has to agree with me about traditional marriage. I'm not going to infringe on any rights of gay couples, any more than I would expect or want them to infringe on me. My point is, if anyone believes in fundamental conservative principles, I am going to welcome him or her in our tent. It would be terrible for Republicans to lose any group of Americans simply because we might not agree with who someone loves.

Let's all focus on what we do agree about. We need to stop playing small ball and focus on the big picture. We need to win elections, and we can't do that if we aren't united and if we don't stay on point!

No doubt, one of the touchiest issues in American politics is the issue of abortion. That is a tough one, but I do believe that all politicians should hold their ground on issues they have a strong conviction about. "Never trust a politician who abandons his or her convictions." I believe conservatives should always hold their ground on whatever their convictions are. I know I said that I don't much consider social issues when I vote, and I don't. When I say that, what I mean is that so long as a politician sees eye to eye with me on low taxes, smaller government, and strong national defense, he or she will likely earn my vote regardless of his or her position on other issues, unless there is another candidate who agrees with me on all of those priorities, plus everything else I believe, so long as that candidate is electable. That said, I don't consider abortion a "social issue." Abortion is definitely a moral issue that most people have very strong convictions about, one way or the other. Abortion is also a legal issue, and politicians should vote their conscience and stand on their convictions, whatever those convictions may be.

When social conservatives are attacked for supporting legislation that restricts late-term abortion, I might suggest that they remind those progressives who are on the attack, of the atrocities of Dr. Kermit Gosnell, the Philadelphia abortion doctor who was sentenced to three life sentences for killing an aborted baby that he described as so big it could "walk to the bus." Gosnell was convicted of first-degree murder in the deaths of three babies born alive, then stabbed with scissors. He pled guilty and accepted the three life sentences to spare him the death penalty. Philadelphia District Attorney Seth Williams said about Gosnell: "Any doctor who cuts into the necks, severing the spinal cords, of living, breathing babies who would survive with proper medical attention is a murderer and a monster." No doubt. Gosnell was running nothing short of an abortion mill and making millions off of giving late-term abortions to young inner-city moms. Gosnell is the poster child for supporting strong legislation restricting late-term abortion.

I noticed that the liberal Left was completely silent about the rights of all the babies Dr. Gosnell was convicted of murdering.

All of that said, Republicans would be well served to tone down any rhetoric about abortion. We need to understand just how polarizing an issue abortion is and not give this issue to our opponents, who would gladly exploit the "one-issue" voters, by attacking pro-life conservatives as having a war on women. That is a ridiculous argument, if you ask me; I mean, I'm not sure how someone's belief that life begins at conception constitutes a "war on women."

Roe v. Wade (the Supreme Court ruling of January 22, 1973, that legalized abortion) was settled over forty years ago. While I may disagree with the high court ruling, there is something called *stare decisis*, a legal principle by which judges are obligated to respect the precedent established by prior decisions. In other words, it means that the subject is settled law. The longer a precedent stands, the more credence a justice is required to give it in considering the precedent as "settled law." The words originate from the phrasing of the principle in the Latin maxim *stare decisis et non quieta movere*: "to stand by decisions and not disturb the undisturbed." In legal contexts, this is understood to mean that courts should generally abide by precedent and not disturb settled matters. *Roe v. Wade* would be difficult if not impossible to overturn, and social conservatives who would like to see *Roe v. Wade* overturned would be well advised for now, to choose their battles wisely.

Speaking of Supreme Court rulings, conservatives would be very well advised to keep their eye on the real ball that can move the country in one direction or another. The Supreme Court was created in 1789 by Article III of the US Constitution, which stipulates that the "judicial Power of the United States, shall be vested in one supreme Court" together with any lower courts Congress may establish. When I say that we need to keep our eye on the ball, what I'm saying is that conservatives must stay focused not only on 2014, but even more importantly we must stay focused on 2016. During the next president's term, we will likely have at least four Supreme Court justices retire: Antonin Scalia (born in 1936), Anthony Kennedy (born in 1936), Ruth Bader Ginsburg (born in 1933), and Stephen Breyer (born in 1938). Scalia is a strong conservative vote, Kennedy is a swing vote, and Ginsburg and Breyer are both liberal votes. A Supreme Court justice is appointed by the president and confirmed by Congress, and they are appointed for a life term or until a justice chooses to retire. Assuming none of the justices pass away or retire in the next two years, our next president could really shape the high court for many years to come. If conservatives aren't able to win in 2016 and progressive liberals are able shape the Supreme Court, America as we've known it will be gone forever.

RINOs (Republicans in name only) would do well to join their fellow conservatives and prove once and for all that they really are fiscal conservatives by supporting a balanced budget amendment to the US Constitution. In 1995 House Republicans came close to passing a balanced budget amendment to our Constitution; but for the defection of Sen. Mark Hatfield (R-OR), the bill would have passed the House with a two thirds vote. Sen. Tom Daschle (D-SD) defected in his support of the bill in the Senate, so the bill failed.

Thomas Jefferson wrote in 1798: "I wish it were possible to obtain a single amendment to our Constitution. I would be willing to depend on that alone for the reduction for the administration of our government; I mean an additional article taking from the Federal Government the power of borrowing." The first balanced budget amendment, however, was not proposed until 1936, when Rep. Harold Knutson (R-MN) introduced House Joint Resolution 579 proposing a per-capita limit on federal debt. We came close again in 1982, but then Speaker Thomas "Tip" O'Neill (D-MA) inevitably killed the bill.

So how do we balance the budget? Budget Chairman, Representative Paul Ryan has produced a number of viable budgets that would balance the budget in about ten years. But here's another thought; we adopt the "Penny Plan." Everyone should be able to tighten his or her belt enough to live with one penny less. If we could get lawmakers to simply cut a penny from every dollar the government spends each year for six years and cap government spending at 18 percent of GDP (gross domestic product), we would balance our budget in less than ten years. It really is just that simple. It is high time that Americans realize that for every $2 our government brings in, it is spending $3. That is totally unsustainable, and it is a moral imperative that we live within our means.

If our government had a balanced budget amendment, we wouldn't be in this terrible situation we find ourselves in today. It would prevent the kind of out-of-control government we have today and protect us from our own demise. Businesses have to balance their budgets, families have to balance theirs, and even the states have to balance their budgets; the federal government should have to do so as well. Democrats, however, recognize that the threat of a balanced budget amendment would prevent their progressive big government ideology, so few Democrats can find their way to support it. All the more reason to pass it.

Republicans need to support sweeping tax reform. The right tax reform and tax reductions would spur our economy and create growth more quickly than anything else. My vote would be to do away with the IRS altogether and support either a flat tax or a national sales tax. We are "taxed enough already." President Obama has already proved that we can't spend our way out of this hole we're in; the only way is to earn our way out of it, and that starts with sweeping tax reform!

We also must repeal and replace Obamacare. Health care is obviously a very hot-button topic. And as much as I oppose Obamacare, or the Affordable Care Act, Republicans have got to unite around a health care reform bill that addresses a lot of serious concerns. Open up health care markets across state lines. Obviously the issue of covering preexisting conditions and protections from cancelation must be a high priority consideration in any new health care reform.

Some level of tort reform might need to be a consideration, but let's not use the term "tort reform" too loosely. I'm all for trying to do away with frivolous lawsuits, but who's to say which lawsuits are frivolous and which ones aren't? Let's not lose sight of the fact that jury awards for injured parties are one thing that keeps the free market in check, and caps on jury awards would be a bean counters dream. Corporations would know with certainty the downside for bad or irresponsible behavior, and if the advantages outweighed the downside, look out. I do believe that it is very important that injured persons or parties should be able to be justly compensated for losses or injury, because that is what holds businesses like health care providers and other free market businesses, accountable. The fact that you can't easily sue the federal government or government employees is one of the problems with big government and certainly contributes to their lack of accountability.

Overly burdensome government regulations have stifled our economic recovery and have crippled many businesses. I certainly recognize the need for some regulation and the importance of protecting our environment. But there has got to be a reasonable balance. Part of that reasonable balance must recognize the necessity of America's global competitiveness on the world stage. The sad truth is that if America as a country could eliminate 100 percent of any air pollution we produce, it wouldn't put a dent in the global pollution problem. That doesn't mean that we shouldn't act responsibly and even take the lead for the rest of the world, but we have got to consider the reality of the world economy.

Under the Obama administration's complete lack of leadership, our military has been severely weakened. Obama plans to cut our military budget to pre–World War II levels. Our readiness, or lack thereof, certainly caught us with our pants down on September 11, 2011, when we found ourselves under attack in Benghazi, Libya, and, according to the Obama administration, we didn't have any military assets available to provide any assistance. If we don't have military assets in such a hot spot as the Middle East on the eleven-year anniversary of the attacks on our homeland, we are in pretty sad shape. Terrorists are running ramped, like wildfire across the Middle East and Obama's complete lack of leadership have made America impotent to do anything meaningful about it. This would be the worst time in America's history for us to cut back our military readiness. President Obama's mere suggestion that he thinks that would be a good idea, shows just how completely clueless he really is.

What's happened in Iraq is inexcusable. Forty-five hundred of our brave soldiers lost their lives liberating Iraq, and we spent over a trillion dollars in American treasure. We had won the war and were on the path to a reasonably democratic ally in the Middle East, and what does Obama do? He cuts and runs and lets everything we gave our blood, sweat, and treasure achieving fall down the tubes. He's dead set on doing the very same thing in Afghanistan, and if Iraq and Afghanistan are turned over to our enemies, may God help us all! Republicans need to adamantly support our military and make every effort to repair the damage President Obama has done to America around the world. When America doesn't lead around the world, it quickly creates a vacuum that will quickly be filled by our enemies, who would do us harm.

America's allies no longer trust us, and our enemies no longer respect or fear us. One need look no further than the conflict in Ukraine, with Russian President Vladimir Putin ignoring any warnings from Barack Obama, as Putin invades his sovereign neighbor, and is complicit in shooting down a commercial air-liner and killing 298 innocent victims.

My biggest concern blocking the light at the end of the tunnel is the fact that we have been so weakened as a country by the failed policies of this administration. Mark my words about this, and I pray to God that I am wrong about this prediction: America will suffer another 9/11 type of terrorist on our homeland within the next few years. I suspect that the attack may eclipse the attacks of 2001. Again, I pray to God that I am wrong about this, but the complete and utter impotence of the Obama administration has so weakened America and emboldened our enemies that we would be naïve as a country if we didn't realize that our enemy recognizes we are on the canvas, out of breath, bruised and battered, with little will to defend ourselves or strike back. This may not happen by the end of Obama's term, but very likely within the first few years of a new administration before any new president has the time needed to repair all of the damage he will inherit from the Obama administration. Make no mistake, our enemies have been emboldened and know that they now have two more years left to build their organizations, train their fellow terrorists, and strategize their next attack on America. The terrorist group ISIS who has already taken over half of Iraq and half of Syria, have already as much as told us that they intend to attack America.

So let's talk about the bright light that could be shining on our economy if we would embrace it. Energy is going to prove to be our country's saving grace! We just need to get the progressive ideology out of power. Due to new innovations in drilling for oil and natural gas, America has become the world's largest producer of natural gas, and, according to the International Energy Agency (IEA), the United States is on track to soon take over as the largest producer of oil in the world, beating out Saudi Arabia by the year 2020, and it could well be energy independent by the year 2030. The 1990s boomed economically not necessarily because of any political party in power, but because the Internet and technology boomed! Energy is the tech boom of our coming generation. If we are able to develop a safe but very aggressive energy policy, we may well be able to earn our way out of the mess we are in. Why has it taken over five years to get any approval on the Keystone Pipeline? Progressive government, plain and simple. I say, let's build the pipeline, then drill, baby, drill.

The brightest light around the corner is that the American people have had a full taste of progressivism and would have to be blind not to see the damage it has caused. This puts the political winds at the backs of conservatives. Not only do Republicans have the wind at their backs in the coming elections, they have the facts and the statistics. Forget about the Obama administration being scandal ridden and the Democrats' complete lack of demand for accountability from the president and their turning a blind eye to all of the corruption that the American people are finally opening their eyes to. Republicans would be well advised to stay focused on the facts, because the facts are definitely in favor of the Republicans and their smaller government, lower taxes philosophy.

The report card is in and the evidence is obvious that states led by Republican governors have outperformed nearly every state led by a Democratic governor. In a May 2013 study of all states in the United States and which state ranks the highest in economic potential, virtually all of the top ten are states that voted for the GOP.

The study, called "Red States, Poor States," was the sixth in a continuing series from the ALEC (American Legislative Exchange Council) and rated the states using fifteen factors, some of which included minimum wage laws, labor policies, and rates of taxation. The top of the list was Utah. ALEC's Jonathan Williams said, "The real key to Utah is low tax rates, but more than that a predictable tax climate. Utah legislators are very conscientious about the fact that they don't' spend beyond their means and also they don't make changes in tax policy retroactively. They make changes very gradually and they generally make them in a lower tax direction." Williams added that the worst ten states were more likely high-tax "blue" states that had stringent restrictions on business. New York and Vermont were at the bottom of the list in the latest survey. According to the ALEC study, the state with the greatest economic growth from 2001 thru 2011 was Texas, and the worst was Michigan. The numbers for growth were derived from the state's job growth, gross state product growth, and population shifts.

Twenty-nine of the fifty states are run by Republicans governors, and most have a Republican majority among lawmakers. One could easily make the argument that because of the majority of states are run by Republicans, with good fiscal policies, that is what has helped keep the country from sinking into a double-dip recession due to the Obama policies.

Republicans may well have more than just the political winds at their backs, as well as a great report card in the states with Republican leadership. The Democrats' presumptive presidential nominee appears to be the same presumptive nominee the Democrats had in 2008, before Hillary Clinton was stunned by an unknown Barack Obama, who surprised the Clinton political machine by beating her in the '08 Democratic primaries.

Our next Commander in Chief will likely inherit the most difficult job that any president since Harry Truman inherited. The economy is still struggling along, and our military has been gravely jeopardized by the Obama administration's policies. Islamic terrorists, such as ISIS or ISIL, or whatever they are calling themselves; definitely present a very clear and present danger to the world and America. Contrary to President Obama calling ISIS a "junior varsity team", back in January 2014, ISIS is definitely no "JV" team. They are very well funded, disciplined, and organized, and they intend to kill Americans as they have already demonstrated by decapitating American journalist James Foley, and posting the beheading on U-Tube. I have little doubt that ISIS will strike the US homeland, sometime in the near future. They have already promised us that they will be attacking us at home. I know that this country is war weary, but that can't be an excuse to turn a blind eye and sit on our hands. The Islamic terrorists are currently on a battle field in Syria and Iraq, and if we don't offensively and aggressively confront them there now, we will undoubtedly be forced to defensively confront them at home. It would be much better for America to fight and defeat them in Iraq, than to fight them in the streets of America. I know that most Americans are opposed to war, and certainly opposed to having US military "boots on the ground", but no US president should ever take that option off of the table. Mark my words, if we don't eradicate these Islamic terrorists now, we will live to regret it. In the words of Ronald Reagan, "Peace through strength", it doesn't work any other way, and America desperately needs another Ronald Reagan.

We have got to keep our eye on the ball. We have to win elections and take America back. We can't win elections if we are constantly fighting among ourselves. We need to put forth solid conservative ideas and get our messaging on point. And for goodness' sake, we have got to put up the very best candidates, and make sure that they are well vetted! The next couple of elections are way too important, and America needs strong, conservative leadership.

I remember when I was in sixth grade and Jimmy Carter had just gotten elected, and I distinctly remember a girl classmate jumping up and down in excitement as we headed down the hall to our classroom. I obviously didn't know much if anything about politics, other than Richard Nixon's historic resignation over Watergate a few years earlier, and Gerald Ford being the only president not to win a presidential election when he lost his election bid against Carter, most likely due to his pardoning of Nixon. In any event, I distinctly recall wondering what on earth made a peanut farmer qualified to be the president of the United States. But heck, I was just a kid and didn't know any better one way or the other, but it did make me wonder. Unfortunately the majority of Americans failed to connect the dots, the same dots that I as a sixth grader at least thought enough to question.

I vividly recall the very same thought going through my head the day America thought that a community organizer with absolutely no management experience whatsoever could possibly be qualified to be the president of the United States and the commander in chief of the most powerful military in history. Unfortunately, half of America failed to connect those pretty glaring dots, not just once, but twice! I have little doubt that now in hindsight, and after six years of utter incompetence, there are darn few Americans who don't have buyer's remorse. But hey, I do have to give it to Mr. Obama, he sure can give one heck of a speech.

Here is the silver lining, the light at the end of the tunnel, so to speak. Four years of Jimmy Carter was a huge wake-up call for most Americans. Those four dark years of Jimmy Carter gave us Ronald Reagan, who went on to be one of the greatest presidents in modern history. Barack Obama may well prove to be the best thing that ever happened to conservatism in America. If four years of Jimmy Carter gave us Ronald Reagan, eight years of Barack Obama may well result in America electing a very strong and conservative leader. Obama's dire experiment in progressive government has been exposed for what it is: a complete failure! God knows that America will need a very strong leader in the White House to get us out of this dire mess we now find ourselves in.

"We the people" may well have a very unique opportunity before us. The perfect storm, if you will, to reverse all of the damage that's been done to our country and our economy during this lost decade we have endured. What do I mean? As I said earlier in this chapter when referring to immigration, in the words of Rahm Emanuel, "Don't ever let a good crisis go to waste." America is in the midst of a terrible crisis. Much worse than the crisis that gave us the era of Reid, Pelosi, and Obama, the era that has now exposed the damaging unintended consequences of progressivism. America is teetering on the edge of the cliff and staring into the abyss. American voters may not know exactly what needs to happen, but they have at least figured out that something different does need to happen. They may not know exactly what it is that they do want, but they know that this isn't it.

Big government has been exposed for what it is. One need only look at the VA to understand that big government may not quite be the best thing since sliced bread. Not only has the VA scandal exposed big government for what it is, it has also exposed nationalized health care for what it is and what it could easily be, and it's a pretty ugly picture.

The IRS has also exposed the corruption and incompetence of big government and the overwhelming and overreaching power that the IRS does has. I do think Americans may want to reconsider whether the IRS should be in control of our health care system, as it is with the Affordable Care Act. Now might be the best chance in history to have sweeping changes to the IRS tax code, or, even better yet, to abolish the IRS and go to a much simpler tax code or a flat tax, or even a national sales tax.

The crisis along our southern border may have exposed the shambles our immigration policy is really in. This may well have created the very best opportunity to finally secure our southern border and pass some real immigration reform. Our southern border not only jeopardizes our national security; it has become a humanitarian crisis, and fortunately Americans tend to quickly pay attention to a humanitarian crisis.

A failure of American leadership around the world, has the world in utter chaos, and in flames. The disasters and national embarrassments that America has had around the world may be a wake-up call to Americans that maybe it's not such a good thing to weaken our military. Maybe it's not such a good thing for our allies not to be able to depend on us, and maybe it's not such a good thing for our enemies not to fear us. And maybe Americans finally have a better understanding of why the world is a much safer place with America as a strong leader around the world. Certainly a strong leader can make that case to the American public, and I believe that America is ready to embrace the importance of a strong military, strong and decisive leadership, and a strong America.

Our exploding national debt and out-of-control spending may finally be the wake-up call that America has been needing to get a balanced budget amendment passed into law. It may also have given us a narrow window of opportunity to have a serious conversation about some reasonable adjustments to entitlements to ensure our sovereignty for all future generations.

So, maybe there is a glimmer of hope, a light at the end of the tunnel.

CHAPTER TWENTY THREE

Our Founding Fathers: The Declaration

I think our Founding Fathers would be turning over in their graves right now if they knew what we've allowed to happen to America. One historic document that everyone has heard of but few probably ever remember reading greatly emphasizes what our Founding Fathers did for "we the people." This historic document lead to America's independence from Great Brittan. We the people of the United States of America owe it to our Founding Fathers to take our country back and get our house in order so that what they sacrificed for this nation will not have been in vain. I think it's fitting to end this book by using the last few chapters to share the three most important documents in American history: the Declaration of Independence, the US Constitution, and the Bill of Rights. If you have never read these historic documents, or if you haven't read them since junior high school history class, I would very much encourage you to do so now.

I've read these historic documents on a number of occasions over the past few years; in fact, the last time I read these documents, I realized just how disappointed our Founding Fathers would be if they were here today, and that is what inspired me to write this book. I must say, as I sat and typed out each word of these historic documents, word for word, it was powerful and emotional. It made me angry about what "we the people" have taken for granted and what we've allowed to happen to this great country of ours. It also, however, gave me hope, strength, and encouragement that we can take our country back and make America the exceptional pillar of democracy that our Founding Fathers envisioned America would become. We the people of the United States of America owe it to our Founding Fathers to make it happen!

In a letter written to George III, the king of Great Britain, our Founding Fathers said enough is enough and declared America's independence.

Note: You may notice what appear to be typos or errors, but the English language has had some changes in the past two centuries and some words and punctuation have evolved. This document is written exactly the way Thomas Jefferson, Benjamin Franklin, John Adams, Robert Livingston, and Roger Sherman wrote it over two hundred years ago.

From the US National Archives and Records Administration.

IN CONGRESS, July 4, 1776

The unanimous Declaration of the thirteen united States of America,

When in the course of human events, it becomes necessary for one people to dissolve the political bands which have connected them with another, and to assume among the powers of the earth, the separate and equal station to which the Laws of Nature and Nature's "God entitle them, a decent respect to the opinions of mankind requires that they should declare the cause which impel them to the separation.

We hold these truths to be self-evident, that all men are created equal, that they are endowed by their Creator with certain unalienable Rights, that among these are Life, Liberty and the pursuit of Happiness. – That to secure these rights, Governments are instituted among Men, deriving their just powers from the consent of the governed, – That whenever any Form of Government becomes destructive of these ends, it is the Right of the People to alter or to abolish it, and to institute new Government, laying its foundation on such principles and organizing its powers in such form, as to them shall seem most likely to affect their Safety and Happiness,. Produce, indeed, will dictate that Governments long established should not be changed for light and transient causes; and accordingly all experience hath shewn, that mankind are more disposed to suffer, while evils are sufferable, than to right themselves by abolishing the forms to which they are accustomed. But when a long train of abuses and usurpations, pursuing invariably the same Object evinces a design to reduce them under absolute Despotism, it is their right, it is their duty, to throw off such Government, and to provide new Guards for their future security. – Such has been the patient sufferance of these Colonies; and such is now the necessity which constrains them to alter their former System of Government. The history of the present King of Great Britain is a history of repeated injuries and usurpations, all having in direct object the establishment of an absolute Tyranny over these States. To prove, this let Facts be submitted to a candid world.

He has refused his Assent to Laws, the most wholesome and necessary for the public good. He has forbidden his Governors to pass Laws of immediate and pressing importance, unless suspended in their operation till his Assent should be obtained; and when so suspended, he has utterly neglected to attend to them.

He has refused to pass other Laws for the accommodation of large districts of people, unless those people would relinquish the right of Representation in the Legislature, a right inestimable to them and formidable to tyrants only.

He has called together legislative bodies at places unusual, uncomfortable, and distant from the depository of their public Records, for the sole purpose of fatiguing them into compliance with his measures.

He has dissolved Representative Houses repeatedly, for opposing with manly firmness his invasions on the rights of the people.

He has refused for a long time, after such dissolutions, to cause others to be elected; whereby the Legislative powers, incapable of Annihilation, have returned to the People at large for their exercise; the State remaining in the mean time exposed to all the dangers of invasion from without, and convulsions within.

He has endeavoured to prevent the population of these States; for that purpose obstructing the Laws for Naturalization of Foreigners; refusing to pass others to encourage their migration hither, and raising the conditions of new Appropriations of Lands.

He has obstructed Administration of Justice, by refusing his assent to Laws for establishing Judiciary powers.

He has made Judges dependent on his Will alone, for the tenure of their offices, and the amount and payment of their salaries.

He has erected a multitude of New Offices, and sent hither swarms of Officers to harass our people, and eat out their substance.

He has kept among us, in times of peace, Standing Armies without the Consent of our legislatures.

He has affected to render Military independent of and superior to the Civil power.

He has combined with others to subject us to a jurisdiction foreign to our constitution, and unacknowledged by our laws; giving his Assent to their Acts of pretended Legislation:

For Quartering large bodies of armed troops among us:

For protecting them, by a mock Trial, from punishment for any Murders which they should commit on the Inhabitants of these States:

For cutting off our Trade with all parts of the world:

For imposing Taxes on us without our Consent:

For depriving us in many cases, of the benefits of Trial by Jury:

For transporting us beyond Seas to be tried for pretended offences:

For abolishing the free System of English Laws in a neighbouring Province, establishing therein an Arbitrary government, and enlarging its Boundaries so as to render it at once an example and fit instrument for introducing the same absolute rule into the Colonies:

For taking away our Charters, abolishing our most valuable Laws, and altering fundamentally the Forms of our Government:

For suspending our own Legislatures, and declaring themselves invested with power to legislate for us in all cases whatsoever.

He has abdicated Government here, by declaring us out of his Protection and waging War against us.

He has plundered our seas, ravaged our Coasts, burnt our towns, and destroyed the lives of our people.

He is at this time transporting large Armies of foreign Mercenaries to compleat the works of death, desolation and tyranny, already begun with circumstances of Cruelty & perfidy scarcely paralleled in the most barbarous ages, and totally unworthy the Head of a civilized nation.

He has constrained our fellow Citizens taken Captive on the high Seas to bear Arms against their Country, to become the executioners of their friends and Brethren, or to fall themselves by their Hands.

He has excited domestic insurrections amongst us, and has endeavoured to bring on the inhabitants of our frontiers, the merciless Indian Savages, whose known rule of warfare, is an undistinguished destruction of all ages, sexes and conditions.

In every stage of these Oppressions We have Petitioned for Redress in the most humble terms: Our repeated Petitions have been answered only by repeated injury. A Prince whose character is thus marked by every act which may define a Tyrant, is unfit to be the Ruler of a free people.

Nor have We been wanting in attentions to our Brittish brethren. We have warned them from time to time of attempts by their legislature to extend an unwarrantable Jurisdiction over us. We have reminded them of the circumstances of our emigration and settlement here. We have appealed to their native justice and magnanimity, and we have conjured them by the ties of our common kindred to disavow these usurpations, which, would inevitably interrupt our connections and correspondence. They too have been deaf to the voice of justice and consanguinity. We must, therefore, acquiesce in the necessity, which denounces our Separation, and hold them, as we hold the rest of mankind, Enemies in War, in Peace Friends.

We, therefore, the Representatives of the united States of America, in General Congress, assembled, appealing to the Supreme Judges of the world for the rectitude of our intentions, do, in the Name, and by Authority of the good People of these Colonies, solemnly publish and declare, That these United Colonies are, and of Right ought to be Free and Independent States; that they are Absolved from all Allegiance to the British Crown, and that all political connection between them and the State of Great Britain, is and ought to be totally dissolved; and that as Free and Independent States, they have full Power to levy War, conclude Peace, contract Alliances, establish Commerce, and to do all other Acts and Things which Independent States may of right do. And for the support of this Declaration, with a firm reliance on the protection of divine Providence, we mutually pledge to each other our Lives, our Fortunes and our sacred Honor.

This letter, the declaration of our independence, was signed by fifty-six representatives of what would become the United States of America. It was first read to the public at high noon on July 8, 1776, in the Old State House Yard in Philadelphia (in the building that is now Independence Hall).

We the People
Article 1

CHAPTER TWENTY FOUR

We the People:
The Constitution

I can't think of any better way to end this book than to recite the Declaration of Independence, the Constitution of the United States, and the Bill of Rights. Far too many Americans have forgotten where we came from and what our Founding Fathers sacrificed so that "we the people" could have the life they have afforded us. We need to remind our elected officials that the Constitution and the Bill of Rights aren't just some irritating pieces of paper; these historic documents are what make our democracy exceptional and make America the greatest country on earth.

From the US National Archives and Records Administration:

Note: The following text is a transcription of the Constitution in its original form. Items that are underlined have since been amended or superseded. You may note what appear to be typos or errors; however, spelling and punctuation in the English language have evolved in the past two centuries, and this document is written exactly as it was written by Thomas Jefferson, James Madison, and Thomas Paine over two hundred years ago.

The Constitution of the United States

We the People of the United States, in Order to form a more perfect Union, establish Justice, insure domestic Tranquility, provide for the common defence, promote the general Welfare, and secure the Blessings of Liberty to ourselves and our Posterity, do ordain and establish this Constitution of the United States of America.

Article. 1.

Section. 1.

All legislative Powers herein granted shall be vested in a Congress of the United States, which shall consist of a Senate and House of Representatives.

Section. 2.

The House of Representatives shall be composed of Members chosen every second Year by the People of the several States, and the Electors in each State shall have the Qualifications requisite for Electors of the most numerous Branch of the State Legislature.

No Person shall be a Representative who shall not have attained to the Age of twenty five Years, and been seven Years a Citizen of the United States, and who shall not, when elected, be an inhabitant of that state in which he shall be chosen.

Representatives and direct Taxes shall be apportioned among the several States which may be included within this Union, according to their respective Numbers, which shall be determined by adding to the whole Number of free Persons, including those bound to Service for a Term of Years, and excluding Indians not taxed, three fifths of all other Persons. The actual Enumeration shall be made within three Years after the first Meeting of the Congress of the United States, and within every subsequent Term of ten Years, in such Manner as they shall by Law direct. The Number of Representatives shall not exceed one for every thirty Thousand, but each State shall have at Least one Representative; and until such enumeration shall be made, the State of New Hampshire shall be entitled to chuse three, Massachusetts eight, Rhode-Island and Providence Plantations one, Connecticut five, New-York six, New Jersey four, Pennsylvania eight, Delaware one, Maryland six, Virginia ten, North Carolina five, South Carolina five, and Georgia three.

When vacancies happen in the Representation from any State, the Executive Authority thereof shall issue Writs of Election to fill such Vacancies.

The House of Representatives shall chuse their Speaker and other Officers: and shall have the sole Power of Impeachment.

Section. 3.

The Senate of the United States shall be composed of two Senators from each State, chosen by the Legislature thereof for six Years: and each Senator shall have one Vote.

Immediately after they shall be assembled in Consequence of the first Election, they shall be divided as equally as may be into three Classes. The Seats at the Expiration of the fourth Year, and of the third Class at the Expiration of the sixth Year, so that one third may be chosen every second Year; and if Vacancies happen by Resignation, or otherwise, during the Recess of the legislature of any State, the Executive thereof may make temporary Appointments until the next Meeting of the legislature, which shall then fill such Vacancies.

No Person shall be a Senator who shall not have attained to the Age of thirty Years, and been nine Years a Citizen of the United States, and who shall not, when elected, be an inhabitant of that State for which he shall be chosen.

The Vice President of the United States shall be President of the Senate, but shall have no Vote, unless they be equally divided.

The Senate shall chuse their other Officers, and also a president pro tempore, in the Absence of the Vice President, or when he shall exercise the Office of President of the United States.

Judgment in Cases of Impeachment shall not extend further than to removal from Office, and disqualification to hold and enjoy any Office of honor, Trust or Profit under the United States: but the Party convicted shall nevertheless be liable and subject to Indictment, Trial Judgment and Punishment, according to Law.

Section. 4.

The Times, Places and Manner of holding Elections for Senators and Representatives, shall be prescribed in each State by the Legislature thereof; but the Congress may at any time by Law make or alter such Regulations, except as to the Places of chusing Senators.

The Congress shall assemble at least once in every Year, and such Meeting shall be on the first Monday in December, unless they shall by Law appoint a different Day.

Section. 5.

Each House shall be the Judge of the Elections, Returns and Qualifications of its own Members, and a majority of each shall constitute a Quorum to do Business; but a smaller Number may adjourn from day to day, and may be authorized to compel the Attendance of absent Members, in such Manner, and under such Penalties as each house may provide.

Each House may determine the Rules of its Proceedings, punish its Members of disorderly Behaviour, and, with the Concurrence of two thirds, expel a Member.

Each House shall keep a Journal of its Proceedings, and from time to time publish the same, excepting such Parts as may in their Judgment require Secrecy; and the Yeas and Nays of the Members of either House on any question shall, at the Desire of one fifth of those Present, be entered on the Journal.

Neither House, during the Session of Congress, shall without the Consent of the other, adjourn for more than three days, nor to any other Place than that in which the two Houses shall be sitting.

Section. 6.

The Senators and Representatives shall receive a Compensation for their Services, to be ascertained by Law, and paid out of the Treasury of the United States. They shall in all Cases, except Treason, Felony and Breach of the Peace, be privileged from Arrest during their Attendance at the Session of their respective Houses, and in going to and returning from the same; and for any Speech or Debate in either House, they shall not be questioned in any other Place.

No Senator or Representative shall, during the Time for which he was elected, be appointed to any civil office under the Authority of the United States, which shall have been created, or the Emoluments whereof shall have been increased during such time; and no Persons holding any Office under the United States, shall be a Member of either House during his Continuance in Office.

Section. 7.

All Bills for raising Revenue shall originate in the House of Representatives and the Senate, shall, before it become a Law, be presented to the President of the United States: if he approve he shall sigh it, but if not he shall return it, with his Objections to the House in which it shall have originated, who shall enter the Objections at large on their Journal, and proceed to reconsider it. If after such Reconsideration two thirds of that House shall agree to pass the Bill, it shall be sent, together with the Objections, to the other House, by which it shall likewise be reconsidered, and if approved by two thirds of that House, it shall become a Law. But in all Such Cases the Votes of both Houses shall be determined by yeas and Nays, and the Names of the Persons voting for and against the Bill shall be entered on the Journal of each House respectively. If any Bill shall not be returned by the President within ten Days (Sundays excepted) after it shall have been presented to him, the Same shall be a Law, in like Manner as if he had signed it, unless the congress by their Adjournment prevent its Return, in which Case it shall not be a Law.

Every Order, Resolution, or Vote to which the concurrence of the Senate and the House of Representatives may be necessary (except on a question of Adjournment) shall be presented to the President of the United States; and before the Same shall take Effect, shall be approved by him, or being disapproved by him, shall be repassed by two thirds the Senate and the House of Representatives, according to the Rules and Limitations prescribed in the Case of a Bill.

Section. 8.

The Congress shall have Power To lay and collect Taxes, Duties, Imposts and Excises, to pay the Debts and provide for the common Defence and general Welfare of the United States; but all Duties, imposts and Excises shall be uniform throughout the United States;

To borrow Money on the credit of the United States;

To regulate Commerce with foreign Nations, and among the several States, and with the Indian Tribes;

To establish an uniform Rule of Naturalization, and uniform Laws on the subject of Bankruptcies throughout the United States;

To Coin Money, regulate the Value thereof, and of foreign Coin, and fix the Standard of Weights and Measures;

To Provide for the Punishment of counterfeiting the securities and current Coin of the United States.

To establish Post Office and post Roads;

To promote the Progress of Science and useful Arts, by securing for limited Times to Authors and Inventors the exclusive Right to their respective Writings and Discoveries;

To constitute Tribunals inferior to the supreme Court;

To define and punish Piracies and Felonies committed on the high Seas, and Offences against the Law of Nations;

To declare War, grant Letters of Marque and Reprisal, and make Rules concerning Captures on Land and Water;

To raise and support Armies, but no Appropriation of Money to that Use shall be for a longer Term than two Years;

To provide and maintain a Navy;

To make Rules for the Government and Regulation of the land and naval Forces;

To provide for calling forth the Militia to execute the Laws of the Union, suppress Insurrections and repel Invasions;

To provide for organizing, armies, and disciplining, the Militia, and for governing such Part of them as may be employed in the Service of the United States, reserving to the States respectively, the appointment of the Officers, and the Authority of training the Militia according to the discipline prescribed by Congress;

To exercise exclusive Legislation in all Cases whatsoever, over such District (not exceeding ten Miles square) as my, by Cession of particular States, and the Acceptance of Congress, become the Seat of the Government of the United States, and to exercise like Authority over all Places purchased by the Consent of the Legislature of the States in which the Same shall be, for the Erection of Forts, Magazines, Arsenals, dock-Yards, and other needful Buildings; - And To Make all Laws which shall be necessary and proper for carrying into Execution the foregoing Powers, and all other Powers vested by this Constitution in the Government of the United States, or in any Department or Officer thereof.

Section. 9.

The Migration or Importation of such Persons as any of the States now existing shall think proper to admit, shall not be prohibited by the Congress prior to the Year one thousand eight hundred and eight, but a Tax or duty may be imposed on such Importation, not exceeding ten dollars for each Person.

The Privilege of the Writ of Habeas Corpus shall not be suspended, unless when in Cases of Rebellion or Invasion the public Safety may require it.

No Bill of Attainder or ex post facto Law shall be passed.

No Capitation, or other direct, Tax shall be laid, <u>unless in Proportion to the Census or enumeration herein before directed to be taken.</u>

No Tax or Duty shall be laid on Articles exported from any State.

No Preference shall be given by any Regulation of Commerce or Revenue to the Ports of one State over those of another; nor shall Vessels bound to, or from, one State, be obliged to enter, clear, or pay Duties in another.

No Money shall be drawn from the Treasury, but in Consequence of Appropriations made by Law; and a regular Statement and Account of the Receipts and Expenditures of all public Money shall be published from time to time.

No Title of Nobility shall be granted by the United States; And no Person holding any Office of Profit or Trust under them, shall, without the Consent of the Congress, accept of any present, Emolument, Office, or Title, of any kind whatever, from any King, Prince, or foreign State.

Section. 10.

No State shall enter into any Treaty, Alliance, or Confederation; grant Letters of Marque and Reprisal; coin Money; emit bills of Credit; make any Thing but gold and silver Coin a Tender of Payment of Debts; pass any Bill of Attainder, ex post facto Law, or Law impairing the Obligation of Contracts, or grant any Title of Nobility.

No State shall, without the consent of Congress, lay any Imposts or Duties on Imports or Exports, except what may be absolutely necessary for executing it's inspection Laws; and the net Produce of all Duties and Imposts, laid by any State on Imports or Exports, shall be for the Use of the Treasury of the United States; and all such Laws shall be subject to the Revision and Controul of the Congress.

No State shall, without the consent of Congress, lay any Duty of Tonnage, keep Troops, or Ships of War in time of Peace, enter into any Agreement or Compact with another State, or with a foreign Power, or engage in War unless actually invaded, or in such imminent Danger as will not admit of delay.

Article. II.

Section. 1.

The executive Power shall be vested in a President of the United States of America. He shall hold his office during the Term of four years, and, together with the Vice President, chosen for the same Term, be elected, as follows;

Each State shall appoint, in such Manner as the Legislature thereof may direct, a Number of Electors, equal to the whole Number of Senators and Representatives to which the State may be entitled in the Congress; but no Senator or Representative, or Person holding an Office of Trust or Profit under the United States, shall be appointed an Elector.

The Electors shall meet in their representative States, and vote by Ballot for two Persons, of whom one at least shall not be an inhabitant of the same State with themselves. And they shall make a List of all the Persons voted for, and of the Number of Votes for each; which List they shall sign and certify, and transmit sealed to the Seat of the government of the United States, directed to the President of the Senate. The President of the Senate shall, in the Presence of the Senate and House of Representatives, open all Certificates, and the Votes shall then be counted. The Person having the greatest Number of Votes shall be the President, if such Number be a Majority of the whole Number of Electors appointed; and if there be more than one who have such Majority, and have an equal Number of Votes, then the House of Representatives shall immediately chuse by Ballot one of them for President; and if no Persons have a Majority, then from the five highest on the List the said House shall in like Manner chuse the President. But in chusing the President, the Votes shall be taken by States, the Representation from each State having one Vote; A quorum for this purpose shall consist of a Member or Members from two thirds of the States, and a Majority of all the States shall be necessary to a Choice. In every Case, after the Choice of the President, the Person having the greatest Number of Votes of the Electors shall be the Vice President. But if there should remain two or more who have equal Votes, the Senate shall chuse from them by Ballot the Vice President.

The Congress may determine the Time of chusing the Electors, and the Day on which they shall give their Votes; which Day shall be the same throughout the United States. No Person except a natural born Citizen, or a Citizen of the United States, at the time of the Adoption of this Constitution, shall be eligible to the Office of President; neither shall any Person be eligible to that Office who shall not have attained the Age of thirty five Years, and been fourteen Years a Resident within the United States.

In Case of the Removal of the President from Office, or if his Death, Resignation, or Inability to discharge the Powers and Duties of the said Office, the Same shall devolve on the Vice President, and the Congress may by Law provide for the case of Removal, Death, Resignation or inability, both of the President and Vice president, declaring what Officer shall then act as President, and such Officer shall act accordingly, until Disability be removed, or a President shall be elected.

The President shall, at stated Times, receive for his Services a Compensation, which shall neither be increased nor diminished during the Period for which he shall have been elected, and he shall not receive within that Period any other Emolument from the United States, or any of them.

Before he enter on the Execution of his Office, he shall take the following Oath or Affirmation; — "I do solemnly swear (or affirm) that I will faithfully execute the Office of President of the United States, and will to the best of my Ability, preserve, protect and defend the Constitution of the United States."

Section. 2.

The President shall be Commander in Chief of the Army and Navy of the United States, and of the Militia of the several States, when called into the actual Service of the United States; he may require the Opinion, in writing, of the principal Officer in each of the executive Departments, upon any Subject relating to the Duties of their respective Offices, and he shall have Power to grant Reprieves and Pardons for Offences against the United States, except in Cases of Impeachment.

He shall have Power, by and with the Advice and Consent of the Senate, to make Treaties, provided two thirds of the Senators present concur; and he shall nominate, and by and with the Advice and Consent of the Senate, shall appoint Ambassadors, other public Ministers and Consultants, Judges of the supreme Court, and all other Officers of the United States, whose Appointments are not herein otherwise provided for, and which shall be established by Law; but the congress may by law vest the Appointment of such inferior Officers, as they think proper, in the President alone, in the Courts of Law, or in the Heads of Departments.

The President shall have Power to fill up all Vacancies that may happen during the Recess of the Senate, by granting Commission which shall expire at the End of their next Session.

Section. 3.

He shall from time to time give to the Congress information of the State of the Union, and recommend to their Consideration such Measures as he shall judge necessary and expedient; he may, on extraordinary Occasions convene both Houses, or either of them, and in Case of Disagreement between them, with Respect to the Time of Adjournment, he may adjourn them to such Time as he shall think proper; he shall receive Ambassadors and other public Ministers; he shall take Care that the Laws be faithfully executed, and shall Commission all the Officers of the United States.

Section. 4.

The President, Vice president and civil Officers of the United States, shall be removed from Office on Impeachment for, and Conviction of, Treason, Bribery, or other high Crimes and Misdemeanors.

Article III

Section. 1.

The judicial Power of the United States shall be vested in one supreme Court, and in such inferior Courts as the Congress may from time to time ordain and establish. The judges, both of the supreme and inferior Courts, shall hold their Offices during good Behaviour, and shall, at stated Times, receive for their Services a Compensation, which shall not be diminished during their continuance in Office.

Section. 2.

The judicial Power shall extend to all Cases, in Law and Equity, arising under this Constitution, the Laws of the United States, and Treaties made, or which shall be made, under their Authority; — to all Cases affecting Ambassadors, other public Ministers and Consuls; — to all cases of admiralty and maritime Jurisdiction; — to Controversies to which the United States shall be a Party; — to Controversies between two or more States; — between a State and Citizens of another State, — between

Citizens of different States, and between a State, or the citizens thereof, and foreign States, Citizens or Subjects.

In all Cases affecting Ambassadors, other public Ministers and Consuls, and those in which a State shall be Party, the supreme Court shall have original Jurisdiction. In all the other Cases before mentioned, the supreme Court shall have appellate Jurisdiction, both as to Law and Fact, with such Exceptions, and under such Regulations as the Congress shall make.

The Trial of all Crimes, except in Cases of impeachment, shall be by Jury; and such Trial shall be held in the State where the said Crimes shall have been committed; but when not committed within any State, the Trial shall be at such Place or Places as the Congress may by Law have directed.

Section. 3.

Treason against the United States, shall consist only in levying War against them, or in adhering to their Enemies, giving them Aid and comfort. No Person shall be convicted of Treason unless on the Testimony of two Witnesses to the same overt Act, or on Confession in open Court.

The Congress shall have Power to declare the Punishment of Treason, but no Attainder of Treason shall work corruption of Blood, or Forfeiture except during the Life of the Person attained.

Article IV

Section. 1.

Full Faith and Credit shall be given in each State to the public Acts, Records, and judicial Proceedings of every other State. And the congress may by general Laws prescribe the Manner in which such Acts, Records and Proceedings shall be provided, and the Effect thereof.

Section. 2.

The Citizens of each State shall be entitled to all Privileges and Immunities of Citizens of the several States.

A Person charged in any State with Treason, Felony, or other Crime, who shall flee from Justice, and be found in another State, shall on Demand of the executive Authority of the State from which he fled, be delivered up, to be removed to the State having Jurisdiction of Crime.

No Person held to Service or Labour in one State, under the Laws thereof, escaping into another, shall in Consequence of any Law or Regulation therein, be discharged from such Services or Labour, but shall be delivered up on Claim of the Party to whom such Service or Labour may be due.

Section. 3.

New States may be admitted by the Congress into this Union; but no new State shall be formed or erected within the Jurisdiction of another State; nor any State be formed by the Junction of two or more States, or Parts of States, without the Consent of the Legislature of the States concerned as well as of the Congress.

The congress shall have Power to dispose of and make all needful Rules and Regulations respecting the Territory of other Property belonging to the United States; and nothing in this Constitution shall be so construed as to prejudice any Claims of the United States, or of any particular State.

Section. 4.

The United States shall guarantee to every State in the Union a Republican Form of Government, and shall protect each of them against Invasion; and on Application of the Legislature, or of the Executive (when the Legislature cannot be convened), against domestic Violence.

Article. V.

The Congress, whenever two thirds of both Houses shall deem it necessary, shall propose Amendments to this Constitution, or, on the Application of the Legislatures of two thirds of the several States, shall call a Convention for proposing Amendments, which, in either Case, shall be valid to all Intents and purposes, as Part of this Constitution, when ratified by the Legislatures of three fourths of the several States, or by Conventions in three fourths thereof, as the one or the other Mode of Ratification may be proposed by the Congress; Provided that no Amendment which may be made prior to the Year One thousand eight hundred and eight shall in any Manner affect the first and fourth Clauses in the Ninth Section of the first Article; and that no State, without its Consent, shall be deprived of its equal Suffrage in the Senate.

Article. VI.

All Debts contracted and Engagements entered into, before the Adoption of this Constitution, shall be as valid against the United States under this Constitution, as under the Confederation.

This Constitution and the Laws of the United States which shall be made in Pursuance thereof; and all Treaties made, or which shall be made, under the Authority of the United States, shall be the supreme Law of the Land; and the Judges in every State shall be bound thereby, any Thing in the Constitution or Laws of any State to the Contrary notwithstanding.

The Senators and Representatives before mentioned, and the Members of the several State Legislatures, and all executive and judicial Officers, both of the United States and the several States, shall be bound by Oath or Affirmation, to support this Constitution; but no religious Test shall ever be requir3d as a Qualification to any Office or public Trust under the United States.

Article. VII.

The Ratification of the conventions of nine States, shall be sufficient for the Establishment of this Constitution between the States so ratifying the Same.

The Word, "the, "being interlined between the seventh and eighth Lines of the first Page, the Word "Thirty" being partly written on an Erazure in the fifteenth Line of the first Page, The Words "is tried" being interlined between the thirty second and thirty third Lines of the first Page and the Word "the" being interlined between the forty third and forty fourth Lines of the second Page.

Attest William Jackson Secretary Done in Convention by the Unanimous Consent of the States present the Seventeenth Day of September in the Year of our Lord one thousand seven hundred and Eighty seven and the Independence of the United States of America the Twelfth in witness whereof We have hereunto subscribed our names.

G. Washington, President and deputy from Virginia Also signed by thirty-eight other representatives from Delaware, Maryland, Virginia, North Carolina, South Carolina, Georgia, New Hampshire, Massachusetts, Connecticut, New York, New Jersey, and Pennsylvania.

Congress OF THE United States

CHAPTER TWENTY FIVE

That Irritating Little Document: The Bill of Rights

Note; the phrase "That Irritating Little Document", is in sarcastic reference to the fact that all too often progressive law makers find the bill of rights to be very irritating to them, because it stops them in their tracks from completely dismantling all of our rights as Americans.

The Bill of Rights:

The Preamble to the Bill of Rights

Congress of the United States

Begun and held at the city of New-York, on Wednesday the fourth of March, one thousand seven hundred and eighty nine

THE Conventions of a number of the States, having at the time of their adopting the Constitution, expressed a desire, in order to prevent misconstruction or abuse of its powers, that further declaratory and restrictive clauses should be added: And as extending the ground of public confidence in the Government, will best ensure the beneficent ends of its institution.

RESOLVED by the Senate and House of Representatives of the Unites States of America, in Congress assembled, two thirds of both Houses concurring, that the following Articles be proposed to the Legislatures of the several States, as amendments to the Constitution of the United States, all or any of which Articles, when ratified by three fourths of the said Legislatures, to be valid to all intents and purposes, as part of the said Constitution: viz.

ARTICLES in addition to, and Amendment of the constitution of the United States of America, proposed by Congress, and ratified by the Legislatures of the several States, pursuant to the fifth Article of the original Constitution.

Note: The following text is a transcription of the first ten amendments to the Constitution in their original form. These amendments were ratified December 15, 1791, and form what is known as the "Bill of Rights."

Amendment I

Congress shall make no law respecting an establishment of religion, or prohibiting the free exercise thereof; or abridging the freedom of speech, or of the press; or the right of the people peaceably to assemble, and to petition the Government for a redress of grievances.

Amendment II

A well regulated Militia, being necessary to the security of a free State, the right of the people to keep and bear Arms, shall not be infringed.

Amendment III

No Soldier shall, in time of peace be quartered in any house, without the consent of the Owner, nor in time of war, but in a manner to be prescribed by law.

Amendment IV

The right of the people to be secure in their persons, houses, papers, and effects, against unreasonable searches and seizures, shall not be violated, and no Warrants shall issue, but upon probable cause, supported by Oath or affirmation, and particularly describing the place to be searched, and the persons or things to be seized.

Amendment V

No person shall be held to answer for a capital, or otherwise infamous crime, unless on a presentment or indictment of a Grand Jury, except in cases arising in the land or naval forces, or in the Militia, when in actual service in time of War or public danger; nor shall any person subject for the same offence to be twice put in jeopardy of life or limb; nor shall be compelled in any criminal case to be a witness against himself, nor be deprived of life, liberty, or property, without due process of law; nor shall private property be taken for public use, without just compensation.

Amendment VI

In all criminal prosecutions, the accused shall enjoy the right to a speedy and public trial, by an impartial jury of the State and district wherein the crime shall have been committed, which district shall have been previously ascertained by law, and to be informed of the nature and cause of the accusation; to be confronted with the witnesses against him; to have compulsory process for obtaining witnesses in his favor, and to have the Assistance of Counsel for his defence.

Amendment VII

In Suits at common law, where the value in controversy shall exceed twenty dollars, the right of trial by jury shall be preserved, and no fact tried by a jury, shall otherwise re-examined in any Court of the United States, than according to the rules of the common law.

Amendment VIII

Excessive bail shall not be required, nor excessive fines imposed, nor cruel and unusual punishments inflicted.

Amendment IX

The enumeration in the Constitution, of certain rights, shall not be construed to deny or disparage others retained by the people.

Amendment X

The powers not delegated to the United States by the Constitution, nor prohibited by it to the States, are reserved to the States respectively, or to the people.

Amendments XI - XXVII (11 – 27)

In addition to the original ten amendments, the constitution has been amended only seventeen more times in over two centuries and more than a hundred Congresses. It is a true testament to the Constitution that it has stood the test of time, and a real testament to the foresight of our Founding Fathers.

It's amazing to me that today's politicians pass two-thousand-page bills such as the Affordable Care Act, which affects one sixth of our economy, and most of them do not even read the bill. And, I believe there is something inherently wrong with politicians writing and passing legislation in a format that most of "we the people" can't even understand. Yet our Founding Fathers, knowing that they served "we the people," made sure to pass the most important legislation in history in a format that is easy to read, makes good common sense, and is short enough that it doesn't take up more than a few chapters of a book.

The Final Word

Thank you for taking the time to read this book, I sincerely hope you got something positive from it. Please note that I will be updating this book at the end of Barack Obama's presidency, which will hopefully be the beginning of a new America, with conservative leadership. I pray God that when Barack Obama leaves office that it will finally, be the end of "the Lost Decade".

All of the problems we face as a country aren't going to fix themselves. It is up to us to be the foot soldiers in this fight, and this is a fight that we cannot afford to give up on, nor can we afford to lose it. I am just one concerned American who has only one single vote, so I realize that my "just voting" isn't going to amount to much in any upcoming election. Don't get me wrong, I am certainly not minimizing the importance of every vote; I'm merely pointing out the importance of us all doing more than just casting a vote.

I do have a voice, and so do you. That's why I wrote this book: to express my voice and concerns. The events that have taken place that have brought America to the edge of the cliff, staring down into the abyss, are overwhelming for sure. Unfortunately people only get little bits and pieces along the way, and most of the important pieces get lost in the shuffle and forgotten about. With this book, I've tried to put as many of those important pieces as possible together in some organized fashion to tell the whole story, in hopes that you come away with a clearer understanding of the facts that got us here, so that we can all do everything in our power to reverse the course on which we are headed and never allow it to happen ever again.

Knowledge is power, and the only way we are going to fuel the power to take our country back, is to make sure that "we the people" know all of the facts, and have the knowledge so we can empower ourselves to effectuate real change. Knowledge is power, and the only way we are going to fuel the power to take our country back is to make sure that "we the people" know all of the facts, and have the knowledge, so we can empower ourselves to effectuate real change. I would ask that you please join me in this cause, and recommend this book to as many of your friends, family members, and associates as possible through Facebook, Twitter, or any other social media, regardless of their political leanings.

I began each chapter with a fitting quote from one of our Founding Fathers, and I think it is appropriate that we end this book with another quote from one of our Founding Fathers;
"A morsel of genuine History is a thing so rare as to be always valuable." —Thomas Jefferson, 1817

I say let's make some genuine history! There has never been a more important time in the history of our republic to take our country back and put it on the path to prosperity. There may also never be a more opportune time for us to make that a reality. The future of America, and the future of our children and grandchildren depend on it. Let's "Make it Happen!"

Godspeed,

Merlyn Vandervort

Sources and Credits

Chapter 1
Wikipedia, Bing Images, the Daily Caller

Chapter 2
Wikipedia, RT USA, the USDEBTCLOCK.org, Bing Images, CNBC, *National Review*

Chapter 3
Wikipedia, Bing Images, Fox News

Chapter 4
Wikipedia, Fox News, Gateway Pundit, Bing Images, Wall Street, and the Financial Crisis

Chapter 5
DiscovertheNetworks.org, *The Hill*, Wikipedia, Bing Images, Breitbart, WND, Poligu, the *Washington Times*, *National Review*

Chapter 6

The Fiscal Times, The Foundry, Wikipedia, *Encyclopedia Britannica*, *Forbes*, Minyanville, New Deal or Raw Deal, Bing Images, the American Conservative, FDR, the New Deal, and Expansion of Federal Power

Chapter 7

The *Weekly Standard*, Wikipedia, Fox Nation, the *New Yorker*, Stimulus Waste, Recovery.gov, Bing Images, the Blaze, The Freeman, Breitbart, American Thinker

Chapter 8

Pimco, CNBC, *Washington Post*, Politico, Fact Checker, Front Page Mag, Bing Images, Fox News, News Max, Wikipedia

Chapter 9

News Max, CNN US, Fox News, Bing Images, the *Washington Post*, Huff Post, *New York Times*

Chapter 10

Wikipedia, Renew America, Bing Images, the tea party, the Tea Party Patriots website

Chapter 11

The National Interest, Fox News, the Daily Caller, the Fact Checker, the *New York Times*, *Washington Post*, CNN, Bing Images, Wikipedia, AllenWest.com, *New York Post*, WJCA, *National Journal*, *Weekly Standard*, *Los Angeles Times*, Daily Beast, Rand.org, CNS News

Chapter 12

Business Insider, Wikipedia, Bing Images, CNN Politics, Breitbart, *US News*

Chapter 13
The New Media Journal, Conservative Daily, Bing Images, Fox News, Breitbart, the *Washington Times*

Chapter 14
Breitbart, Associated Press, Fox Business, Bing Images, *US News*, *Forbes*, *Washington Examiner*, the Blaze, ABC News, CNN, Daily Signal

Chapter 15
The *Weekly Standard*, CBS News, Bing Images, *Washington Times*, CNN Politics, Fox News, the Blaze

Chapter 16
Real Clear Politics, Bing Images, CNN, the Daily Beast, *Forbes*, WND, Fox News, CBS

Chapter 17
Free Republic, Bing Images, WND

Chapter 18
Cato.org, Fox News, Bing Images, WND

Chapter 19
Fox News, Breitbart, Washington Post, Bing Images, ABC News

Chapter 20
Fox News, NY Daily News, Bing Images, CNN, Wikipedia, WND, the Examiner, ABC News, the Washington Post, the New York Times.

Chapter 21
Politico, Fox News, the Daily Beast, CNN, Reuters, US News, Bing Images, Bloomberg

Chapter 22
NPR, ABC News, Wikipedia, Heritage, Fox News, the Daily Beast, the Daily Signal, the New York Times, Bing Images

Chapter 22
The US National Archives

Chapter 23
The US National Archives

Chapter 24
The US National Archives

(Note; photos and images were obtained thru Bing Images, all are Creative Commons Licensing System, for commercial use and distribution)